SWEDEN

13TH EDITION

Where to Stay and Eat
for All Budgets

Must-See Sights
and Local Secrets

Ratings You Can Trust

Portions of this book appear in *Fodor's Scandinavia*

Fodor's Travel Publications   New York, Toronto, London, Sydney, Auckland
www.fodors.com

FODOR'S SWEDEN
Editor: Nuha E. Ansari

Editorial Production: Tom Holton
Editorial Contributors: Christina Knight, Rob Hincks, Karin Palmquist
Maps: David Lindroth, *cartographer;* Bob Blake and Rebecca Baer, *map editors*
Design: Fabrizio La Rocca, *creative director;* Guido Caroti, *art director;* Melanie Marin, *senior picture editor*
Production/Manufacturing: Colleen Ziemba
Cover Photo (Stockholm): Bildhuset AB/Photonica

ISBN 1-4000-1341-0

ISSN 1528-3070

Thirteenth Edition

SPECIAL SALES
Fodor's Travel Publications are available at special discounts for bulk purchases for sales promotions or premiums. Special editions, including personalized covers, excerpts of existing guides, and corporate imprints, can be created in large quantities for special needs. For more information, contact your local bookseller or write to Special Markets, Fodor's Travel Publications, 1745 Broadway, New York, New York 10019. Inquiries from Canada should be directed to your local Canadian bookseller or sent to Random House of Canada, Ltd., Marketing Department, 2775 Matheson Boulevard East, Mississauga, Ontario L4W 4P7. Inquiries from the United Kingdom should be sent to Fodor's Travel Publications, 20 Vauxhall Bridge Road, London SW1V 2SA, England.

AN IMPORTANT TIP & AN INVITATION
Although all prices, opening times, and other details in this book are based on information supplied to us at press time, changes occur all the time in the travel world, and Fodor's cannot accept responsibility for facts that become outdated or for inadvertent errors or omissions. So **always confirm information when it matters,** especially if you're making a detour to visit a specific place. Your experiences—positive and negative—matter to us. If we have missed or misstated something, **please write to us.** We follow up on all suggestions. Contact the Sweden editor at editors@fodors.com or c/o Fodor's at 1745 Broadway, New York, New York 10019.

PRINTED IN THE UNITED STATES OF AMERICA

10 9 8 7 6 5 4 3 2 1

DESTINATION SWEDEN

I n the towns and cities of Scandinavia's largest country, contemporary architecture sits side by side with dramatic designs of a bygone era. Stockholm, one of Europe's most breathtaking capitals, is built on a series of islands. Its ultramodern skyscrapers are just a short walk from twisting, medieval streets. In the fairy-tale province of Dalarna, red-painted farmhouses line the shores of pristine, sun-dappled lakes. Swedes spend their summer in the southern provinces, on sandy beaches in resort towns, and exploring medieval châteaus. Untamed rivers cut through the wide open spaces of the isolated moorlands of the north, and glacier-topped mountains neighbor vast forests of pine, spruce, and birch. This is a land of contrasts, of bustling cities existing side by side with areas of untamed natural beauty, and a place where modern, European democracy coexists with a strong affection for monarchy.

Karen Cure, Editorial Director

CONTENTS

Maps

CloseUps

ABOUT THIS BOOK

There's no doubt that the best source for travel advice is a like-minded friend who's just been where you're headed. But with or without that friend, you'll have a better trip with a Fodor's guide in hand. Once you've learned to find your way around its pages, you'll be in great shape to find your way around your destination.

SELECTION

Our goal is to cover the best properties, sights, and activities in their respective categories, as well as the most interesting communities to visit. We make a point of including local food-lovers' hot spots as well as neighborhood options, and we avoid all that's touristy unless it's really worth your time. You can go on the assumption that everything you read about in this book is recommended whole-heartedly by our writers and editors. Flip to On the Road with Fodor's to learn more about who they are. It goes without saying that no property mentioned in the book has paid to be included.

RATINGS

Orange stars ★ denote sights and properties that our editors and writers consider the very best in the area covered by the entire book. These, the best of the best, are listed in the Fodor's Choice section in the front of the book. Black stars ★ highlight the sights and properties we deem Highly Recommended, the don't-miss sights within any region. Fodor's Choice and Highly Recommended options in each region are usually listed on the title page of the chapter covering that region. Use the index to find complete descriptions. In cities, sights pinpointed with numbered map bullets ❶ in the margins tend to be more important than those without bullets.

SPECIAL SPOTS

Pleasures & Pastimes focuses on types of experiences that reveal the spirit of the destination. Watch for Off the Beaten Path sights. Some are out of the way, some are quirky, and all are worth your while. If the munchies hit while you're exploring, look for Need a Break? suggestions.

TIME IT RIGHT

Wondering when to go? Check On the Calendar up front and chapters' Timing sections for weather and crowd overviews and best days and times to visit.

SEE IT ALL

Use Fodor's exclusive Great Itineraries as a model for your trip. (For a good overview of the entire destination, follow those that begin the book, or mix regional itineraries from several chapters.) In cities, Good Walks guide you to important sights in each neighborhood; ▶ indicates the starting points of walks and itineraries in the text and on the map.

BUDGET WELL

Hotel and restaurant price categories from ¢ to $$$$, are defined in the opening pages of each chapter—expect to find a balanced selection for every budget. For attractions we always give standard adult admission fees; reductions are usually available for children, students, and senior citizens. Look in Discounts & Deals in Smart Travel Tips for information on destination-wide ticket schemes. Want to pay with plastic? AE, D, DC, MC, V following restaurant and hotel listings indicate whether American Express, Discover, Diner's Club, MasterCard, or Visa are accepted.

BASIC INFO

Smart Travel Tips lists travel essentials for the entire area covered by the book; city- and region-specific basics end each chapter. To find the best way to get around, see the transportation section; see individual modes of travel ("By Car," "By Train") for details. We assume you'll check Web sites or call for particulars.

ON THE MAPS Maps throughout the book show you what's where and help you find your way around. Black- and orange-numbered bullets ❶ ❶ in the text correlate with bullets on maps.

BACKGROUND In general, we give background information within the chapters in the course of explaining sights as well as in CloseUp boxes and in Understanding Sweden, at the end of the book. To get in the mood, review the suggestions in Books & Movies. The glossary can be invaluable.

FIND IT FAST Within the book chapters are arranged in a roughly anticlockwise geographic direction starting with Stockholm. Chapters are divided into small regions, within which towns are covered in logical geographical order; attractive routes and interesting places between towns are flagged as En Route. Heads at the top of each page help you find what you need within a chapter.

DON'T FORGET Restaurants are open for lunch and dinner daily unless we state otherwise; we mention dress only when there's a specific requirement and reservations only when they're essential or not accepted—it's always best to book ahead. Hotels have private baths, phones, TVs, and air-conditioning and operate on the European Plan (a.k.a. EP, meaning without meals). We always list facilities but not whether you'll be charged extra to use them, so when pricing accommodations, find out what's included.

SYMBOLS

Many Listings

★ Fodor's Choice
★ Highly recommended
⊠ Physical address
✦ Directions
🕮 Mailing address
☎ Telephone
🖷 Fax
⊕ On the Web
✉ E-mail
🎟 Admission fee
☉ Open/closed times
⚑ Start of walk/itinerary
Ⓜ Metro stations
▱ Credit cards

Outdoors

🏌 Golf
⛺ Camping

Hotels & Restaurants

🏨 Hotel
🛏 Number of rooms
♦ Facilities
🍽 Meal plans
✗ Restaurant
⌛ Reservations
🏛 Dress code
🚭 Smoking
🍸 BYOB
✗🏨 Hotel with restaurant that warrants a visit

Other

🐾 Family-friendly
🛈 Contact information
⇨ See also
⊠ Branch address
☞ Take note

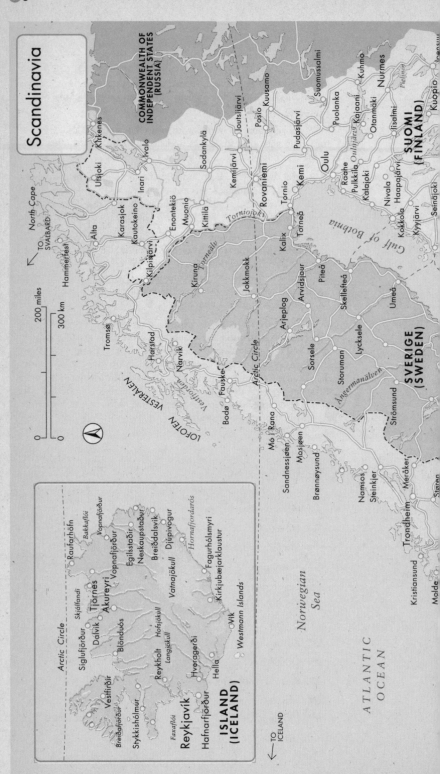

Scandinavia

200 miles

300 km

TO SVALBARD

North Cape

Hammerfest
Kirkenes
Ulsjoki
Alta
Karasjok
Inari
Ivalo
Kautokeino
Kilpisjärvi
Enontekiö
Muonio
Kittilä
Sodankylä
Posio
Joutsijärvi
Kuusamo
Suomussalmi
Kuhmo
Nurmes
Kemijärvi
Puolanka
Rovaniemi
Otanmäki
Iisalmi
Kuopio
Kaiaani
Pudasjärvi
Oulu
Raahe
Pulkkila Oulujärvi
Kalajoki
Nivala
Haapajärvi
Kokkola
Kyyjärvi
Seinäjoki

COMMONWEALTH OF INDEPENDENT STATES (RUSSIA)

Torniojoki
Tornio
Kemi
Torneå
Kalix
Kiruna
Jokkmokk
Arvidsjaur
Piteå
Skellefteå
Umeå
Arjeplog
Sorsele
Lycksele
Storuman
Strömsund
Ångermanälven

Tromsø
Harstad
Narvik
Fauske
Bodø
Mo i Rana
Mosjøen
Sandnessjøen
Brønnøysund
Namsos
Steinkjer
Trondheim

SVERIGE (SWEDEN)

Arctic Circle

Gulf of Bothnia

SUOMI (FINLAND)

LOFOTEN
VESTERÅLEN
Vestfjorden

Meråker
Stjørn
Molde
Kristiansund

Norwegian Sea

ATLANTIC OCEAN

TO ICELAND

ISLAND (ICELAND)

Arctic Circle

Raufarhöfn
Bakkafjói
Vopnafjörður
Skjálfandi
Þórshöfn
Akureyri
Egilsstaðir
Neskaupstaður
Breiðdalsvik
Djúpivogur
Hornafjarðarós
Fagurhólsmyri
Kirkjubæjarklaustur
Vik
Westmann Islands
Hella
Hvergagerði
Hafnarfjörður
Reykjavik
Reykholt
Langjökull
Hofsjökull
Vatnajökull
Blönduós
Dalvik
Siglufjörður
Vestfirðir
Ísafjörður
Stykkishólmur
Faxaflói
Breiðafjörður
Tjörnes
Vopnafjörður

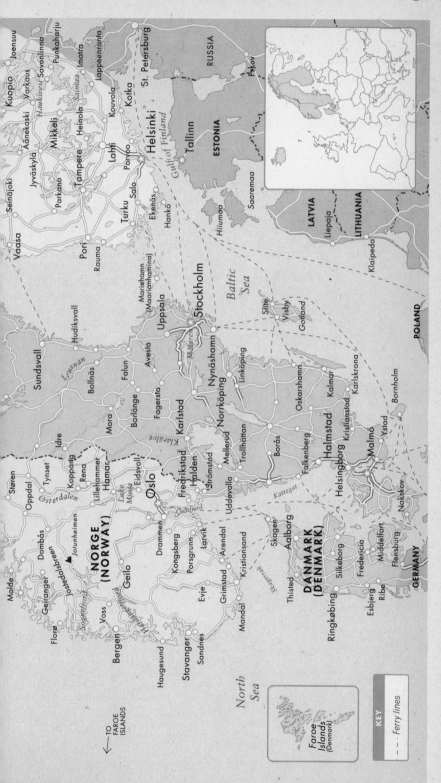

KEY

- - - Ferry lines

Faroe Islands
(Denmark)

TO FAROE ISLANDS

North Sea

NORGE (NORWAY)

DANMARK (DENMARK)

GERMANY

POLAND

LITHUANIA

LATVIA

ESTONIA

RUSSIA

Baltic Sea

Gulf of Finland

Sweden

Arctic Circle

Norwegian Sea

Riksgränsen
Kiruna

Luleälven Gällivare
Jokkmokk

Arjeplog
Töre
Tärneå
Kalix
Arvidsjaur
Tärnaby
Sorsele
Luleå
Storuman
Piteå
Lycksele
Skellefteå
Åsele
Umeälven
Umeå
Strömsund

Åre

Östersund

Tännäs
Sundsvall
Ljungan

Idre
Hudiksvall

Bollnäs
Mora
Söderhamn

Falun
Gävle
Borlänge
Avesta
Fagersta
Karlstad
Uppsala
Västerås
Mälaren
Stockholm
Mellerud
Örebro
Strömstad
Vänern
Uddevalla
Trollhättan
Norrköping
Vättern
Göteborg
(Gothenburg)
Linköping
Borås
Jönköping
Nässjö
Visby
Falkenberg
Värnamo
Oskarshamn
Halmstad
Växjö
Gotland
Helsingborg
Kalmar
Öland
Malmö
Karlskrona
Kristianstad
DENMARK
Trelleborg
Ystad

NORWAY

FINLAND

Gulf of Bothnia

Åland

Gulf of Finland

ESTONIA

Gotska Sandön

Baltic Sea

Gulf of Riga

LATVIA

LITHUANIA

0   50 miles
0   75 km

ON THE ROAD WITH FODOR'S

A trip takes you out of yourself. Concerns of life at home completely disappear, driven away by more immediate thoughts—about, say, what marvels will beguile the next day or where you'll have dinner. That's where Fodor's comes in. We make sure that you know all your options, so that you don't miss something that's around the next bend just because you didn't know it was there. Because the best memories of your trip might well have nothing to do with what you came to Sweden to see, we guide you to sights large and small all over the country. You might set out to see the islands and parks of Stockholm, but back at home you find yourself unable to forget your boat trip on the Göta Canal, or exploring the Arctic heathland of the north. With Fodor's at your side, serendipitous discoveries are never far away.

Our success in showing you every corner of Sweden is a credit to our extraordinary writers. Although there's no substitute for travel advice from a good friend who knows your style, our contributors are the next best thing—the kind of people you would poll for travel advice if you knew them.

British journalist Rob Hincks primarily writes and edits for food and travel magazines in Sweden and England. Rob has lived in Stockholm since 2000, but through his Swedish wife, Mikaela, his associations with the country go back much farther.

Growing up in the north of Sweden, Karin Palmquist used to dread summer vacations when her parents would pack the camper with kids and pets and slowly make their way down to her grandparents' house in the south, stopping at every church and archeological site on the way. Yet, somehow, those road trips awoke in her a lifelong love for travel. Now a freelance writer for newspapers including the *Washington Times* and *Washington Post,* Karin roams the globe for six months a year. She spends the rest of her time in Washington, D.C., her adopted home.

With 449,963 square km (173,731 square mi) for only 8.8 million residents, almost all Sweden's citizens have the space to live as they choose. The capital, Stockholm, is on the west coast. To the south of the city is the province of Småland, a densely forested land with isolated villages, and well known for producing fine crystal glassware. Sweden's southernmost province, Skåne, has thriving farms, sand beaches, castles and manor houses; it's where Swedes go for summer vacations. Göteborg, Sweden's second largest city, is on the west coast. The Göta Canal stretches between Göteborg and Stockholm. The north of Sweden, in contrast, is a land of vast spaces, of heaths and moors, craggy peaks and fast-flowing rivers.

(1) Stockholm

Stockholm, one of Europe's most beautiful capitals, is built on 14 small islands, at the place where the waters of Lake Mälaren rush into the Baltic. Bustling, skyscraper-lined boulevards are a short walk from twisting medieval streets in this modern yet pastoral city.

(2) Side Trips from Stockholm

In the area surrounding the capital but in easy reach of it are many small, historically significant islands, most of them crowned with castles. These make for great day trips and are reachable by boat or train. Farther afield is the island of Gotland, with its Viking remains and wilderness preserves, and the pretty university town of Uppsala.

(3) The Bothnian Coast

The Bothnian Coast is a rugged, windswept finger of land that runs up the eastern side of Sweden between Stockholm and the northern wilderness. Its grand 19th-century towns and cities testify to the wealth that industry brought in the last few decades, and its tiny fishing villages and ancient religious communities point to the more isolated times that preceded it. Its majestic fjords overlook the Gulf of Bothnia, and many Swedes keep holiday homes here. The capital of the county is Gävle, which makes a good base from which to explore the region.

(4) Göteborg

Sweden's second-largest city, Göteborg, is on the west coast. A Viking port in the 11th century, today the city is home to the Scandinavium, an indoor arena; Nordstan, one of Europe's largest indoor shopping malls; and Liseberg, Scandinavia's largest amusement park.

(5) Side Trips from Göteborg

A cruise on the Göta Canal, which stretches from Stockholm, in the east, to Göteborg, in the west, provides a notable coast-to-coast journey through the Swedish countryside. North of Göteborg, the Bohuslän region has a rocky coastline dotted with attractive fishing villages—it also has uncrowded beaches, making it a wonderful area to explore in summer.

(6) The South & the Kingdom of Glass

South of Göteborg, in the densely forested Småland province, are isolated villages whose names are bywords for fine crystal glassware: Kosta, Orrefors, Boda, and Skruf.

Skåne, the country's southernmost province, and the other southern provinces have a significantly different heritage than the rest of the country. Part of Denmark until 1658, the area still has its own distinct dialect. Known as Sweden's best area for crops, this is a lush, expansive countryside with many farms. It is a place of exceptional beauty, ranging from the coastal headlands of Mölle and the Kullaberg National Park to lovely nature reserves and the urban capital, Malmö. Historic castles abound, reminding you that there has always been an aristocracy in Sweden.

7 **Dalarna: The Folklore District**

Dalarna, the central region of Sweden, is considered the most typically Swedish and traditional of all the country's 24 provinces. It's a place of forests, mountains, and lakes, with red-painted wooden farmhouses dotting the countryside. Swedes gather there for Midsummer Day celebrations, when they dress in folk costumes and sing traditional songs. Falun is the capital of the region.

8 **Norrland & Norrbotten**

The north of Sweden, Norrland, is a place of wide-open spaces. Golden eagles soar above snowcapped crags; huge salmon fight their way up wild, tumbling rivers; rare orchids bloom in Arctic heathland; wild rhododendrons splash the land with color. It's where the nomadic indigenous peoples of Europe, the Sámi, live, and it's where you go to experience the midnight sun in Sweden.

Sweden is made up of 21 counties. In the southeast is Stockholm county, which includes the capital of the same name. The industrial seaport city of Göteborg and the neighboring west-coastal counties of Bohuslän and Halland (the so-called Swedish Riviera) form another region, along with Värmland and Dalsland, on the Norwegian border. The southernmost part of Sweden, a lovely mix of farmland, forests, and châteaus, includes Skåne, Småland (the Kingdom of Glass), Blekinge, Västergötland, Östergötland, and the island of Öland. Dalarna, the country's heartland, is centered on Lake Siljan and the town of Mora; this is where Swedish folklore and traditions are most visible. To the north of Stockholm is the Bothnian Coast, a land of dramatic cliffs, fjords, and port towns that appear timeless. The northern half of Sweden, called Norrland and including the counties of Lappland and Norrbotten, is a great expanse consisting mostly of mountains and wilderness; here the hardy Sámi (also known as Lapps) herd reindeer. Many hardy visitors come to see the midnight sun.

Sampling all of Sweden's far-flung variety is best suited to a traveler with either no time constraints or an exceedingly generous purse. The few representative stops below, however, can make even a short visit worthwhile.

Numbers in the text correspond to numbers in the margin and black bullets on the maps. We list at least one hotel for each of the towns on the itinerary.

Stockholm & Environs

3 days. Spend two days in the capital city, ▦ **Stockholm**; one of these days may be spent on a boat trip in the archipelago or on Lake Mälaren. A night at the opera will set the scene, or, for the more budget-conscious traveler, some people-watching over a beer or two downtown. On the third day either visit ▦ **Göteborg**—a port town since the Viking era, marked with attractive boulevards, canals, and important museums— by high-speed train, or fly to ▦ **Mora**, in the heart of Sweden's folklore country, Dalarna. A summertime dip in Lake Siljan will bring freshness and clarity to your travel-worn senses. You could also fly to ▦ **Gotland** for a quick island adventure. The warm climate, golden, cliff-lined beaches, and delicious local lamb specialties make it difficult to leave.

Stockholm to Göteborg

5 days. Start with two days in ▦ **Stockholm**; add a third day if you want to make a side trip to ▦ **Uppsala**, Sweden's principal university town, along the banks of the Fyris River. You can take a long boat journey out into the archipelago, sleeping in a small waterside cabin. On day four fly to ▦ **Mora** and rent a car for a drive around Lake Siljan, or fly to **Skellefteå** for a glimpse of northern Sweden's devout religious past and its musically innovative present. On day five fly to ▦ **Göteborg**.

North to South

10 days. You can tackle this itinerary using public transportation. Start with three days in ▦ **Stockholm**, which will allow you to really get to know the city. Urban bustle, cultural highlights, and pastoral calm can all be absorbed in this time. On day four take the high-speed train to ▦ **Göteborg** and stay two nights and perhaps take the chance to sail out in the west-coast archipelago. It's not as big as Stockholm's archipelago, but the locals will tell you it is much more beautiful. On day six take the train to ▦ **Kalmar**, with Sweden's best-preserved Renaissance castle, via ▦ **Växjö**, the starting place for many of Sweden's

1 million immigrants to America in the 19th century, now the finishing place for many family-tree-tracing pilgrimages. From Kalmar catch the ferry to ☒ **Gotland**. On day eight return to Stockholm. Spend day nine flying to either ☒ **Mora** or ☒ **Kiruna**, the northernmost city in Sweden. Alternatively, from **Gotland** you could spend a couple of days taking the train up the **Bothnian Coast** to experience wild seas, pine-clad islands, tiny fishing villages, and grand towns built on 19th-century industrial fortunes. Stay in ☒ **Gävle,** ☒ **Sundsvall,** or ☒ **Umeå.** Return to Stockholm on day 10.

The official tourist season—when hotel rates generally go down and museum and castle doors open—runs from mid-May through mid-September. This is Sweden's balmiest time of year; summer days are sunny and warm, nights refreshingly cool. (Summer is also mosquito season, especially in the north, but also as far south as Stockholm.) The whole country goes mad for Midsummer Day, in the middle of June. Many attractions close in late August, when the schools reopen at the end of the Swedish vacation season. The colors of autumn fade out as early as September, when the rainy season begins. The weather can be bright and fresh in the spring and fall (although spring can bring lots of rain), and many visitors prefer sightseeing when there are fewer people around. Winter comes in November and stays through March, sometimes longer. In Sweden this season is an Alpine affair, with sub-zero temperatures. The days can be magnificent when the snow is fresh, the sky a brilliant Nordic blue, and the air crystal fresh. Although many of the more traditional attractions are closed, there is skiing, skating, ice fishing, sleigh riding, and myriad other winter activities on offer throughout the country.

Climate

Sweden has typically unpredictable northern European summer weather, but as a general rule, it is likely to be warm but not hot from May until September. In Stockholm the weeks just before and after Midsummer offer almost 24-hour light, and in the far north, above the Arctic Circle, the sun doesn't set at all between the end of May and the middle of July. Below are average daily maximum and minimum temperatures for Stockholm.

Forecasts **Weather Channel Connection** ☎ 900/932–8437, 95¢ per minute from a Touch-Tone phone ⊕ www.weather.com.

STOCKHOLM

Jan.	30F	–1C	May	57F	14C	Sept.	59F	15C
	23	–5		43	6		48	9
Feb.	30F	–1C	June	66F	19C	Oct.	48F	9C
	23	–5		52	11		41	5
Mar.	37F	3C	July	72F	22C	Nov.	41F	5C
	25	–4		57	14		34	1
Apr.	46F	8C	Aug.	68F	20C	Dec.	36F	2C
	34	1		55	13		28	–2

ON THE CALENDAR

WINTER	
Nov.	The Stockholm Film Festival brings world-class films, directors, and actors to the city. The Stockholm Open tennis tournament attracts top players for an indoor tournament at the Kungliga Tennishallen. The Stockholm International Horse Show, held at the Globen sports center, is a big draw.
Nov. 11	St. Martin's Day is celebrated primarily in the southern province of Skåne. Roast goose is served, accompanied by *svartsoppa*, a bisque made of goose blood and spices.
Dec.	For each of the four weeks of Advent, which leads up to Christmas, a candle is lighted in a four-prong candelabra.
Dec. 10	Nobel Day sees the presentation of the Nobel prizes by the king of Sweden at a glittering banquet held in Stadshuset, Stockholm's City Hall.
Dec. 13	On Santa Lucia Day young girls are selected to be "Lucias"; they wear candles—today usually electric substitutes—in their hair and sing hymns with their handmaidens and "star boys" at ceremonies around the country.
Dec. 24	Christmas Eve is the principal day of the Christmas celebration. Traditional Christmas dishes include ham, rice porridge, and lutefisk (dried cod soaked in lye and then boiled).
Dec. 31	New Year's Eve is the Swedes' occasion to set off an astounding array of fireworks. Every household has its own supply, and otherwise quiet neighborhood streets are full of midnight merrymakers.
Jan. 13	Knut signals the end of Christmas festivities and the "plundering" of the Christmas tree: trinkets are removed from the tree, edible ornaments gobbled up, and the tree itself thrown out.
Feb.	A market held in Jokkmokk features both traditional Sámi (Lapp) artifacts and plenty of reindeer. It begins on the first Thursday and runs through Saturday. On Shrove Tuesday special buns called *semlor*—lightly flavored with cardamom and filled with almond paste and whipped cream—are traditionally placed in a dish of warm milk, topped with cinnamon, and eaten.
SPRING	
Mar. (first Sun.)	The Vasalopp Ski Race goes 90 km (56 mi) from Sälen to Mora in Dalarna and attracts entrants from all over the world.
Apr.	On Maundy Thursday, which marks the beginning of the Easter celebrations, small girls dress up as witches and hand out "Easter letters" for small change or candy. *Påskris,* twigs tipped with brightly dyed feathers, decorate homes. On April 30, for the Feast of Valborg, bonfires are lighted to celebrate the end of winter. The liveliest celebrations involve the students of the university cities of Uppsala, 60 km (37 mi) north of Stockholm, and Lund, 16 km (10 mi) north of Malmö.

May 1	Labor Day marches and rallies are held nationwide, and politicians give speeches in town squares. Tjejtrampet, one of the world's largest bicycle races for women, takes place in May as well.
June	In early June the Restaurant Festival fills Stockholm's Kungsträdgården with booths offering inexpensive international and Swedish cuisine. Also in June is the Stockholm Marathon. Midsummer Eve and Day celebrations are held on the Friday evening and Saturday that fall between June 20 and 26. Swedes raise maypoles decorated with floral garlands and sing, play games, and dance all night long. Traditional celebrations, open to the public, are held every year at Skansen in Stockholm. In mid-June comes the Hultsfred Festival, in southern Sweden. It's the country's largest, and wildest, rock festival, with major acts from all over the world.
June 6	National Day is celebrated, with parades, speeches, and band concerts nationwide.
SUMMER	
July	Since 1983 the Stockholm Jazz Festival has brought in the world's best jazz and blues musicians for a five-day festival of music and good cheer. It's held on Skeppsholmen, on a stage behind the Moderna Museet.
Aug.	Crayfish are a delicacy in Sweden, and the second Wednesday of August marks the Crayfish Premiere, when friends gather to eat them at outdoor parties.

PLEASURES & PASTIMES

Beaches

Beaches in Sweden range from wide and sandy strands, on the western side of the country, to steep and rocky shores, on the eastern side, from oceanfront to lakefront, from resorts to remote nature preserves. The area most favored for the standard sunbathing and wave-frolicking vacation is known as the Swedish Riviera, on the coast south of Göteborg. Wherever you go, a dip in the east's brackish Baltic or the west's wild Atlantic is a bracing experience that will set your pulse racing.

Dining

The nation's standard home-cooked meal is basically peasant fare—sausages, potatoes, wild game, fish, and other hearty foods to ward off the winter cold. Yet Sweden has also produced the *smörgåsbord,* a generous and artfully arranged buffet featuring both hot and cold dishes. Fish—fresh, smoked, or pickled—is a Swedish specialty; herring and salmon both come in myriad preparations.

Recently, restaurants in the larger cities have begun offering innovative dishes that combine the ingredients and simplicity of traditional Swedish cuisine with Mediterranean, Asian, and Caribbean influences, a fusion trend that dovetails with an increase in the number of foreign restaurants popping up throughout Sweden. Despite the popularity of such culinary endeavors, it's still easy to find *Husmanskost* (home-cooking) recipes, which are often served in restaurants as a *dagens rätt* (daily special) at lunch. Examples are *pyttipanna* (literally, "bits in the pan"—beef and potato hash topped with a fried egg); pea soup with pancakes, a traditional meal on Thursday; and, of course, *kötbullar,* Swedish meatballs, served with lingonberry jam, a creamy brown sauce, and mashed potatoes.

Look for *kräftor* (crayfish), boiled with dill, salt, and sugar, then cooled overnight; they are most popular in August. Swedes eat kräftor with hot buttered toast, caraway seeds, and schnapps or beer. Autumn heralds an exotic assortment of mushrooms and wild berries. Trout and salmon are common, as are various cuts of elk and reindeer. To the foreign palate, the best of Norrland's culinary specialties is undoubtedly *löjrom,* pinkish caviar from a species of Baltic herring, eaten with chopped onions and sour cream, and the various desserts made from the bittersweet cloudberries that thrive here.

Ice-Skating

Sweden produces some of the best hockey players in the world. Just look at Peter Forsberg and Mats Sudin, both stars of the National Hockey League. But there's another, slightly more unusual type of ice-skating that is also big in Sweden. In *långfärdsskridsåkning* (long-distance skating), extralong skate blades are strapped onto mountaineering boots. This allows the skaters to travel great distances in long, smooth strides. It's especially popular in the Stockholm archipelago when the water between islands is frozen.

Lodging

Service in a Swedish hotel, no matter the price category, is always unfailingly courteous and efficient. Accommodations on the expensive side offer great charm and beauty, but the advantages of location held by less luxurious establishments shouldn't be overlooked. The woodland setting of a camper's *stuga* (small wooden cottage) may be just as desirable and memorable as the gilded antiques of a downtown hotel.

In summer many discounts, special passes, and summer packages are available. Some offer discounts approaching 50%. Weekend rates are also considerably cheaper. Sweden Hotel's ScanPlus Hotel pass costs SKr 90 and gives discounts of 15%–50%, depending on the hotel. Also, if you stay four nights in a row, you get your fifth night free.

Vandrarhem (hostels), also scrupulously clean and well run, are more expensive than elsewhere in Europe. The Swedish Touring Club (STF, ⊕ www.stfturist.se) has 315 hostels and 40 mountain cabins nationwide, most with four- to six-bed family rooms, around 100 with running hot and cold water. They are open to anyone regardless of age. Prices are about SKr 100 per night for members of STF or organizations affiliated with Hostelling International. Nonmembers are charged an additional SKr 35 per night. STF publishes an annual hostel handbook. The Swedish Hostel Association also has a Web site with information in English (⊕ www.svif.se).

Sailing

Deep at heart, modern Swedes are still seafaring Vikings. Sweden's cultural dependence on boats runs so deep that a popular gift at Christmas is candles containing creosote, providing the comforting scent of dock and hull for when sailors can't be on their boats—which is most of the year. In summer thousands of craft jostle among the islands of the archipelago and clog the lakes and rivers. Statistics claim there are more than 250,000 boats in the Stockholm archipelago alone. Boating opportunities are plentiful, from hourly rentals to chartered cruises in anything from kayaks to motor launches to huge luxury ferry liners.

Skiing

Sweden is a skiing nation, with plenty of major mountains for downhill skiing and snowboarding and endless trials for Nordic skiing. The best areas are in the north, with Åre offering the most challenging terrain and Sälen better for families. One of Sweden's legendary sports heroes is Ingemar Stenmark, the champion downhill skier who dominated the sport in the 1970s. Today Pernilla Wiberg is the queen of the slopes.

Tennis

When Björn Borg began to win Wimbledon with almost monotonous regularity, Sweden became a force in world tennis. As such, the country is filled with indoor and outdoor courts, and major competitions—notably the Stockholm Open—take place regularly. One of the most unusual is the annual Donald Duck Cup, in Båstad, for children ages 11–15; ever since the young Björn won a Donald Duck trophy, the tournament has attracted thousands of youngsters who hope to imitate his success.

The sights, restaurants, hotels, and other travel experiences on these pages are our editors' top picks—our Fodor's Choices. They're the best of their type in the area covered by the book—not to be missed and always worth your time. In the destination chapters that follow, you will find all the details.

LODGING

$$$–$$$$　**Berns, Stockholm.** Discreet lighting; modern Italian furniture; and swank marble, granite, and wood inlays all work together to bring art-deco style to Berns, which has been open for business since the days of Strindberg.

$$$–$$$$　**Diplomat, Stockholm.** You never feel the Diplomat has to try too hard; Euro-chic meets quiet efficiency in an effortlessly stylish art-nouveau showpiece.

$$$$　**Grand Hotel, Stockholm.** The city's showpiece, an 1874 landmark, is luxurious and has a glassed-in veranda overlooking the harbor.

$$$　**Radisson SAS Grand Hotel, Saltsjöbaden.** A white-stone confection in the fashionable Victorian resort outside Stockholm. The grandeur is pleasantly faded, the service perfectly deft.

$–$$$　**Villa Källhagen, Stockholm.** Peaceful grace, natural light, an affinity with the changing seasons and one of Sweden's best restaurants— all this is just minutes from bustling downtown Stockholm.

$$　**Elite Plaza, Göteborg.** The palatial 1889 exterior encloses a stylish modern hotel with luxury and quiet elegance. All the original details remain, from stucco ceilings to the English mosaic floor.

$$　**Hotel Continental, Ystad.** The Continental is grand inside and out. The remarkable foyer has marble chandeliers and marble pillars and stairs. Every room is bright, modern, and unique.

$–$$　**Grand Hotel, Mölle.** It's not the plushest hotel in the world, but the turreted Grand has a cordial staff and an unrivaled view of the town below. The hotel's restaurant is also excellent.

BUDGET LODGING

¢–$$　**Columbus Hotel, Stockholm.** Ideal for a quiet vacation, the Columbus is an oasis of calm in the busy urban streets of Södermalm.

$　**Hotel Gustav Wasa, Stockholm.** Right next to Odenplan Square, the Gustav Wasa is a great budget option, a friendly hotel in the heart of downtown.

$　**Hotel Winn, Falun.** Built in rustic Dalarna style, this small, cozy hotel in the town center is the place to unwind after a long day's sightseeing.

$　**Marina Plaza, Helsingborg.** The use of space, style, and elegance— especially in the loftlike atrium—lends a decidedly modern appeal to this lodging.

$	**Pärlan, Stockholm.** Entering the Pearl, a bed-and-breakfast on a quiet street in Östermalm, is like walking into a home from the 19th century.
$	**Royal, Göteborg.** Small, family owned, and traditional, the Royal is a taste of old-fashioned Swedish elegance in the center of bustling Göteborg.
¢	**Hotel Dalecarlia, Tällberg.** There's a homey feel to this first-class hotel, which has good lake views, a spa and fitness center, and wonderful food.
¢	**Rum i Backen, Vaxholm.** This pretty, early-20th-century wooden house on Vaxholm's main street is a charming, family-run B&B with just one guest room.

RESTAURANTS

$$$–$$$$	**Edsbacka Krog, Stockholm.** Traditional Swedish cuisine is taken to new heights at this phenomenal restaurant in an old inn just outside town.
$$$–$$$$	**Wedholms Fisk, Stockholm.** The traditional Swedish fare here, especially the fresh fish, is simple but outstanding.
$$$	**Bon Lloc, Stockholm.** Enjoy Mediterranean-influenced Swedish cuisine at this elegant restaurant.
$$$	**Fredsgatan 12, Stockholm.** Stockholm's politicians and style mavens gather here for the Swedish-Asian fare, which is some of the best grub in town.
$$$	**Le Village, Göteborg.** The food here is exceptional, especially the seasonal meat dishes. If you like any of the furnishings, you can buy them from the store next door.
¢–$$$	**Tranan, Stockholm.** The food here is Swedish with a touch of French, and is so good it'll make you want to keep coming back.
$–$$	**Cyrano, Göteborg.** A little piece of southern France in Sweden, this superb, authentically Provençal bistro is an absolute must.
$–$$	**Salt & Brygga, Malmö.** Not only is the Mediterranean cooking here done with organic produce, but ecologically-friendly materials have been used for everything from the wall paint to the table linens and the staff's uniforms.

BUDGET RESTAURANTS

¢–$	**Herman's, Stockholm.** Try the buffet-style vegetarian meals at this Södermalm institution.
¢–$	**Il Forno, Stockholm.** Go to Il Forno for some of the best brick-oven pizza north of the Mediterranean—be sure to sit outside in summer.
¢	**Jukkasjärvi Wärdshus, Jukkasjärvi.** The Norrland cuisine—characterized by reindeer, wild berries, mushrooms, dried and smoked meats, salted fish, fermented herring, and rich sauces using thick creams—is suberb at this hotel restaurant.

¢ **Köpmangården, Sunne.** If you blink, you may miss this tiny bar and restaurant on a residential street, serving delicious, hearty meals.

¢–$$ **Pelican, Stockholm.** This traditional, working-class drinking hall serves hearty Swedish fare and lots of beer.

$ **Lottas, Ystad.** The steak is beautifully cooked and presented at this typical southern Swedish restaurant.Castles and Palaces

CASTLES & PALACES

Drottningholms Slott, Stockholm. One of the most delightful European palaces, this is a kind of miniature Versailles, full of insights into how mid-18th-century royalty lived.

Kalmar Slott, Småland. Sweden's best-preserved Renaissance castle is set on a commanding site on the Baltic shore. Sections of it date back 800 years.

Kungliga Slottet, Stockholm. In this magnificent granite edifice you can tour the State Apartments; the Royal Armory; and the Treasury, where the crown jewels are kept.

Tjolöholms Slott, Tjolöholm, Swedish Riviera. This eccentric castle, built at the turn of the 20th century by a Scottish manufacturer, has amazing interiors full of what were then state-of-the-art touches.

MUSEUMS & MONUMENTS

Carl Larsson Gården, Sundborn. The cottage here contains an exceptional assortment of beautiful rooms and works of art.

Marinmuseum, Karlskrona. One of the oldest museums in Sweden, opened in 1752, the Naval Museum is a UNESCO Heritage Site.

Motala Motormuseum. Packed with pristine cars and the paraphernalia of bygone days, the Motor Museum brings the past to life with music and a sense of fun.

Nationalmuseum, Stockholm. The museum's collection of paintings and sculptures is made up of about 12,500 works, with an emphasis on Swedish and Nordic art.

Stadshuset, Stockholm. A trip to the top of the tower of this ornate building, is rewarded by a breathtaking panorama of the city and Riddarfjärden.

Skansen, Stockholm. Farmhouses, windmills, barns, and churches are just some of the buildings brought from around the country and preserved in this museum.

Vasamuseet, Stockholm. The *Vasa*, a warship that sank on its maiden voyage in 1628, was raised nearly intact in 1961 and now has its own museum.

Zorn Museet, Mora. Many fine paintings by Anders Zorn (1860–1920), Sweden's leading impressionist painter, are displayed in this museum next to the beautiful house he built in his hometown.

CHURCHES

Domkyrkan, Lund, the South. A seat of religious power in Sweden since 1103, this monumental cathedral also manages to seem gracious. The astrological clock, with moving mechanical figures, is not to be missed.

Leksands Kyrka, Leksand, Dalarna. Sweden's largest village church is also one of its prettiest. The shaded churchyard opens out onto a stunning view across Lake Silja.

Skellefteå Landskyrka, Skellefteå, Bothnian Coast. Set in a 400-room "village" built to house a traveling congregation, this striking neo-classical church is a reminder of northern Sweden's staunch Christian past. Its 800-year-old Romanesque Maria carving is one of the few of its kind left in the world.

Heligkorskyrkan i Dalby, near Lund. Founded in 1060, this is the oldest stone church in Sweden. It retains many of its original features, including the exposed brick within the church, and a renowned baptismal font.

PARKS & GARDENS

Trädgårdsföreningens Park, Göteborg. You'll find beautiful open green spaces at the Horticultural Society Park, as well as a magnificent rose garden, and a butterfly house.

Rosendals Trädgårder This gorgeous slice of greenery is a perfect place to spend a few hours on a late summer afternoon. When the weather's nice, people flock to the garden café.

Sofiero Slott, Helsingborg. The park of Sofiero Palace is a delight, filled with more than 10,000 samples of 300 kinds of rhododendron, various statues donated by international artists, greenhouses, and a large English garden

Bergianska Trädgården, Stockholm. The beautiful Bergianska Botanical Gardens, on a peninsula extending out into the small bay of Brunnsvik, can provide a wonderful break from the city.

QUINTESSENTIAL SWEDEN

Cruising on a steamship in the Stockholm archipelago.

Dogsledding in Norrland.

Happening upon the Midsummer celebrations around Lake Silja.

Hiking around the island of Ørland, with its ancient runic stones, nature reserve, and extraordinary birdlife.

Picnicking at sunset on the coastal cliffs beside the mysterious Ales Stones, near Ystad, which still mystify archaeologists to this day.

Watching a Lucia procession at Christmastime.

SMART TRAVEL TIPS

Finding out about your destination before you leave home means you won't squander time organizing everyday minutiae once you've arrived. You'll be more streetwise when you hit the ground as well, better prepared to explore the aspects of Sweden that drew you here in the first place. The organizations in this section can provide information to supplement this guide; contact them for up-to-the-minute details, and consult the A to Z sections that end each chapter for facts on the various topics as they relate to Sweden's many regions. Happy landings!

AIR TRAVEL

BOOKING

When you book **look for nonstop flights and remember that "direct" flights stop at least once.** Try to avoid connecting flights, which require a change of plane. For more booking tips and to check prices and make on-line flight reservations, log on to www.fodors.com.

CARRIERS

All major cities and towns are linked with regular flights by Scandinavian Airlines System (SAS). Malmö Aviation also has service between Stockholm, Göteborg, and Malmö. Most Swedish airports are a long way from city centers but are served by fast and efficient bus service. From North America, American, Delta, Finnair, Iceland Air, Lufthansa, SAS, United, and other major airlines serve Stockholm's Arlanda International Airport and Göteborg's Landvetter Airport. From the United Kingdom, Stockholm and Göteborg are served by SAS, British Airways, British Midland, and Ryan Air.

Airlines and Contacts American ☎ 800/433-7300 ⊕ www.aa.com. **British Airways** ☎ 020/88974000 ⊕ www.british-airways.com. **British Midland** ☎ 01332/854000 in the U.K ⊕ www.flybmi.com. **Delta** ☎ 800/221-1212 ⊕ www.delta.com. **Finnair** ☎ 800/950-5000 ⊕ www.finnair.com. **Iceland Air** ☎ 800/223-5500 ⊕ www.icelandair.com. **Lufthansa** ☎ 800/645-3880 ⊕ www.lufthansa.com. **Ryan Air** ☎ 0871/2460000 in the U.K., 0155/202240 in Sweden ⊕ www.ryanair.com. **SAS** ☎ 0770/727727 in Sweden, 020/77344020 in the U.K., 800/433-7300 in the U.S. ⊕ www.scandinavian.net. **United** ☎ 800/241-6522 ⊕ www.united.com.

CHECK-IN & BOARDING

Always **ask your carrier about its check-in policy.** Plan to arrive at the airport about 2 hours before your scheduled departure time for domestic flights and 2½ to 3 hours before international flights.

Assuming that not everyone with a ticket will show up, airlines routinely overbook planes. When everyone does, airlines ask for volunteers to give up their seats. In return, these volunteers usually get a certificate for a free flight and are rebooked on the next flight out. If there are not enough volunteers, the airline must choose who will be denied boarding. The first to get bumped are passengers who checked in late and those flying on discounted tickets, so **get to the gate and check in as early as possible,** especially during peak periods.

Always **bring a government-issued photo I.D. to the airport;** even when it's not required, a passport is best.

CUTTING COSTS

Intra-Scandinavian air travel is usually expensive. If you want to economize, look into the Visit Scandinavia Fare offered by SAS. One coupon costs about $69, but they vary greatly depending on routing and destination—generally, the cost rises the farther north the destination, up to about $200. The coupons are valid for destinations within Denmark, Norway, and Sweden and also between Sweden and Finland. They are sold only in the United States and only to non-Scandinavians. Coupons can be used year-round for a maximum of three months and must be purchased in conjunction with transatlantic flights.

The **SAS Visit Scandinavia/Europe Air Pass** offers up to eight flight coupons for one-way travel within and between Scandinavian cities (and participating European cities such as Frankfurt, Paris, and London). Most one-way tickets for domestic travel within each Scandinavian country cost $65; one-way fares between Scandinavian countries are usually $75, unless you are venturing into the far north, Lapland, Iceland, or Greenland (these flights range from $115 to $225). These passes can be bought only in conjunction with a round-trip ticket between North America and Europe on SAS and must be used within three months of arrival. SAS also provides family fares—children between 2 and 17 and a spouse can receive 50% off the full fare of business-class tickets with the purchase of one full-fare business-class ticket. Contact SAS for information.

The least expensive airfares to Scandinavia must usually be purchased in advance and are nonrefundable.

It's smart to **call a number of airlines,** and when you are quoted a good price, **book it on the spot**—the same fare may not be available the next day. Always **check different routings** and look into using different airports. Travel agents, especially low-fare specialists (⇨ Discounts & Deals), are helpful.

Consolidators are another good source. They buy tickets for scheduled international flights at reduced rates from the airlines, then sell them at prices that beat the best fare available directly from the airlines, usually without restrictions. Sometimes you can even get your money back if you need to return the ticket. Carefully read the fine print detailing penalties for changes and cancellations, and **confirm your consolidator reservation with the airline.**

🔲 **Consolidators** AirlineConsolidator.com ☎ 888/468-5385 ⊕ www.airlineconsolidator.com; for international tickets. **Best Fares** ☎ 800/576-8255 or 800/576-1600 ⊕ www.bestfares.com; $59.90 annual membership. **Cheap Tickets** ☎ 800/377-1000 or 888/922-8849 ⊕ www.cheaptickets.com. **Expedia** ☎ 800/397-3342 or 404/728-8787 ⊕ www.expedia.com. **Hotwire** ☎ 866/468-9473 or 920/330-9418 ⊕ www.hotwire.com. **Now Voyager Travel** ✉ 45 W. 21st St., 5th floor, New York, NY 10010 ☎ 212/459-1616 🖷 212/243-2711 ⊕ www.nowvoyagertravel.com. **Onetravel.com** ⊕ www.onetravel.com. **Orbitz** ☎ 888/656-4546 ⊕ www.orbitz.com. **Priceline.com** ⊕ www.priceline.com. **Travelocity** ☎ 888/709-5983, 877/282-2925 in Canada, 0870/111-7060 in the U.K. ⊕ www.travelocity.com.

ENJOYING THE FLIGHT

For more legroom, **request an emergency-aisle seat.** Don't sit in the row in front of the emergency aisle or in front of a bulkhead, where seats may not recline. If you have dietary concerns, **ask for special meals when booking.** These can be vegetarian, low-cholesterol, or kosher, for example. On long flights, try to maintain a normal routine, to help fight jet lag. At night, **get some sleep.** By day, **eat light meals, drink water** (not alcohol), and **move around the cabin** to stretch your legs. Many airlines offer in-flight exercise videos or information sheets, designed to promote well-being in the air. For additional jet-lag tips consult *Fodor's FYI: Travel Fit & Healthy* (available at bookstores everywhere).

FLYING TIMES

Flying time from New York to Stockholm is eight hours. From London's Heathrow Airport flying time to Stockholm is 2¼ hours. From Sydney and major cities in New Zealand, the flight to any Scandinavian country will last more than 20 hours and will require at least one transfer.

HOW TO COMPLAIN

If your baggage goes astray or your flight goes awry, complain right away. Most carriers require that you **file a claim immediately.** The Aviation Consumer Protection Division of the Department of Transportation publishes *Fly-Rights,* which discusses airlines and consumer issues and is available on-line. You can also find articles and information on mytravelrights.com, the Web site of the nonprofit Consumer Travel Rights Center.

Airline Complaints **Aviation Consumer Protection Division** ✉ U.S. Department of Transportation, C-75, Room 4107, 400 7th St. SW, Washington, DC 20590 ☎ 202/366-2220 ⊕ airconsumer.ost.dot.gov. **Federal Aviation Administration Consumer Hotline** ✉ for inquiries: FAA, 800 Independence Ave. SW, Washington, DC 20591 ☎ 800/322-7873 ⊕ www.faa.gov.

AIRPORTS

Sweden's major gateway, **Arlanda International Airport,** is 41 km (26 mi) north of Stockholm. Göteborg's **Landvetter Airport** is 26 km (16 mi) from the city.

Airport Information **Arlanda International Airport** ☎ 46/87976100 ⊕ www.lfv.se. **Landvetter Airport** ☎ 46/31941100 ⊕ www.lfv.se.

BIKE TRAVEL

Cycling is a very popular sport in Sweden and the south of the country, with its low-lying, flat landscape, is perfect for the more genteel cyclist. All major towns and cities are well provided with cycle paths and designated cycle lanes. Bike-rental costs average around SKr 100 per day. Tourist offices and the Swedish Touring Association have information about cycling package holidays that include bike rentals, overnight accommodations, and

meals. The Swedish bicycling organization, Cykelfrämjandet (National Cycle Association), publishes a free English-language guide to cycling trips.

Cykelfrämjandet ✉ Thuleg. 43, 113 53 Stockholm ☎ 08/54591030 Mon.-Thurs. 9-noon 📠 08/54591039 ⊕ www.cykelframjandet.a.se. **Swedish Touring Association** (STF) ✉ Box 25, 101 20 Stockholm ☎ 08/4632200 📠 08/6781938 ⊕ www.meravsverige.se.

BOAT & FERRY TRAVEL

A rewarding way to see Sweden is from the many ferryboats that ply the archipelagos and main lakes. In Stockholm visitors should buy a special *Båtluffarkort* (Inter Skerries Card, SKr 385) from Waxholmsbolaget. This card allows you 16 days of unlimited travel on the archipelago ferryboats. There are excellent links between Harwich, in the United Kingdom, and Göteborg, and between Newcastle, also in the United Kingdom, and Göteborg, aboard DFDS Seaways ferries. The Viking Lines and Silja Lines also have overnight ferries to Helsinki, Finland, both of them offering great bargains for one- and two-day round-trips. A word of warning though—the Helsinki boats are often filled with graduating students and other young Swedes taking right-of-passage cruises. If you are looking for a peaceful boat crossing, a quick glass of wine and a quiet night, find another route.

Taking a ferry is not only fun; it is often necessary in Scandinavia. Many companies arrange package trips, some offering a rental car and hotel accommodations as part of the deal. The word *ferry* can be deceptive; generally, those vessels so named are more like small-scale cruise ships, with several dining rooms, sleeping quarters, shopping, pool and sauna, and entertainment.

Ferry crossings often last overnight. The trip between Copenhagen and Oslo, for example, takes approximately 16 hours; most lines leave about 5 PM and arrive about 9 the next morning. The direct cruise between Stockholm and Helsinki takes 12 hours, usually leaving about 6 PM and arriving the next morning at 9. Trips from Germany to Oslo and Helsinki generally take about 20 hours; crossings to Reykjavík from Bergen tend to last about two days (25 hours to the Faroe Islands, and another 24 hours to Iceland). The shortest ferry route runs between Helsingør, Denmark, and Helsingborg, Sweden; it takes only 20 minutes.

CAR FERRIES

Travel by car in Scandinavia often necessitates travel by ferry. Some well-known vehicle and passenger ferries run between Copenhagen, Denmark, and Malmö, Sweden; between Helsingør, Denmark, and Helsingborg, Sweden; between Copenhagen and Göteborg, Sweden; and between Stockholm, Sweden, and Helsinki, Finland. The Helsingør/Helsingborg ferry (ScandLines) takes only 20 minutes; taking a car costs between SKr 255 and SKr 275 (about $24–$26 or £16–£18.50) one-way. Transporting a car between Stockholm and Helsinki costs about € 52 during high season and € 29 during low season (about $47 and $26 or £32 and £18). Round-trip fares are cheaper, and on weekends the Øresund Runt pass (for crossing between Copenhagen and Malmö in one direction and Helsingborg and Helsingør in the other) costs only SKr 475 (about $45 or £31).

🛈 Boat & Ferry Information Color Line ✉ Box 30, DK-9850 Hirsthals, Denmark ☎ 45/99-56-20-00 🖷 45/99-56-20-20, ✉ Hjortneskaia, Box 1422 Vika, N-0115 Oslo, Norway ☎ 47/22-94-44-00 🖷 47/22-83-04-30, ✉ Color Scandi Line, Torksholmen, S-45 200 Strømstad, Sweden ☎ 46/52662000 🖷 46/52614669, ✉ Color Line GmbH, Postfach 6080, 24121 Kiel, Germany ☎ 49/431-7300-300 🖷 49/431-7300-400 ⊕ www.colorline.no. **Scand-Lines** ✉ Box 1, DK-3000 Helsingør, Denmark ☎ 45/33-15-15-15 🖷 45/33-15-10-20, ✉ Knutpunkten 43, S-252 78 Helsingborg, Sweden ☎ 46/42186100 🖷 46/42186049, ⊕ www.scandlines.com.

FERRIES FROM ENGLAND

The chief operator between England and many points within Scandinavia, Holland, and Germany is DFDS Seaways, with ships connecting Harwich and Newcastle to Esbjerg, Denmark; Kristiansand, Norway; and Amsterdam. Fjordline offers the only direct service from England to Bergen and northern Norway.

PLYING SCANDINAVIAN WATERS

Connections from Denmark to Norway and Sweden are available through DFDS and the Stena Line. Fjord Line sails along the magnificent west coast of Norway. Connections to the Faroe Islands and Iceland from Norway and Denmark are available through the Smyril Line. Silja Lines and Viking Lines offer a variety of cruises to Finland, with departures from Stockholm to Mariehamn, in the Åland archipelago, Turku (Åbo) and Helsinki (Helsingfors), and a crossing from Umeå to Vaasa.

🛈 Major Operators DFDS Seaways ✉ Sankt Annae Plads 30, DK-1295 Copenhagen, Denmark ☎ 45/33-42-33-42 🖷 45/33-42-33-41, ✉ DFDS Seaways Travel Centre, Scandinavia House, Parkeston, Harwich, Essex CO12 4QG ☎ 44/8705-333-000 🖷 44/1255-244-382, ✉ DFDS Seaways USA Inc., 6555 NW 9th Ave., Suite 207, Fort Lauderdale, FL 33309 ☎ 800/533-3755 🖷 954/491-7958, ✉ Box 8895, Scandiahamnen, S-402 72 Göteborg, Sweden ☎ 46/31650610 ⊕ www.seaeurope.com. **Fjord Line** ✉ Skoltegrunnskaien, Box 7250, N-5020 Bergen, Norway ☎ 47/55-54-88-00 🖷 47/55-54-86-01 ✉ Tyne Commission Quay, North Shields NE29 6EA, Newcastle, England ☎ 44/191-296-1313 🖷 44/191-296-1540 ⊕ www.fjordline.com. **Silja Line** ✉ Mannerheimintie 2, 00100 Helsinki, Finland ☎ 358/9-18041 🖷 358/9-1804279 ✉ Kungsgatan 2, S-111 43 Stockholm, Sweden ☎ 46/86663512 or 46/8222140, 🖷 46/86119162 or 46/92316066, ✉ c/o DFDS Seaways, Scandinavia House, Parkeston Quay, Harwich, Essex, England CO12 4QG ☎ 44/1255-240-240 🖷 44/255-244-382, ✉ c/o Norwegian Coastal Voyage, Inc./Bergen Line Service, 405 Park Ave., New York 10022 ☎ 212/319-1300 or 800/323-7436 🖷 212/319-1390 ⊕ www.silja.com/english. **Smyril Line** ✉ J. Brocksgøta 37, Box 370, FO-110 Tórshavn, Faroe Islands ☎ 298/34-59-00 🖷 298/34-59-50, ✉ Slottsgate 1, Box 4135 Dreggen, N-5835 Bergen, Norway ☎ 47/55-32-09-70 🖷 47/55-96-02-72 ⊕ www.smyril-line.com. **Stena Line** ✉ Trafikhamnen, DK-9900 Frederikshavn, Denmark ☎ 45/96-20-02-00 🖷 45/96-20-02-80, ✉ PB 764, Sentrum, N-0106 Oslo, Norway ☎ 47/23-17-91-00 🖷 47/23-17-90-60 ✉ Stena Line AB, S-405 19 Göteborg, Sweden ☎ 46/317040000 🖷 46/31858595 ⊕ www.stenaline.com. **Viking Line** ✉ Mannerheimintie 14, 00100 Helsinki ☎ 358/9-12351 🖷 358/9-647075 ⊕ www.vikingline.fi.

BUSINESS HOURS

BANKS & OFFICES

Banks are officially open weekdays 9:30–3, but many stay open until 5 on most weekdays and until 6 on Thursday. The bank at Arlanda International Airport is open every day with extended hours, and the Forex and Valuta Specialisten currency-exchange offices also have extended hours. Most banks operate a numbered-ticket system for lining up: take a number and wait your turn. Ticket machines are always somewhere near a bank's doors. Make exchanging money your first task to avoid a frustratingly long wait. More and more Swedes use Internet banking for daily cash transactions, and, strange as it may seem, it is not uncommon to come across cashless bank branches. These are more often found in smaller towns and villages, so it is worth checking before traveling.

MUSEUMS & SIGHTS

The opening times for museums vary widely, but most are open from 10 to 4 Tuesday–Sunday. Consult the guide in *På Stan,* the entertainment supplement published in *Dagens Nyheter's* Friday edition, or *What's On,* a monthly entertainment listings guide published in Swedish and English by the Swedish tourism authorities. It's available for free at hotels, tourist centers, and some restaurants.
🔳 Web Sites **På Stan** ⊕ www.dn.se/pastan. **What's On** ⊕ www.stockholmtown.se.

SHOPS

Shops are generally open weekdays from 9, 9:30, or 10 until 6 and Saturday from 10 to 1 or 4. Most large department stores stay open later in the evening, and some open on Sunday. Several supermarkets open on Sunday, and there are a number of late-night food shops such as the 7-Eleven chain. Systembolaget, Sweden's liquor monopoly and therefore the only place to buy alcohol, is open weekdays from 10 to 6, with extended hours until 7 on Thursday and Saturday from 10 to 2. Most Sytembolagets display their product behind glass. Customers take a numbered ticket and order at a counter from which their choice is collected when their number is called. Unless time is very definitely on your hands, avoid buying alcohol on a Friday, when the wait can be as long as an hour.

BUS TRAVEL

There is excellent bus service between all major towns and cities. Consult the *Yellow Pages* under "Bussresearrangörer" for the telephone numbers of the companies concerned. Recommended are the services offered to different parts of Sweden from Stockholm by Swebus. For local bus journeys, when buying a single ticket only, it is usual to pay the driver on boarding. Longer journeys and coupons or multiple tickets should be purchased before your journey from the relevant bus company.
🔳 Bus Information **Interbus** ☎ 08/7279000. **Svenska Buss** ☎ 0771/676767 ⊕ www.svenskabuss. se. **SwebusExpress** ☎ 0200/218218 ⊕ www. express.swebus.se.

CAMERAS & PHOTOGRAPHY

The *Kodak Guide to Shooting Great Travel Pictures* (available at bookstores everywhere) is loaded with tips.
🔳 Photo Help **Kodak Information Center** ☎ 800/ 242-2424.

CAR RENTAL

Major car-rental companies such as Avis, Bonus, Budget, Europcar, and Hertz have facilities in all major towns and cities as well as at airports. Various service stations also offer car rentals, including Q8, Shell, Statoil, and Texaco. See the *Yellow Pages* under "Biluthyrning" for telephone numbers and addresses. Renting a car is a speedy business in Sweden with none of the usual lengthy documentation and vehicle checks; show your passport, license, and credit card, pick up the key, and away you go. Although this is a plus if you are in a hurry, if you feel more comfortable being shown around your car before you drive, just ask and most companies will oblige.

Rates in Stockholm begin at $75 a day and $190 a week for a manual-drive economy car without air-conditioning and with unlimited mileage. This does not include tax on car rentals, which is 25% in Sweden. A service charge also is usually added, which ranges from $15 to $25.
🔳 Major Agencies **Alamo** ☎ 800/522-9696, 020/ 8759-6200 in the U.K. ⊕ www.alamo.com. **Avis** ☎ 800/331-1084, 800/879-2847 in Canada, 02/ 9353-9000 in Australia, 09/525-1982 in New Zealand, 0870/606-0100 in the U.K. ⊕ www.avis. com. **Budget** ☎ 800/527-0700, 0870/156-5656 in the U.K. ⊕ www.budget.com. **Dollar** ☎ 800/800-6000, 0124/622-0111 in the U.K., where it's affiliated with Sixt, 02/9223-1444 in Australia ⊕ www.dollar. com. **Hertz** ☎ 800/654-3001, 800/263-0600 in Canada, 020/8897-2072 in the U.K., 02/9669-2444 in Australia, 09/256-8690 in New Zealand ⊕ www. hertz.com **National Car Rental** ☎ 800/227-7368, 020/8680-4800 in the U.K. ⊕ www.nationalcar.com.

CUTTING COSTS

To get the best deal, **book through a travel agent who will shop around.** Do **look into wholesalers,** companies that do not own fleets but rent in bulk from those that do and often offer better rates than traditional car-rental operations. Payment must be made before you leave home.

Wholesalers Auto Europe ☎ 207/842-2000 or 800/223-5555 🖶 207/842-2222 ⊕ www.autoeurope.com. **Europe by Car** ☎ 212/581-3040 or 800/223-1516 🖶 212/246-1458 ⊕ www.europebycar.com. **DER Travel Services** ✉ 9501 W. Devon Ave., Rosemont, IL 60018 ☎ 800/782-2424 🖶 800/282-7474 for information, 800/860-9944 for brochures ⊕ www.dertravel.com. **Kemwel Holiday Autos** ☎ 800/678-0678 🖶 914/825-3160 ⊕ www.kemwel.com.

INSURANCE

When driving a rented car you are generally responsible for any damage to or loss of the vehicle. Before you rent, see what coverage your personal auto-insurance policy and credit cards provide.

Before you buy collision coverage, check your existing policies—you may already be covered. However, collision policies that car-rental companies sell for European rentals usually do not include stolen-vehicle coverage.

REQUIREMENTS & RESTRICTIONS

Ask about age requirements: Several countries require drivers to be over 20 years old, but some car-rental companies require that drivers be at least 25. In Scandinavia your own driver's license is acceptable for a limited time; check with the country's tourist board before you go. An International Driver's Permit is a good idea; it's available from the American or Canadian Automobile Association or, in the United Kingdom, from the Automobile Association or Royal Automobile Club.

SURCHARGES

Before you pick up a car in one city and leave it in another, **ask about drop-off charges or one-way service fees,** which can be substantial. Note, too, that some rental agencies charge extra if you return the car before the time specified in your contract. To avoid a hefty refueling fee, **fill the tank just before you turn in the car,** but be aware that gas stations near the rental outlet may overcharge.

CAR TRAVEL

The Øresundsbron, the new 8-km (5-mi) bridge between Malmö and Copenhagen, simplifies car travel and makes train connections possible between the two countries. Ferry service is cheaper but slower—it takes 45 minutes to make the crossing.

Sweden has an excellent highway network of more than 80,000 km (50,000 mi). The fastest routes are those with numbers prefixed with an *E* (for "European"), some of which are the equivalent of American highways or British motorways. The size of the country compared to its population means that most roads are relatively traffic free. However, rush hour around major cities can bring traffic jams and holdups of frustrating proportions.

Also be aware that there are relatively low legal blood-alcohol limits and tough penalties for driving while intoxicated in Scandinavia; Sweden, Iceland, and Finland have zero-tolerance laws. Penalties include license suspension and fines or imprisonment, and the laws are sometimes enforced by random police roadblocks in urban areas on weekends. In addition, an accident involving a driver who has an illegal blood-alcohol level usually voids all insurance agreements, making the driver responsible for all medical bills and collision damage.

In a few remote areas in northern Sweden, road conditions can be unpredictable, and careful planning is required for safety's sake. Several mountain and highland roads in these areas close during winter—when driving in such remote areas, especially in winter, it is best to let someone know your travel plans. It is also wise to **use a four-wheel-drive vehicle** and to **travel with at least one other car** in these areas.

AUTO CLUBS

In Australia Australian Automobile Association ☎ 02/6247-7311.
In Canada Canadian Automobile Association (CAA) ☎ 613/247-0117.
In New Zealand New Zealand Automobile Association ☎ 09/377-4660.
In the U.K. Automobile Association (AA) ☎ 0990/500-600. **Royal Automobile Club (RAC)** ☎ 0990/722-722 for membership, 0345/121-345 for insurance.
In the U.S. American Automobile Association ☎ 800/564-6222.

EMERGENCY SERVICES

The Larmtjänst organization, run by a confederation of Swedish insurance companies, provides a 24-hour breakdown service. Its phone numbers are listed in the *Yellow Pages*.

GASOLINE

Sweden has some of the highest gasoline rates in Europe, about SKr 10 per liter (about SKr 38 per gallon). Lead-free gasoline is readily available. Gas stations are self-service: pumps marked SEDEL are automatic and accept SKr 20 and SKr 100 bills; pumps marked KASSA are paid for at the cashier; the KONTO pumps are for customers with credit cards.

PARKING

Parking meters and, increasingly, timed ticket machines operate in larger towns, usually between 8 AM and 6 PM. The fee varies from about SKr 6 to SKr 35 per hour. Parking garages in urban areas are mostly automated, often with machines that accept credit cards; LEDIGT on a garage sign means space is available. Many streets in urban areas are cleaned weekly at a designated time on a designated day, during which time parking is not allowed, not even at meters. Times are marked on a yellow sign at each end of the street. Try to avoid getting a parking ticket, which can come with fines of SKr 300–SKr 700.

ROAD CONDITIONS

All main and secondary roads are well surfaced, but some minor roads, particularly in the north, are gravel.

ROAD MAPS

If you plan on extensive road touring, consider buying the *Vägatlas över Sverige*, a detailed road atlas published by the Mötormännens Riksförbund, available at bookstores for around SKr 300.

RULES OF THE ROAD

Drive on the right, and—no matter where you sit in a car—seat belts are mandatory. You must also have at least low-beam headlights on at all times. Cars rented or bought in Sweden will have automatic headlights, which are activated every time the engine is switched on. Signs indicate five basic speed limits, ranging from 30 kph (19 mph), in school or playground areas, to 110 kph (68 mph), on long stretches of E roads.

CHILDREN IN SWEDEN

In Sweden children are to be seen *and* heard and are genuinely welcome in most public places. This includes restaurants and bars, most of which will offer baby and infant chairs.

If you are renting a car, don't forget to **arrange for a car seat** when you reserve. For general advice about traveling with children, consult *Fodor's FYI: Travel with Your Baby* (available in bookstores everywhere).

DISCOUNTS

Children are entitled to discount tickets (often as much as 50% off) on buses, trains, and ferries throughout Scandinavia, as well as reductions on special City Cards. A parent with a buggy or stroller travels free on local buses in Sweden's towns and cities. On SAS children age 2–12 pay 75%, children under two 10%, of an adult round-trip airfare. There are no restrictions on children's fares when booked in economy class. "Family fares," available only in business class, are also worth looking into (⇨ Cutting Costs *under* Air Travel).

With the Scanrail Pass (⇨ Train Travel)—good for rail journeys throughout Scandinavia—children under age 4 travel free (on lap); those ages 4–11 pay half fare, and those ages 12–25 can get a Scanrail Youth Pass, providing a 25% discount off the adult fare.

FLYING

If your children are age 2 or older, **ask about children's airfares.** As a general rule, infants under 2 not occupying a seat fly at greatly reduced fares or even for free. When booking, **confirm carry-on allowances** if you're traveling with infants. In general, for babies charged 10% of the adult fare you are allowed one carry-on bag and a collapsible stroller; if the flight is full, the stroller may have to be checked or you may be limited to less.

Experts agree that it's a good idea to use safety seats aloft for children weighing less than 40 pounds. Airlines set their own policies: U.S. carriers usually require that the child be ticketed, even if he or she is young enough to ride free, since the seats must be strapped into regular seats. Do **check your airline's policy about using safety seats during takeoff and landing.** And since safety seats are not allowed everywhere in the plane, get your seat assignments early.

When reserving, **request children's meals or a freestanding bassinet** if you need them. But note that bulkhead seats, where you must sit to use the bassinet, may lack an overhead bin or storage space on the floor. For all airlines servicing Scandinavia, it is necessary to reserve children's and infant meals at least 24 hours in advance; travel of an unaccompanied minor should be confirmed at least three days prior to the flight.

LODGING

Most hotels in Scandinavia allow children under a certain age to stay in their parents' room at no extra charge, but others charge for them as extra adults; be sure to **find out the cutoff age for children's discounts.**

SIGHTS & ATTRACTIONS

Places that are especially appealing to children are indicated by a rubber-duckie icon (🦆) in the margin.

CONSUMER PROTECTION

Whenever shopping or buying travel services in Scandinavia, **pay with a major credit card,** if possible, so you can cancel payment or get reimbursed if there's a problem. If you're doing business with a particular company for the first time, **contact your local Better Business Bureau and the attorney general's offices** in your state and (for U.S. businesses) the company's home state as well. Have any complaints been filed? Finally, if you're buying a package or tour, always **consider travel insurance** that includes default coverage (⇨ Insurance).

⛵ BBBs Council of Better Business Bureaus ✉ 4200 Wilson Blvd., Suite 800, Arlington, VA 22203 ☎ 703/276-0100 🖷 703/525-8277 ⊕ www. bbb.org.

CRUISE TRAVEL

You can go on one of the highly popular four-day cruises of the Göta Canal, which traverse rivers, lakes, and, on the last lap, the Baltic Sea. A lovely waterway, the Göta Canal with its 65 locks links Göteborg, on

the west coast, with Stockholm, on the east. Cruise participants travel on fine old steamers, some of which date almost to the canal's opening, in 1832. The oldest and most desirable is the *Juno*, built in 1874. Prices start at SKr 6,100 for a bed in a double cabin. For more information contact the Göta Canal Steamship Company.

To learn how to plan, choose, and book a cruise-ship voyage, check out Cruise How-To's on www.fodors.com.

⛵ Cruise Lines Göta Canal Steamship Company ✉ Box 272, S401 24 Göteborg ☎ 03/1806315 🖷 03/1158311 ⊕ www.gotacanal.se.

CUSTOMS & DUTIES

When shopping, **keep receipts** for all purchases. Upon reentering the country, **be ready to show customs officials what you've bought.** If you feel a duty is incorrect or object to the way your clearance was handled, note the inspector's badge number and ask to see a supervisor. If the problem isn't resolved, write to the appropriate authorities, beginning with the port director at your point of entry.

IN AUSTRALIA

Australian residents who are 18 or older may bring home $A400 worth of souvenirs and gifts (including jewelry), 250 cigarettes or 250 grams of tobacco, and 1,125 ml of alcohol (including wine, beer, and spirits). Residents under 18 may bring back $A200 worth of goods. Prohibited items include meat products. Seeds, plants, and fruits need to be declared upon arrival.

⛵ Australian Customs Service Regional Director ✉ Box 8, Sydney, NSW 2001, Australia ☎ 02/9213-2000 🖷 02/9213-4000 ⊕ www.customs.gov.au.

IN CANADA

Canadian residents who have been out of Canada for at least seven days may bring home C$750 worth of goods duty-free. If you've been away fewer than seven days but more than 48 hours, the duty-free allowance drops to C$200; if your trip lasts 24–48 hours, the allowance is C$50. You may not pool allowances with family members. Goods claimed under the C$750 exemption may follow you by mail; those claimed under the lesser exemptions must accompany you. Alcohol and tobacco products may be included in the seven-day and 48-hour exemptions but not in the 24-hour exemption. If you meet the age requirements of the province or territory through which you reenter Canada, you may bring in, duty-free, 1.14 liters (40 imperial ounces) of wine or liquor *or* 24 12-ounce cans or bottles of beer or ale. If you are 19 or older you may bring in, duty-free, 200 cigarettes and 50 cigars. Check ahead of time with the Canada Customs Revenue Agency or the Department of Agriculture for policies regarding meat products, seeds, plants, and fruits.

You may send an unlimited number of gifts worth up to C$60 each duty-free to Canada. Label the package UNSOLICITED GIFT—VALUE UNDER $60. Alcohol and tobacco are excluded.

🚩 **Canada Customs and Revenue Agency** ⊠ 2265 St. Laurent Blvd. S, Ottawa, Ontario K1G 4K3, Canada ☎ 204/983-3500 or 506/636-5064, 800/461-9999 in Canada ⊕ www.ccra-adrc.gc.ca.

IN NEW ZEALAND

Homeward-bound residents 17 or older may bring back $700 worth of souvenirs and gifts. Your duty-free allowance also includes 4.5 liters of wine or beer; one 1,125-ml bottle of spirits; and either 200 cigarettes, 250 grams of tobacco, 50 cigars, or a combination of the three up to 250 grams. Prohibited items include meat products, seeds, plants, and fruits.

🚩 **New Zealand Customs** Custom House ⊠ 50 Anzac Ave., Box 29, Auckland, New Zealand ☎ 09/300-5399 🖶 09/359-6730 ⊕ www.customs.govt.nz.

IN SWEDEN

Travelers 21 or older entering Sweden from non-EU countries may import duty-free 1 liter of liquor and 2 liters of fortified wine; 2 liters of wine or 15 liters of beer; 200 cigarettes or 100 grams of cigarillos or 50 cigars or 250 grams of tobacco; 50 grams of perfume; ¼ liter of aftershave; and other goods whose total value does not exceed SKr 1,700. Travelers from the United Kingdom or other EU countries may import duty-free 1 liter of liquor or 3 liters of fortified wine; 5 liters of wine; 15 liters of beer; 300 cigarettes or 150 cigarillos or 75 cigars or 400 grams of tobacco; and other goods, including perfume and aftershave, of any value.

IN THE U.K.

If you are a U.K. resident and your journey was wholly within the European Union,

you probably won't have to pass through customs when you return to the United Kingdom. If you plan to bring back large quantities of alcohol or tobacco, check EU limits beforehand. In most cases, if you bring back more than 200 cigars, 3,200 cigarettes, 10 liters of spirits, 110 liters of beer, and/or 90 liters of wine, you have to declare the goods upon return.

From countries outside the European Union, including Iceland and Norway, you may bring home, duty-free, 200 cigarettes or 50 cigars; 1 liter of spirits or 2 liters of fortified or sparkling wine or liqueurs; 2 liters of still table wine; 60 milliliters of perfume; 250 milliliters of toilet water; plus £145 worth of other goods, including gifts and souvenirs. If you are from a non-EU country, items prohibited to bring with you on your return include meat products, seeds, plants, and fruits.

🚩 **HM Customs and Excise** ⊠ St. Christopher House, Southwark, London, SE1 OTE, U.K. ☎ 020/7928-3344 ⊕ www.hmce.gov.uk.

IN THE U.S.

U.S. residents who have been out of the country for at least 48 hours (and who have not used the $400 allowance or any part of it in the past 30 days) may bring home $400 worth of foreign goods duty-free.

U.S. residents age 21 and older may bring back 1 liter of alcohol duty-free. In addition, regardless of your age, you are allowed 200 cigarettes and 100 non-Cuban cigars. Antiques, which the U.S. Bureau of Customs and Border Protection defines as objects more than 100 years old, enter duty-free, as do original works of art done entirely by hand, including paintings, drawings, and sculptures.

You may also mail or ship packages home duty-free: up to $200 worth of goods for personal use, with a limit of one parcel per addressee per day (except alcohol or tobacco products or perfume worth more than $5); label the package PERSONAL USE and attach a list of its contents and their retail value. Do not label the package UNSOLICITED GIFT or your duty-free exemption will drop to $100. Mailed items do not affect your duty-free allowance on your return.

🚩 **U.S. Customs Service** ⊠ 1300 Pennsylvania Ave. NW, Room 6.3D, Washington, DC 20229 ⊕ www.customs.gov ☎ 202/354-1000 inquiries

✉ complaints c/o 1300 Pennsylvania Ave. NW, Room 5.4D, Washington, DC 20229 ✉ registration of equipment c/o Office of Passenger Programs ☎ 202/927–0530.

DISABILITIES & ACCESSIBILITY

Facilities for travelers with disabilities in Scandinavia are generally good, and most major tourist offices offer special booklets and brochures on travel and accommodations. Most Scandinavian countries have organizations that offer advice to travelers with disabilities and can give information on public and local transportation, sights and museums, hotels, and special-interest tours. Notify and make all local and public transportation and hotel reservations in advance to ensure a smooth trip.

F Local Resources **DHR De Handikappades Riksförbund** ✉ Box 47305, Katrinebergsvägen 6, 100 74 Stockholm, Sweden ☎ 46/86858000 ⊕ www.dhr.se/english.htm.

LODGING

Best Western in Stockholm has properties with wheelchair-accessible rooms. If wheelchair-accessible rooms on other floors are not available, ground-floor rooms are provided.

F Wheelchair-Friendly Chain **Best Western** ☎ 800/528–1234.

RESERVATIONS

When discussing accessibility with an operator or reservations agent, **ask hard questions.** Are there any stairs, inside *or* out? Are there grab bars next to the toilet *and* in the shower/tub? How wide is the doorway to the room? To the bathroom? For the most extensive facilities, **opt for newer accommodations.**

SIGHTS & ATTRACTIONS

Although most major attractions in Stockholm present no problems, windy cobblestone streets, especially in the Gamla Stan (Old Town), may be challenging for travelers with disabilities.

TRANSPORTATION

With advance notice most airlines, buses, and trains can arrange assistance for those requiring extra help with boarding. Contact each company you will be using at least one week in advance or, ideally, when you book.

Confirming ahead is especially important when planning travel to less populated regions. Not all of the smaller planes and ferries often used in such areas are accessible.

F Complaints **Aviation Consumer Protection Division** (⇨ Air Travel) for airline-related problems. **Civil Rights Office** ✉ U.S. Department of Transportation, Departmental Office of Civil Rights, S-30, 400 7th St. SW, Room 10215, Washington, DC 20590 ☎ 202/366–4648 🖶 202/366–9371 ⊕ www.dot.gov/ost/docr/index.htm for problems with surface transportation. **Disability Rights Section** ✉ U.S. Department of Justice, Civil Rights Division, Box 66738, Washington, DC 20035-6738 ☎ 202/514–0301 or 800/514–0301, 202/514–0383 TTY, 800/514–0383 TTY 🖶 202/307–1198 ⊕ www.usdoj.gov/crt/ada/adahom1.htm for general complaints.

TRAVEL AGENCIES

In the United States, the Americans with Disabilities Act requires that travel firms serve the needs of all travelers. Some agencies specialize in working with people with disabilities.

F Travelers with Mobility Problems **Access Adventures** ✉ 206 Chestnut Ridge Rd., Scottsville, NY 14624 ☎ 716/889–9096 ✉ dltravel@prodigy.net, run by a former physical-rehabilitation counselor. **CareVacations** ✉ No. 5, 5110–50 Ave., Leduc, Alberta T9E 6V4, Canada ☎ 780/986–6404 or 877/478–7827 🖶 780/986–8332 ⊕ www.carevacations.com, for group tours and cruise vacations. **Flying Wheels Travel** ✉ 143 W. Bridge St., Box 382, Owatonna, MN 55060 ☎ 507/451–5005 or 800/535–6790 🖶 507/451–1685 ⊕ www.flyingwheelstravel.com.

DISCOUNTS & DEALS

Be a smart shopper and **compare all your options** before making decisions. A plane ticket bought with a promotional coupon from travel clubs, coupon books, and direct-mail offers or on the Internet may not be cheaper than the least expensive fare from a discount ticket agency. And always keep in mind that what you get is just as important as what you save.

DISCOUNT RESERVATIONS

To save money, **look into discount reservations services** with toll-free numbers, which use their buying power to get a better price on hotels, airline tickets, even car rentals. When booking a room, always **call the hotel's local toll-free number** (if one is available) rather than the central reservations number—you'll often get a better price. Always ask about special packages or corporate rates.

When shopping for the best deal on hotels and car rentals, **look for guaranteed exchange rates,** which protect you against a falling dollar. With your rate locked in, you won't pay more, even if the price goes up in the local currency.

Airline Tickets ☎ **800/247-4537.**

Hotel Rooms International Marketing & Travel Concepts ☎ **800/790-4682** ⊕ **www.imtc-travel. com. Players Express Vacations** ☎ **800/458-6161** ⊕ **www.playersexpress.com. Steigenberger Reservation Service** ☎ **800/223-5652** ⊕ **www.srs-worldhotels.com. Travel Interlink** ☎ **800/888-5898** ⊕ **www.travelinterlink.com. Turbotrip.com** ☎ **800/ 473-7829** ⊕ **www.turbotrip.com.**

PACKAGE DEALS

Don't confuse packages and guided tours. When you buy a package, you travel on your own, just as though you had planned the trip yourself. Fly/drive packages, which combine airfare and car rental, are often a good deal. If you **buy a rail/drive pass,** you may save on train tickets and car rentals. All Eurail- and Europass holders get a discount on Eurostar fares through the Channel Tunnel. Also check rates for Scanrail Passes (⇨ Train Travel).

EATING & DRINKING

Sweden's major cities offer a full range of dining choices, from traditional to international restaurants. Outside the cities, restaurants are usually more local in influence, but most use good, fresh ingredients. Investments in training and successes in international competitions have spurred restaurant quality to fantastic heights in Sweden, and it easily competes among other major European countries in the gourmet stakes. It is worth remembering, though, that for many years eating out was prohibitively expensive for many Swedes, giving rise to a home socializing culture that still exists today. For this reason many smaller towns and rural areas are bereft of anything approaching a varied restaurant scene. The restaurants we list are the cream of the crop in each price category. Properties indicated by an ✕▣ are lodging establishments whose restaurant warrants a special trip.

CUTTING COSTS

Restaurant meals are big-ticket items throughout Scandinavia, but there are ways to keep the cost of eating down. Take full advantage of the large buffet breakfast often included in the cost of a hotel room. At lunch look for a "menu" that offers a set two- or three-course meal for a set price, often including bread and salad, or limit yourself to a hearty appetizer. Some restaurants now include a trip to the salad bar in the dinner price. At dinner pay careful attention to the price of wine and drinks, since the high tax on alcohol raises these costs considerably. For more information on affordable eating, *see* Money Matters.

CATEGORY	COST*
$$$$	over SKr 370
$$$	SKr 250–SKr 370
$$	SKr 130–SKr 250
$	under SKr 130

per person for a main course at dinner

MEALS & SPECIALTIES

The surrounding oceans and plentiful inland lakes and streams provide Scandinavian countries with an abundance of fresh fish and seafood: salmon, herring, trout, and seafood delicacies are mainstays and are prepared in countless ways. Elk, deer, reindeer, and lamb feed in relatively unspoiled areas in Iceland and northern Norway, Sweden, and Finland and have the succulent taste of wild game. Berries and mushrooms are still harvested from the forests; sausage appears in a thousand forms, as do potatoes and other root vegetables such as turnips, radishes, rutabagas, and carrots. Some northern tastes may seem a bit unusual, such as the fondness for pickled and fermented fish—to be sampled carefully at first—and a universal obsession with sweet pastries, ice cream, and chocolate.

Also novel for the visitor might be the use of fruit in main dishes and soups, of sour milk on breakfast cereal, and of preserved fish paste as a spread for crackers, along with the ever-present tasty whole-grain crisp breads and hearty ryes. The Swedish *smörgåsbord* (a kind of buffet meal) is less common these days but is still the traveling diner's best bet for breakfast. A smörgåsbord usually comes with a wide range of cheeses, fresh fish, and vegetables alongside meat and breads and other starches.

MEALTIMES

Unless otherwise noted, the restaurants listed in this guide are open daily for lunch and dinner. Most Swedes take all their meals early, particularly outside of urban areas. It is not uncommon for lunch to be taken at 11 AM and dinner at 6 PM. For this reason many restaurants close their kitchens earlier than their southern European counterparts. Lovers of late dining should stick to the city.

RESERVATIONS & DRESS

Reservations are always a good idea: we mention them only when they're essential or not accepted. Book as far ahead as you can, and reconfirm as soon as you arrive. We mention dress only when men are required to wear a jacket or a jacket and tie.

WINE, BEER & SPIRITS

In Scandinavia the markup on alcoholic beverages by restaurants is often very high—with drinks selling for as much as four times the standard retail price.

ELECTRICITY

To use electric-powered equipment purchased in the United States or Canada, **bring a converter and adapter.** The electrical current in Scandinavia is 220 volts, 50 cycles alternating current (AC); wall outlets take Continental-type plugs, with two round prongs.

If your appliances are dual-voltage, you'll need only an adapter. Don't use 110-volt outlets marked FOR SHAVERS ONLY for high-wattage appliances such as blow-dryers. Most laptops operate equally well on 110 and 220 volts and so require only an adapter.

EMBASSIES

🏴 Australia ✉ Sergels Torg 12 ☎ 08/6132900.
🏴 Canada ✉ Tegelbacken 4, Box 16129, 10323 Stockholm ☎ 08/4533000.
🏴 New Zealand ✉ Nybrog. 34, Stockholm ☎ 08/50632000.
🏴 United Kingdom ✉ Skarpög. 68, 11593 Stockholm ☎ 08/6713000.
🏴 United States ✉ Strandv. 101, 11589 Stockholm ☎ 08/7835300.

EMERGENCIES

Anywhere in Sweden, dial 112 for emergency assistance.

HOLIDAYS

In general, all Scandinavian countries celebrate New Year's Eve and New Year's Day, Good Friday, Easter Sunday and Easter Monday, May Day (May 1; celebrated as Labor Day in many countries), Midsummer Eve and Midsummer Day (although its date varies by country), and Christmas (as well as Christmas Eve and Boxing Day, the day after Christmas). In addition, Sweden has the following holidays: Epiphany, Jan. 6; Ascension; Pentecost Monday, All Saints' Day (observed the first Sat. after Oct. 30).

On major holidays such as Christmas, most shops close or operate on a Sunday schedule. On the eves of such holidays, many shops are also closed all day or are open with reduced hours.

On May Day the city centers are usually full of people, celebrations, and parades. During Midsummer, at the end of June, locals flock to the lakes and countryside to celebrate the beginning of long summer days with bonfires and other festivities.

INSURANCE

The most useful travel-insurance plan is a comprehensive policy that includes coverage for trip cancellation and interruption, default, trip delay, and medical expenses (with a waiver for preexisting conditions).

Without insurance you will lose all or most of your money if you cancel your trip, regardless of the reason. Default insurance covers you if your tour operator, airline, or cruise line goes out of business. Trip-delay covers expenses that arise because of bad weather or mechanical delays. Study the fine print when comparing policies.

If you're traveling internationally, a key component of travel insurance is coverage for medical bills incurred if you get sick on the road. Such expenses are not generally covered by Medicare or private policies. U.K. residents can buy a travel-insurance policy valid for most vacations taken during the year in which it's purchased (but check preexisting-condition coverage).

British and Australian citizens need extra medical coverage when traveling overseas.

Always **buy travel policies directly from the insurance company**; if you buy them from a cruise line, airline, or tour operator that goes out of business you probably will not be covered for the agency or operator's default, a major risk. Before making any purchase, **review your existing health and homeowner's policies** to find what they cover away from home.

F Travel Insurers In the U.S.: **Access America** ✉ 6600 W. Broad St., Richmond, VA 23230 ☏ 800/284-8300 🖷 804/673-1491 ⊕ www.etravelprotection.com. **Travel Guard International** ✉ 1145 Clark St., Stevens Point, WI 54481 ☏ 715/345-0505 or 800/826-1300 🖷 800/955-8785 ⊕ www.travelguard.com. **F** Insurance Information In the U.K.: **Association of British Insurers** ✉ 51–55 Gresham St., London EC2V 7HQ, U.K. ☏ 020/7600-3333 🖷 020/7696-8999 ⊕ www.abi.org.uk. In Canada: **RBC Travel Insurance** ✉ 6880 Financial Dr., Mississauga, Ontario L5N 7Y5, Canada ☏ 905/791-8700, 800/668-4342 in Canada 🖷 905/816-2498 ⊕ www.royalbank.com. In Australia: **Insurance Council of Australia** ✉ Level 3, 56 Pitt St., Sydney NSW 2000 ☏ 02/9253-5100 🖷 02/9253-5111 ⊕ www.ica.com.au. In New Zealand: **Insurance Council of New Zealand** ✉ Level 7, 111–115 Customhouse Quay, Box 474, Wellington, New Zealand ☏ 04/472-5230 🖷 04/473-3011 ⊕ www.icnz.org.nz.

LANGUAGE

Swedish is closely related to Danish and Norwegian. After *z,* the Swedish alphabet has three extra letters, *å, ä,* and *ö,* something to bear in mind when using the phone book. Another phone-book alphabetical oddity is that *v* and *w* are interchangeable; Wittström, for example, comes before Vittviks, not after. And after all that, you'll be happy to know that most Swedes are happy to speak English.

LODGING

The lodgings we list are the cream of the crop in each price category. We always list the facilities that are available—but we don't specify whether they cost extra: when pricing accommodations, always ask what's included and what costs extra.

Sweden offers a variety of accommodations, from simple bed-and-breakfasts, campsites, and hostels to hotels of the highest international standard. In the larger cities lodging ranges from first-class business hotels run by SAS, Sheraton, and Scandic to good-quality tourist-class hotels, such as RESO, Best Western, Scandic Budget, and Sweden Hotels, to a wide variety of single-entrepreneur hotels. In the countryside look for independently run inns and motels, known as guesthouses. In addition, farm holidays increasingly have become available to tourists, and Sweden has organizations that can help plan stays in the countryside.

Before you leave home, **ask your travel agent about discounts** (⇨ Hotels *under* Lodging), including summer hotel checks for Best Western, Scandic, and Inter Nor hotels, and enormous year-round rebates at SAS hotels for travelers over 65. All EuroClass (business-class) passengers can get discounts of at least 10% at SAS hotels when they book through SAS.

Two things about hotels usually surprise North Americans: the relatively limited dimensions of Scandinavian beds and the generous size of Scandinavian breakfasts. Scandinavian double beds are often about 60 inches wide or slightly less, close in size to the U.S. queen size. King-size beds (72 inches wide) are difficult to find and, if available, require special reservations.

Older hotels may have some rooms described as "double" that in fact have one double bed plus one foldout sofa big enough for two people. This arrangement is occasionally called a combi-room but is being phased out.

Many older hotels, particularly the country inns and independently run smaller hotels in the cities, do not have private bathrooms. Inquire about this ahead of time if this is important to you.

Scandinavian breakfasts resemble what many people would call lunch, usually including breads, cheeses, marmalade, hams, lunch meats, eggs, juice, cereal, milk, and coffee. Generally, the farther north you go, the larger the breakfasts become. Breakfast is usually included in hotel rates.

Make reservations whenever possible. Even countryside inns, which usually have space, are sometimes packed with vacationing Europeans.

Assume that hotels operate on the **European Plan** (EP, with no meals) unless we specify that they use the **Continental Plan** (CP, with a Continental breakfast),

Modified American Plan (MAP, with breakfast and dinner), or the **Full American Plan** (FAP, with all meals).

CATEGORY	COST*
$$$$	over SKr 2,800
$$$	SKr 1,900–SKr 2,800
$$	SKr 1,000–SKr 1,900
$	under SKr 1,000

All prices are for two people in a standard double room, including breakfast, service charge, and tax.

CUTTING COSTS

Ask about high and low seasons when making reservations since different countries define their tourist seasons differently. Some hotels lower prices during tourist season, whereas others raise them during the same period. In Sweden many hotels offer lower prices on weekends and during the summer months, some by as much as 50%.

If you are visiting a city in Sweden it is worth looking at accommodation outside the city limits. This is where you will find the best budget lodging and good transport links and the relatively small Swedish cities means a trip downtown never takes too long.

Hotels in Sweden offer Inn Checks, or prepaid hotel vouchers, for accommodations ranging from first-class hotels to country cottages. These vouchers, which must be purchased from travel agents or from the Scandinavian Tourist Board before departure, are sold individually and in packets for as many nights as needed and offer savings of up to 50%. Most countries also offer summer bargains for foreign tourists; winter bargains can be even greater. For further information about Scandinavian hotel vouchers, contact the Scandinavian Tourist Board.

ProSkandinavia checks can be used in 400 hotels across Scandinavia (excluding Iceland) for savings up to 50% for reservations made usually no earlier than 24 hours before arrival, although some hotels allow earlier bookings. One check costs about $40. Two checks will pay for a double room at a hotel, one check for a room in a cottage. The checks can be bought at many travel agencies in Scandinavia or ordered from **ProSkandinavia** (✉ Akersgt. 11, N-0158 Oslo, Norway

☎ 47/22–41–13–13 🖷 47/22–42–06–57 ⊕ www.proskandinavia.com).

APARTMENT & VILLA RENTALS

With 250 chalet villages with high standards, Sweden enjoys popularity with its chalet accommodations, often arranged on the spot at tourist offices. Many are organized under the auspices of the Swedish Touring Association (STF). DFDS Seaways in Göteborg arranges package deals that combine a ferry trip from Britain across the North Sea and a stay in a chalet village.
🗗 **Rental Contacts DFDS Seaways** ☎ 031/650600, 01912/936262 within the U.K. **Swedish Touring Association** ☎ 08/4632200 🖷 08/6781938 ⊕ www.meravsverige.se.

CAMPING

There are 760 registered campsites nationwide, many close to uncrowded swimming places and with fishing, boating, or canoeing; they may also offer bicycle rentals. Prices range from SKr 70 to SKr 130 per 24-hour period. Many campsites also offer accommodations in log cabins at various prices, depending on the facilities offered. Most are open between June and September, but about 200 remain open in winter for skiing and skating enthusiasts. Sveriges Campingvårdernas Riksförbund (Swedish Campsite Owners' Association or SCR) publishes, in English, an abbreviated list of sites; contact the office for a free copy.
🗗 **Sveriges Campingvårdernas Riksförbund** ✉ Box 255, 451 17 Uddevalla ☎ 0522/642440 🖷 0522/642430 ⊕ www.camping.se.

FARM & COTTAGE HOLIDAYS

The old-fashioned farm or countryside holiday, long a staple for Scandinavian city dwellers, is becoming increasingly available to tourists. In general, you can choose to stay on the farm itself and even participate in daily activities, or you can opt to rent a private housekeeping cottage. Contact the local tourist board or Swedish Farm Holidays for details.
🗗 **Swedish Farm Holidays** ✉ Box 8, S-668 21 Ed, Sweden ☎ 46/53412075 🖷 46/53461011 ⊕ www.bopalantgard.org.

HOME EXCHANGES

If you would like to exchange your home for someone else's, **join a home-exchange**

organization, which will send you its updated listings of available exchanges for a year and will include your own listing in at least one of them. It's up to you to make specific arrangements.

📶 **Exchange Clubs HomeLink International** ✉ Box 47747, Tampa, FL 33647 ☎ 813/975-9825 or 800/638-3841 🖷 813/910-8144 ⊕ www.homelink. org ✍ $106 per year. **Intervac U.S.** ✉ Box 590504, San Francisco, CA 94159 ☎ 800/756-4663 🖷 415/ 435-7440 ⊕ www.intervacus.com ✍ $93 yearly fee includes one catalog and on-line access.

HOSTELS

No matter what your age, you can **save on lodging costs by staying at hostels.** In some 4,500 locations in more than 70 countries around the world, Hostelling International (HI), the umbrella group for a number of national youth-hostel associations, offers single-sex, dorm-style beds and, at many hostels, rooms for couples and family accommodations. Membership in any HI national hostel association, open to travelers of all ages, allows you to stay in HI-affiliated hostels at member rates; one-year membership is about $25 for adults (C$26.75 in Canada, £9.30 in the U.K., $30 in Australia, and $30 in New Zealand); hostels run about $10–$25 per night. If a hostel has nearly filled up, members have priority over others; members are also eligible for discounts around the world, even on rail and bus travel in some countries.

📶 **Organizations Hostelling International–American Youth Hostels** ✉ 733 15th St. NW, Suite 840, Washington, DC 20005 ☎ 202/783-6161 🖷 202/ 783-6171 ⊕ www.hiayh.org. **Hostelling International–Canada** ✉ 400–205 Catherine St., Ottawa, Ontario K2P 1C3, Canada ☎ 613/237-7884, 800/663-5777 in Canada 🖷 613/237-7868 ⊕ www. hostellingintl.ca. **Youth Hostel Association of England and Wales** ✉ Trevelyan House, 8 St. Stephen's Hill, St. Albans, Hertfordshire AL1 2DY, U.K. ☎ 0870/8708808 🖷 01727/844126 ⊕ www. yha.org.uk. **Youth Hostel Association Australia** ✉ 10 Mallett St., Camperdown, NSW 2050, Australia ☎ 02/9565-1699 🖷 02/9565-1325 ⊕ www.yha. com.au. **Youth Hostels Association of New Zealand** ✉ Level 3, 193 Cashel St., Box 436, Christchurch, New Zealand ☎ 03/379-9970 🖷 03/ 365-4476 ⊕ www.yha.org.nz.

HOTELS

All hotels listed have private baths unless otherwise noted.

Major hotels in larger cities cater mainly to business clientele and can be expensive; weekend rates are more reasonable and can even be as low as half the normal price. Prices are normally on a per-room basis and include all taxes and service charges and usually breakfast. Apart from the more modest inns and the cheapest budget establishments, private baths and showers are standard.

Whatever their size, almost all Swedish hotels provide scrupulously clean accommodations and courteous service. Since many Swedes go on vacation during July and through early August, make your hotel reservations in advance, especially if staying outside the city areas during that time. Some hotels close during the winter holidays as well; call ahead for information.

An official annual guide, *Hotels in Sweden,* published by and available free from the Swedish Travel and Tourism Council, gives comprehensive information about hotel facilities and prices. Countryside Hotels comprises 35 select resort hotels, some of them restored manor houses or centuries-old inns. Hotellcentralen is an independent agency that makes advance telephone reservations for any Swedish hotel at no cost. The Sweden Hotels group has about 100 independently owned hotels and its own classification scheme—with a letter assigned according to a hotel's facilities.

Major hotel groups like Best Western, Radisson SAS, RESO, Scandic, and Sweden Hotels also have their own central reservations services.

📶 **Best Western** ☎ 020/792752. **Countryside Hotels** ✉ Box 69, 830 13 Åre ☎ 06/4751860 🖷 06/4751920. **Hotellcentralen** ✉ Centralstation, 111 20 ☎ 08/7892425 🖷 08/7918666. **Radisson SAS** ☎ 02/0797592. **RESO** ☎ 08/4114040. **Scandic** ☎ 08/51751700. **Sweden Hotels** ☎ 020/770000. 📶 **Toll-Free Numbers Best Western** ☎ 800/528-1234 ⊕ www.bestwestern.com. **Choice** ☎ 800/ 221-2222 ⊕ www.choicehotels.com. **Comfort Inn** ☎ 800/228-5150 ⊕ www.comfortinn.com. **Hilton** ☎ 800/445-8667 ⊕ www.hilton.com. **Holiday Inn** ☎ 800/465-4329 ⊕ www.basshotels.com. **Quality Inn** ☎ 800/228-5151 ⊕ www.qualityinn. com. **Radisson** ☎ 800/333-3333 ⊕ www. radisson.com. **Sheraton** ☎ 800/325-3535 ⊕ www.starwoodhotels.com.

MAIL & SHIPPING

POSTAL RATES

Postcards and letters up to 20 grams can be mailed for SKr 8 within Sweden, SKr 10 to destinations within Europe, and SKr 10 to the United States and all other countries.

MONEY MATTERS

Prices throughout this guide are given for adults. Substantially reduced fees are almost always available for children, students, and senior citizens. For information on taxes, *see* Taxes.

Here is an idea what you'll pay for food and drink in Sweden: a cup of coffee, SKr 25–SKr 35; a beer, SKr 40–SKr 55; a mineral water, SKr 12–SKr 25; a cheese roll, SKr 25–SKr 50; pepper steak à la carte, SKr 120–SKr 190; a cheeseburger, SKr 60; and pizza, starting at SKr 40.

Be aware that sales taxes can be very high, but foreigners can get some refunds by shopping at tax-free stores (⇨ Taxes). City cards can save you transportation and entrance fees in many of the larger cities.

You can **reduce the cost of food by planning.** Breakfast is often included in your hotel bill; if not, you may wish to buy fruit, sweet rolls, and a beverage for a picnic breakfast. Electrical devices for hot coffee or tea should be bought abroad. When purchasing, make sure they conform to the local current.

Opt for a restaurant lunch instead of dinner, since the latter tends to be significantly more expensive. Instead of beer or wine, **drink tap water**—liquor can cost four times the price of the same brand in a store—but do specify tap water, as the term *water* can refer to soft drinks and bottled water, which are also expensive. Throughout Scandinavia the tip is included in the cost of your meal.

In most of Scandinavia, liquor and strong beer (over 3% alcohol) can be purchased only in state-owned shops, at very high prices, during weekday business hours, usually 9:30–6, and in some areas on Saturday until mid-afternoon. A midsize bottle of whiskey in Sweden, for example, can easily cost SKr 250 (about $35). Weaker beers and ciders are usually available in grocery stores in Scandinavia.

ATMS

The 1,200 or so blue Bankomat cash dispensers nationwide have been adapted to take some foreign cards, including Master-Card, Visa, and bank cards linked to the Cirrus network. You may encounter some complications on remote machines. It's best to use those that are next to major bank offices. For more information contact Bankomatcentralen in Stockholm or your local bank. American Express has cash and traveler's check dispensers; there's also an office at Stockholm's Arlanda Airport.

🚹 **American Express** ⊠ Birger Jarlsg. 1 ☎ 020/793211 toll-free. **Bankomatcentralen/CEK AB** ☎ 08/7255700.

CREDIT CARDS

Throughout this guide, the following abbreviations are used: **AE,** American Express; **DC,** Diners Club; **MC,** MasterCard; and **V,** Visa.

CURRENCY

The unit of currency is the krona (plural kronor), which is divided into 100 öre and is written as SKr or SEK. Coins come in SKr 1, SKr 5, and SKr 10. Bank notes come in denominations of SKr 20, SKr 50, SKr 100, SKr 500, and SKr 1,000. At press time the exchange rates for the krona was SKr 9 to the U.S. dollar, SKr 6 to the Canadian dollar, SKr 13 to the British pound sterling, SKr 9 to the Euro, SKr 6 to the Australian dollar, SKr 5 to the New Zealand dollar, and SKr 1 to the South African rand.

CURRENCY EXCHANGE

Traveler's checks and foreign currency can be exchanged at banks all over Sweden and at post offices displaying the NB EX-CHANGE sign. Be sure to have your passport with you when exchanging money at a bank.

OUTDOORS & SPORTS

BOATING & SAILING

Swedes love to be on the water, whether sailing in the Stockholm archipelago or kayaking along the rocky west coast. STF publishes a Swedish-language annual guide to all the country's marinas. Svenska Kanotförbundet (Swedish Canoeing Association) publishes a similar booklet. For information on sailing throughout the country, including information on how to rent or charter boats yourself, contact the Svenska Seglarförbundet (Swedish Sailing Association).

Svenska Kanotförbundet (Swedish Canoeing Association) ⊠ Idrotts Hus, 123 87 Farsta ☎ 08/6056565 ⊕ www.svenskidrott.se/kanot. **Svenska Seglarförbundet** (Swedish Sailing Association) ⊠ af Pontins väg 6, 115 21 Stockholm ☎ 08/4590990 ⊕ www.ssf.se.

GOLF

Sweden has 365 golf clubs; you can even play by the light of the midnight sun at Boden, in the far north, and there are a number of ice courses, too, offering winter challenges. Wherever you play, all Swedish golf courses require you to show a handicap certificate. Svenska Golfförbundet (the Swedish Golfing Association) publishes an annual guide in Swedish; it costs around SKr 100, including postage.

Svenska Golfförbundet ⊠ Box 84, 182 11 Danderyd ☎ 08/6221500 🖶 08/7558439 ⊕ www.golf.se.

SKIING

There are plenty of downhill and crosscountry facilities in Sweden. The bestknown resorts are in the country's western mountains: Åre, in the north, with 29 lifts; Idre Fjäll, to the south of Åre, offering accommodations for 10,000; and Sälen, in the folklore region of Dalarna. You can ski through May at Riksgränsen, in the far north. Most of Sweden's skiing resorts also offer a host of other winter activities, from skating to ice fishing, for the nonskiers in the family.

TENNIS

Tennis is popular throughout the country, and courts are fairly easy to find. Contact Svenska Tennisförbundet (Swedish Tennis Association) for information.

Svenska Tennisförbundet ⊠ Lidingöv. 75, Box 27915, 115 94 Stockholm ☎ 08/6679770 🖶 08/6646606 ⊕ www.tennis.se.

PACKING

Check *Fodor's How to Pack* (available in bookstores everywhere) for more tips.

CHECKING LUGGAGE

You are allowed one carry-on bag and one personal article, such as a purse or a laptop computer. Make sure that everything

you carry aboard will fit under your seat or in the overhead bin. Get to the gate early, so you can board as soon as possible, before the overhead bins fill up.

PASSPORTS & VISAS

When traveling internationally, **carry your passport** even if you don't need one (it's always the best form of I.D.) and **make two photocopies of the data page** (one for someone at home and another for you, carried separately from your passport). If you lose your passport, promptly call the nearest embassy or consulate and the local police.

ENTERING SCANDINAVIA

All U.S. citizens, even infants, need only a valid passport to enter any Scandinavian country for stays of up to three months.

PASSPORT OFFICES

The best time to apply for a passport or to renew is in fall and winter. Before any trip, check your passport's expiration date, and, if necessary, renew it as soon as possible.

Australian Citizens Australian Passport Office ☎ 131-232 ⊕ www.dfat.gov.au/passports.

Canadian Citizens Passport Office ☎ 819/994-3500, 800/567-6868 in Canada ⊕ www.dfait-maeci.gc.ca/passport.

New Zealand Citizens New Zealand Passport Office ☎ 04/494-0700 ⊕ www.passports.govt.nz.

U.K. Citizens London Passport Office ☎ 0870/521-0410 ⊕ www.ukpa.gov.uk for fees and documentation requirements and to request an emergency passport.

U.S. Citizens National Passport Information Center ☎ 900/225-5674, calls are 35¢ per minute for automated service, $1.05 per minute for operator service ⊕ www.travel.state.gov/npicinfo.html.

SENIOR-CITIZEN TRAVEL

To qualify for age-related discounts, **mention your senior-citizen status up front** when booking hotel reservations (not when checking out) and before you're seated in restaurants (not when paying the bill). When renting a car, ask about promotional car-rental discounts, which can be cheaper than senior-citizen rates.

TRAIN TRAVEL

Seniors over 60 are entitled to discount tickets (often as much as 50% off) on buses, trains, and ferries throughout

Scandinavia, as well as reductions on special City Cards. Eurail offers discounts on Scanrail and Eurail train passes (⇨ Train Travel).

🎫 Educational Programs **Elderhostel** ✉ 11 Ave. de Lafayette, Boston, MA 02111-1746 ☎ 877/426-8056 🖷 877/426-2166 ⊕ www.elderhostel.org.

SHOPPING

Prices in Scandinavia are never low, but quality is high, and specialties are sometimes less expensive here than elsewhere. Scandinavian design in both furniture and glassware is world renowned. Swedish crystal, Icelandic sweaters, Danish Lego blocks and furniture, Norwegian furs, and Finnish fabrics—these are just a few of the items to look for. Keep an eye out for sales, called *rea* in Swedish. Most shops in Sweden will gift-wrap items for you if you ask.

STUDENTS IN SCANDINAVIA

🎫 IDs & Services **Council Travel (CIEE)** ✉ 205 E. 42nd St., 15th floor, New York, NY 10017 ☎ 212/822-2700 or 888/268-6245 🖷 212/822-2699 ⊕ www. councilexchanges.org for mail orders only, in the United States. **Travel Cuts** ✉ 187 College St., Toronto, Ontario M5T 1P7, Canada ☎ 416/979-2406, 800/667-2887 in Canada 🖷 416/979-8167 ⊕ www. travelcuts.com.

TAXES

VALUE-ADDED TAX

All hotel, restaurant, and departure taxes and the value-added tax (VAT; called *moms* all over Scandinavia) are automatically included in prices. The VAT is 25%; non-EU residents can obtain a 15% refund on goods of SKr 200 or more. To receive your refund at any of the 15,000 stores that participate in the tax-free program, you'll be asked to fill out a form and show your passport. The form can then be turned in at any airport or ferry customs desk. Keep all your receipts and tags; occasionally, customs authorities ask to see your purchases, so pack them where they will be accessible.

Note: Tax-free sales of alcohol, cigarettes, and other luxury goods have been abolished among EU countries, with Sweden, Finland, and Denmark among the last to adopt these regulations. Finland's Åland Islands have some special rights under the EU and therefore allow tax-free sales for

ferries in transit through its ports. All Sweden–Finland ferry routes now pass through the islands, de facto continuing the extremely popular tax-free sales for tourists. Air travel to the Scandinavia EU member states (Sweden, Finland, Denmark), as well as Norway, no longer allows tax-free sales.

Global Refund is a VAT refund service that makes getting your money back hassle-free. The service is available Europe-wide at 130,000 affiliated stores. In participating stores **ask for the Global Refund form** (called a Shopping Cheque). Have it stamped like any customs form by customs officials when you leave the European Union (be ready to show customs officials what you've bought). Then take the form to one of the more than 700 Global Refund counters—conveniently located at every major airport and border crossing—and your money will be refunded on the spot in the form of cash, a check, or a credit to your credit-card account (minus a small percentage for processing).

🎫 **Global Refund** ✉ 99 Main St., Suite 307, Nyack, NY 10960 ☎ 800/566-9828 🖷 845/348-1549 ⊕ www.globalrefund.com.

TELEPHONES

Post offices do not have telephone facilities, but there are plenty of pay phones. Long-distance calls can be made from special telegraph offices called *Telebutik,* marked TELE.

AREA & COUNTRY CODES

Sweden's country code is 46. When phoning Sweden from outside the country, drop the first 0 from the number. Swedish phone numbers vary in their number of digits.

DIRECTORY & OPERATOR ASSISTANCE

🎫 **Directory Assistance** ☎ 118118, 118119 for international calls. **Operator Assistance** ☎ 90200, 0018 for international calls.

INTERNATIONAL CALLS

To make an international call, dial 00, followed by the country code and then your number. Access codes for various international companies are listed below.

LONG-DISTANCE SERVICES

AT&T, MCI, and Sprint access codes make calling long distance relatively convenient, but you may find the local access number blocked in many hotel rooms. First ask the hotel operator to connect you. If the hotel operator balks, ask for an international operator, or dial the international operator yourself. One way to improve your odds of getting connected to your long-distance carrier is to travel with more than one company's calling card (a hotel may block Sprint, for example, but not MCI). If all else fails, call from a pay phone.

Access Codes **AT&T USADirect** ☎ 020/795611. **MCI Call USA** ☎ 020/0895438. **Sprint Express** ☎ 020/799011.

LOCAL CALLS

A local call costs a minimum of SKr 2. For calls outside the locality, dial the area code (see telephone directory). Public phones are of three types: one takes SKr 1 and SKr 5 coins (newer public phones also accept SKr 10 coins); another takes only credit cards; and the last takes only the prepaid *Telefonkort* (telephone card).

MOBILE PHONES

Scandinavia has been one of the world leaders in mobile phone development; nearly half of those in Scandinavia own a cellular phone. Although standard North American cellular phones will not work in Scandinavia, most Scandinavian capitals have several companies that rent cellular phones to tourists. Contact the local tourist offices for details.

PHONE CARDS

A Telefonkort, available at Telebutik, Pressbyrån (large blue-and-yellow newsstands), or hospitals, costs SKr 35, SKr 60, or SKr 100. If you're making numerous domestic calls, the card saves money. Many pay phones in downtown Stockholm and Göteborg take only these cards; so it's a good idea to carry one.

TIME

Sweden is one hour ahead of Greenwich mean time (GMT) and six hours ahead of eastern standard time (EST).

TIPPING

In addition to the 12% value-added tax, most hotels usually include a service charge of 15%; it is not necessary to tip unless you have received extra services.

Similarly, a service charge of 13% is usually included in restaurant bills. It is a custom, however, to leave small change when buying drinks. Taxi drivers and hairdressers expect a tip of about 10%.

TOURS & PACKAGES

Because everything is prearranged on a prepackaged tour or independent vacation, you spend less time planning—and often get it all at a good price.

BOOKING WITH AN AGENT

Travel agents are excellent resources. But it's a good idea to collect brochures from several agencies, as some agents' suggestions may be influenced by relationships with tour and package firms that reward them for volume sales. If you have a special interest, **find an agent with expertise in that area**; the American Society of Travel Agents (ASTA; ⇨ Travel Agencies) has a database of specialists worldwide.

Make sure your travel agent knows the accommodations and other services of the place being recommended. Ask about the hotel's location, room size, beds, and whether it has a pool, room service, or programs for children, if you care about these. Has your agent been there in person or sent others whom you can contact?

Do some homework on your own, too: local tourism boards can provide information about lesser-known and small-niche operators, some of which may sell only direct.

Tour-Operator Recommendations **American Society of Travel Agents** (⇨ Travel Agencies). **National Tour Association** (NTA) ✉ 546 E. Main St., Lexington, KY 40508 ☎ 859/226-4444 or 800/682-8886 🖷 859/226-4404 🌐 www.ntaonline.com. **United States Tour Operators Association** (USTOA) ✉ 342 Madison Ave., Suite 1522, New York, NY 10173 ☎ 212/599-6599 or 800/468-7862 🖷 212/599-6744 🌐 www.ustoa.com.

BUYER BEWARE

Each year consumers are stranded or lose their money when tour operators—even large ones with excellent reputations—go out of business. So **check out the operator.** Ask several travel agents about its reputation, and try to **book with a company that has a consumer-protection program.** (Look for information in the company's brochure.) In the United States, members of the National Tour

Association and the United States Tour Operators Association are required to set aside funds to cover your payments and travel arrangements in the event that the company defaults. It's also a good idea to choose a company that participates in the American Society of Travel Agents' Tour Operator Program (TOP); ASTA will act as mediator in any disputes between you and your tour operator.

Remember that the more your package or tour includes the better you can predict the ultimate cost of your vacation. Make sure you know exactly what is covered, and **beware of hidden costs.** Are taxes, tips, and transfers included? Entertainment and excursions? These can add up.

SIGHTSEEING TOURS

Stockholm Sightseeing runs a variety of sightseeing tours of Stockholm. Also contact local tourist offices.

Fees & Schedules Stockholm Sightseeing ✉ Skeppsbron 22 ☎ 08/57814020.

TRAIN TRAVEL

From London the British Rail European Travel Center can be helpful in arranging connections to Sweden's SJ (Statens Järnvägar), the state railway.

SJ has a highly efficient network of comfortable electric trains. On nearly all long-distance routes there are buffet cars and, on overnight trips, sleeping cars and couchettes in both first- and second class. Seat reservations are advisable, and on some trains—indicated with *R, IN,* or *IC* on the timetable—they are compulsory. An extra fee of SKr 15 is charged to reserve a seat on a trip of less than 150 km (93 mi); on longer trips there is no extra charge. Reservations can be made right up to departure time. The high-speed X2000 train has been introduced on several routes; the Stockholm–Göteborg run takes just under three hours. Travelers younger than 19 years travel at half fare. Up to two children younger than 12 years may travel free if accompanied by an adult.

CUTTING COSTS

SJ cooperates with a number of local traffic systems, allowing you to buy one ticket, called a *Tågplusbiljett,* that works on trains, buses, and subways. Speak with the reservations people about what kind of combination you are interested in and where you'd like to travel. The Eurail and InterRail passes are both valid in Sweden. SJ also organizes reduced-cost package trips in conjunction with local tourist offices. Details are available at any railway station or from SJ.

Consider a Scanrail Pass, available for travel in Denmark, Sweden, Norway, and Finland for both first- and second-class train travel: you may have five days of unlimited travel in any two-month period ($366 first class/$271 second class); 10 days of unlimited travel in two months ($488/$362); or 21 consecutive days of unlimited train travel ($567/$420). With the Scanrail Pass you also enjoy travel bonuses, including free or discounted ferry, boat, and bus travel and a Hotel Discount Card that allows 10%–30% off rates for select hotels June–August.

Passengers ages 12–25 can **buy Scanrail Youth Passes** ($254 first class/$188 second class, five travel days in two months; $341/$253 for 10 travel days in two months; $394/$292 for 21 days of unlimited travel).

Those over age 60 can **take advantage of the Scanrail Senior Pass,** which offers the travel bonuses of the Scanrail Pass and discounted travel ($324 first class/$240 second class, five days; $434/$322, 10 days; $502/$372, for 21 consecutive days). Buy Scanrail passes through Rail Europe and travel agents.

For car and train travel, price the Scanrail'n Drive Pass: in 15 days you can get five days of unlimited train travel and two days of car rental (choice of three car categories) with unlimited mileage in Denmark, Norway, and Sweden. You can purchase extra car-rental days and choose from first- or second-class train travel. Individual rates for two adults traveling together (compact car: $385 first class/$308 second class) are considerably lower (about 25%) than those for single adults; the third or fourth person sharing the car needs to purchase only a Scanrail pass.

In Scandinavia you can **use EurailPasses,** which provide unlimited first-class rail travel, in all of the participating countries for the duration of the pass. If you plan to rack up the miles, get a standard pass. These are available for 15 days ($580), 21 days ($762), one month ($946), two months ($1,338), and three months ($1,654). Eurail- and EuroPasses are available through travel agents and Rail Europe.

If you are an adult traveling with a youth under age 26 and/or a senior, **consider buying a EurailSaver Pass**; this entitles you to second-class train travel at the discount youth or senior fare, provided that you are traveling with the youth or senior at all times. A Saver pass is available for $498 (15 days), $648 (21 days), and $804 (one month); two- and three-month fares are also available.

In addition to standard EurailPasses, **ask about special rail-pass plans.** Among these are the Eurail YouthPass (for those under age 26), a Eurail FlexiPass (which allows a certain number of travel days within a set period), the Euraildrive Pass, and the EuroPass Drive (which combines travel by train and rental car).

Whichever pass you choose, remember that you must **purchase your pass before you leave** for Europe.

Many travelers assume that rail passes guarantee them seats on the trains they wish to ride. Not so. You need to **book seats ahead even if you are using a rail pass**; seat reservations are required on some European trains, particularly high-speed trains, and are a good idea on trains that may be crowded—particularly in summer on popular routes. You will also need a reservation if you purchase sleeping accommodations.

🚆 Train Information **British Rail European Travel Center** ✉ Victoria Station, London ☎ 020/78342345. **DER Travel Services** ☎ 800/782-2424. **Rail Europe** ☎ 800/848-7245. **Statens Järnvägar, or SJ** ✉ Central Station, Vasag. 1 ☎ 08/7622000 or 0771/757575.

🚆 Where to Buy Rail Passes **CIT Tours Corp.** ✉ 342 Madison Ave., Suite 207, New York, NY 10173 ☎ 212/697-2100, 800/248-8687, 800/248-7245 in western U.S. ⊕ www.cit-tours.com. **DER Travel Services** ✉ Box 1606, Des Plaines, IL 60017 ☎ 800/782-2424 🖷 800/282-7474 ⊕ www.dertravel.com. **Rail Europe** ✉ 226–230 Westchester Ave., White Plains, NY 10604 ☎ 800/438-7245, 914/682-5172, or 416/602-4195 ✉ 2087 Dundas E, Suite 105, Mississauga, Ontario L4X 1M2 ☎ 800/438-7245, 914/682-5172, or 416/602-4195 ⊕ www.raileurope.com.

TRAVEL AGENCIES

A good travel agent puts your needs first. Look for an agency that has been in business at least five years, emphasizes customer service, and has someone on staff who specializes in your destination. In addition, **make sure the agency belongs to a professional trade organization.** The American Society of Travel Agents (ASTA)—the largest and most influential in the field with more than 20,000 members in some 140 countries—maintains and enforces a strict code of ethics and will step in to help mediate any agent-client dispute if necessary. ASTA (whose motto is "Without a travel agent, you're on your own") also maintains a Web site that includes a directory of agents. (If a travel agency is also acting as your tour operator, *see* Buyer Beware *in* Tours & Packages.)

🚆 Local Agent Referrals **American Society of Travel Agents (ASTA)** ✉ 1101 King St., Suite 200, Alexandria, VA 22314 ☎ 800/965-2782 24-hr hot line 🖷 703/739-7642 ⊕ www.astanet.com. **Association of British Travel Agents** ✉ 68-71 Newman St., London W1T 3AH, U.K. ☎ 020/7637-2444 🖷 020/7637-0713 ⊕ www.abtanet.com. **Association of Canadian Travel Agents** ✉ 130 Albert St., Suite 1705, Ottawa, Ontario K1P 5G4, Canada ☎ 613/237-3657 🖷 613/237-7052 ⊕ www.acta.net. **Australian Federation of Travel Agents** ✉ Level 3, 309 Pitt St., Sydney NSW 2000, Australia ☎ 02/9264-3299 🖷 02/9264-1085 ⊕ www.afta.com.au. **Travel Agents' Association of New Zealand** ✉ Level 5, Paxus House, 79 Boulcott St., Box 1888, Wellington 10033, New Zealand ☎ 04/499-0104 🖷 04/499-0827 ⊕ www.taanz.org.nz.

VISITOR INFORMATION

🚆 Tourist Information **Stockholm Information Service (Sverigehuset)** ✉ Hamng. 27, Box 7542, 103 93 Stockholm ☎ 08/7892490. **Swedish Travel and Tourism Council** ✉ 73 Welbeck St., London W1S 8AN ☎ 020/79359784 in the U.K. 🖷 020/79355853 ✉ 655 3rd Ave., 18th floor, New York, NY 10017 ☎ 212/885-9700 🖷 212/697-0835 ✉ Box 3030, Kungsg. 36, 103 61 Stockholm ☎ 08/7255500 🖷 08/7255531.

🚆 U.S. Government Advisories **U.S. Department of State** ✉ Overseas Citizens Services Office, Room 4811 N.S., 2201 C St. NW, Washington, DC 20520 ☎ 202/647-5225 for interactive hot line ⊕ travel.state.gov/travel/html; enclose a self-addressed, stamped, business-size envelope.

WEB SITES

Do check out the World Wide Web when planning your trip. You'll find everything from weather forecasts to virtual tours of famous cities. Be sure to **visit Fodors.com** (⊕ www.fodors.com), a complete travel-planning site. You can research prices and book plane tickets, hotel rooms, rental cars, vacation packages, and more. In addition, you can post your pressing questions in the Travel Talk section. Other planning tools include a currency converter and weather reports, and there are loads of links to travel resources.

SWEDISH RESOURCES

Swedish Travel & Tourism Council (⊕ www.visitsweden.org). **City of Stockholm** (⊕ www.stockholm.se/english).

STOCKHOLM

1

FODOR'S CHOICE

Bergianska Trädgården, *Universitet*

Hotel Gustav Wasa, *Downtown Stockholm*

Kungliga Slottet, *Gamla Stan*

Nationalmuseum, *City*

Rosendals Trädgården, *Djurgården*

Stadshuset, *Kungsholmen*

Villa Källhagen, *Downtown Stockholm*

Fredsgatan 12 *restaurant, City*

Tranan, *restaurant in Vasastan*

Il Forno, *restaurant in Vasastan*

Herman's, *restaurant in Södermalm*

Bon Lloc, *restaurant in Norrmalm*

Pelican, *restaurant in Södermalm*

Columbus Hotel, *Södermalm*

Diplomat hotel, *Östermalm*

Grand Hotel, *City*

Pärlan hotel, *Östermalm*

Hennes & Mauritz, *City*

Ordning & Reda, *City*

Many other great hotels and restaurants enliven Stockholm. For other favorites, look for the black stars as you read this chapter.

POSITIONED WHERE THE WATERS OF Lake Mälaren rush into the Baltic, Stockholm is one of Europe's most beautiful capitals. Nearly 1.6 million people live in the greater Stockholm area, yet it remains a quiet, almost pastoral city.

Built on 14 small islands joined by bridges crossing open bays and narrow channels, Stockholm is a handsome, civilized city filled with parks, squares, and airy boulevards, yet it is also a bustling modern metropolis. Glass-and-steel skyscrapers abound, but you are never more than a short walk from twisting medieval streets and waterside walkways.

The first written mention of Stockholm dates from 1252, when a powerful regent named Birger Jarl (d. 1266) built a fortified castle and township here. King Gustav Vasa (1496–1560) took it over in 1523, and King Gustavus Adolphus (1594–1632) made it the heart of an empire a century later.

During the Thirty Years' War (1618–48), Sweden gained importance as a Baltic trading state, and Stockholm grew commensurately. But by the beginning of the 18th century, Swedish influence had begun to wane and Stockholm's development had slowed. It did not revive until the industrial revolution, when the hub of the city moved north from Gamla Stan.

Nowadays most Stockholmers live in high-rise suburbs that branch out to the pine forests and lakesides around the capital. They are linked by a highly efficient infrastructure of roads, railways, and a subway system that is one of the safest in the world. Air pollution is minimal, and the city streets are relatively clean and safe.

EXPLORING STOCKHOLM

Although Stockholm is built on a group of islands adjoining the mainland, the waterways between them are so narrow and the bridges so smoothly integrated that the city really does feel more or less continuous. The island of Gamla Stan and its smaller neighbors, Riddarholmen and Helgeandsholmen, form what can be called the town center. South of Gamla Stan, Södermalm spreads over a wide area, its many art galleries and bars attracting a slightly bohemian crowd. North of Gamla Stan is Norrmalm, the financial and business heart of the city. West of Norrmalm is the island of Kungsholmen, site of the Stadshuset (city hall) and most of the city government offices. East of Norrmalm is Östermalm, an old residential neighborhood where many of the embassies and consulates are found. Finally, between Östermalm and Södermalm lies the island of Djurgården, once a royal game preserve, now the site of lovely parks and museums such as Skansen, the open-air cultural heritage park.

Modern Stockholm

The area bounded by Stadshuset, Hötorget, Stureplan, and the Kungliga Dramatiska Teatern (nicknamed Dramaten) is essentially Stockholm's downtown, where the city comes closest to feeling like a bustling metropolis. Shopping, nightlife, business, traffic, dining, festivals—all are at their most intense in this part of town.

A Good Walk

Start at the redbrick **Stadshuset** ❶ ☞, a powerful symbol of Stockholm. Cross the bridge to Klara Mälarstrand and follow the waterfront to Drottninggatan. Take a left and continue along this popular shop-lined pedestrian street north to the hub of the city, **Sergels Torg** ❷. The **Kulturhuset** ❸ is in the imposing glass building on the southern side of Sergels

Torg. Farther north on Drottninggatan is the market-filled **Hötorget** ④. The intersection of Kungsgatan and Sveavägen, where the Konserthuset (Concert Hall) stands, is one of the busiest pedestrian crossroads in town.

Head north up Sveavägen for a brief detour to see the spot where Prime Minister Olof Palme was assassinated in 1986. A plaque has been laid on the right-hand side of the street, just before the intersection with Olof Palmes Gata; his grave is in Adolf Fredrik's Kyrkogård, a few blocks farther on. Continue north along Sveavägen until you reach the large intersection of Odengatan and Sveavägen. On your left will be **Stockholms Stadsbiblioteket** ⑤. Go back down Sveavägen and turn right up Tegnérgatan to find **Strindbergsmuseet Blå Tornet** ⑥, where playwright August Strindberg lived from 1908 to 1912. Return to Hötorget by way of Drottninggatan.

Next, walk east along Kungsgatan, one of Stockholm's main shopping streets, to Stureplan. On this street is Sturegallerian, an elegant mall. Head southeast along Birger Jarlsgatan—named for the nobleman generally credited with founding Stockholm around 1252—where there are still more interesting shops and restaurants. When you reach Nybroplan, take a look at the grand **Kungliga Dramatiska Teatern** ⑦.

Heading west up Hamngatan, stop in at **Hallwylska Museet** ⑧ for a tour of the private collection of Countess von Hallwyl's treasures. Continue along Hamngatan to **Kungsträdgården** ⑨, a park since 1562. Outdoor cafés and restaurants are clustered by this leafy spot, a summer venue for public concerts and events. At the northwest corner of the park is Sverigehuset, or Sweden House, the tourist center; on the opposite side of Hamngatan is the NK department store.

TIMING   Allow about 4½ hours for the walk, plus an hour each for guided tours of Stadshuset and Hallwylska Museet (September–June, Sunday only). The Strindbergsmuseet Blå Tornet is closed Monday.

What to See

⑧ **Hallwylska Museet** (Hallwyl Museum). This private late-19th-century palace with imposing wood-panel rooms houses a collection of furniture, paintings, and musical instruments in a bewildering mélange of styles assembled by Countess von Hallwyl, who left it to the state upon her death. ✉ *Hamng. 4, Normalm* ☎ *08/51955599* ⊕ *www.hallwylskamuseet.se* 🎫 *SKr 65* ☉ *Guided tours only. Tours in English July and Aug., daily at 1; Sept.–June, Sun. at 1.*

★ ④ **Hötorget** (Hay Market). Once the city's hay market, this is now a popular gathering place with an excellent outdoor fruit-and-vegetable market. Also lining the square are the Konserthuset (Concert Hall), the PUB department store, and a multiscreen cinema Filmstaden Sergel. ✉ *Just west of Sveaväg, Normalm.*

> **need a break?** Stop at the food hall **Kungshallen** (✉ Hötorget opposite Filmstaden Sergel, Normalm ☎ 08/218005) and choose from Swedish and international goodies. Or get a window table at the café inside Filmstaden Sergel.

③ **Kulturhuset** (Culture House). Since it opened in 1974, architect Peter Celsing's cultural center, a glass-and-stone monolith on the south side of Sergels Torg, has become a symbol of Stockholm and of the growth of modernism in Sweden. Stockholmers are divided on the aesthetics of this building—most either love it or hate it. Here there are exhibitions for children and adults, a library, a theater, a youth center, an exhibition center, and a restaurant. Head to Café Panorama, on the top

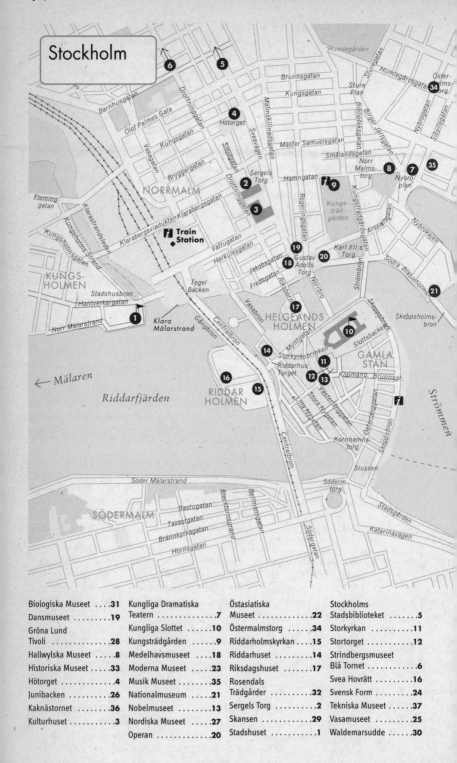

Stockholm

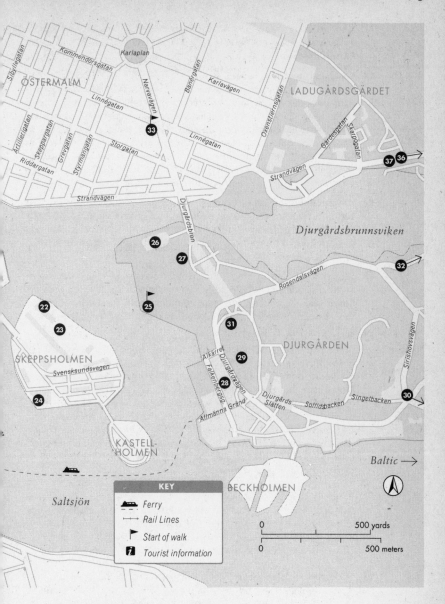

ÖSTERMALM

Sibyllegatan
Kommendörsgatan
Karlaplan
Narvavägen
Banérgatan
Karlavägen

LADUGÅRDSGÄRDET

Linnégatan
Artillerigatan
Skeppargatan
Grevgatan
Styrmansgatan
Storgatan
33
Linnégatan
Oxenstiernsgatan
Gärdesgatan
Sturegatan

Riddargatan
Strandvägen
37 **36**

Strandvägen

Djurgårdsbron
Djurgårdsbrunnsviken

26
27
Rosendalsvägen
32

22
25
31
DJURGÅRDEN
23
Sirishovsvägen

SKEPPSHOLMEN
Svensksundsvägen
Alkärret
Djurgårdsvägen
29

24
Falkenbergsg.
28
Djurgårds Slätten
Solfidsbacken
Singelbacken
30
Allmänna Gränd

KASTELL-
HOLMEN

Baltic →

BECKHOLMEN

Saltsjön

KEY	
🚢	Ferry
┼┼┼	Rail Lines
⚑	Start of walk
🛈	Tourist information

0   500 yards
0   500 meters

floor, to savor traditional Swedish cuisine and a great view of Sergels Torg down below. ⊠ *Sergels Torg 3, City* ☎ *08/50831508* ⊕ *www. kulturhuset.stockholm.se.*

❼ Kungliga Dramatiska Teatern (Royal Dramatic Theater). Locally known as Dramaten, the national theater stages works by the likes of Strindberg and other playwrights of international stature in a grand appealing building whose facade and gilded statuary look out over the city harbor. The theater gave its first performance in 1788, when it was located at Bollhuset on Slottsbacken, next to the Royal Palace. It later moved to Kungsträdgården, spent some time in the Opera House, and ended up at its present location in 1908. Performances are in Swedish. ⊠ *Nybroplan, Östermalm* ☎ *08/6670680* ⊕ *www.dramaten.se.*

☺ ❾ Kungsträdgården (King's Garden). This is one of Stockholm's smallest yet most central parks. Once the royal kitchen garden, it now hosts a large number of festivals and events each season. The park has numerous cafés and restaurants, a playground, and, in winter, an ice-skating rink. ✛ *Between Hamng. and the Operan.*

❷ Sergels Torg. Named after Johan Tobias Sergel (1740–1814), one of Sweden's greatest sculptors, this busy junction in Stockholm's center is dominated by modern, functional buildings and a sunken pedestrian square with subterranean connections to the rest of the neighborhood.

⚑ ❶ Stadshuset (City Hall). The architect Ragnar Östberg, one of the founders
FodorsChoice of the National Romantic movement, completed Stockholm's city hall
★ in 1923. Headquarters of the city council, the building is functional but ornate: its immense **Blå Hallen** (Blue Hall) is the venue for the annual Nobel Prize dinner, Stockholm's principal social event. A trip to the top of the 348-foot tower, most of which can be achieved by elevator, is rewarded by a breathtaking panorama of the city and Riddarfjärden. ⊠ *Hantverkarg. 1, Kungsholmen* ☎ *08/50829000* ⊕ *www.stockholm. se* ☒ *SKr 45, tower SKr 20* ☉ *Guided tours only. Tours in English, June–Aug., daily 10, 11, noon, and 2; Sept., daily 10, noon, and 2; Oct.–May, daily 10 and noon.*

> **need a break?** After climbing the Stadshuset tower, relax on the fine grass terraces that lead down to the bay and overlook Lake Mälaren. Or have lunch in **Stadshuskällaren** (City Hall Cellar; ☎ 08/6505454), where the annual Nobel Prize banquet is held. You can also head a few blocks down Hantverkargatan to find several good small restaurants.

❺ Stockholms Stadsbiblioteket (Stockholm City Library). Libraries aren't always a top sightseeing priority, but the Stockholm City Library is among the most captivating buildings in town. Designed by the famous Swedish architect E. G. Asplund and completed in 1928, the building's cylindrical, galleried main hall gives it the appearance of a large birthday cake. Inside is an excellent "information technology" center with free Internet access—and lots of books, too. ⊠ *Sveav. 73, Vasastan* ☎ *08/50831100* ⊕ *www.ssb.stockholm.se* ☉ *Mon.–Thurs. 10–7, Fri. 10–6, Sat. noon–4.*

★ ❻ Strindbergsmuseet Blå Tornet (Strindberg Museum, Blue Tower). Hidden away over a grocery store, this museum is dedicated to Sweden's most important author and dramatist, August Strindberg (1849–1912), who resided here from 1908 until his death four years later. The interior has been expertly reconstructed with authentic furnishings and other objects, including one of his pens. The museum also houses a library, printing press, and picture archives, and it is the site of literary, musical, and theatrical events. ⊠ *Drottningg. 85, Norrmalm* ☎ *08/4115354* ⊕ *www.*

strindbergsmuseet.se ✉ *SKr 40* ☉ *Sept.–May, Tues. noon–7, Wed.–Sun. noon–4, June–Aug., Tues.–Fri. 11–4, weekends noon–4.*

Gamla Stan & Skeppsholmen

Gamla Stan (Old Town) sits between two of Stockholm's main islands and is the site of the medieval city. Just east of Gamla Stan is the island of Skeppsholmen, whose narrow, twisting cobble streets are lined with superbly preserved old buildings.

A Good Walk

Start at the waterfront edge of Kungsträdgården and walk across Strömsbron to **Kungliga Slottet** ⑩ ▶, where you can see the changing of the guard at noon every day. Walk up the sloping cobblestone drive called Slottsbacken and bear right past the Obelisk to find the main entrance to the palace. Stockholm's 15th-century Gothic cathedral, **Storkyrkan** ⑪, stands at the top of Slottsbacken, but its entrance is at the other end, on Trångsund.

Following Källargränd from the Obelisk or Trångsund from Storkyrkan, you will reach the small square called **Stortorget** ⑫, marvelously atmospheric amid magnificent old merchants' houses. Stockholm's Börshuset (Stock Exchange), which currently houses the **Nobelmuseet** ⑬, fronts the square.

Walk past Svartmangatan's many ancient buildings, including the Tyska Kyrkan, or German Church, with its resplendent oxidized copper spire and airy interior. Continue along Svartmangatan and take a right on Tyska Stallplan to Prästgatan, and just to your left will be Mårten Trotzigs Gränd; this lamplighted alley stairway leads downhill to Järntorget. From here take Västerlånggatan back north across Gamla Stan, checking out the pricey fashion boutiques, galleries, and souvenir shops along the way.

Cut down Storkyrkobrinken to the 17th-century Dutch baroque **Riddarhuset** ⑭. A short walk takes you over Riddarholmsbron to Riddarholmen—Island of Knights—on which stands **Riddarholmskyrkan** ⑮. Also on Riddarholmen is the white 17th-century palace that houses the **Svea Hovrätt** ⑯. Returning across Riddarholmsbron, take Myntgatan back toward Kungliga Slottet and turn left onto Stallbron and cross the bridge. You'll then pass through the refurbished stone **Riksdagshuset** ⑰ on Helgeandsholmen, Holy Ghost Island. Another short bridge returns you to Drottninggatan; take a right onto Fredsgatan and walk until you reach **Medelhavsmuseet** ⑱, on the left, just before Gustav Adolfs Torg. Right there on the square is the **Dansmuseet** ⑲.

The **Operan** ⑳ occupies the waterfront between Gustav Adolfs Torg and Karl XII's Torg (part of Kungsträdgården). A little farther along, on Södra Blasieholmshamn, a host of tour boats docks in front of the stately Grand Hotel. Pass the Grand and visit the **Nationalmuseum** ㉑. Cross the footbridge to the idyllic island of Skeppsholmen, the location of the **Östasiatiska Museet** ㉒, with a fine collection of Buddhist art. Also on Skeppsholmen is the **Moderna Museet** ㉓, which is in the same complex that houses the **Arkitekturmuseet**. To the southwest is **Svensk Form** ㉔, a design museum. The adjoining island, Kastellholmen, is a pleasant place for a stroll, especially on a summer evening, with views of the Baltic harbor and Djurgården's lighted parks.

TIMING   Allow three hours for the walk, double that if you want to tour the various parts of the palace. The Nationalmuseum and Östasiatiska Museet will take up to an hour each to view. Note that Kungliga Slottet is closed Monday off-season, and Stockholms Leksaksmuseum, Moderna Museet,

STOCKHOLM'S ARCHITECTURAL PROCESSION

AS IN MANY OTHER SWEDISH CITIES, a single afternoon walk in Stockholm offers a journey through centuries of architectural change and innovation. There are, of course, the classics. Take Kungliga Slottet (Royal Palace) on Gamla Stan. Designed by Nicodemus Tessin the Younger and built between 1690 and 1704, it's a rather austere palace—no domes, no great towers—and yet it commands a certain respect sitting so regally over the water. Nearby, on Riddarholmen, observe the gorgeous, medieval Riddarholmskyrkan (Riddarholm Church), with its lattice spire pointed toward the heavens. And let's not forget Drottningholm, a 17th-century châteauesque structure—designed by Tessin the Elder and finished by his son— that has been the home of the royal family since 1981. Also at Drottningholm is the Court Theater (1766), which, remarkably, still contains its original interior and fully functional stage machinery.

Stadshuset (city hall) is also a must-see on any architectural walking tour. Completed in 1923, the building contains more than 8 million bricks and 19 million gilded mosaic tiles. Each year the Nobel Prize ceremony is held in the building's Blå Hallen (Blue Hall). Built a few years later is Stadsbiblioteket (City Library), designed by Eric Gunnar Asplund—one of Sweden's most renowned architects. The library's eye-pleasing yet simple design foreshadows the funkis (functionalist) movement that Gunnar helped spearhead in the 1920s and '30s.

Skattehuset (Tax House), also known as Skatteskrapan (a play on the word skyscraper), is hard to miss, looming mercilessly as it does over Södermalm. Completed in the early 1950s as part of an attempt to consolidate the nation's tax offices, the singularly dull, gray, 25-story building is often criticized for having ruined the southern skyline of Stockholm. Except for the annual siege of thousands of Stockholmers flooding it with last-minute tax declarations every May, the building sees few visitors.

Farther south, another architectural oddity plagues—or enhances, depending on whom you ask—the skyline. Globen (the Globe), the world's largest spherical building, looks something like a colossal golf ball or a futuristic space-station still awaiting its launch into orbit. Unveiled in 1988, it's the main arena in Stockholm for indoor sporting events (especially hockey) and rock concerts. Despite debates concerning its aesthetics (or lack thereof), a look at the cables and beams inside reveals Globen's architecture marvel.

Another much debated architectural undertaking is Hötorgscity, across from the highly influential Kulturhuset at Sergels Torg. This postwar compound of five 18-story buildings was constructed in the mid-'50s and shares the oppressive style of its near-contemporary, the Skatteskrapan. Hötorgscity was built to house retail stores and offices and thus bring more commerce to downtown Stockholm. The project failed. A significant chunk of historic Stockholm was lost. Vandalized by ne'er-do-wells and ignored by prospective tenants, the buildings were shut down in the '70s, although today there is a renewed interest in the top floors of the buildings, especially among young business owners.

What is most striking about the buildings that make up Stockholm's architectural portfolio is their collective diversity. You'll glean a particularly remarkable sense of this if you in one day you visit buildings that collectively encompass all the architectural styles. Centuries of history involving both failures and successes are reflected in the styles these structures represent. Every building in Stockholm, new or old, tells a story.

Nationalmuseum, and Östasiatiska Museet are always closed Monday. The Riddarhuset is open weekdays only; off-season, hit the Riddarholmskyrkan on a Wednesday or weekend.

What to See

Arkitekturmuseet. The Museum of Architecture uses models, photos, and drawings to tell the long and interesting story of Swedish architecture. Certain buildings shed light on specific periods, including the Stockholm Town Hall, Vadstena Castle, and the Helsingborg Concert House. The museum also hosts lectures, debates, and architectural tours of the city. ⊠ *Skeppsholmen* ☎ *08/58727000* ⊕ *www.arkitekturmuseet. se* ⊠ *Free* ⊙ *Tues. and Thurs. 11–8, Fri.–Sun. 11–6.*

⑲ **Dansmuseet** (Museum of Dance). Close to the Royal Opera House, the Museum of Dance has a permanent collection that examines dance, theater, and art from Asia, Africa, and Europe. Such artists as Fernand Léger, Francis Picabia, Giorgio de Chirico, and Jean Cocteau are represented in the exhibitions. The Rolf de Maré Study Centre has a vast collection of dance reference materials, including about 4,000 books and 3,000 videos. ⊠ *Gustav Adolfs torg 22–24, City* ☎ *08/4417650* ⊕ *www. dansmuseet.nu* ⊠ *SKr 50* ⊙ *Weekdays 11–4, weekends noon–4.*

Järntorget (Iron Square). Named after its original use as an iron and copper marketplace, this square was also the venue for public executions. ⊠ *Intersection of Västerlångg and Österlångg, Gamla Stan.*

▶ ⑩ **Kungliga Slottet** (Royal Palace). Designed by Nicodemus Tessin, the Royal
Fodor'sChoice Palace was completed in 1760 and replaced the previous palace that had
★ burned here in 1697. Just three weeks later, Tessin—who had also designed the previous incarnation, submitted his drawings for the new palace to the Swedish government. The rebuilding was finally completed, exactly according to Tessin's designs, 60 years later. The four facades of the palace each have a distinct style: the west is the king's, the east the queen's, the south belongs to the nation, and the north represents royalty in general. Watch the changing of the guard in the curved terrace entrance, and view the palace's fine furnishings and Gobelin tapestries on a tour of the **Representationsvän** (State Apartments). To survey the crown jewels, which are no longer used in this self-consciously egalitarian country, head to the **Skattkammaren** (Treasury). The **Livrustkammaren** (Royal Armory) has an outstanding collection of weaponry, coaches, and royal regalia. Entrances to the Treasury and Armory are on the Slottsbacken side of the palace. ⊠ *Gamla Stan* ☎ *08/4026130* ⊕ *www. royalcourt.se* ⊠ *State Apartments SKr 70, Treasury SKr 70, Royal Armory SKr 70 combined ticket for all areas SKr 110* ⊙ *State Apartments and Treasury May–Aug., daily 10–4; Sept.–Apr., Tues.–Sun. noon–3. Armory May–Aug., daily 11–4; Sept.–May, Tues.–Sun. 11–4.*

⑱ **Medelhavsmuseet** (Mediterranean Museum). During the 1700s this building housed the Royal Courts. Then, in the early 1900s, the vast interior of the building was redesigned to resemble the Palazzo Bevilaqua i Bologna, Italy. The collection has a good selection of art from Asia as well as from ancient Egypt, Greece, and Rome. In the Gold Room you can see fine gold, silver, and bronze jewelry from the Far East, Greece, and Rome. ⊠ *Fredsg. 2, City* ☎ *08/51955380* ⊕ *www.medelhavsmuseet. se* ⊠ *SKr 50* ⊙ *Tues. 11–8, Wed.–Fri. 11–4, weekends noon–5.*

★ ㉓ **Moderna Museet** (Museum of Modern Art). Reopened in its original venue on Skeppsholmen, the museum's excellent collection includes works by Picasso, Kandinsky, Dalí, Brancusi, and other international artists. You can also view examples of significant Swedish painters and sculptors and an extensive section on photography. The building itself is striking. Designed by the well-regarded Spanish architect Rafael Moneo, it has seemingly endless hallways of blond wood and walls of glass. ✉ *Skepp-sholmen, City* ☎ *08/51955200* ⊕ *www.modernamuseet.se* ✉ *Free* ⊙ *Tues.–Thurs. 11–8, Fri.–Sun. 11–6.*

㉑ **Nationalmuseum.** The museum's collection of paintings and sculptures
is made up of about 12,500 works. The emphasis is on Swedish and Nordic art, but other areas are well represented. Look especially for some fine works by Rembrandt. The print and drawing department is also impressive, with a nearly complete collection of Edouard Manet prints. ✉ *Södra Blasieholmshamnen, City* ☎ *08/51954300* ⊕ *www. nationalmuseum.se* ✉ *SKr 75* ⊙ *Jan.–Aug., Tues. 11–8, Wed.–Sun. 11–5; Sept.–Dec., Tues. and Thurs. 11–8, Wed., Fri., and weekends 11–5.*

⑬ **Nobelmuseet.** The Swedish Academy meets at Börshuset (the Stock Exchange) every year to decide the winner of the Nobel Prize for literature. The building is also the home of the Nobel Museum. Along with exhibits on creativity's many forms, the museum displays scientific models, shows films, and has a full explanation of the process of choosing prizewinners. The museum does a good job covering the controversial selections made over the years. It's a must for Nobel Prize hopefuls and others. ✉ *Börshuset, Stortorget, Gamla Stan* ☎ *08/232506* ⊕ *www. nobelprize.org/nobelmuseum* ⊙ *Wed.–Mon. 10–6, Tues. 10–8.*

⑳ **Operan** (Opera House). Stockholm's baroque Opera House is almost more famous for its restaurants and bars than for its opera and ballet productions, but that doesn't mean an evening performance should be missed. There's not a bad seat in the house. For just SKr 35 you can even get a listening-only seat (with no view). Still, its food and drink status can't be denied. It has been one of Stockholm's artistic and literary watering holes since the first Operakällaren restaurant opened on the site in 1787. ✉ *Gustav Adolfs Torg, City* ☎ *08/248240* ⊕ *www. operan.se.*

㉒ **Östasiatiska Museet** (Museum of Far Eastern Antiquities). If you have an affinity for Asian art and culture, don't miss this impressive collection of Chinese and Japanese Buddhist sculptures and artifacts. Although some exhibits are displayed with little creativity, the pieces themselves are always worthwhile. The more than 100,000 pieces that make up the holdings here include many from China's Neolithic and Bronze ages. ✉ *Skeppsholmen, City* ☎ *08/51955750* ⊕ *www.mfea.se* ✉ *Free* ⊙ *Tues. noon–8, Wed.–Sun. noon–5.*

⑮ **Riddarholmskyrkan** (Riddarholm Church). Dating from 1270, the Grey Friars monastery is the second-oldest structure in Stockholm and has been the burial place for Swedish kings for more than 400 years. The redbrick structure, distinguished by its delicate iron-fretwork spire, is rarely used for services: it's more like a museum now. The most famous figures interred within are King Gustavus Adolphus, hero of the Thirty Years' War, and the warrior King Karl XII, renowned for his daring invasion of Russia, who died in Norway in 1718. The most recent of the 17 Swedish kings to be put to rest here was Gustav V, in 1950. The different rulers' sarcophagi, usually embellished with their monograms, are visible in the small chapels dedicated to the various dynasties. ✉ *Rid-darholmen* ☎ *08/4026130* ✉ *SKr 20* ⊙ *May–Aug., daily 10–4; Sept., weekends noon–3.*

⑭ **Riddarhuset.** Completed in 1674, the House of Nobles was used for parliamentary assemblies and administration during the four-estate parliamentary period that lasted until 1866. Since then Swedish nobility has continued to meet here every three years for administrative meetings. Hanging from its walls are 2,325 escutcheons, representing all the former noble families of Sweden. The building has excellent acoustic properties and is often used for concerts. ⊠ *Riddarhustorget 10, Gamla Stan* ☏ *08/7233990* ⊕ *www.riddarhuset.se* 🖅 *SKr 40* ☉ *Weekdays 11:30–12:30.*

⑰ Riksdagshuset (Parliament Building). When in session, the Swedish Parliament meets in this 1904 building. Above the entrance, the architect placed sculptures of a peasant, a burgher, a clergyman, and a nobleman. Take a tour of the building not only to learn about Swedish government but also to see the art within. In the former First Chamber are murals by Otte Sköld illustrating different periods in the history of Stockholm, and in the current First Chamber a massive tapestry by Elisabet Hasselberg Olsson, *Memory of a Landscape,* hangs above the podium. ⊠ *Riksg. 3A, Gamla Stan* ☏ *08/7864000* ⊕ *www.riksdagen.se* 🖅 *Free* ☉ *Tours in English late June–late Aug., weekdays 12:30 and 2; late Aug.–late June, weekends 1:30. Call ahead for reservations.*

off the beaten path

STOCKHOLMS LEKSAKSMUSEUM – In Södermalm, Stockholm's Toy Museum has a collection of toys and dolls from all over the world, as well as a children's theater with clowns, magicians, storytellers, and puppet shows. The museum is near the Mariatorget subway station, two stops south of Gamla Stan. ⊠ *Mariatorget 1, Södermalm* ☏ *08/64044492* 🖅 *SKr 40* ☉ *Tues.–Fri. 10–4, weekends noon–4.*

⑪ Storkyrkan. Swedish kings were crowned in the 15th-century Great Church as late as 1907. Today its main attractions are a dramatic wooden statue of St. George slaying the dragon, carved by Bernt Notke of Lübeck in 1489, and the *Parhelion* (1520), the oldest-known painting of Stockholm. ⊠ *Trångsund 1, Gamla Stan* ☏ *08/7233016* ☉ *Sept.–Apr., daily 9–4; May–Aug., daily 9–6.*

⑫ Stortorget (Great Square). Here in 1520 the Danish king Christian II ordered a massacre of Swedish noblemen. The slaughter paved the way for a national revolt against foreign rule and the founding of Sweden as a sovereign state under King Gustav Vasa, who ruled from 1523 to 1560. One legend holds that if it rains heavily enough on the anniversary of the massacre, the old stones still run red. ⊠ *Near Kungliga Slottet, Gamla Stan.*

need a break?

As you stroll along the busy shopping street of Västerlånggatan, you may suddenly notice the strong smell of waffles. That would be the fresh waffle-cones being made at **Café Kåkbrinken** (⊠ Västerlång. 41, on corner of Kåkbrinken near Stortorget, Gamla Stan), which serves the best (and biggest) ice-cream cones in the Old Town.

⑯ Svea Hovrätt (Swedish High Court). The Swedish High Court commands a prime site on the island of Riddarholmen, on a quiet and restful quayside. Sit on the water's edge and watch the boats on Riddarfjärden (Bay of Knights) and, beyond it, Lake Mälaren. From here you can see the lake, the stately arches of Västerbron (West Bridge) in the distance, the southern heights, and above all, the imposing profile of the city hall, which appears almost to be floating on the water. At the quay you may see one of the Göta Canal ships. ⊠ *Riddarholmen* ☉ *Not open to public.*

㉔ Svensk Form (Swedish Form). This museum emphasizes the importance of Swedish form and design, although international works and trends are also covered. Exhibits include everything from chairs to light fixtures to cups, bowls, and silverware. Find out why Sweden is considered a world leader in industrial design. Every year the museum gives out a prestigious and highly coveted design award called Utmärkt Svenskt Form (Outstanding Swedish Design). The winning objects are then exhibited in the fall. ⊠ *Skeppsholmen Holmamiralens väg 2, Skeppsholmen, City* ☎ *08/6443303* ⊕ *www.svenskform.se* ☉ *Tues. and Thurs. noon–7, Fri.–Sun. noon–5.*

Djurgården & Skansen

Djurgården is Stockholm's pleasure island: on it are the outdoor museum Skansen, the Gröna Lund amusement park, and the *Vasa*, a 17th-century warship raised from the harbor bed in 1961, as well as other delights.

A Good Walk

You can approach Djurgården from the water aboard the small ferries that leave from Slussen at the southern end of Gamla Stan. In summer ferries also leave from Nybrokajen, or New Bridge Quay, in front of the Kungliga Dramatiska Teatern. Alternatively, starting at the theater, stroll down the Strandvägen quayside—taking in the magnificent old sailing ships and the fine views over the harbor—and cross Djurgårdsbron, or Djurgården Bridge, to the island. Your first port of call should be the **Vasamuseet** ㉕ ▸, with its dramatic display of splendid 17th-century warships. If you have children in tow, be sure to visit **Junibacken** ㉖, just off Djurgårdsbron. Return to Djurgårdsvägen to find the entrance to the **Nordiska Museet** ㉗, worth a visit for insight into Swedish folklore.

Continue on Djurgårdsvägen to the amusement park **Gröna Lund Tivoli** ㉘, where Stockholmers of all ages come to play. Beyond the park, cross Djurgårdsvägen to **Skansen** ㉙.

From Skansen continue on Djurgårdsvägen to Prins Eugens Väg and follow the signs to the beautiful late-19th-century **Waldemarsudde** ㉚. On the way back to Djurgårdsbron, take the small street called Hazeliusbacken around to the charmingly archaic **Biologiska Museet** ㉛. From the museum walk toward Djurgårdsbron and then take a right on Rosendalsvägen. Signs on this street lead to **Rosendals Trädgårder** ㉜, which has beautiful gardens and a delightful café. From here you can stroll back along the water toward the city.

TIMING   Allow half a day for this tour, unless you're planning to turn it into a full-day event with lengthy visits to Skansen, Junibacken, and Gröna Lund Tivoli. The Vasamuseet warrants two hours, and the Nordiska and Biologiska museums need an hour each. Waldemarsudde requires another half hour. Gröna Lund Tivoli is closed from mid-September to late April. The Nordiska Museet closes Monday, and the Biologiska Museet and Waldemarsudde are closed Monday off-season.

What to See

🐾 ㉛ **Biologiska Museet** (Biological Museum). The Biological Museum, in the shadow of Skansen, exhibits preserved animals in various simulated environments. The museum itself, unchanged since its 19th-century opening, is a delightful look into the past. ⊠ *Hazeliusporten, Djurgården* ☎ *08/4428215* ⊕ *www.skansen.se* ☒ *SKr 30* ☉ *Apr.–Sept., daily 10–4; Oct.–Mar., Tues.–Sun. 10–3.*

🐾 ㉘ **Gröna Lund Tivoli.** Smaller than Copenhagen's Tivoli or Göteborg's Liseberg, this amusement park is a clean, well-organized pleasure garden with rides, attractions, and restaurants. If you're feeling especially daring, try the Power Tower. At 350 feet (80 meters), it's Europe's tallest free-fall amusement-park ride. Concerts are held here all summer long, drawing top performers from Sweden and around the world. ⊠ *Allmänna Gränd 9, Djurgården* ☎ *08/58750100* ⊕ *www.tivoli.se* ✆ *SKr 60, not including tickets or passes for rides* ☉ *Late Apr.–mid-Sept., daily. Hrs vary but are generally noon–11 PM. Call ahead for specific information.*

★ ☺ ㉖ **Junibacken.** In this storybook house you travel in small carriages through the world of children's book writer Astrid Lindgren, creator of the irrepressible character Pippi Longstocking. Lindgren's tales come alive as various scenes are revealed. It's perfect for children ages 5 and up. ⊠ *Galärvarsv., Djurgården* ☎ *08/58723000* ⊕ *www.junibacken.se* ✆ *SKr95* ☉ *June–Aug., daily 9–6; Sept.–May, Wed.–Sun. 10–5.*

☺ ㉗ **Nordiska Museet** (Nordic Museum). An imposing late-Victorian structure housing peasant costumes from every region of the country and exhibits on the Sámi (pronounced *sah*-mee)—Lapps, the formerly seminomadic reindeer herders who inhabit the far north and many other aspects of Swedish life. Families with children should visit the delightful "village life" play area on the ground floor. ⊠ *Djurgårdsv. 6–16, Djurgården* ☎ *08/51956000* ⊕ *www.nordm.se* ✆ *SKr 60* ☉ *Tues. and Thurs. 10–8, Wed. and Fri.–Sun. 10–5.*

㉜ **Rosendals Trädgårder** (Rosendal's Garden). This gorgeous slice of greenery is a perfect place to spend a few hours on a late summer afternoon. When the weather's nice, people flock to the garden café, which is in one of the greenhouses, to enjoy tasty pastries and salads made from the locally grown vegetables. Pick your own flowers from the vast flower beds (paying by weight) or take away produce from the farm shop. ⊠ *Rosendalsterrassen 12, Djurgården* ☎ *08/6622814* ✆ *Free* ☉ *May–Sept., daily 11–6; Oct.–Apr., call ahead for hrs.*

FodorśChoice
★

★ ☺ ㉙ **Skansen.** The world's first open-air museum, Skansen was founded in 1891 by philologist and ethnographer Artur Hazelius, who is buried here. He preserved examples of traditional Swedish architecture brought from all parts of the country, including farmhouses, windmills, barns, a working glassblower's hut, and churches. Not only is Skansen a delightful trip out of time in the center of a modern city, but it also provides insight into the life and culture of Sweden's various regions. In addition, the park has a zoo, carnival area, aquarium, theater, and cafés. ⊠ *Djurgårdsslätten 4951, Djurgården* ☎ *08/4428000* ⊕ *www.skansen.se* ✆ *Park and zoo costs vary according to day of week, but are approximately SKr 30 Sept.–Apr. and SKr 60 May–Aug., aquarium SKr 60* ☉ *Oct.–Apr., daily 10–4; May, daily 10–8; June–Aug., daily 10–10; Sept., daily 10–5.*

need a break?
The **Cirkus Theater** (⊠ Djurgårdsslätten, Djurgården ☎ 08/58798750), on Hazeliusbacken right near the entrance to Skansen, has a lovely terrace café. If you want something a bit more hearty, head to **Hasselbacken Hotel** (⊠ Hazeliusbacken 20, Djurgården ☎ 08/51734300) and dine on its terrace.

⚑ ★ ㉕ **Vasamuseet** (Vasa Museum). The warship *Vasa* sank 10 minutes into its maiden voyage in 1628, consigned to a watery grave until it was raised from the seabed in 1961. Its hull was preserved by the Baltic mud, free of the worms that can eat through ships' timbers. Now largely restored to her former glory (however short-lived it may have been), the man-of-war resides in a handsome museum. Daily tours are available year-round. ⊠ *Galärvarvsv., Djurgården* ☎ *08/51954800* ⊕ *www.vasamuseet.se* ✆ *SKr 70* ☉ *Thurs.–Tues. 10–5, Wed. 10–8.*

㉚ **Waldemarsudde.** This estate, Djurgården's gem, was bequeathed to the Swedish people by Prince Eugen upon his death, in 1947. It maintains an important collection of Nordic paintings from 1880 to 1940, in addition to the prince's own works. ⌧ *Prins Eugens väg 6, Djurgården* ☎ *08/54583700* ⊕ *www.waldemarsudde.com* ⌧ *SKr 75* ☉ *May–Aug., Tues.–Wed. and Fri.–Sun. 11–5, Thurs. 11–8; Sept.–Apr., Tues.–Wed. and Fri. 11–4, Thurs. 11–8, weekends 11–4.*

Östermalm & Kaknästornet

Marked by waterfront rows of Renaissance buildings with palatial rooftops and ornamentation, Östermalm is a quiet residential section of central Stockholm, its elegant streets lined with museums and fine shopping. On Strandvägen, or Beach Way, the boulevard that follows the harbor's edge from the busy downtown area to the staid diplomatic quarter, you can choose one of three routes. The waterside walk, with its splendid views of the city harbor, bustles with tour boats and sailboats. Parallel to the walk (away from the water) is a tree-shaded walking and bike path. Walk, rollerblade, or ride a bike down the middle, and you just might meet the occasional horseback rider, properly attired in helmet, jacket, and high polished boots. Take the route farthest from the water, and you will walk past upscale shops and expensive restaurants.

A Good Walk

Walk east from the Kungliga Dramatiska Teatern, in Nybroplan, along Strandvägen until you get to Djurgårdsbron, an ornate little bridge that leads to the island of Djurgården. Resist going to the park, and instead turn left up Narvavägen and walk along the right-hand side until you reach Oscars Kyrka. Cross the street and continue up the left side until you reach the **Historiska Museet** ㉝ ▶. From here it's only a short walk farther up Narvavägen to Karlaplan, a pleasant circular park with a fountain. Go across or around the park to find Karlavägen. Heading northwest along this long boulevard, you'll pass by many small shops and galleries. At Nybrogatan turn left (this intersection is beyond the limits of the Stockholm map). Be sure to take some time to check out the exclusive furniture stores on your way down to **Östermalmstorg** ㉞, where there's an excellent indoor food market. Cut across the square and take a right down Sibyllegatan to the **Musik Museet** ㉟, installed in the city's oldest industrial building. Within the same block is the **Armémuseum.** Then go back to Nybroplan, where you can catch Bus 69 going east to **Kaknästornet** ㊱ for a spectacular view of Stockholm from the tallest tower in Scandinavia. From here walk back toward town along Djurgårdsbrunnsvägen until you reach **Tekniska Museet** ㊲.

TIMING   This tour requires a little more than a half day. You'll want to spend about an hour in each of the museums. The bus ride from Nybroplan to Kaknästornet takes about 15 minutes, and the tower merits another half hour. The Historiska and Musik museums are closed Monday, and the Millesgården is closed Monday off-season.

What to See

Armémuseum. The large Military Museum covers everything from Sweden's early might as a kingdom to its unique, neutral military position during the 20th century. The castle guards and military band marches from this square every day on its walk to the Royal Palace on Gamla Stan. ⌧ *Riddarg. 13, Östermalm* ☎ *08/7889560* ⊕ *www.armemuseum. org* ⌧ *SKr 60* ☉ *Tues. 11–8, Wed.–Sun. 11–4.*

need a
break?

For some of the best baguettes and croissants outside Paris, stop by **Riddarbageriet** (⌧ Riddarg. 15, Östermalm) near the Armémuseum. Bread in Stockholm doesn't get any better than this: they deliver to the king and queen and many of the city's best restaurants. You can also get great coffee, sandwiches, and pastries. The bakery is closed in July.

▶ **③③ Historiska Museet** (Museum of National Antiquities). Viking treasures and the Gold Room are the main draw, but well-presented temporary exhibitions also cover various periods of Swedish history. The gift shop here is excellent. ⊠ *Narvav. 13–17, Östermalm* ☎ *08/51955000* ⊕ *www. historiska.se* ☒ *SKr 50* ⊙ *Tues.–Wed. and Fri.–Sun. 11–5, Thurs. 11–8.*

③⑥ Kaknästornet (Kaknäs TV Tower). The 511-foot-high Kaknäs radio and television tower, completed in 1967, is the tallest building in Scandinavia. Surrounded by satellite dishes, it is also used as a linkup station for a number of Swedish satellite TV channels and radio stations. Eat a meal in a restaurant 426 feet above the ground and enjoy panoramic views of the city and the archipelago. ⊠ *Mörkakroken off Djurgårdsbrunnsv., Djurgården* ☎ *08/6672180* ☒ *SKr 30* ⊙ *June–Aug., daily 9 AM–10 PM; Sept.–May, daily 10–9.*

off the beaten path

MILLESGÅRDEN – This gallery and sculpture garden north of the city is dedicated to the property's former owner, American-Swedish sculptor Carl Milles (1875–1955). On display throughout the property are Milles's own unique works, and inside the main building, once his house, is his private collection. On the terrace is the beautiful Anne's House, designed by famous Austrian designer Josef Frank, where Milles spent the final years of his life. The setting is exquisite: sculptures top columns on terraces in a magical garden high above the harbor and the city. Millesgården can be easily reached via subway to Ropsten, where you catch the Lidingö train and get off at Herserud, the second stop. The trip takes about 30 minutes. ⊠ *Carl Milles väg 2, Lidingö* ☎ *08/4467580* ⊕ *www. millesgarden.se* ☒ *SKr 75* ⊙ *May–Sept., daily 10–5; Oct.–Apr., Tues.–Fri. noon–4, weekends 11–5.*

③⑤ Musik Museet. Inside what was the military's bread bakery from the 17th century to the mid-1900s, the Music Museum has more than 6,000 instruments in its collection, with the focus on items from 1600 to 1850. Its 18th-century woodwind collection is internationally renowned. The museum also holds jazz, folk, and world music concerts. Children are invited to touch and play some of the instruments, and the motion-sensitive "Sound Room" lets you produce musical effects simply by gesturing and moving around. ⊠ *Sibylleg. 2, Östermalm* ☎ *08/51955490* ⊕ *www.musikmuseet.se* ☒ *SKr 50* ⊙ *Tues.–Sun. 11–4.*

③④ Östermalmstorg. The market square and its neighboring streets represent old, established Stockholm. **Saluhall** is more a collection of boutiques than an indoor food market; the fish displays can be especially intriguing. At the other end of the square, **Hedvig Eleonora Kyrka**, a church with characteristically Swedish faux-marble painting throughout its wooden interior, is the site of frequent lunchtime concerts in spring and summer. ⊠ *Nybrog. at Humlegårdsg., Östermalm.*

need a break?

The little restaurants inside the **Saluhall** (⊠ Östermalmstorg, Östermalm) offer everything from takeout coffee to sit-down meals.

③⑦ Tekniska Museet. Only a 10-minute bus ride from the city, the Museum of Science and Technology has a huge Machinery Hall displaying cars, bicycles, and even airplanes. There are also exhibits on technology in the home and the history of the printed word in Sweden (the first book dates from 1483). Teknorama, the museum's science center, encourages children and young adults to learn more about the natural sciences and technology. There are also a café and gift shop. ⊠ *Museiv. 7, Djurgårdsbrunnsv., Djurgården* ☎ *08/4505600* ⊕ *www.tekniskamuseet.se* ✉ *SKr 60; free Wed. night* ⊙ *Mon.–Tues. and Thurs.–Fri. 10–5, Wed. 10–8, weekends 11–5.*

Outside the City

There are a number of excellent sites only a short bus or subway ride from the city center, many of which can be combined. Trips to nearly all these places could be done in a morning or afternoon and even added on to the other walks.

What to See

Fodor'sChoice **Bergianska Trädgården.** The beautiful Bergianska Botanical Gardens, on
★ a peninsula extending out into the small bay of Brunnsvik, can provide a wonderful break from the city. They are only a short subway ride away. Paths weave along the water in the open park area. Visit Edvard Anderson's modern Växthus (Greenhouse) for its impressive Mediterranean and tropical environments. The century-old Victoriahuset (Victoria House) contains tropical plants as well and has one of the best collections of water plants in the world. ⊠ *Frescativ., near the university, Universitet* ☎ *08/156545* ⊕ *www.bergianska.se* ✉ *Park is free, Greenhouse SKr 40, Victoria House SKr 10* ⊙ *Park daily yr-round; Victoria House May–Sept., daily 11–4, weekends 11–5; Greenhouse daily 11–5.*

Fjärilshuset (Butterfly and Bird House). After a short bus ride and a nice walk through the magnificent Haga Park, you could be in a room filled with hundreds of tropical butterflies. In the bird room, hundreds of birds of 40 species fly freely. The Haga Park itself is impressive and worth a lengthy stroll, but be sure to combine it with a trip to this feather-filled oasis. ⊠ *Take Bus 515 from the Odenplan subway stop, Haga* ☎ *08/7303981* ⊕ *www.fjarilshuset.se* ✉ *SKr 70* ⊙ *Apr.–Sept., Tues.–Fri. 10–4, weekends 11–5:30; Oct.–Mar., Tues.–Fri. 10–3, weekends 11–4.*

☺ **Naturhistoriska Riksmuseet and Cosmonova** (Museum of Natural History). Founded in 1739 by the famous Swedish botanist Linnaeus and his colleagues at the Science Academy, the museum has been in its present location near the university since 1916. The last decade has brought much rebuilding and other improvements. Exhibits include "Life in Water," "Marvels of the Human Body," and "Space Adventure." Cosmonova shows science and nature films in Sweden's only IMAX theater. The subway ride to the Universitet stop takes less than 10 minutes from the city center. ⊠ *Frescativ. 40, Universitet* ☎ *08/51954040* ⊕ *www.nrm.se* ✉ *SKr 65* ⊙ *Fri.–Wed. 10–7, Thurs. 10–8; Cosmonova mid-May–end of May and Aug.–Sept., Tues.–Sun.; June–July, daily 10–7.*

Tyresö Slottet (Tyresö Castle). After a quick, 20-minute bus ride from southern Stockholm, you'll find yourself in the gorgeous Romantic gardens that surround this castle, built in the 1660s. The Nordic Museum led the renovations that restored the grounds to their late-1800s glory. The main building is filled with elaborate salons, libraries, and studies, and the west wing has a nice café and restaurant. Be sure to leave time for both the castle and gardens. ⊠ *Take Bus 805 from Gullmarsplan to Tyresö Slott, Tyresö* ☎ *08/7700178* ⊕ *www.nordm.se/slott* ✉ *SKr 70* ⊙ *Sept.–Oct., daily 11–3; June 22–Aug. 19, Tues.–Sun. 11–4. Tours at noon, 1, and 2.*

Ulriksdals Slott (Ulriksdals Castle). Construction on the castle began in 1640, but it was during the first half of the 1700s that the castle took on the look that it has today. Built in the Renaissance style, the castle is most closely associated with King Gustav Adolf and Queen Louise, who in 1923 added a famous living room designed by Carl Malmsten. The Dutch Renaissance chapel from the mid-1800s is still used for masses, weddings, and concerts. ✉ *Take Bus 503 from Bergshamra subway stop, on the Red Line, Ulriksdal* ☎ *08/4026130* ⊕ *www.royalcourt. se/ulriksdal* 🖼*SKr 50* ☉ *Mid-May–Aug., Tues.–Sun. noon–4; Sept., weekends noon–4.*

WHERE TO EAT

Stockholm's restaurant scene rivals that of any major European capital, with upscale restaurants offering creative menus at trendy modern locations. The best bring foreign innovations to bear on Sweden's high-quality raw ingredients. The city's top restaurants will charge accordingly, but you aren't likely to leave disappointed. Of course, there are also plenty of less expensive restaurants with traditional Swedish cooking. Among Swedish dishes, the best bets are wild game and fish, particularly salmon, and the smörgåsbord buffet, which usually offers a good variety at an inexpensive price. Reservations are often necessary on weekends.

Prices

WHAT IT COSTS In Swedish Kronor				
$$$$	**$$$**	**$$**	**$**	**¢**
AT DINNER over 420	250–420	150–250	100–150	below 100

Prices are for a main course at dinner.

Downtown Stockholm & Beyond

★ **$$$–$$$$** ✕ **Edsbacka Krog.** In 1626 Edsbacka, just outside town, became Stockholm's first licensed inn. Its exposed rough-hewn beams, plaster walls, and open fireplaces still give it the feel of a resting post for the gentry, and careful modernization has created all the comforts you would expect at this end of the restaurant scale. Chef Christer Lindström interprets Swedish cuisine creatively. Ease into the meal with seared lobster served with a compote of root crops, followed by roasted breast and liver of wild duck with pear sauce. ✉ *Sollentunav. 220, Sollentuna* ☎ *08/963300* ⊟ *AE, DC, MC, V* ☉ *Closed Sun. and Mon.*

★ **$$$–$$$$** ✕ **Wedholms Fisk.** Noted for its fresh seafood dishes, Wedholms Fisk is appropriately set by a bay in Stockholm center. High ceilings, large windows, and tasteful modern paintings from the owner's personal collection create a spacious, sophisticated space. The traditional Swedish cuisine, which consists almost exclusively of seafood, is simple but outstanding. Try the poached sole in basil sauce or the scallops gratinéed with leeks. ✉ *Nybrokajen 17, City* ☎ *08/6117874* ⊟ *AE, DC, MC, V* ☉ *Closed Sun. and July.*

$$–$$$$ ✕ **Operakällaren.** Open since 1787, the haughty grande dame of Stockholm is more a Swedish institution than a seat of gastronomic distinction. Thick carpeting, shiny polished brass, and handsome carved-wood chairs and tables fill the room. The crystal chandeliers are said to be Sweden's finest, and the high windows on the south side have magnificent views of the Royal Palace. The restaurant is famed for its seasonal smörgåsbord, offered from early June through Christmas. Coveted selections include pickled herring, *rollmops* (rolled herring), reindeer and elk (in season), and ice cream with cloudberry sauce. In summer the veranda opens as the Operabryggan Café, facing Kungsträdgården and the waterfront. Around the corner in the same building is the restaurant's *backficka,* a pleasantly active bar/restaurant with a less expensive menu.

CloseUp

A SWEDISH TOAST

MANY OF THOSE WHO HAVE NEVER SEEN SWEDEN *have nonetheless conjured an often nearsighted image of what they think it is like: Nordic woodlands, crystalline-featured women, Greta Garbo, sexual freedom, and lives lived within rigid, formal constraints. There's some truth to the latter image of Swedish formality. So let's take a look at it.*

Please take a seat as an invited guest at the dining table. It is set with a crisp white tablecloth, perfectly polished silver, a candelabra, napkins, and crystal glasses. The wine is chilled, and nothing is out of place. Your hostess, a woman, of course, is the shimmering image of household perfection.

Nowhere more than at the dining table will you encounter the unspoken truths of Swedish formality, especially in the toast. In Australia or New Zealand it is scarcely de rigueur and may be accompanied by a drawling "G'day, mate." In Britain it is all stiff upper lip and chivalry. In the United States the rules are as diverse as the cultures that populate it. But in Sweden there is only one way to toast, its protocol very specific and universally followed. Do not touch your glass yet, even though it is full and you are nervous. Never do this. You must wait until one of the hosts, usually the man, lifts his glass to all. Do not drink. Everyone must reply to the proffered "skål" (or cheers) with a collective "skål." Then you will all tilt your glasses to the host and hostess. Delayed eye contact is imperative before, during and after the measured sip of appreciation. Don't empty the glass. The meal has commenced.

From here on in during the dinner, toasting will still play a role, but the procedure is individualized and personal. Guests will toast each other. You are free to toast anyone but the hostess. She can toast anyone she pleases. This is a safeguard against hostess inebriation. The temptation, of course, is for everyone to intermittently toast her in thanks. But this could leave her floundering on the floor, a run in her stockings, and a hand on her husband's best friend's knee. This is not seemly behavior in Swedish society.

The roots of this alcohol-related tradition may lie with the Vikings. They always lived in peril, and no one could be trusted. The rule was to toast your "friend" with full eye contact and an arm behind the back to prevent a quick slitting of the throat. Later, state control would become big in Sweden; alcohol was once banned to stop the poor from brewing their potatoes into freedom-inducing alcohol; later alcohol was limited to stave off social and health problems. Even today you can buy wine and spirits only in government-controlled liquor stores, called Systembolagett. Caution is part of the Swedish nature, and the alcohol rituals show it.

Back at the dinner table, most of the rules will not be unfamiliar to you, simply practiced in a more accentuated form.

I will leave you with your hosts now. You can find your way from here. As a foreigner you will be granted some leeway in strictly adhering to the customs. But whatever you do, do not take the bottle as you leave. From that transgression there is certainly no way back.

⊠ *Operahuset, Jakobs Torg 2, City* ☏ *08/6765800* ⚠ *Reservations essential* ⋔ *Jacket and tie* ▤ *AE, DC, MC, V* ◷ *Main dining room closed in July.*

$$–$$$$ ✕ **Restaurangen.** This restaurant gained its fine reputation in large part due to its flavor-based menu. Diners build three-, five-, or seven-course meals from 20 flavors, 15 of which are salty and five of which are sweet. Thus, chili, coriander, and vanilla would result in a chicken spring roll with mint dipping sauce, seafood and tofu with lemongrass juice, and vanilla ice cream with a waffle and fresh strawberries. Each flavor has a letter next to it that corresponds to the wine-list offerings that are recommended to best complement the flavor. The restaurant, with its blond wood, beige and brown fabrics, and red- and cream-color walls, was created by three students from Stockholm's prestigious Beckman's School of Design. ⊠ *Oxtorgsg. 14, City* ☏ *08/220952* ▤ *AE, DC, MC, V* ◷ *Closed Sun.*

$$$ ✕ **Bon Lloc.** With an elegant and spacious dining area and a creative
Fodor'sChoice   Mediterranean-influenced menu, Bon Lloc has established itself as one
★   of the hottest restaurants in town. The menu uses common ingredients like ham and cod to create dishes that recall Catalonia as much as Sweden. The extensive wine list offers an excellent selection of European wines. The interior's light-brown wood and mosaic tiles allude to Mediterranean styles while still evoking Swedish simplicity, much as the food does. ⊠ *Regeringsg. 111, Norrmalm* ☏ *08/6606060* ⚠ *Reservations essential* ▤ *AE, DC, MC, V* ◷ *Closed Sun.*

$$$ ✕ **Fredsgatan 12.** The government crowd files into this funky restaurant
Fodor'sChoice   at lunch; a more casual yet stylish crowd is there at night. All come here
★   to enjoy what is probably some of the best food in town. The young chef Melker Andersson works his magic here, creating Swedish-, Asian-, and European-inspired dishes that defy convention and positively demand enjoyment. The menu offers creative combinations, such as rabbit *taquitos* (filled tortillas rolled up and deep-fried) or asparagus Caesar salad with scallops and tiger prawns. When ordering a cocktail, choose a flavor such as mint and sugar or lemon-cherry and then an alcohol of your choice with which to mix it. From the bar you can get a nice view into the kitchen of this popular restaurant—always a good sign of a place that values its food. ⊠ *Fredsg. 12, City* ☏ *08/248052* ▤ *AE, DC, MC, V* ◷ *Closed Sun.*

★ $$$ ✕ **Ulriksdals Wärdshus.** The lunchtime smörgåsbord at this country inn can't be beat. Built in the park of an 18th-century palace in 1868, the traditionally decorated inn overlooks orchards and a peaceful lake. It's an expensive restaurant, but the impeccable service and outstanding cuisine make a splurge here worthwhile. Menu highlights include monkfish with a ragout of gnocchi, samphire, and lovage and seared sweetbread served with veal-shank ravioli, endive, and foie gras. The restaurant's cellar is listed in Guinness world records as the most complete in the world. There are more than 500 bottles of the top five Bordeaux chateaux from the 20th century, nearly one for every year for every wine. ⊠ *Ulriksdals Slottspark, Solna* ☏ *08/850815* ⚠ *Reservations essential* ⋔ *Jacket required* ▤ *AE, DC, MC, V* ◷ *No dinner Sun.*

$$–$$$ ✕ **Riche.** This Stockholm establishment was for many years an exclusive club. Today the elegance and style remain, but the diners are from a much broader pool. Eat in the casual glassed-in veranda on wicker chairs, or move inside to the main dining room for more formal dining. For the ultimate in posh tradition, book a table at the Teatergrillen, in the back: members of the Swedish royal family are fans, too. All three sections serve Swedish and French cuisine. Upstairs is a chill-out space where DJs play late night and you can buy simple smørrebrød (open-

face sandwiches) until 2 AM. ⊠ *Birger Jarlsg. 4, Östermalm* ☎ *08/54503560* 🖃 *AE, DC, MC, V* ☉ *Closed Sun.*

$$–$$$ ✕ **Stallmästaregården.** A historic old inn with an attractive courtyard and garden, Stallmästaregården is in Haga Park, just north of Norrtull, about 15 minutes by car or bus from the city center. Fine summer meals are served on a tented terrace overlooking the waters of Brunnsviken. Specialties include poached fillet of Dover sole with black *tagliolini* and lobster sauce. ⊠ *Norrtull near Haga; take Bus 52 to Stallmästaregården, Haga* ☎ *08/6101300* 🖃 *AE, DC, MC, V* ☉ *Closed Sun.*

$–$$$ ✕ **Storstad.** A lighter and less expensive menu is served in the bar area of this popular hangout, which looks out on the street through wide arching windows. In the sparse but inviting dining room in the back you might try the sweet-corn soup with truffle pasta and Parmesan cheese before moving on to meat specialties such as fried duck breast with honey-baked beets, mushroom spring rolls, and port syrup. The wine list is excellent and especially strong on French and Californian wines. ⊠ *Odeng. 41, Vasastan* ☎ *08/6733800* ⌨ *Reservations essential* 🖃 *AE, DC, MC, V* ☉ *No lunch. Closed Sun.*

¢–$$$ ✕ **Tranan.** There's something about Tranan that makes you want to go
Fodor'sChoice   back. The food is Swedish with a touch of French and is consistently
★   very good. The stark walls covered with old movie posters and the red-and-white-checked tablecloths are reminders of the days when it was a workingman's beer parlor. Try the *biff rydberg*—fillet of beef, fried potatoes, horseradish, and egg yolk—it's a Swedish classic. The bar downstairs has DJs and live music and gets packed to bursting on weekends. ⊠ *Karlbergsv. 14, Vasastan* ☎ *08/52728100* 🖃 *AE, DC, MC, V* ☉ *No lunch weekends.*

★ $$ ✕ **Prinsen.** Still in the same location as when it opened in 1897, the Prince serves both traditional and modern Swedish cuisine. The interior is rich with mellow, warm lighting; dark wood paneling; and leather chairs and booths. The staff is as delightfully starched as the white aprons they wear. On the walls are black-and-white oil paintings of famous people done by one of the long-serving staff members, as well as paintings by local artists that came into the restaurant's possession when they were used as payment to settle tabs. The restaurant is known for its scampi salad and wild-game dishes. Downstairs are a bar and a space for larger parties. ⊠ *Mäster Samuelsg. 4, City* ☎ *08/6111331* 🖃 *AE, DC, MC, V* ☉ *No lunch weekends.*

$$ ✕ **Rolfs Kök.** Small and modern, Rolfs is a casual restaurant serving excellent Swedish-French cuisine to an eclectic mix of businesspeople and theater and arts folks. The chairs and the salt and pepper shakers hang on hooks on the wall above each table. Go for the lingonberry-glazed reindeer fillet with cauliflower; root vegetables and smoked chili pepper; or a feta cheese salad with lime, soy, and chili-fried chicken. ⊠ *Tegnérg. 41, Norrmalm* ☎ *08/101696* 🖃 *AE, DC, MC, V* ☉ *No lunch weekends.*

$$ ✕ **Stockholms Matvarufabriken.** Although it's a bit hard to find, tucked away as it is on a side street, Stockholm's Food Factory is well worth seeking out. The popular bistro restaurant, serving French, Italian, and Swedish cuisine, is packed full on the weekends as young and old come to enjoy the exposed-brick, candlelighted dining room and varied menu: here omelets are taken to new levels with ingredients such as truffles and asparagus. Brown-paper tablecloths and kitchen cloths used as napkins set the informal tone. ⊠ *Idung. 12, Vasastan* ☎ *08/320704* 🖃 *AE, DC, MC, V.*

$$ ✕ **Sturehof.** This massive complex of a restaurant with two huge bars is a complete social, architectural, and dining experience amid wood paneling, leather chairs and sofas, and distinctive lighting fixtures.

There's a bar directly facing Stureplan where you can sit on a summer night and watch Stockholmers gather at the nearby Svampen, a mushroomlike concrete structure that has doubled as the city's meeting point for years. In the elegant dining room fine Swedish cuisine is offered. Upstairs is the O-Bar, a dark and smoky lounge filled well into the night with young people and loud music. ⊠ *Stureplan 2, City* ☎ *08/4405730* ⊟ *AE, DC, MC, V.*

$$ ✕ **Undici.** First Tomas Brolin was a hero to the Swedish people on the soccer field; now he's a hero on the Stockholm restaurant scene. Undici is one of the city's most popular places, both to eat and hang out. A small seating area in the front is good for finalizing that business deal, while curved leather banquettes along the wall are better for festive groups of six or seven. The dining room in back is decked out in fine dark woods and white linens and serves a combination of northern Swedish and northern Italian cuisine. Dishes have included such standouts as lamb fillet with cannelloni and *rimmat lammlägg* (salt-cured lamb) with goat cheese, spinach, and spicy merguez sausage. ⊠ *Stureg. 22, Norrmalm* ☎ *08/6616617* ⊟ *AE, DC, MC, V* ☯ *Closed Sun. No lunch Sat.*

$$ ✕ **Wasahof.** Across the street from Vasaparken, and just a short walk from Odenplan, Wasahof feels like an authentic bistro, but the cooking actually mixes Swedish, French, and Italian recipes. The pleasantly rustic space and good food have attracted all kinds of culturati—actors, writers, journalists—for some time. Seafood is a specialty here—this is the place in Stockholm to get oysters. ⊠ *Dalag. 46, Vasastan* ☎ *08/323440* ⊟ *AE, DC, MC, V* ☯ *Closed Sun.*

$–$$ ✕ **Dramatenrestaurangen Frippe.** Connected to Lillascenen, the smaller stage that's behind the Royal National Theater, this is the perfect place to grab a bite before a performance. One wall is covered in black-and-white photos of the theater's most famous actors, and posters of major productions line the bar, behind which is the open kitchen. Bar stools along the window allow for great people-watching. The food is a modern take on *husmanskost*, traditional Swedish cooking. Try the classic Isterband sausage with creamy parsley potatoes. ⊠ *Nybrog./Almlöfsg., City* ☎ *08/6656142* ⊟ *AE, DC, MC, V* ☯ *No lunch weekends.*

$–$$ ✕ **East.** Just off Stureplan, East is one of the city's culinary hot spots, offering enticing contemporary pan-Asian fare from Thailand, Japan, Korea, and Vietnam. Order a selection of appetizers to get a sampling of this cross-cultural cooking. East is a perfect spot to have dinner before a night on the town. Try the Luxor: chicken, tiger shrimp, and egg noodles with peanuts, mint leaves, and coconut sauce. The bar area at this vibrant restaurant turns into a miniclub at night, with soul and hip-hop on the turntables. ⊠ *Stureplan 13, Norrmalm* ☎ *08/6114959* ⊟ *AE, DC, MC, V.*

$–$$ ✕ **Halv trappa plus gård.** This hip restaurant is exactly what its name suggests: two half floors plus a pleasant courtyard. Owned by the same two guys who run Halv Grek Plus Turk (Half Greek plus a Turk), the retro vibe harks back to the '70s. The menu emphasizes fish, most of it done with a Mediterranean flair. The staff is good-hearted and professional. When possible, eat in the courtyard, but book a table, since there are only 10 out there. ⊠ *Lästmakarg. 3, City* ☎ *08/6110277* ⊟ *AE, DC, MC, V* ☯ *Closed Sun. No lunch.*

$–$$ ✕ **Kjellsons.** Kjellsons is a bar first and a restaurant second, but this doesn't mean the menu is short on high-caliber dishes (to say nothing of fine drinks). Appetizers include an excellent pea soup (a Swedish tradition) and a delicious avocado-and-smoked ham salad—most of the fare is traditional Swedish. And be sure to ask for a basket of cracker bread—it comes with a tube of the famous caviar. In summer there's outdoor seating. ⊠ *Birger Jarlsg. 36, City* ☎ *08/6110045* ⊟ *AE, DC, MC, V.*

$–$$ ✕**Norrlands Bar & Grill.** If it's people you like, then this is the place. Downstairs is a restaurant and cocktail bar, upstairs a bar and terrace. Both floors are always busy. The food is Swedish with Mediterranean influences, the cocktails are superb, and the dining room is sleek and contemporary. Norrlands has produced a cookbook and a drink book, both of which are best-sellers. ⊠ *Norrlandsg. 24, Norrmalm* ☎ *08/6118810* ⊟ *AE, DC, MC, V* ☺ *Closed Sun.*

¢–$$ ✕**Roppongi.** Although far from downtown and not exactly in the most happening area, Roppongi's adventurous, creative menu and quality fish make it the best sushi place in Stockholm. This means it's almost always packed, so be ready to share the stripped-down space with other sushi lovers. The shrimp tempura rolls will leave you drooling for more and the *tamaki* cones are plump and bursting with flavor. ⊠ *Hantverkarg. 76, Kungsholmen* ☎ *08/6501772* ⊟ *AE, DC, MC, V* ☺ *No lunch weekends.*

¢–$ ✕**Il Forno.** You might not expect to find brick-oven pizza in Sweden, but Il Forno serves some of the best you'll find north of the Mediterranean. Choose from more than 25 combinations, all of which use only the freshest ingredients and a tasty, crunchy crust. The kitchen also churns out a number of pasta dishes and sells many varieties of Italian olives, olive oil, and other fine foods. As much Italian as Swedish is spoken here. Sit outside when possible—the interior can feel a bit stuffy. ⊠ *Atlasg. 9, Vasastan* ☎ *08/319049* ⊟ *AE, DC, MC, V.*

FodorsChoice
★

Gamla Stan & Skeppsholmen

★ $$$–$$$$ ✕**Franska Matsalen.** This classic French restaurant in the Grand Hotel serves the best true French cuisine in the city—plus, you can enjoy an inspiring view of Gamla Stan and the Royal Palace across the inner harbor waters. The menu changes five times a year, but the emphasis is always on Swedish ingredients. They're used to create such dishes as pike perch with oxtail and truffles. The lofty measure of opulence here is commensurate with the bill. ⊠ *Grand Hotel, Södra Blasieholmsh. 8, City* ☎ *08/6793584* ⌁ *Reservations essential* 🏛 *Jacket required* ⊟ *AE, DC, MC, V* ☺ *Closed weekends.*

★ $$$–$$$$ ✕**Pontus in the Green House.** After working for some time under the guidance of the famous chef Erik Lallerstedt—who owned this exquisite restaurant when it was called Eriks—Pontus has taken over operations. You can still count on traditional fare of the haute variety, with a concentration on meat and fish dishes. The menu has both traditional Swedish and contemporary international cuisines. Everything is delicious, and expensive. For a calmer dining experience, choose a corner table upstairs; the ground floor always bustles. You'll be dining among Sweden's rich and famous. For a cheaper menu of traditional Swedish dishes, and slightly less fanfare, sit at the bar downstairs. ⊠ *Österlångg. 17, Gamla Stan* ☎ *08/238500* ⊟ *AE, DC, MC, V* ☺ *Closed Sun. No lunch Sat.*

$$$ ✕**Den Gyldene Freden.** Sweden's most famous old tavern has been open for business since 1722. Every Thursday the Swedish Academy meets here in a private room on the second floor. The haunt of bards and barristers, artists and adpeople, Freden could probably serve sawdust and still be popular, but the food and staff are worthy of the restaurant's hallowed reputation. The cuisine has a Swedish orientation, but Continental influences spice up the menu. Season permitting, try the oven-baked fillets of turbot served with chanterelles and crêpes; the gray hen fried with spruce twigs and dried fruit is another good selection. ⊠ *Österlångg. 51, Gamla Stan* ☎ *08/248760* ⊟ *AE, DC, MC, V* ☺ *Closed Sun. No lunch.*

$$–$$$ ✕**Källaren Diana.** This atmospheric Gamla Stan cellar dates from the Middle Ages. During the first part of the 18th century the building was used as a warehouse and owned by Jonas Alströmer, the scientist who introduced the potato to Sweden—by stealing two bags from England. Today the warehouse is a restaurant that uses the best indigenous ingredients from the Swedish forests and shores. Try the oven-roasted pheasant with calvados and grapes or the grilled fillet of reindeer with pepper sauce and honey-glazed salsify. ⊠ *Brunnsgränd 2–4, Gamla Stan* ☎ *08/107310* ▤ *AE, DC, MC, V* ☉ *Closed Sun.*

$–$$$ ✗ **Eriks Bakficka.** A favorite among Östermalm locals, Erik's Bakficka is a block from the elegant waterside, a few steps down from street level. Owned by the well-known Swedish chef Erik Lallerstedt (who also owns Gondolen), the restaurant serves Swedish dishes, including a delicious baked fillet of char with spring onions and green pea sauce. No smoking is allowed in the main dining room (a policy that's rare in Stockholm). A lower-priced menu is served in the pub section, where smoking is still allowed. ⊠ *Fredrikshovsg. 4, Östermalm* ☎ *08/6601599* ▤ *AE, DC, MC, V* ☉ *Closed in July.*

$–$$$ ✗ **Mårten Trotzig.** This contemporary functional space is both a dining room and a bar. The short menu demonstrates the chef's imagination, blending multicultural recipes in intriguing ways. Try the yellow- and red-tomato salad with arugula pesto, and then move on to the flounder fillet with artichoke hearts, asparagus, and a light grapefruit sauce. In a beautiful plant-lined courtyard, less expensive lunch specials are served. The staff is young, the service professional. ⊠ *Västerlångg. 79, Gamla Stan* ☎ *08/4422530* ▤ *AE, DC, MC, V* ☉ *Closed Sun.*

★ **¢–$$$** ✗ **Koh Phangan.** Creative food is served until midnight at this lively Thai restaurant, where you'll be seated in individual "huts," each with a special name and style. The entire restaurant is decked out in colored lights, fake palm fronds, and trinkets from Thailand. Recorded jungle sounds play in the background. Sign up for a table on the chalkboard next to the bar when you arrive. Although you can expect at least an hour-long wait on weekends, the food is well worth it. Grilled fish and seafood with extravagant, spicy sauces are the specialty. ⊠ *Skåneg. 57, Södermalm* ☎ *08/6425040* ⌦ *Reservations not accepted* ▤ *AE, DC, MC, V.*

$$ ✗ **Källaren Aurora.** Elegant, if a little stuffy, this Gamla Stan cellar restaurant is set in a beautiful 17th-century house. Its largely foreign clientele—most often busloads of tourists dropped off for a meal—enjoys top-quality Swedish and international cuisines served in small rooms. Charcoal-grilled spiced salmon, veal Parmesan, and orange-basted halibut fillet are all good. ⊠ *Munkbron 11, Gamla Stan* ☎ *08/219359* ▤ *AE, DC, MC, V* ☉ *No lunch. Closed in July.*

$–$$ ✗ **Grill Ruby.** This American-style barbecue joint (at least as American as it is possible to be in Gamla Stan) is just a cobblestone's throw away from the statue of St. George slaying the dragon. Next door to its French cousin, Bistro Ruby, Grill Ruby skips the escargot and instead focuses on steaks and fish grills. The grilled steak with french fries and béarnaise sauce is delicious. On Sunday an American-style brunch is served, where you can enjoy huevos rancheros and a big Bloody Mary while blues and country music drift from the speakers. ⊠ *Österlångg. 14, Gamla Stan* ☎ *08/206015* ▤ *AE, DC, MC, V.*

$–$$ ✗ **Hannas Krog.** This bohemian neighborhood restaurant is almost always filled with locals. Although it may not be as supertrendy as it was a decade ago, it remains a Södermalm hot spot. Diners are serenaded at 10 minutes to the hour by a mooing cow that emerges from the cuckoo clock just inside the door. The dishes—from Caribbean shrimp to Provençal lamb—are all flavorful. The crowds that gather here don't manage to slow down the consistent service. The bar in the basement is loud but pleasant. Local live bands play there on occasion. ⊠ *Skåneg. 80, Södermalm* ☎ *08/6438225* ▤ *AE, DC, MC, V* ☉ *No lunch weekends and July.*

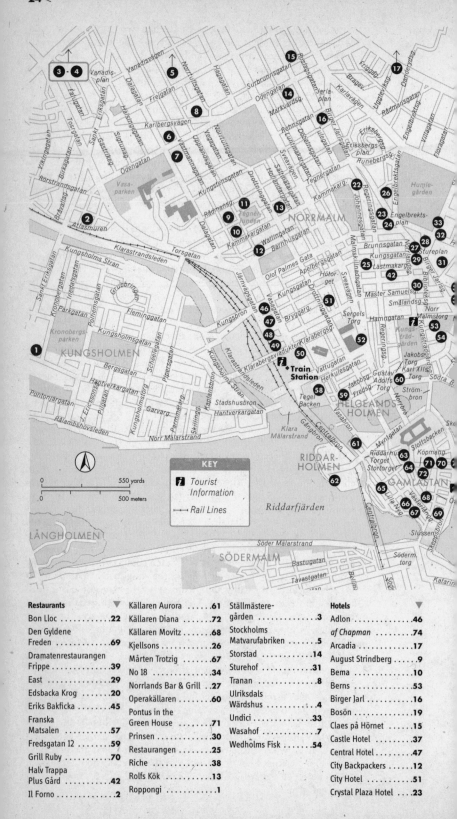

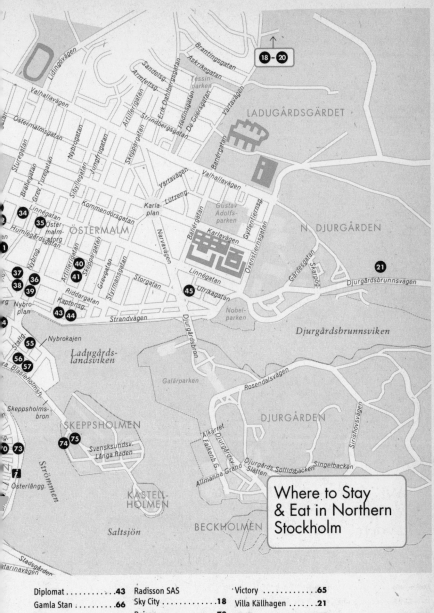

Where to Stay & Eat in Northern Stockholm

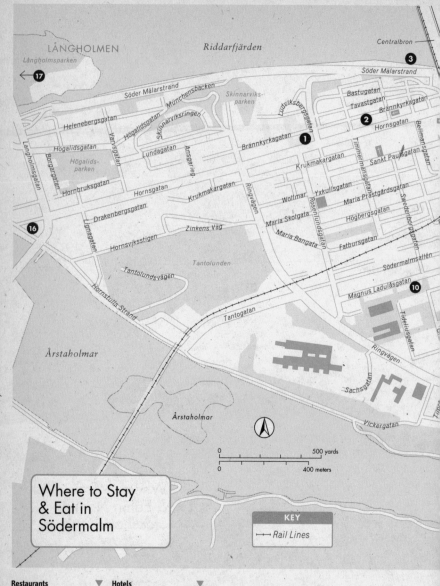

Where to Stay & Eat in Södermalm

KEY

— Rail Lines

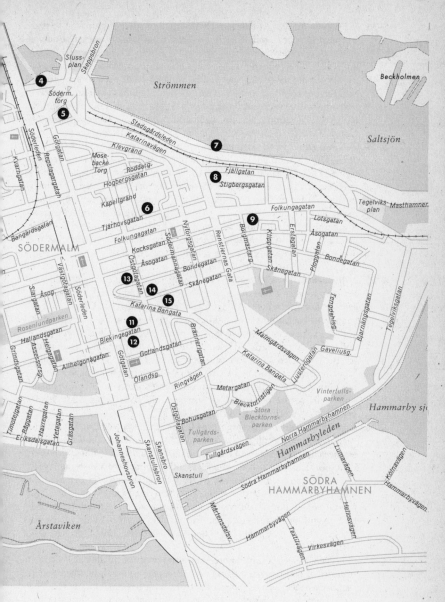

$-$$ ✕ **Källaren Movitz.** At first glance Movitz looks like nothing more than a typical European pub, which is exactly what it is upstairs. But downstairs it's a restaurant serving Swedish cuisine with French and Italian influences. The refined table settings and abundant candlelight reflecting off the curves of the light yellow walls of what used to be a potato cellar in the 1600s make this an elegant place to dine. The reindeer steak with mushroom sauce and currant jelly is delicious, as is the pasta stuffed with smoked salmon, shrimp, and ricotta cheese. ✉ *Tyska Brinken 34, Gamla Stan* ☎ *08/209979* ▭ *AE, DC, MC, V* ☉ *Closed Sun.*

$-$$ ✕ **Opus.** Don't let the stripped-down, albeit charming, small space fool you—Opus's food packs a big-time punch and has earned it a reputation as a top French restaurant in town. Everything is prepared with intense care by the French-born and -trained cook and is served attentively by his Polish wife. Together they own this popular little restaurant, where the sauces are unbeatable. Try the pork fillet with chanterelle sauce or the perch fillet with avocado sauce to find out for yourself. As the restaurant has only 10 tables, be sure to call ahead. ✉ *Blekingeg. 63, Södermalm* ☎ *08/6446080* ⌂ *Reservations essential* ▭ *AE, DC, MC, V* ☉ *Closed Sun. No dinner Mon.*

¢-$$ ✕ **Humlehof.** If you're feeling extra hungry and a bit tight on funds, go straight to this Bavarian restaurant serving traditional Swedish and eastern European dishes. Start by ordering an ice-cold Czech or Austrian draft beer, a bowl of what has to be the best goulash in Stockholm, and the *schweizer* (Swiss-style) schnitzel, which is as big as your face and served with salad and fried potatoes. If schnitzel's not your thing, try the pan-fried Haloumi cheese with sun-dried tomatoes, summer salad, and garlic bread. A TV in the corner above the bar means a sports-bar crowd gathers when a game is on, but it's never out of control and only adds to the restaurant's cheeriness. ✉ *Folkungag. 128, Södermalm* ☎ *08/6410302* ▭ *AE, DC, MC, V.*

¢-$$ ✕ **no18.** Despite being a high-profile bar and restaurant, no18 remains casual and informal. Walk in, and to your left are tables and low leather chairs across from a bar that curves to a set of stairs. Go up to the colorful dining room, which extends farther into a lush courtyard open in summer. In the basement are a large bar and an open area for dancing. A less expensive menu has club sandwiches, burgers, and Caesar salad, but if you want to go all the way, try the good ol' entrecôte with béarnaise sauce and fries or a chicken fillet with olive-and-basil risotto. ✉ *Linnég. 18, Östermalm* ☎ *08/6621018* ▭ *AE, DC, MC, V* ☉ *Closed Sun.*

¢-$$ ✕ **Pelican.** Beer, beer, and more beer is the order of the day at Pelican, a Fodor's Choice traditional working-class drinking hall, a relic of the days when Södermalm was the dwelling place of the city's blue-collar brigade. Today's more bohemian residents find it just as enticing, with the unvarnished wood-paneled walls, faded murals, and glass globe lights fulfilling all their down-at-the-heel pretensions. The food here is some of the best traditional Swedish fare in the city. The meatballs and the knuckle of ham with three mustards are legendary. ✉ *Blekingeg. 40, Södermalm* ☎ *08/55609090* ⌂ *No reservations* ▭ *AE, DC, MC, V* ☉ *Closed Sun.*

$ ✕ **Restaurang Ho's.** Walk into this hidden gem of a Chinese restaurant and something about it just feels right. Nothing fancy—Ho's lets its authentic, intensely flavored food speak for itself. With more than 100 choices, the menu is never-ending and includes Chinese takes on duck, squid, scallops, pork, chicken, beef, and tofu. The stir-fried squid with green and red peppers in black-bean sauce packs a serious punch. Finish with a classic fried banana and ice cream. ✉ *Hornsg. 151, Södermalm* ☎ *08/844420* ▭ *AE, DC, MC, V* ☉ *Closed Mon.*

¢–$ ✗ **Herman's.** Herman's is a haven for vegetarians out to get the most bang
Fodor'sChoice for their kronor. The glassed-in back deck and open garden both pro-
★ vide spectacular views of the water and Gamla Stan. The food is always
served buffet style and includes various vegetable and pasta salads, warm
casseroles, and such entrées as Indonesian stew with peanut sauce and
vegetarian lasagna. The fruit pies and chocolate cakes and cookies are
delicious. ⊠ *Fjällg. 23A, Södermalm* ☎ *08/6439480* ▭ *MC, V.*

¢–$ ✗ **Indira.** This busy Indian restaurant about a block off Götgatanhas has
an overwhelming 60 meal choices. The food is cheap and delicious and
the service fast. Order as soon as you enter and find a seat at one of the
mosaic-coated tables. There are a number of tables in the basement as
well, so don't leave right away if it looks packed on the first floor. The
chicken korma, with raisins and cashews, is fantastic, and the honey-
saffron ice cream is a perfect end to a meal. ⊠ *Bondeg. 3B, Södermalm*
☎ *08/6414046* ▭ *AE, DC, MC, V.*

¢ ✗ **Jerusalem Grill House.** Enter this wild grill, and it may be hard to believe you're still in Stockholm. The men behind the counter sing along
to the music blaring from the sound system, and the menu is in both
Swedish and Arabic. On the walls are surreal landscape paintings, odd
sculptures, and loads of hookahs—in fact, there are five or six pipes that
the regulars use to smoke their tobacco. Falafel, chicken kebabs, gyros,
mixed fried-vegetable plates, lamb fillets—they've got it all, as well as
authentic Arabic tea and coffee. Late on weekend nights it's packed with
hungry partygoers. ⊠ *Hornsg. 92, Södermalm* ☎ *08/6684131* ▭ *No
credit cards.*

WHERE TO STAY

All rooms in the hotels reviewed below are equipped with shower or
bath unless otherwise noted. Some hotels close during the winter holidays; call ahead if you expect to travel during that time.

Prices

Although Stockholm has a reputation for prohibitively expensive hotels, great deals can be found during the summer, when prices are substantially lower and numerous discounts are available. More than 50
hotels offer the "Stockholm Package," which includes accommodations
for one night, breakfast, and the *Stockholmskortet,* or Stockholm Card,
which entitles the cardholder to free admission to museums and travel
on public transport. Details are available from travel agents, tourist bureaus, and the **Stockholm Information Service** (⊠ Box 7542, 103 93 Stockholm ☎ 08/7892400 🖷 08/7892450). Also try **Hotellcentralen**
(⊠ Centralstation, 111 20 Stockholm ☎ 08/7892425 🖷 08/7918666);
the service is free if you go in person, but a fee applies if you call.

WHAT IT COSTS In Swedish Kronor				
$$$$	$$$	$$	$	¢
FOR 2 PEOPLE above 2,900	2,300–2,900	1,500–2,300	1,000–1,500	under 1,000

Prices are for two people in a standard double room in high season.

Downtown Stockholm & Beyond

$$$$ ▣ **Royal Viking (Radisson SAS).** For the weary traveler, the Royal Viking's
location right next to the central station is a gift; fall off the airport train
and into the comfortable beds. When you awake, enjoy the attractive
natural textiles and artwork, sturdy writing desks, separate seating
areas, and plush robes in the large bathrooms. Triple-glazed windows

and plenty of insulation keep traffic noise to a minimum. The large atrium lobby and split-level lounge, extensively renovated in 2002, take the edge off what was previously another faceless international business hotel. But if it's business you want, there is a business-class SAS check-in counter in the lobby. ⊠ *Vasag. 1 City, 101 24* ☎ *08/50654000* 📠 *08/ 50654001* ⊕ *www.radissonsas.com* 🛏 *319 rooms* ⚐ *Restaurant, bar, minibars, no-smoking rooms, indoor pool, sauna, convention center* ⊟ *AE, MC, V.*

$$$$ 🏨 **Sheraton Hotel and Towers.** Popular with business executives, the Sheraton is also an ideal hotel for the tourist on a generous budget looking for comfort and luxury. English is the main language at the restaurant and bar, which fill up at night once the piano player arrives. The lobby is vast and modern. There's a gift shop selling Swedish crystal and international newspapers. Rooms have hardwood floors, leather chairs, thick rugs, and sturdy, fine wood furniture. The big buffet breakfast is not included in room rates. ⊠ *Tegelbackan 6 City, 101 23* ☎ *08/ 4123400* 📠 *08/4123409* ⊕ *www.sheratonstockholm.com* 🛏 *449 rooms* ⚐ *2 restaurants, piano bar, sauna, gym, casino* ⊟ *AE, DC, MC, V.*

★ **$$$–$$$$** 🏨 **Berns Hotel.** This cozy yet subtly ultramodern hotel was a hot spot when it opened its doors in the late 19th century and retains that status today. You can breakfast in the Red Room, immortalized by August Strindberg's novel of the same name; the hotel was one of his haunts. The restaurant and bar is a joint venture with restaurant entrepreneur and designer Terence Conran. Rates include the use of a nearby fitness center with a pool. ⊠ *Näckströmsg. 8 City, 111 47* ☎ *08/56632000* 📠 *08/56632201* ⊕ *www.berns.se* 🛏 *65 rooms, 3 suites* ⚐ *Restaurant, bar, no-smoking rooms, meeting room* ⊟ *AE, DC, MC, V.*

$$–$$$$ 🏨 **Scandic Hotel Anglais.** This '60s hotel, directly across from the Royal Library and the tree-filled Humlegården, is popular among North American business travelers and tourists. It's in the center of almost everything—shopping, sightseeing, and major businesses. The clean, pleasant rooms have wall-to-wall carpeting and furniture. An agreement with Sturebadet, Stockholm's most exclusive bathhouse, gives hotel guests access to their excellent facilities, which include tile pools from the turn of the 20th century. At night in Scandic's piano bar you'll hear more English than anything else. ⊠ *Humlegårdsg. 23,* ☎ *08/51734000* 📠 *08/51734011* ⊕ *www.scandichotels.se* 🛏 *212 rooms* ⚐ *2 restaurants, piano bar, meeting rooms* ⊟ *AE, DC, MC, V.*

$$$ 🏨 **Nordic Hotel.** Next to the central station, this modern center for the business traveler is actually two hotels—Nordic Light and Nordic Sea—in one. The first focuses on simplicity. Rooms are a mix of dark wood, gray flannel, and black-and-white tile, with adjustable spotlights in the ceiling. Nordic Sea uses lighter wood with lots of blue fabric and mosaic tiles to create a Mediterranean touch. A huge aquarium in the lobby holds exotic fish, and you can chill out in Stockholm's only ice bar, where the temperature never rises above freezing. Both hotels are clean and bright and provide excellent service. ⊠ *Vasaplan City 101 37* ☎ *08/50563000* 📠 *08/50563060* ⊕ *www.nordichotels.se* 🛏 *542 rooms* ⚐ *2 bars, 2 lounges, meeting rooms* ⊟ *AE, DC, MC, V.*

$$$ 🏨 **Radisson SAS SkyCity Hotel.** Right in the center of Arlanda Airport's SkyCity complex, this hotel is equipped and tastefully furnished. If your room faces the runway, you can watch the planes take off and land (the extensive soundproofing makes them seem to do so quietly). If you're flying out very early in the morning or are stuck with a layover in Stockholm, this is the ideal airport hotel. ⊠ *Arlanda Airport, 190 45* ☎ *08/50674000* 📠 *08/50674001* ⊕ *www.radissonsas.com* 🛏 *230 rooms* ⚐ *Restaurant, bar, no-smoking rooms, gym, meeting room* ⊟ *AE, DC, MC, V.*

$$$ ⊞ **Sergel Plaza.** The lobby in this stainless-steel-paneled hotel is welcoming, with cane chairs set up in a pleasant, skylighted seating area. The bright rooms are practical but tend to lack the luxury that the price tag may lead you to expect. In fact, the run-of-the-mill furnishings and a tad too much gray make it a bit dull. But its central location on the main pedestrian mall makes it a great base if you're not going to spend much time at the hotel. For breakfast there is an international buffet or a Japanese breakfast; the Anna Rella Restaurant serves innovative Swedish and international dishes. At night the piano bar behind the lobby fills with guests. ⊠ *Brunkebergstorg 9, 103 27* ☎ *08/51726300* 🖷 *08/51726311* ⊕ *www. scandic-hotels.se* ⤶ *405 rooms* ⌂ *Restaurant, bar, no-smoking rooms, sauna, shops, casino, convention center* ☐ *AE, DC, MC, V.*

$$–$$$ ⊞ **Birger Jarl.** At this high-design hotel the lobby doubles as a modern-art gallery, with frequently changing exhibitions. Some rooms have been individually designed by several of the country's top designers: it costs extra to stay in these. Most rooms are not large, but all are well furnished and have nice touches, such as heated towel racks in the bathrooms; all double rooms have bathtubs. Four family-style rooms have extra floor space and sofa beds. You can choose your breakfast from an extensive buffet just off the lobby, but room service is also available. ⊠ *Tuleg. 8, 104 32* ☎ *08/6741800* 🖷 *08/6737366* ⊕ *www.birgerjarl. se* ⤶ *225 rooms* ⌂ *Coffee shop, no-smoking rooms, sauna, meeting room* ☐ *AE, DC, MC, V.*

$$–$$$ ⊞ **Crystal Plaza Hotel.** Housed in one of Stockholm's oldest hotel buildings (1895), the Crystal Plaza, with a circular tower and peach walls, is sure to catch the eye of anyone walking down Birger Jarlsgatan. Most rooms have a mix of birch-wood furniture, hardwood floors with small rugs, and the requisite hotel artwork on the walls. Rooms facing the inner courtyard can be a bit quieter than those on the street. If you want only the best, throw down a little extra money for one of the circular tower rooms, two of which have balconies. The hotel's location, just a stone's throw from the hip bars of Stureplan and downtown shopping, makes it an ideal place for folks looking to have quick access to a good time in the city. ⊠ *Birger Jarlsg. 35, 111 45* ☎ *08/4068800* 🖷 *08/241511* ⊕ *www.crystalplaza.aos.se* ⤶ *112 rooms* ⌂ *Restaurant, bar, breakfast room* ☐ *AE, DC, MC, V.*

★ $$–$$$ ⊞ **Lydmar Hotel.** Only a 10-minute walk from the downtown hub of Sergels Torg and a stone's throw from Stureplan, the epicenter of Stockholm's nightlife, the Lydmar is more than just a hotel—it's also one of the trendiest bars in town. Even if you don't stay here, be sure to take a ride in the elevator, in which you can choose from eight kinds of elevator music, all of (believe it or not) quality. The lobby lounge is alive on weekends with jazz and with DJs spinning the latest club music. The hotel reception is hidden away at the back of the bar, much to the amusement of the locals, who can sit for ages watching the bemused tourists wander aimlessly among the cool cocktail drinkers. ⊠ *Stureg. 10, 114 36* ☎*08/56611300* 🖷*08/56611301* ⊕*www.lydmar.se* ⤶*61 rooms, 5 suites* ☐ *AE, DC, MC, V.*

$$–$$$ ⊞ **Scandic Hotel Continental.** In city center across from the train station, the Continental is a reliable hotel that's especially popular with Americans. Rooms have a minibar, trouser press, and satellite television. An extravagant Scandinavian buffet is served in the Gustavian breakfast rooms. ⊠*Klara Vattugränd 4, 101 22* ☎*08/51734200* 🖷*08/517342311* ⊕ *www.scandic-hotels.com* ⤶ *268 rooms* ⌂ *Restaurant, bar, no-smoking rooms, sauna, meeting room* ☐ *AE, DC, MC, V.*

$–$$$ ✕⊞ **Villa Källhagen.** The changing seasons are on display in this beautiful country hotel, reflected through the huge windows, glass walls, and bedroom skylights. Originally an inn, dating to 1810, an extension was

★

added in 1994, with natural light the main focus. Rooms are spacious and furnished in light woods and natural fabrics. It's only a few minutes from the city center, but its woodland surroundings can put you a million miles away. The restaurant also relies heavily on the seasons, serving a delicious blend of fresh Swedish ingredients cooked with a French influence. ☒ *Djurgårdsbrunnsv. 10, 115 27* ☎ *08/6650300* 🖷 *08/ 6650399* ⊕ *www.kallhagen.se* 📞 *20 rooms* ♧ *Restaurant, brasserie, bar, no-smoking rooms, meeting room* ⊟ *AE, DC, MC, V.*

$$ 🔲 **Adlon.** Although in a building dating from 1884, the Adlon considers itself a high-tech business hotel. All rooms, which are rather undistinguished, offer Internet connections. The hotel's proximity to downtown Stockholm and the central station make it ideal for the business traveler hoping to find some time to explore while in town. Despite traffic, rooms on the street remain quiet. Rates are cheaper if rooms are booked via the Web. ☒ *Vasag. 42, 111 20* ☎ *08/4026500* 🖷 *08/208610* ⊕ *www.adlon.se* 📞 *78 rooms* ♧ *Breakfast room, no-smoking rooms, meeting rooms* ⊟ *AE, DC, MC, V.*

$$ 🔲 **Central Hotel.** Less than 300 yards from the central station, this practical hotel is a good option for both business and pleasure travelers. The rooms are fairly small, but all face a pleasant, quiet courtyard. And thanks to extra sound insulation, the chaos of Vasagatan remains outside the room. Bathrooms have showers only. ☒ *Vasag. 38, 101 20* ☎ *08/ 56620800* 🖷 *08/247573* ⊕ *www.centralhotel.se* 📞 *93 rooms* ♧ *In-room data ports, no-smoking rooms, meeting room* ⊟ *AE, DC, MC, V.*

$$ 🔲 **City.** This large modern-style hotel is near the city center and Hötorget Market, making it ideal for shopping and sightseeing (or movie watching, since it's also close to a movie complex). Rooms are filled with modern, no-frills furniture. Some have hardwood floors. Breakfast is served in the atrium Winter Garden restaurant. ☒ *Slöjdg. 7, 111 81* ☎ *08/ 7237200* 🖷 *08/7237209* ⊕ *www.rica.cityhotels.se* 📞 *293 rooms* ♧ *Restaurant, no-smoking rooms, sauna, meeting room* ⊟ *AE, DC, MC, V* ⦿ *BP.*

$$ ✕🔲 **Claes på Hörnet.** This may be the most exclusive—and smallest—
★ hotel in town, with only 10 rooms in a former 1739 inn. The rooms, comfortably furnished with period antiques, go quickly (book three or so months in advance, especially around Christmas). The restaurant ($$) is worth visiting even if you don't spend the night: its old-fashioned dining room serves Swedish and Continental dishes such as outstanding *strömming* (Baltic herring) and cloudberry mousse cake. Reservations are essential. Note that the restaurant is closed in July. ☒ *Surbrunnsg. 20, 113 48* ☎ *08/165130* 🖷 *08/6125315* 📞 *10 rooms* ♧ *Restaurant* ⊟ *AE, DC, MC, V.*

$$ ✕🔲 **Stockholm Plaza Hotel.** On one of Stockholm's foremost streets for shopping and entertainment, and only a short walk from the city's nightlife and business center, this hotel is ideal if you want to be in a central location. The building was built in 1884, and the Elite hotel chain took over in 1984. Rooms are furnished in an elegant, traditional manner and are reasonably sized. The restaurant, Vassa Egen, is one of the best in the city, a bright, elegant domed dining room serving exquisite modern Scandinavian cuisine. ☒ *Birger Jarlsg. 29, Downtown 103 95* ☎ *08/56622000* 🖷 *08/56622020* ⊕ *www.elite.se* 📞 *151 rooms* ♧ *Restaurant, bar, meeting rooms* ⊟ *AE, DC, MC, V.*

$$ 🔲 **Tegnérlunden.** A quiet city park fronts this modern hotel, a 10-minute walk along shop-lined Sveavägen from the downtown hub of Sergels Torg. Although the rooms are small and sparsely furnished, they are clean and well maintained. The lobby is bright with marble, brass, and greenery, as is the sunny rooftop breakfast room. ☒ *Tegnérlunden 8, 113 59*

☎ *08/54545550* 🖷 *08/54545551* ⊕ *www.swedenhotels.se* ➲ *103 rooms* ⚫ *Breakfast room, no-smoking rooms, sauna, meeting room* 🖃 *AE, DC, MC, V.*

$ 🏨 **Arcadia.** On a hilltop near a large waterfront nature preserve, this converted dormitory is within 15 minutes of downtown by bus or subway or 30 minutes on foot along pleasant shopping streets. Rooms are furnished in a spare, neutral style, with plenty of natural light. The adjoining restaurant serves meals on the terrace in summer. To get here, take Bus 43 to Körsbärsvägen. ⊠ *Körsbärsv. 1, 114 89* ☎ *08/56621500* 🖷 *08/56621501* ⊕ *www.arcadia.elite.se* ➲ *82 rooms* ⚫ *Restaurant* 🖃 *AE, DC, MC, V.*

$ 🏨 **August Strindberg.** A narrow frescoed corridor leads from the street to the flagstone courtyard, into which the hotel's restaurant expands in summer. Parquet flooring and high ceilings distinguish the rooms, which are otherwise plainly furnished. Kitchenettes are available; some rooms can be combined into family apartments. The four floors have no elevator. ⊠ *Tegnérg. 38, 113 59* ☎ *08/325006* 🖷 *08/209085* ➲ *19 rooms* ⚫ *Restaurant, kitchenettes (some)* 🖃 *AE, DC, MC, V.*

$ 🏨 **Hotel Gustav Wasa.** The Gustav Wasa, named after the first king of
FodorśChoice Sweden, is right next to Odenplan Square. The hotel is in a 19th-century
★ residential building and has fairly large, bright rooms with herringbone hardwood floors, original trim and details along the ceilings, and a funky blend of antiques and furniture that's more modern. Ask for a room with a window out to the street in order to get a direct view of the grand Gustav Wasa Church and the Odenplan. The other available view, of the inner courtyard, is much less exciting. The downtown location and lower prices make this an excellent place for budget travelers who prefer a friendly hotel. ⊠ *Västmannag. 61, 113 25* ☎ *08/343801* 🖷 *08/307372* ⊕ *www.hotel.wineasy.se/gustav.vasa* ➲ *33 rooms* 🖃 *AE, DC, MC, V.*

¢ 🏨 **Bema.** This small hotel is relatively central, on the ground floor of an apartment block near Tegnérlunden park. Room have a modern Swedish style, with beech-wood furniture. One four-bed family room is available. Breakfast is served in your room. Given the price, it's difficult to beat. ⊠ *Upplandsg. 13, 111 23* ☎ *08/232675* 🖷 *08/205338* ➲ *12 rooms* 🖃 *AE, DC, MC, V.*

Gamla Stan & Skeppsholmen

$$$$ 🏨 **Grand Hotel.** The city's showpiece hotel is an 1874 landmark on the
FodorśChoice quayside at Blasieholmen, just across the water from the Royal Palace.
★ Visiting political dignitaries, Nobel Prize winners, and movie stars come to enjoy its gracious charm, which extends from the grand public rooms to the comfortable, luxurious bedrooms. One of the hotel's most alluring features is a glassed-in veranda overlooking the harbor, where an excellent smörgåsbord buffet is served. Guests have access to the high-class Sturebadet Health Spa nearby, and there is a small gym area in the hotel. Franska Matsalen, the hotel's main restaurant, serves French cuisine and is ranked as one of the best in Sweden. ⊠ *Södra Blasieholmshamnen 8, Box 16424, City 103 27* ☎ *08/6793500* 🖷 *08/6118686* ⊕ *www.grandhotel.se* ➲ *310 rooms, 21 suites* ⚫ *2 restaurants, bar, no-smoking rooms, sauna, fitness center, shops, meeting room* 🖃 *AE, DC, MC, V.*

$$–$$$$ 🏨 **Radisson SAS Strand Hotel.** An art nouveau monolith, built in 1912 for the Stockholm Olympics, this hotel has been completely and tastefully modernized. It's on the water across from the Royal Dramatic Theater, directly in front of the quay, where many of the boats leave for the archipelago. It's also only a short walk from the Old Town and the museums on Skeppsholmen. No two rooms are alike, but all are furnished with simple and elegant furniture, offset by white woodwork and hues of moss green and cocoa brown. The Piazza restaurant has an outdoor feel to it: Italian cuisine is the specialty, and the wine list is superb. An SAS check-in counter for business-class travelers adjoins the main reception area. ✉ *Nybrokajen 9, Box 16396, City 103 27* ☎ *08/50664000* 🖷 *08/6112436* ⊕ *www.radissonsas.com* ↩ *152 rooms* ⚲ *Restaurant, no-smoking rooms, sauna, meeting room* ⊟ *AE, DC, MC, V.*

$$–$$$ 🏨 **Lady Hamilton.** As charming as its namesake, Lord Nelson's mistress, the Lady Hamilton is a modern hotel inside a 15th-century building. Swedish antiques fill the guest rooms and common areas. Romney's *Bacchae* portrait of Lady Hamilton hangs in the foyer, where she also supports the ceiling in the form of a large smiling figurehead from an old ship. The breakfast room, furnished with captain's chairs, looks out onto the lively cobblestone street, and the subterranean sauna rooms, in whitewashed stone, provide a secluded fireplace and a chance to take a dip in the building's original, medieval well. ✉ *Storkyrkobrinken 5, Gamla Stan 111 28* ☎ *08/50640100* 🖷 *08/50640110* ⊕ *www.lady-hamilton.se* ↩ *34 rooms* ⚲ *Bar, breakfast room, no-smoking rooms, sauna, meeting room* ⊟ *AE, DC, MC, V.*

★ **$$–$$$** 🏨 **Reisen.** On the waterfront in Gamla Stan, this hotel opened in 1819. The rooms looking out over the water are fantastic, and for a small supplement you can get a room with a private sauna and Jacuzzi. There is a fine Italian restaurant with a grill, tea and coffee service in the library, and what is reputed to be the best piano bar in town. A small swimming pool, dominated by businessmen cooling off after the sauna, is built under the medieval arches of the foundations. ✉ *Skeppsbron 12–14, Gamla Stan 111 30* ☎ *08/223260* 🖷 *08/201559* ⊕ *www.firsthotels.com* ↩ *144 rooms* ⚲ *Restaurant, piano bar, no-smoking floor, indoor pool, sauna, meeting room* ⊟ *AE, DC, MC, V.*

$$ 🏨 **Gamla Stan.** The feel of historical Stockholm living is rarely more prevalent than in this quiet hotel tucked away on a narrow street in one of the Gamla Stan's 17th-century houses. All rooms are decorated in the Gustavian style, with hardwood floors, Oriental rugs, and antique furniture. A short walk from the Gamla Stan metro stop, it's a perfect home base for later exploring. ✉ *Lilla Nyg. 25, Gamla Stan* ☎ *08/7237250* 🖷 *08/7237259* ⊕ *www.rica.cityhotels.se* ↩ *51 rooms* ⚲ *No-smoking floor, meeting room* ⊟ *AE, DC, MC, V.*

$$ 🏨 **Lord Nelson.** The owners of the Lady Hamilton and the Victory run this small hotel with a nautical theme right in the middle of Gamla Stan. Rooms are only a touch larger than cabins—but service is excellent. Noise from traffic in the pedestrian street outside can be a problem during the summer. ✉ *Västerlångg. 22, Gamla Stan 111 29* ☎ *08/50640120* 🖷 *08/50640130* ⊕ *www.lord-nelson.se* ↩ *31 rooms* ⚲ *Café, no-smoking room, sauna, meeting room* ⊟ *AE, DC, MC, V.*

$$ 🏨 **Victory.** Slightly larger than its brother and sister hotels, the Lord Nelson and Lady Hamilton, this extremely atmospheric Gamla Stan building dates from 1640. The theme is nautical, with items from the HMS *Victory* and Swedish antiques. Each room is named after a 19th-century sea captain. The noted Lejontornet restaurant keeps an extensive wine cellar. ✉ *Lilla Nyg. 5, Gamla Stan 111 28* ☎ *08/50640000* 🖷 *08/50640010* ⊕ *www.victory-hotel.se* ↩ *48 rooms* ⚲ *Restaurant, bar, no-smoking floor, 2 saunas, meeting room* ⊟ *AE, DC, MC, V.*

$–$$ 🏨 **Mälardrottningen.** One of the more unusual establishments in Stockholm, Mälardrottningen, a Sweden Hotels property, was once Barbara Hutton's yacht. Since 1982 it has been a quaint and pleasant hotel, with a crew as service conscious as any in Stockholm. Tied up on the freshwater side of Gamla Stan, it is minutes from everything. The small suites are suitably decorated in a navy-blue-and-maroon nautical theme. Some of the below-deck cabins are a bit stuffy, but in summer you can take your meals out on deck. The ship's chief assets are novelty and absence of traffic noise. ✉ *Riddarholmen 4, Riddarholmen 111 28* ☎ *08/ 54518780* 🖷 *08/243676* 🛏 *59 cabins* ⚐ *Restaurant, bar, grill, no-smoking rooms, sauna, meeting room* ☰ *AE, DC, MC, V.*

Östermalm

$$$–$$$$
FodorsChoice
★
🏨 **Diplomat.** Within easy walking distance of Djurgården, this elegant hotel is less flashy than most in its price range but oozes a certain European chic, evident in its subtle, tasteful designs and efficient staff. The building is a turn-of-the-20th-century town house that housed foreign embassies in the 1930s and was converted into a hotel in 1966. Rooms are all individual but have fresh colors, clean lines, and subtle hints of floral prints in common, and those in the front, facing the water, have magnificent views over Stockholm Harbor. The T-Bar, formerly a rather staid tearoom and restaurant, is now one of the trendiest bars among the city's upper crust. The second-floor bar is ideal for a break from sightseeing. ✉ *Strandv. 7C, Östermalm 104 40* ☎ *08/4596800* 🖷 *08/ 4596820* ⊕ *www.diplomathotel.com.* 🛏 *128 rooms* ⚐ *Restaurant, bar, no-smoking room, sauna, meeting room* ☰ *AE, DC, MC, V.*

$$$
🏨 **Hotel Esplanade.** Right on the water and only a few buildings down from Stockholm's Royal Dramatic Theater, Hotel Esplanade is a beautiful hotel with a real touch of old Stockholm. Originally a guesthouse operated by an elderly woman, the inn now has owners who have sought to maintain its hominess—you'll probably be offered a glass of fine brandy in the lounge when you check in. Rooms are individually decorated with antiques, and some offer water views. Breakfast is served in the original art nouveau–style breakfast room. Be sure to call well ahead to book a room, since many regulars return every year. ✉ *Strandv. 7A, Östermalm 114 56* ☎ *08/6630740* 🖷 *08/6625992* ⊕ *www. hotelesplanade.se* 🛏 *34 rooms* ⚐ *Breakfast room, lobby lounge, sauna* ☰ *AE, DC, MC, V.*

$$–$$$
🏨 **Castle Hotel.** On a backstreet just off Birgar Jarlsgatan, this centrally located hotel has been in operation since the 1930s. The owners are great jazz enthusiasts, and the hotel has hosted such jazz greats as Dizzy Gillespie, Chet Baker, and Benny Carter. Rooms are done with art deco furnishings but are on the diminutive side. Showing the spirit of the jazz theme along with a propensity for a good pun are the names of the two suites: Suite Georgia Brown and Suite Lorraine. ✉ *Riddarg. 14, Östermalm 114 35* ☎ *08/6795700* 🖷 *08/6112022* ⊕ *www.castle-hotel.se* 🛏 *50 rooms, 2 suites* ⚐ *Restaurant, meeting room* ☰ *AE, DC, MC, V.*

$$–$$$
🏨 **Mornington.** Just off the main square of Östermalm, the Mornington is close to both the nightlife of Stureplan and the downtown business district. The lobby, bar, and restaurant area are hip places to hang out, and there's a lovely little library of more than 4,000 books (mostly in Swedish) spread throughout the lobby; you can borrow them during your stay. All rooms have hardwood floors and elegant furniture, but ask for a renovated room on the sixth or seventh floor—the older rooms are a bit worn out. ✉ *Nybrog. 53, Östermalm 102 44* ☎ *08/50733000* 🖷 *08/50733039* ⊕ *www.mornington.se* 🛏 *140 rooms* ⚐ *Restaurant, bar, no-smoking rooms, sauna, steam room, solarium, meeting room* ☰ *AE, DC, MC, V.*

★ **$$**
🏨 **Wellington.** From the outside the building resembles the Industrihuset (Industry House) across the street, but inside is a delightful hotel with polite, professional staff and quality service. It's in a quiet residential area in Östermalm near the Hedvig Eleonora Church and cemetery, a calm home

base from which to enjoy the city. Rooms are modern and fresh with hard-wood floors. Rooms facing the inner courtyard have balconies. Ask for a room on the top floor for a great view of the neighborhood's rooftops. The breakfast buffet is top-notch, serving all the Swedish classics, including pickled herring. ☒ *Storg. 6, Östermalm 114 51* ☎ *08/6670910* 🖷 *08/6671254* ⊕ *www.wellington.se* 🖅 *60 rooms* ॰ *Bar, breakfast room, in-room data ports, sauna, meeting rooms* ⊟ *AE, MC, V.*

★ **$–$$** 🖭 **Örnsköld.** Right in the heart of the city, this hidden gem feels like an old private club, from its brass-and-leather lobby to the Victorian-style furniture in the moderately spacious, high-ceiling rooms. Rooms over-looking the courtyard are quieter, but those facing the street—not a par-ticularly busy one—are sunnier. The hotel is frequented by actors appearing at the Royal Theater next door. ☒ *Nybrog. 6, Östermalm 114 34* ☎ *08/6670285* 🖷 *08/6676991* 🖅 *30 rooms* ⊟ *AE, MC, V.*

$ 🖭 **Pärlan.** The name of this hotel means the "Pearl" and that's exactly what it is. On the second floor of an early-19th-century building on a quiet street, the Pärlan is a friendly alternative to the city's bigger ho-tels. Furniture throughout is a mix of fine antiques and flea market bar-gains, making it quirky and homey. A balcony looking out over the inner courtyard is a perfect spot for eating breakfast, which is served buffet style in the kitchen every morning. Be sure to admire the ultra-Swedish tile oven in the corner of the dining room. If you want to get a feel for what it's like to really live in this neighborhood, this is your best bet. Book far in advance because the rooms are almost always full. ☒ *Skep-perg. 27, Östermalm 114 52* ☎ *08/6635070* 🖷 *08/6677145* 🖅 *9 rooms* ⊟ *AE, MC, V.*

FodorśChoice ★ (margin)

Södermalm

$$$ 🖭 **Hilton Hotel Slussen.** Working with what appears to be a dubious lo-cation (atop a tunnel above a six-lane highway), the Hilton has pulled a rabbit out of a hat. Built on special noise- and shock-absorbing cush-ions, the hotel almost lets you forget about the highway. The intrigu-ing labyrinth of levels, separate buildings, and corridors is filled with such unique details as a rounded stairway lighted from between the steps. The guest rooms are exquisitely designed and modern, with plenty of stainless steel and polished-wood inlay to accent the maroon color scheme. The Eken restaurant and bar serves food indoors and out. If you eat or drink too much, there's a gym with excellent facilities. The hotel is at Slussen, easily accessible from downtown. ☒ *Guldgränd 8, Södermalm 104 65* ☎ *08/51735300* 🖷 *08/51735311* ⊕ *www.scandic. se* 🖅 *264 rooms* ॰ *2 restaurants, piano bar, no-smoking rooms, indoor pool, hair salon, sauna, gym, meeting room* ⊟ *AE, DC, MC, V.*

★ **$$** 🖭 **Anno 1647.** Named for the date the building was erected, this small, pleasant hotel is a piece of Stockholm history. Rooms vary in shape, but all have original, well-worn pine floors with 17th-century-style ap-pointments. There's no elevator in this four-story building. The bar and café are a popular local hangout. The menu is international. Guest DJs control the sound waves. ☒ *Mariagränd 3, Södermalm 116 41* ☎ *08/4421680* 🖷 *08/4421647* 🖅 *42 rooms, 30 with bath* ॰ *Snack bar* ⊟ *AE, DC, MC, V.*

$–$$ 🖭 **Alexandra.** This economy hotel to the south of Gamla Stan is a five-minute walk from the subway and only a few stops from the city cen-ter. Rooms are fairly big but have a definite late-1980s look. There are a number of cheaper rooms, adjacent to the parking garage and with-out windows. ☒ *Magnus Ladulåsg. 42, Södermalm 118 27* ☎ *08/840320* 🖷 *08/7205353* 🖅 *68 rooms, 5 2-room suites* ॰ *Breakfast room, no-smoking rooms, sauna* ⊟ *AE, DC, MC, V.*

¢–$$ ☒ **Columbus Hotel.** Just a few blocks from busy Götgatan, the Colum-
Fodor'sChoice   bus is an oasis of calm in the busy urban streets of Södermalm. Built in
★   1780, it was originally a brewery, then a jail, then a hospital, then a tem-
porary housing area. Since 1976 the beautiful building, with its large,
tranquil inner courtyard, has been a hotel. Rooms have wide beams, pol-
ished hardwood floors, antique furniture, and bright wallpaper and fab-
rics. Many look out over the courtyard, others on the nearby church.
In summer breakfast is served outside. The peace and quiet this hotel
provides, even though it's close to all the action, makes it ideal for a va-
cation. ☒ *Tjärhovsg. 11, Södermalm 116 21* ☎ *08/6441717* 🖷 *08/
7020764* ⊕ *www.columbus.se* ⇜ *64 rooms, 36 with bath* ⚲ *Bar, café*
▤ *AE, MC, V.*

¢–$ ☒ **Pensionat Oden, Söder.** Clean, inexpensive, and centrally located, this
bed-and-breakfast is on the second floor of a 19th-century building. Horns-
gatan, the street it's on, is Södermalm's busiest and filled with pubs, restau-
rants, and shops. Rooms have hardwood floors, Oriental rugs, and an
odd blend of new and old furniture. A kitchen is available for use. The
hotel is popular with parents visiting their children in college, academ-
ics traveling on a budget, and backpackers. Book rooms well in advance,
especially during the holidays. ☒ *Hornsg. 66B, Södermalm* ☎ *08/
6124349* 🖷 *08/6124501* ⊕ *www.pensionat.nu* ⇜ *35 rooms, 8 with bath*
⚲ *No-smoking rooms* ▤ *AE, MC, V.*

Youth Hostels

Don't be put off by the "youth" bit: there's actually no age limit. The
standards of cleanliness, comfort, and facilities offered are usually ex-
tremely high.

¢–$ ☒ **Den Röda Båten Mälaren** (The Red Boat). Built in 1914, the *Mälaren*
originally traveled the waters of the Göta Canal under the name of *Sätra.*
Today she has to settle for sitting still in Stockholm as a youth hostel.
The hostel cabins are small but clean and have bunk beds. There are
also four "hotel" rooms, which have private baths and nicer furniture
and details. In the summer the restaurant offers great views of Stock-
holm along with basic, traditional Swedish food. Breakfast costs an ad-
ditional 55 SKr, but sheets are included in your rate. ☒ *Södermälarstrand
kajplats 6, 117 20* ☎ *08/6444385* 🖷 *08/6413733* ⊕ *www.rodabaten.
nu* ⇜ *35 rooms, 4 with bath* ▤ *MC, V.*

¢   ☒ **af Chapman.** This circa-1888 sailing ship, permanently moored in Stock-
holm Harbor just across from the Royal Palace, is a landmark in its own
right. Book early—the place is so popular in summer that finding a bed
may prove difficult. Breakfast (SKr 45) is not included in the room rate;
there are no kitchen facilities. ☒ *Flaggmansv. 8, Skeppsholmen Skepp-
sholmen 111 49* ☎ *08/4632266* 🖷 *08/6117155* ⊕ *www.stfchapman.
com* ⇜ *293 beds, 2- to 6-bed cabins* ⚲ *Café* ☉ *Closed mid-Dec.–mid-
Jan.* ▤ *DC, MC, V.*

¢   ☒ **Bosön.** Out of the way on the island of Lidingö, this hostel is part of
the Bosön Sports Institute, a national training center pleasantly close to
the water. You can rent canoes on the grounds and go out for a paddle.
Breakfast is included in the room rate. There are laundry facilities and
a kitchen you can use. All rooms are clean and fresh. ☒ *Bosön, 181 47
Lidingö* ☎ *08/6056600* 🖷 *08/7671644* ⇜ *70 beds* ⚲ *Cafeteria, sauna,
boating, coin laundry* ▤ *MC, V* ⦿ *BP.*

¢   ☒ **City Backpackers.** You won't find cheaper accommodations closer to
central station than City Backpackers, which has 65 beds. The 19th-
century building typifies the European youth hostel, and this one is well
run. Guests have access to a common kitchen, a lounge with cable TV,
showers, and a courtyard. The seven-person apartment, with its own

kitchen and bathroom, is ideal for a group of young backpackers or an adventurous large family. ✉ *Upplandsg. 2A, Vasastan* ☎ *08/206920* 🖷 *08/100464* ⊕ *www.citybackpackers.se* ↻ *15 rooms* ▤ *MC, V.*

¢ 🔲 *Gustav af Klint.* A "hotel ship" moored at Stadsgården quay, near the Slussen subway station, the *Gustav af Klint* harbors 120 beds in its two sections: a hotel and a hostel. The hostel section has 18 four-bunk cabins and 10 two-bunk cabins; a 14-bunk dormitory is also available from May through mid-September. The hotel section has four single-bunk and three two-bunk cabins with bedsheets and breakfast included. The hostel rates are SKr 120 per person in a four-bunk room and SKr 140 per person in a two-bunk room; these prices do not include bedsheets or breakfast, which are available at an extra charge. All guests share common bathrooms and showers. There are a cafeteria and a restaurant, and you can dine on deck in summer. ✉ *Stadsgårdskajen 153, 116 45* ☎ *08/ 6404077* 🖷 *08/6406416* ↻ *7 hotel cabins, 28 hostel cabins, 28 dormitory beds, all without bath* ⚭ *Restaurant, cafeteria* ▤ *AE, MC, V.*

¢ 🔲 *Långholmen.* This former prison, built in 1724, was converted into a combined hotel and hostel in 1989. The hotel rooms are made available as additional hostel rooms in the summer. Rooms are small, and windows are nearly nonexistent—you *are* in a prison, after all—but that hasn't stopped travelers from flocking here. Each room has 2–5 beds, and all but 10 have bathrooms with shower. The hostel is on the island of Långholmen, which has popular bathing beaches and the Prison Museum. The Inn, next door, serves Swedish home cooking, the Jail Pub offers light snacks, and a garden restaurant operates in the summer. ✉ *Långholmen, Box 9116, 102 72* ☎ *08/6680500* 🖷 *08/7208575* ⊕ *www.langholmen. com* ↻ *254 beds June–Sept., 26 beds Sept.–May* ⚭ *Restaurant, cafeteria, sauna, beach, coin laundry* ▤ *AE, DC, MC, V.*

¢ 🔲 *Skeppsholmen.* This former craftsman's workshop in a pleasant and quiet part of the island was converted into a hostel for the overflow from the *af Chapman,* another hostel an anchor's throw away. Breakfast costs an additional SKr 45. ✉ *Skeppsholmen, 111 49* ☎ *08/4632266* 🖷 *08/6117155* ↻ *155 beds, 2- to 6-bed rooms* ⚭ *Café, coin laundry* ▤ *DC, MC, V.*

Camping

You can camp in the Stockholm area for SKr 80–SKr 130 per night. **Bredäng Camping** (✉ 127 31 Skärholmen ☎ 08/977071) has camping and a youth hostel. Its facilities are excellent and include a restaurant and bar. Fifteen kilometers (9 miles) from Stockholm, in Huddinge, is **Stockholm SweCamp Flottsbro** (✉ 141 25 Huddinge ☎ 08/4499580), where you can camp, play golf, rent canoes and bikes, and hang out on a beach. At **Rösjöbaden Camping** (✉ 192 56 Sollentuna ☎ 08/962184), a short drive north of town, you can fish, swim, and play minigolf and volleyball.

NIGHTLIFE & THE ARTS

Stockholm's nightlife can be broken up into two general groups based on their geography. First, there's Birger Jarlsgatan, Stureplan, and the city end of Kungsträdgården, which are more upscale and trendy, and thus more expensive. At the bars and clubs in this area, it's not unusual to wait in line with people who look like they just stepped off the pages of a glossy magazine. To the south, in Södermalm, things are a bit looser and wilder, but that doesn't mean the bars are any less hip. At night Söder can get pretty crazy—it's louder and more bohemian, and partygoers walk the streets.

In general, on weekends clubs and bars are often packed with tourists and locals, and you might have to wait in line. It's also sometimes hard to distinguish between a bar and nightclub, since many bars turn into clubs late at night. Many establishments will post and enforce a minimum age requirement, which could be anywhere from 18 to 30, depending on the clientele they wish to serve, and they may frown on jeans and sneakers. Your safest bet is to wear dark clothes. Most places are open until around 3 AM.

The tourist guide *What's On* (⊕ www.stockholmtown.com) is available free of charge at most hotels, tourist centers, and some restaurants. It lists the month's events in both English and Swedish. The Thursday editions of the daily newspapers *Dagens Nyheter* (⊕ www.dn.se) and *Svenska Dagbladet* (⊕ www.svd.se) carry current listings of events, films, restaurants, and museums in Swedish. There's also a monthly guide called *Nöjesguiden* (the Entertainment Guide; ⊕ www.nojesguiden.se), which has listings and reviews in Swedish.

Nightlife

Bars & Nightclubs

Go to Stureplan (at one end of Birger Jarlsgatan) on any given weekend night, and you'll see crowds of people gathering around *Svampen* (the Mushroom), a concrete structure that's a roof over pay phones. It's *the* meeting place for people getting ready to go out in this area.

★ Glamour is on the menu at **Brasserie Godot** (⊠ Grev Tureg. 36, Östermalm ☎ 08/6600614), a toned-down chic bar and restaurant known

★ for its excellent cocktail list and hip crowd. **Berns Salonger** (⊠ Berns Hotel, Berzelii Park, City ☎ 08/56632000) has three bars—one in 19th-century style and two modern rooms—plus a huge veranda that's spectacular in the summer. Music here gets so thumping you can hear it down the street. **Folkhemmet** (⊠ Renstiernas Gata 30, Södermalm ☎ 08/6405595), marked by a blue F imitating the T for the subway, is a longtime favorite of the artsy locals. It's friendly and inviting, but be prepared for lots of smoke and a crowded bar. Close to the Mushroom is the casually hip **Lydmar Bar** (⊠ Stureg. 10, Östermalm ☎ 08/56611300), with black-leather couches and chairs and a small stage for bands and DJs. Many people who frequent the bar are in the music business. **Mosebacke Etablissement** (⊠ Mosebacke Torg 3, Södermalm ☎ 08/6419020) is a combined indoor theater, comedy club, and outdoor café with a spectacular view of the city. The crowd here leans toward over-30 hipsters. The **O-bar** (⊠ Stureplan 2, Östermalm ☎ 08/4405730), located upstairs through the restaurant Sturehof, is where the downtown crowd gathers for late-night drinks and music ranging from bass-heavy hip-hop to hard rock. The **Sturehof** itself is a prime location for evening people-watching. The outdoor tables are smack dab in the middle of Stureplan. For what has to be Stockholm's biggest rum collection (more than 64 varieties), slide into **Sjögräs** (Sea Grass; ⊠ Timmermansg. 24, Södermalm ☎ 08/841200), where the drinks go down smoothly to the sounds of reggae. Wander along Götagatan with its lively bars and head for **Snaps/Rangus Tangus** (⊠ Medborgarplatsen, Södermalm ☎ 08/6402868), an India-inspired eatery and cellar lounge/bar in a 300-year-old building. There is live music, and the latest DJs spin here as well. **Sophie's Bar** (⊠ Biblioteksg. 5, City ☎ 08/6118408) is one of Stockholm's major celebrity hangouts. It can be a bit elitist and uptight, probably the reason Madonna checked it out when she was in town. From Sophie's Bar it's a short walk to **Spy Bar** (⊠ Birger Jarlsg. 20, City ☎ 08/6118408), one of Stockholm's most exclusive clubs. It's often filled with local celebrities and lots of glitz and glamour. **Tiger** (⊠ Kungsg. 18, City ☎ 08/244700) is a multilevel club and restaurant with a Latin touch. On the first floor it's all about salsa and *mojitos* (Cuban cocktails made with rum and mint). On the huge second floor the music is anything from hip-hop to house music. Always expect a line and two tough doormen. At Odenplan the basement bar of **Tranan** (⊠ Karlbergsv. 14, Vasastan ☎ 08/52728100) is a fun place to party in semidarkness to anything from ambient music to hard rock. Lots of candles, magazines, and art are inside. A trendy youngish crowd props up the long bar at **WC** (⊠ Skåneg. 51, Södermalm ☎ 08/7022963), with ladies' drink specials on Sunday. Luckily, the only things that'll remind you of the name (which stands for "water closet," or bathroom) are the holes in the middle of the bar stools.

Stockholm can also appease your need for pub-style intimacy. Guinness, ale, and cider enthusiasts rally in the tartan-clad **Bagpiper's Inn** (⊠ Rörstrandsg. 21, Vasastan ☎ 08/311855), where you can get a large selection of bar food. **The Dubliner** (⊠ Smålandsg. 8, City ☎ 08/6797707), probably Stockholm's most popular Irish pub, serves up pub food and hosts live folk music on stage. It's not unusual to see people dancing on the tables. As green as a four-leaf clover, **Limerick** (⊠ Tegnérg. 10, Norrmalm ☎ 08/6731902) is a popular Hibernian watering hole. The very British **Tudor Arms** (⊠ Grevg. 31, Östermalm ☎ 08/6602712) is just as popular as when it opened in 1969. Brits who are missing home cooking will be relieved when they see the menu. **Wirströms Pub** (⊠ Stora Nyg. 13, Gamla Stan ☎ 08/212874) is in labyrinthine 17th-century cellars. Expect lots of smoke, live acoustic music, mostly anglophone patrons, and lots of beer. There are also 130 whiskeys available.

Cabaret

Börsen (⊠ Jakobsg. 6, City ☎ 08/7878500) offers high-quality international cabaret shows. Tucked behind the Radisson SAS near Nybroplan is **Wallmans Salonger** (⊠ Teaterg. 3, City ☎ 08/6116622), where singing and dancing waitstaff and talented stage performers entertain until midnight.

Casinos

Many hotels and bars have a roulette table and sometimes blackjack; games operate according to Swedish rules, which are designed to limit the amount you can lose. **Cosmopol Casino** (⊠ Kungsg. 65, City ☎ 08/7818800) is Stockholm's only international casino; it was opened in 2003 after a relaxation in Sweden's gambling laws. Glitz and glamour abound in the huge chandelier-strung former theater, where games are plentiful and winnings are unlimited; as are losses.

Dance Clubs

Café Opera (⊠ Operahuset, City ☎ 08/6765807), at the waterfront end of Kungsträdgården, is a popular meeting place for young and old alike. It has the longest bar in town, fantastic 19th-century ceilings and details, plus dining and roulette, and major dancing after midnight. The kitchen offers a night menu until 2:30 AM. **Daily News Café** (⊠ Kungsträdgården, City ☎ 08/215655), a glitzy nightclub near Sweden House, is returning to its 1980s popular glory. The crowd here varies depending on the night, with lots of late-night stragglers looking for fun before going home. Down on Stureplan is **Sturecompagniet** (⊠ Stureg. 4, Östermalm ☎ 08/6117800), a galleried, multifloored club where the crowd is young, the dance music is loud, and the lines are long. **Mälarsalen** (⊠ Torkel Knutssonsg. 2, ☎ 08/6581300) caters to the nondrinking jitterbug and fox-trot crowd in Södermalm. **Residence** (⊠ Birger Jarlsg. 29,

Norrmalm ☎08/201411) is a soft-disco nightclub specifically for a thirty- and fortysomething crowd.

Gay Bars

Patricia (✉ Stadsgården, Berth 25, Södermalm ☎ 08/7430570) is a floating restaurant, disco, and bar right next to Slussen. And don't worry—the boat doesn't rock enough to make you sick. All are welcome at **TipTop** (✉ Sveav. 57, Norrmalm ☎ 08/329800), but most of the clientele is gay. Men and women dance nightly to '70s disco and modern techno. Hidden down behind the statue of St. George and the dragon on Gamla Stan, **Mandus Bar och Kök** (✉ Österlångg. 7, Gamla Stan ☎ 08/206055) is a warm and friendly restaurant and bar perfect for drinking and talking late into the night.

Jazz Clubs

The best and most popular jazz venue is **Fasching** (✉ Kungsg. 63, City ☎08/216267), where international and local bands play year-round. The classic club **Nalens** (✉ Regeringsg. 74, City ☎ 08/4533434), which was popular back in the '50s and '60s, is back on the scene with major performances throughout the year; it has three stages. **Stampen** (✉ Stora Nyg. 5, Gamla Stan ☎ 08/205793) is an overpriced but atmospheric club in Gamla Stan with traditional jazz nightly. Get there early for a seat.

Piano Bars

Piano bars are part of Stockholm's nightlife. The **Anglais Bar** (✉ Humlegårdsg. 23, City ☎ 08/51734000), at the Hotel Anglais, is popular on weekends. Most people there are English-speaking international travelers staying at the hotel. The **Clipper Club** (✉ Skeppsbron 1214, Gamla Stan ☎ 08/223260), at the Hotel Reisen, is a pleasant, dark-wood, dimly lighted bar on Gamla Stan.

Rock Clubs

Pub Anchor (✉ Sveav. 90, Norrmalm ☎08/152000), on Sveavägen's main drag, is the city's downtown hard-rock bar. **Krogen Tre Backar** (✉ Tegnérg. 1214, Norrmalm ☎ 08/6734400) is as popular among hard-rock fans as the Pub Anchor is. It's just off Sveavägen. International rock acts often play at **Klubben** (✉ Hammarby Frabriksv. 13, Södermalm ☎ 08/4622200), a small bar and club in the Fryshuset community center south of town.

The Arts

Stockholm's theater and opera season runs from September through May. Both *Dramaten* (the National Theater) and *Operan* (the Royal Opera) shut down in the summer months. When it comes to popular music, big-name acts such as Neil Young, U2, and Eminem frequently come to Stockholm during the summer months while on their European tours. Artists of this type always play at Globen sports arena. For a list of events pick up the free booklet *What's On,* available from hotels and tourist information offices. For tickets to theaters and shows try **Biljettdirekt** (☎077/1707070), at Sweden House (✉ Hamng. 27, City), or any post office.

Classical Music

International orchestras perform at **Konserthuset** (✉Hötorget 8, City ☎08/102110), the main concert hall. The **Music at the Palace series** (☎ 08/102247) runs June through August. Off-season there are weekly concerts by Sweden's Radio Symphony Orchestra at **Berwaldhallen** (Berwald Concert Hall; ✉ Strandv. 69, Östermalm ☎ 08/7845000). After Konserthuset, the best place for classical music is **Nybrokajen 11** (✉Nybrokajen

11, City ☎ 08/071700), where top international musicians perform in relatively small listening halls.

Dance

When it comes to high-quality international dance in Stockholm, there's really only one place to go. **Dansenshus** (✉ Barnhusg. 12–14, Vasastan ☎08/50899090) hosts the best Swedish and international acts, with shows ranging from traditional Japanese dance to street dance and modern ballet. You can also see ballet at the Royal Opera house.

Film

Stockholm has an abundance of cinemas, all listed in the *Yellow Pages* under "Biografer." Current billings are listed in evening papers, normally with Swedish titles; call ahead if you're unsure. Foreign movies are subtitled not dubbed. Most, if not all, movie theaters take reservations over the phone: popular showings can sell out ahead of time. Cinemas are either part of the SF chain or of **SandrewMetronome**. Listings for each can be found on the wall at the theater or in the back of the culture pages of the daily newspapers. **Filmstaden Sergel** (✉ Hötorget, City ☎ 08/56260000) is a 14-screen complex at one end of Hötorget. **Biopalatset and Filmstaden Söder** (✉ Medborgarplatsen, Södermalm ☎ 08/6443100 or 08/56260000) are on the south side of town and have many films from which to choose. If you are interested in smaller theaters with character, try the **Grand** (✉ Sveav. 45, Norrmalm ☎ 08/4112400), a nice little theater with two small screens and not a bad seat in the house. **Röda Kvarn** (✉ Biblioteksg. 5, City ☎ 08/7896073) is a beautiful, old movie theater right near Stureplan. **Zita** (✉ Birger Jarlsg. 37, Norrmalm ☎ 08/232020) is a one-screen theater that shows foreign films. A small restaurant is in the back.

Opera

It is said that Queen Lovisa Ulrika began introducing opera to her subjects in 1755. Since then Sweden has become an opera center of standing, a launchpad for such names as Jenny Lind, Jussi Björling, and ★ Birgit Nilsson. **Operan** (Royal Opera House; ✉ Jakobs Torg 2, City ☎08/248240), dating from 1898, is now the de facto home of Sweden's operatic tradition. **Folkoperan** (✉ Hornsg. 72, Södermalm ☎ 08/6160750) is a modern company with its headquarters in Södermalm. Casting traditional presentation and interpretation of the classics to the wind, the company stages productions that are refreshingly new.

Theater

Kungliga Dramatiska Teatern (Royal Dramatic Theater, called Dramaten; ✉ Nybroplan, City ☎ 08/6670680) sometimes stages productions of international interest, in Swedish, of course. The exquisite **Drottningholms Slottsteater** (Drottningholm Court Theater; ✉ Drottningholm, Drotningholm ☎ 08/6608225) presents opera, ballet, and orchestral music from May to early September; the original 18th-century stage machinery is still used in these productions. Drottningholm, the royal residence, is reached by subway and bus or by a special theater-bus (which leaves from the Grand Hotel or opposite the central train station). Boat tours run here in summer.

SPORTS & THE OUTDOORS

Like all Swedes, Stockholmers love the outdoors and spend a great deal of time doing outdoor sports and activities. Because the city is spread out on a number of islands, you are almost always close to the water. The many large parks, including Djurgården and Haga Park, allow people to quickly escape the hustle and bustle of downtown.

The most popular summertime activities in Stockholm are golf, biking, rollerblading, tennis, and sailing. In the winter people like to ski and ice skate.

Beaches

The best bathing places in central Stockholm are on the island of Långholmen and at Rålambshov, at the end of Norr Mälarstrand. Both are grassy or rocky lakeside hideaways. Topless sunbathing is virtually de rigueur.

Biking & Rollerblading

Stockholm is laced with bike paths, and bicycles can be taken on the commuter trains (except during peak traveling times) for excursions to the suburbs. The bike paths are also ideal for rollerblading. You can rent a bike for between SKr 150 and SKr 250 per day. Rollerblades cost between Skr 80 and SKr 120. Most places require a deposit of a couple thousand kronor. **Cykelfrämjandet** (✉ Thuleg. 43, 113 53 ☎ 08/54591030 ⊕ www.cykelframjandet.a.se), a local bicyclists' association, publishes an English-language guide to cycling trips. City and mountain bikes can be rented from **Cykel & Mopeduthyrning** (✉ Strandv. at Kajplats 24, City ☎ 08/6607959) for SKr 170. Also try **Skepp & Hoj** (✉ Galärvarvsv. 2, Djurgården ☎ 08/6605757), pronounced "ship ahoy," which has nice city cruisers for SKr 250 per day.

Boating

Boating in Stockholm's archipelago is an exquisite summertime activity. From May to September sailboats large and small and gorgeous restored wooden boats cruise from island to island. Both types of boats are available for rental. Walk along the water on Strandvägen, where many large power yachts and sailboats (available for charter) are docked. Sea kayaking has also become increasingly popular and is a delightful way to explore the islands.

Contact **Svenska Seglarförbundet** (Swedish Sailing Association; ✉ af Pontins väg 6, 115 21 ☎ 08/4590990 ⊕ www.ssf.se) for information on sailing. **Svenska Kanotförbundet** (Swedish Canoeing Association; ✉ Idrotts Hus, 123 87 Farsta ☎ 08/6056565 ⊕ www.svenskidrott.se/kanot) has information on canoeing and kayaking. **Capella Skärgårdscatering** (✉ Zirocco, Strandv. Kajplats 20, City ☎ 08/7326850) has a large power yacht available for afternoon and overnight charters for groups of up to 40 people. At the end of Strandvägen, before the bridge to Djurgården, is **Tvillingarnas Båtuthyrning** (✉ Djurgårdsbron, Djurgården ☎ 08/6633739), which has large and small motorboats and small sailboats. **Point 65 N** (✉ Styrmansg. 23, Östermalm), a short walk up from Strandvägen, has high-quality sea kayaks for rent. Its staff will help you get them down and back from the water if it's a two- or three-day rental.

Fitness Centers

Health and fitness is a Swedish obsession. The **Sports Club Stockholm** (✉ City Sports Club, Birger Jarlsg. 6C, City ☎ 08/6798310, ✉ Atlanta Sports Club St. Eriksg. 34, Vasastan ☎ 08/6506625) chain has women's and mixed gym facilities for SKr 90 a day. For a relatively inexpensive massage, try the **Axelsons Gymnastiska Institut** (✉ Gästrikeg. 1012, Vasastan ☎ 08/54545900). **Friskis & Svettis** (✉ St. Eriksg. 54, Vasastan ☎ 08/4297000) is a local chain of indoor and, in summer, outdoor gyms specializing in aerobics; branches are scattered throughout the Stockholm area. Monday through Thursday at 6 PM, from the end of May into late August, it hosts free aerobic sessions in Rålambshovs Park.

Golf

There are numerous golf courses around Stockholm. Greens fees run from about SKr 450 to SKr 650, depending on the club. Contact **Sveriges Golf-förbund** (⊠ Kevingestrand 20, Box 84, 182 11 Danderyd ☎ 08/7315370 ⊕ sfg.golf.se), which is just outside Stockholm, for information. **Stockholms Golfklubb**, which has a midlevel 18-hole course, is there as well. **Lidingö Golfklubb** (⊠ Kyttingev. 2, Lidingö ☎ 08/7317900) has an 18-hole forest-and-park course. It's about a 20-minute drive from the city center. **Ingarö Golfklubb** (⊠ Fogelvik, Ingarö ☎ 08/57028244), which has two 18-hole courses—one midlevel, one difficult—is also about 20 minutes away.

Running

Numerous parks with footpaths dot the central city area, among them **Haga Park** (which also has canoe rentals), **Djurgården,** and the wooded **Liljans Skogen.** A very pleasant public path follows the waterfront across from Djurgården, going east from Djurgårdsbron past some of Stockholm's finest old mansions and the wide-open spaces of Ladugårdsgärdet, a park that's great for a picnic or flying a kite.

Skiing

The **Excursion Shop** (⊠ Sweden House, Kungsträdgården, Stockholm ☎ 08/7892415) has information on skiing as well as other sport and leisure activities and will advise on necessary equipment.

Spectator Sports

The ultramodern, 281-ft **Globen** (⊠ Box 10055, 121 27, Globentorget 2 ☎ 08/7251000), the world's tallest spherical building, hosts such sports as ice hockey and equestrian events. It has its own subway station. Inside the same sports complex as Globen is **Söderstadion** (⊠ Box 10055, 121 27, Globentorget 2 ☎ 08/7251000), the open-air stadium where the Hammarby soccer team plays professional soccer. North of the city is **Råsunda Stadion** (⊠ Box 1216, Solnav. 51, 171 23 Solna ☎ 08/7350935), Stockholm's largest soccer stadium and host to the biggest games between the city's teams.

Swimming

In the town center, **Centralbadet** (⊠ Drottningg. 88, City ☎ 08/54521313) has an extra-large indoor pool, whirlpool, steam bath, and sauna. **Eriksdalsbadet** (⊠ Hammarby slussv. 20, Södermalm ☎ 08/50840250) is the city's largest swimming complex. At Stureplan the exclusive **Sturebadet** (⊠ Sturegallerian, Östermalm ☎ 08/54501500) has a swimming pool, aquatic aerobics, and a sauna.

Tennis

With stars such as Björn Borg and Stefan Edberg, it's impossible for tennis not to be huge in Stockholm. Contact **Svenska Tennisförbundet** (⊠ Lidingöv. 75, Box 27915, 115 94 Stockholm ☎ 08/6679770 🖷 08/6646606 ⊕ www.tennis.se) for information. Borg once played at **Kungliga Tennishallen** (Royal Tennis Hall; ⊠ Lidingöv. 75, Norra Djurgården ☎ 08/4591500), which hosts the Stockholm Open every year. **Tennisstadion**

(✉ Fiskartorpsv. 20, Norra Djurgården ☎ 08/54525254) has well-maintained courts.

SHOPPING

If you like to shop till you drop, then charge on down to any one of the three main department stores in the central city area, all of which carry top-name brands from Sweden and abroad for both men and women. For souvenirs and crafts peruse the boutiques and galleries in Väster-långgatan, the main street of Gamla Stan. For jewelry, crafts, and fine art, hit the shops that line the raised sidewalk at the start of Hornsgatan on Södermalm. Drottninggatan, Birger Jarlsgatan, Biblioteksgatan, Göt-gatan, and Hamngatan also offer some of the city's best shopping.

Department Stores & Malls

★ Sweden's leading department store is **NK** (✉ Hamng. 18–20, across the street from Kungsträdgården, City ☎ 08/7628000); the initials, pronounced enn-*koh,* stand for *Nordiska Kompaniet.* You pay for the high quality here. **Åhléns City** (✉ Klarabergsg. 50, City ☎ 08/6766000) has a selection similar to NK, with slightly better prices. Before becoming a famous actress, Greta Garbo used to work at **PUB** (✉ Drottningg. 63 and Hötorget, City ☎08/4021611), which has 42 independent boutiques. Garbo fans will appreciate the small exhibit on level H2—a collection of photographs begins with her employee ID card.

Gallerian (✉ Hamng. 37, City ☎ 08/7912445), in the city center just down the road from Sergels Torg, is a large indoor mall closely resembling those found in the United States. Toys, shoes, music, a hardware store, designer clothes, and food are among the wares. **Sturegallerian** (✉ Grev Tureg. 9, Östermalm ☎ 08/6114606) is a midsize mall on Stureplan that mostly carries exclusive clothes, bags, and accessories.

Markets

At **Hötorget** there's a lively daily outdoor market where you can buy fresh fruit and vegetables at prices well below those found in grocery stores. It's open from 9 to 6. For a good indoor market hit **Hötorgshallen** (✉ Hötorget, City), directly under Filmstaden. The market is filled with butcher shops, coffee and tea shops, and fresh-fish markets. It closes at 6 PM. If you're interested in high-quality Swedish food, try the classic European ★ indoor market **Östermalms Saluhall** (✉ Östermalmstorg, Östermalm).

Specialty Stores

Auction Houses

Perhaps the finest auction house in town is **Lilla Bukowski** (✉ Strandv. 7, Östermalm ☎ 08/6140800), whose elegant quarters are on the waterfront. **Auktions Kompaniet** (✉ Regeringsg. 47, City ☎ 08/235700) is downtown next to NK. **Stockholms Auktionsverk** (✉ Jakobsg. 10, City ☎ 08/4536700) is under the Gallerian shopping center.

Books

Akademibokhandeln (✉ Mäster Samuelsg. 32, City ☎ 08/6136100 ⊕ www.akademibokhandeln.se) has a large selection of books in English.

If you don't find what you need at Akademibokhandeln, **Hedengrens** (✉ Stureplan 4. Sturegallerian, Östermalm ☎ 08/6115132) is also well stocked, especially with fiction and poetry. **Hemlins** (✉ Västerlångg. 6, Gamla Stan, Gamla Stan ☎ 08/106180) carries foreign titles and antique books.

Gifts

Swedish pottery, jewelry, kitchen items, wooden toys, linens, and cook-books from all over the country are available at **Svensk Hemslöjd** (✉ Sveav. 44, City ☎ 08/232115). Though prices are high at **Vistra** (✉ Kungsg. 55, City ☎ 08/214726), so is the quality of gift items and souvenirs.

Glass

Kosta Boda and Orrefors produce the most popular and well-regarded lines of glassware. The **Crystal Art Center** (✉ Tegelbacken 4, City ☎ 08/217169), near the central station, has a great selection of smaller glass items. **Duka** (✉ Sveav. 24–26, City ☎ 08/104530) specializes in crystal and porcelain at reasonable prices. **NK** carries a wide representative line of Swedish glasswork in its Swedish Shop, downstairs. **Nordiska Kristall** (✉ Kungsg. 9, City ☎ 08/104372), near Sturegallerian, has a small gallery of one-of-a-kind art-glass sculptures as well as plates, vases, glasses, bowls, ashtrays, and decanters. **Svenskt Glas** (✉ Birger Jarlsg. 8, City ☎ 08/7684024), near the Royal Dramatic Theater, carries a decent se-lection of quality Swedish glass, including bowls from Orrefors.

Interior Design

Sweden is recognized globally for its unique design sense and has con-tributed significantly to what is commonly referred to as Scandinavian design. All of this makes Stockholm one of the best cities in the world for shopping for furniture and home and office accessories.

On the corner of Östermalmstorg, in the same building as the market-place, is **Bruka** (✉ Humlegårdsg. 1, Östermalm ☎ 08/6601480), which has a wide selection of creative kitchen items as well as wicker baskets and chairs. In Söder **CBI/Klara** (✉ Nytorgsg. 36, Södermalm ☎ 08/6949240) sells furniture, kitchen items, and other funky things for the home—all made by Swedish and international designers. **David Design** (✉ Nybrog. 7, Östermalm ☎ 08/6119855) sells fine furniture, rugs, mir-rors, and decorative items for the house. **DIS** (✉ Humlegårdsg. 19, Östermalm ☎ 08/6112907) sells heavy dark-wood furniture that has an Asian flair. The rugs and pillowcases are also stunning.

For high-minded, trendy furniture that blends dark woods, stainless steel, and colorfully dyed wools, head to **House** (✉ Humlegårdsg. 14, Östermalm ☎ 08/6611100). There's also a nice assortment of vases and glassware. If you're after the *best* of Scandinavian design (and the most expensive), ★ try **Nordiska Galleriet** (✉ Nybrog. 11, Östermalm ☎ 08/4428360). It has everything from couches and chairs to tables and vases. Slightly out of the way, in the Fridhemsplan neighborhood in western Stockholm, **R.O.O. M.** (✉ Alströmerg. 20, Kungsholmen ☎ 08/6925000) has an impressive assortment of Swedish and international tables, chairs, rugs, pillows, beds—the list goes on. It also has a great book selection, lots of nice ce-ramic bowls and plates, and many decorations and utensils for the kitchen and bathroom. For elegant home furnishings, affluent Stockholmers tend to favor **Svenskt Tenn** (✉ Strandv. 5A, Östermalm ☎ 08/6701600), best known for its selection of designer Josef Franck's furniture and fabrics.

Men's Clothing

Brothers (✉ Drottningg. 53, City ☎ 08/4111201) sells relatively inex-pensive Swedish clothes that are often inspired by the more expensive international brands. For suits and evening suits for both sale and rental, **Hans Allde** (✉ Birger Jarlsg. 58, City ☎ 08/207191) provides good old-fashioned service. For the latest line of fine men's clothing, go to the **Hugo Boss Shop** (✉ Birger Jarlsg. 6, City ☎ 08/6110750). **J. Lindeberg** (✉ Grev Tureg. 9, Östermalm ☎ 08/6786165) has brightly colored clothes in many styles. The golf line has been made famous by Swedish golfer Jesper Parnevik. A great spot for trendy Swedish designs is **Mr. Walker** (✉ Regeringsg. 42, City ☎ 08/7966096). The threads here are fabulous, but be prepared to part with some serious crowns—it's hard to walk out empty-handed. Top men's fashions can be found on the second floor of **NK** (✉ Hamng. 18–20, City ☎ 08/7628000), which stocks everything from outdoor gear and evening wear to swimsuits and workout clothes. The Swedish label **Tiger** (☎ 08/7628772), with a section inside NK, sells fine suits, shoes, and casual wear.

Paper Products

For unique Swedish stationery and office supplies in fun colors and styles, go to **Ordning & Reda** (✉ NK, Hamng. 18–20, City ☎ 08/7628462).

Women's Clothing

Swedish designer **Anna Holtblad** (✉ Grev Tureg. 13, Östermalm ☎ 08/54502220) sells her elegant designs at her own boutique. She specializes in knitted clothes. **Champaigne** (✉ Biblioteksg. 2, City ☎ 08/6118803) has European and Swedish designs that are often discounted. **Filippa K** (✉ Grev Tureg. 18, Östermalm ☎ 08/54588888) has quickly become one of Sweden's hottest designers. Her stores are filled with young women grabbing the latest fashions. The clothes at **Indiska** (✉ Drottningg. 53 and elsewhere, ★ City ☎ 08/109193) are inspired by the bright colors of India. **Kookai** (✉ Biblioteksg. 5, City ☎ 08/6119730) carries trendy, colorful European designs for young women. For lingerie and fashionable clothing at a decent price go to **Twilfit** (✉ Nybrog. 11, Östermalm ☎ 08/6637505 ✉ Sturegallerian 16, Östermalm ☎ 08/6110455 ✉ Gamla Brog. 3638, Norrmalm ☎ 08/201954). **Hennes & Mauritz** (H & M; ✉ Hamng. 22, City ✉ Drottningg. 53 and 56, City ✉ Sergelg. 1 and 22, City ✉ Sergels Torg 12, City ☎ 08/7965500) is one of the few Swedish-owned clothing stores to have achieved international success. Here you can find updated designs at rock-bottom prices. **Polarn & Pyret** (✉ Hamng. 10, Gallerian, Drottningg. 29, City ☎ 08/6709500) carries high-quality Swedish children's and women's clothing. For the modern rebel look, go to **Replay** (✉ Kungsg. 6, City ☎ 08/231416), where the collection covers everything from jeans to underwear. One department store with almost every style and type of clothing and apparel is **NK** (✉ Hamng. 18–20, City ☎ 08/7628000).

STOCKHOLM A TO Z

To research prices, get advice from other travelers, and book travel arrangements, visit www.fodors.com.

AIRPORTS & TRANSFERS

Initially opened in 1960 solely for international flights, Stockholm's Arlanda International Airport now also contains a domestic terminal. The airport is 42 km (26 mi) from the city center; a freeway links the city and airport. The airport is run by Luftfartsverket, a state-owned company. 🏢 **Arlanda International Airport** ✉ 190 45 Stockholm-Arlanda ☎ 08/7976000 📠 08/7978600 🌐 www.arlanda.lfv.se.

AIRPORT TRANSFERS

Travel between Arlanda International Airport and Stockholm has been greatly improved with the completion of the Arlanda Express, a high-speed train service. The yellow-nose train leaves every 15 minutes, travels at a speed of 200 kph (125 mph), and completes the trip from the airport to Stockholm's central station in just 20 minutes; single tickets cost 150 SKr.

Flygbussarna (flight buses) leave both the international and domestic terminals every 10–15 minutes from 6:30 AM to 11 PM and make a number of stops on the way to their final destination at the Cityterminalen at Klarabergsviadukten, next to the central railway station. The trip costs SKr 80 and takes about 35 minutes.

A bus-taxi combination package is available. The bus lets you off by the taxi stand at Haga Forum, Jarva Krog, or Cityterminalen and you present your receipt to the taxi driver, who takes you to your final destination. A trip will cost between SKr 180 and SKr 240, depending on your destination.

For taxis be sure to ask about a *fast pris* (fixed price) between Arlanda and the city. It should be between SKr 350 and SKr 435, depending on the final destination. The best bets for cabs are Taxi Stockholm, Taxi 020, and Taxikurir. All major taxi companies accept credit cards. Watch out for unregistered cabs, which charge high rates and won't provide the same service.

🚗 **Arlanda Express** ✉ Vasag. 11 Box 130, City ☎ 020/222224 ⊕ www.arlandaexpress. com. **Flygbussarna** ☎ 08/6001000 ⊕ www.flygbussarna.com. **Taxi 020** ☎ 020/939393. **Taxikurir** ☎ 08/300000. **Taxi Stockholm** ☎ 08/150000.

BIKE TRAVEL

One of the best ways to explore Stockholm is by bike. There are bike paths and special bike lanes throughout the city, making it safe and enjoyable. Bike rentals will be about SKr 110 per day. One of the best places to ride is on Djurgården. Cykel & Mopeduthyrning and Skepp & Hoj both service that area.

🚲 **Cyke & Mopeduthyrning** (Bike and Moped Rentals) ✉ Standv. kajplats 24, City ☎ 08/6607959. **Skepp & Hoj, Djurgårdsbron** (bike rentals) ✉ Galärvarvsv. 2, Djurgården ☎ 08/6605757.

BOAT & FERRY TRAVEL

Waxholmsbolaget (Waxholm Ferries) offers the *Båtluffarkortet* (Inter-Skerries Card), a discount pass for its extensive commuter network of archipelago boats; the price is SKr 385 for 16 days of unlimited travel. The Strömma Kanalbolaget operates a fleet of archipelago boats that provide excellent sightseeing tours and excursions.

🚢 **Strömma Kanalbolaget** ☎ 08/58714000. **Waxholmsbolaget** ☎ 08/6795830.

BUS TRAVEL TO & FROM STOCKHOLM

All the major bus services, including Flygbussarna, Swebus Express, Svenska Buss, and Interbus, arrive at Cityterminalen (City Terminal), next to the central railway station. Reservations to destinations all over Sweden can be made by calling Swebus.

🚌 **Cityterminalen** ✉ Karabergsviadukten 72, City ☎ 08/4408570. **Interbus** ☎ 08/7279000 ⊕ www.interbus.se. **Swebus Express** ☎ 0200/218218 ⊕ www.express.swebus.se. **Svenska Buss** ☎ 0771/676767 ⊕ www.svenskabuss.se.

BUS TRAVEL WITHIN STOCKHOLM

Late-night bus service connects certain stations when trains stop running. The comprehensive bus network serves out-of-town points of interest, such as Waxholm and Gustavsberg.

CAR RENTAL

Rental cars are readily available in Sweden and are relatively inexpensive. Because of the availability and efficiency of public transport, there is little point in using a car within the city limits. If you are traveling elsewhere in Sweden, you'll find that roads are uncongested and well marked but that gasoline is expensive (about SKr 10 per liter, which is equivalent to SKr 40 per gallon). All major car-rental firms are represented, including Avis, Budget, Hertz, and National. Statoil gas stations also rent out cars, as do local Swedish companies such as Berras and Auto, which can sometimes have better prices than the major companies.

⊞ Major Agencies Auto ⊠ Östgötg. 75, Södermalm ☎ 08/6428040. **Avis** ⊠ Ringv. 90, Södermalm ☎ 08/6449980. **Berras** ⊠ Skepparg. 74, City ☎ 08/6611919. **Budget** ⊠ Klarabergsviadukten 92, City ☎ 020/787787. **Hertz** ⊠ Vasag. 26, City ☎ 08/240720. **National** ⊠ Klarabergsg. 33, City ☎ 08/242655. **Statoil** ☎ 020/252525 throughout Sweden, ⊠ Vasag. 16, City ☎ 08/202064, ⊠ Birger Jarlsg. 68, Norrmalm ☎ 08/211593.

CAR TRAVEL

Approach the city by either the E20 or E18 highway from the west, or the E4 from the north or south. The roads are clearly marked and well sanded and plowed during winter. Signs for downtown read ENTRUM.

Driving in Stockholm is often deliberately frustrated by city planners, who have imposed many restrictions to keep traffic down. Keep an eye out for bus lanes, marked with BUSS on the pavement. Driving in that lane can result in a ticket. Get a good city map, called a Trafikkarta, available at most service stations for around SKr 75.

EMBASSIES

⊞ Australia ⊠ Sergels Torg 12, City ☎ 08/6132900 ⊕ www.austemb.se.

⊞ Canada ⊠ Tegelbacken 4, ☎ 08/4533000 ⊕ www.canadaemb.se.

⊞ New Zealand Consulate-General ⊠ Nybrog. 34, Östermalm ☎ 08/6118090.

⊞ United Kingdom ⊠ Skarpög. 68, Östermalm ☎ 08/6713000 ⊕ www. britishembassy.se.

⊞ United States ⊠ Strandv. 101, Östermalm ☎ 08/7835300 ⊕ www.usis.usemb.se.

EMERGENCIES

Dial 112 for emergencies—this covers police, fire, ambulance, and medical help, as well as sea and air rescue services. Private care is available via CityAkuten. A hospital is called a *sjukhus*, which is Swedish for "sick house," and regular doctors' offices are called *Läkerhuset*. Dentists are listed under under *tandläkare*, or *tandvård*. There is a 24-hour national health service via the emergency number listed below.

⊞ Doctors & Dentists Folktandvården (national dental service) ☎ 020/6875500. **Läkerhuset Hörtorgscity** ⊠ Sveav. 13–15, City ☎ 08/243800. **Läkerhuset Riddargatan 12** ⊠ Riddarg. 12, Östermalm ☎ 08/6797900.

⊞ Emergency Services CityAkuten (Emergency Medical Care) ⊠ Apelbergsg. 48, City ☎ 08/4122961. **CityAkuten Tandvården** (Emergency Dental Care) ⊠ Olof Palmesg. 13A, Norrmalm ☎ 08/4122900.

⊞ Hospitals Ersta sjukhus ⊠ Fjällg. 44, Södermalm ☎ 08/7146100. **Karolinska Sjukhuset** ⊠ Solna (just north of Stockholm), Solna ☎ 08/51770000. **Södersjukhuset** ⊠ Ringv. 52, Södermalm ☎ 08/6161000. **St. Görans Sjukhus** ⊠ Sankt Göransplan 1, Kungsholmen ☎ 08/58701000.

⊞ Police Polisen (Stockholm Police Headquarters) ⊠ Norra Agneg. 33-37, Kungsholmen ☎ 08/4010000.

⊞ 24-Hour Pharmacies C. W. Scheele ⊠ Klarabergsg. 64, City ☎ 08/4548130.

ENGLISH-LANGUAGE MEDIA

BOOKS Many bookshops stock English-language books. Akademibokhandeln has a wide selection of English books, with an emphasis on reference titles. Hedengren's has the best and most extensive selection of English- and other foreign-language books, from fiction to nonfiction, from photography to architecture. NK has a large bookstore with an extensive English-language section.

⊞ Bookstores Akademibokhandeln ⊠ Mäster Samuelsg. 32, near the city center, City ☎ 08/6136100. **Hedengrens** ⊠ Stureplan 4, Sturegallerian shopping complex, Östermalm ☎ 08/6115132. **NK** ⊠ Hamng. 18-20, City ☎ 08/7628000.

RADIO There are two major radio stations with English-language programming in Stockholm. Radio Sweden, part of the state-owned radio company, has news about Sweden in English, daily and weekly English programs, as well as many shows from National Public Radio in the United States and from the BBC in the United Kingdom. You can pick up Radio Sweden at 89.6 FM.

SUBWAY TRAVEL

The subway system, known as T-banan (*Tunnelbanan,* with stations marked by a blue-on-white T), is the easiest and fastest way to get around. Servicing more than 100 stations and covering more than 96 km (60 mi) of track, trains run frequently between 5 AM and 3 AM.

TAXIS

Stockholm's taxi service is efficient but overpriced. If you call a cab, ask the dispatcher to quote you a *fast pris* (fixed price), which is usually lower than the metered fare. Reputable cab companies are Taxi 020, Taxi Stockholm, and Taxikurir. Taxi Stockholm has an immediate charge of SKr 25 whether you hail a cab or order one by telephone. A trip of 10 km (6 mi) should cost about SKr 97 between 6 AM and 7 PM, SKr 107 at night, and SKr 114 on weekends.

🚩 **Taxi 020** ☎ 020/939393. **Taxikurir** ☎ 08/300000. **Taxi Stockholm** ☎ 08/150000.

TOURS

BOAT TOURS Strömma Kanalbolaget runs sightseeing tours of Stockholm. Boats leave from the quays outside the Royal Dramatic Theater, Grand Hotel, and City Hall. Stockholm Sightseeing, which leaves from Skeppsbron in front of the Grand, has four tours, including the "Under the Bridges" and "Historical Canal" tours. Trips last from one to four hours and cost from SKr 100 to SKr 280.

🚩 **City Hall** late May–early Sept. ✉ Hantverkarg. 1, Kungsholmen ☎ 08/50829000. **Stockholm Sightseeing** ✉ Skeppsbron 22, Gamla Stan ☎ 08/57814020 ⊕ www.stockholmsightseeing.com. **Strömma Kanalbolaget** ✉ Skeppsbron 22, Gamla Stan ☎ 08/58714070.

BUS TOURS Open Top Tours offers a narrated bus tour available in a choice of eight languages via individual headphones. The tour, which covers all the main points of interest, leaves each day at 9:20 from the tourist center at Sweden House. More comprehensive tours, taking in museums, Gamla Stan, and city hall, are available through City Sightseeing.

🚩 **City Sightseeing** ✉ Skeppsbron 11, Gamla Stan ☎ 08/58714030 or 08/4117023 ⊕ www.citysightseeing.com. **Open Top Tours** ✉ Hamng. 27, City ☎ 08/6860612. **Sweden House** ✉ Hamng. 27, Box 7542, 103 93 Stockholm ☎ 08/7892490.

PRIVATE GUIDES You can hire your own guide from Stockholm Information Service's Guide Centralen. In summer be sure to book guides well in advance.

🚩 **Guide Centralen** ✉ Sweden House, Hamng. 27, Box 7542, City ☎ 08/7892490 🖷 08/7892491.

WALKING TOURS City Sightseeing runs several tours, including the "Romantic Stockholm" tour of the cathedral and city hall; the "Royal Stockholm" tour, which includes visits to the Royal Palace and the Treasury; and the "Old Town Walkabout," which strolls through Gamla Stan in just over one hour.

🚩 **City Sightseeing** ☎ 08/4117023 ⊕ www.citysightseeing.com.

TRAIN TRAVEL

Both long-distance and commuter trains arrive at the central station in Stockholm on Vasagatan, a main boulevard in the heart of the city. For train information and ticket reservations 6 AM–11 PM, call the SJ number below. There is a ticket and information office at the station where you can make reservations. Automated ticket-vending machines are also available.

Central Station ⊠ Vasag., City ☎ 08/7622000. **Citypendeln** (Commuter Train) ☎ 08/6001000 ⊕ www.citypendeln.se. **SJ** (State Railway Company) ⊠ central station, City ☎ 0771/757575 ⊕ www.sj.se.

TRANSPORTATION AROUND STOCKHOLM

The cheapest way to travel around the city by public transport is to purchase the Stockholmskortet (Stockholm Card). In addition to unlimited transportation on city subway, bus, and rail services, it offers free admission to more than 60 museums and several sightseeing trips. The card costs SKr 220 for 24 hours, SKr 380 for two days, and SKr 540 for three days; you can purchase the card from the tourist center at Sweden House on Hamngatan, from the Hotellcentralen accommodations bureau at the central station, and from the tourist center at Kaknäs Tower.

Stockholm has an excellent bus system, which is operated by SL, the state train company. In 2000 the subway system was bought from SL by Connex, the same company that runs the subways in Paris and London. Tickets for Stockholm subways and buses are interchangeable. Maps and timetables for all city transportation networks are available from the SL information desks at Sergels Torg, the central station, Slussen, and online.

Bus and subway fares are based on zones. All trips in downtown will be SKr 20. As you travel farther out of downtown, zones are added to the fare in increments of SKr 10. Each ticket is good for one hour on both the bus system and the subway. Single tickets are available at station ticket counters and on buses, but it's cheaper to buy an SL Tourist Card from one of the many Pressbyrån newsstands. There's also a pass called a Rabattkupong, valid for both subway and buses; it costs SKr 110 and is good for 10 trips downtown (fewer if you travel in more zones) within the greater Stockholm area. There is no time limit within which the 10 trips must be used. If you plan to travel within the greater Stockholm area extensively during a 24-hour period, you can purchase a 24-hour pass for SKr 80 and a 72-hour pass for SKr 150. The 24-hour pass includes transportation on the ferries between Djurgården, Nybroplan, and Slussen. The 72-hour pass also entitles you to admission to Skansen, Gröna Lund Tivoli, and Kaknäs Tower. Those under 18 or over 65 pay SKr 40 for a one-day pass and SKr 75 for a two-day pass.

Connex ☎ 08/60010000 ⊕ www.connex.nu. **SL** ☎ 08/6001000 ⊕ www.sl.se.

TRAVEL AGENCIES

For a complete listing of travel agencies, check in the *Yellow Pages* under "Resor-Resebyråer," or contact American Express. For air travel contact SAS. SJ, the state railway company, has its main ticket office at central station.

Local Agent Referrals American Express ⊠ Birger Jarlsg. 1, City ☎ 08/6795200, 020/793211 toll free. **SAS** ⊠ Klarabergsviadukten 72, accessible from central station, City ☎ 0710/727727. **SJ** (Statens Järnvägar) ⊠ Vasag. 1, City ☎ 0771/757575.

VISITOR INFORMATION

Tourist Information City Hall June-Aug. ⊠ Hantverkarg. 1, Kungsholmen ☎ 08/50829000. **Fjäderholmarna** ☎ 08/7180100. **Kaknästornet** Kaknäs TV Tower ⊠ Ladugårdsgärdet, Gädet ☎ 08/7892435 ⊕ www.stockholmtown.com. **Stockholm Central Station** ⊠ Vasag., City ☎ 0771/757575. **Stockholm Information Service** Sweden House ⊠ Hamng. 27, Box 7542, 103 93 Stockholm ☎ 08/7892490. **Swedish Travel and Tourism Council** ⊠ Box 3030, Kungsg. 36, 103 61 Stockholm ☎ 08/7255500 ☐ 08/7255531 ⊕ www.visit-sweden.com.

SIDE TRIPS FROM STOCKHOLM

2

FODOR'S CHOICE

Drottningholms Slott, *Drottningholm*

Tre Små Rum restaurant, *Trosa*

Radisson SAS Grand Hotel, *Saltsjöbaden*

Rum i Backen B&B, *Vaxholm*

HIGHLY RECOMMENDED

RESTAURANTS Donners Brunn, *Gotland*

Fjäderholmarnas Krog, *Fjäderholmarna*

HOTELS Bomans, *Vaxholm and the Archipelago*

Jaber, *Uppsala*

Villa Alskog, *Alskog*

SIGHTS Drottningholm

Gripsholms Värdshus & Hotel, *Mariefred*

Tullgarns Slott, *Trosa*

Uppsala Domkyrka, *Uppsala*

SURROUNDING STOCKHOLM is a latticework of small historic islands, most of them crowned with castles straight out of a storybook world. Set aside a day for a trip to any of these; half the pleasure of an island outing is the leisurely boat trip to get there. (Note that the castles can all be reached by alternative overland routes if you prefer the bus or train.) Farther afield is the island of Gotland, whose medieval festival, Viking remains, and wilderness preserves will take you back in time. The university town of Uppsala is another popular day-trip destination; it's a quiet, peaceful place with a wonderful Gothic cathedral that provides an edifying contrast to Stockholm's more energetic character.

Where to Stay & Eat

WHAT IT COSTS In Swedish Kronor				
	$$$$	**$$$**	**$$**	**$**	**¢**
RESTAURANTS	above 420	250–420	150–250	100–150	below 100
HOTELS	above 2,900	2,300–2,900	1,500–2,300	1,000–1,500	under 1,000

Restaurant prices are for a main course at dinner. Hotel prices are for two people in a standard double room in high season.

Drottningholm

★ ❶ *1 km (½ mi) west of Stockholm.*

Fodor'sChoice
★

Occupying an island in Mälaren (Sweden's third-largest lake) some 45 minutes from Stockholm's center, **Drottningholms Slott** (Queen's Island Castle) is a miniature Versailles dating from the 17th century. The royal family once used this property only as a summer residence, but, tiring of the Royal Palace back in town, they moved permanently to one wing of Drottningholm in the 1980s. Designed and built by the same father-and-son team of architects that built Stockholm's Royal Palace, the castle began to be constructed in 1662 on the orders of King Karl X's widow, Eleonora. Today it remains one of the most delightful of European palaces, reflecting the sense of style practiced by mid-18th-century royalty. The interiors, dating from the 17th, 18th, and 19th centuries, are a rococo riot of decoration with much gilding and trompe l'oeil. Most sections are open to the public. ✉ *Drottningholm* ☎ *08/4026280* ⊕ *www.royalcourt.se* 🖃*SKr 50* ☉ *May–Aug., daily 10–4:30; Sept., daily noon–3:30; guided tours in summer only.*

The lakeside gardens of Drottningholms Slott are its most beautiful asset, containing **Drottningholms Slottsteater,** the only complete theater to survive from the 18th century anywhere in the world. Built by Queen Lovisa Ulrika in 1766 as a wedding present for her son Gustav III, the Court Theater fell into disuse after his assassination at a masked ball in 1792 (dramatized in Verdi's opera *Un Ballo in Maschera*). In 1922 the theater was rediscovered; there is now a small theater museum here as well, where you can sign up for a backstage tour and see the original backdrops and stage machinery and some amazing 18th-century tools used to produce such special effects as wind and thunder. To get performance tickets, book well in advance at the box office; the season runs from late May to early September. A word of caution: the seats are extremely hard—take a cushion. ✉ *Drottningholm* ☎ *08/7590406, 08/6608225 box office* ⊕ *www. drottningholmsslottsteater.dtm.se* 🖃 *SKr 50* ☉ *May–June and mid-July–Aug., daily noon–4:30; Sept., daily 1–3:30. Guided tours in English at 12:30, 1:30, 2:30, 3:30, and 4:30.*

Arriving & Departing

Boats bound for Drottningholms Slott leave from Klara Mälarstrand, a quay close to Stadshuset (City Hall). Call **Strömma Kanalbolaget** (⌗ Skeppsbron 22 111 30 ☎ 08/58714000 ⊕ www.strommakanalbolaget.com) for schedules and fares. Alternatively, you can take the T-bana (subway) to Brommaplan, and any of Buses 177, 301–323, or 336 from there. Call **Stockholms Lokal Trafik** (☎ 08/6001000) for details.

Mariefred

❷ *63 km (39 mi) southwest of Stockholm.*

The most delightful way to experience the true vastness of Mälaren is the trip to Mariefred—an idyllic little town of mostly timber houses—aboard the coal-fired steamer of the same name, built in 1903 and still going strong. The town's winding narrow streets, ancient squares, and wooded lakeside paths are all perfect for walking. The **Mariefred Tourist Office** has maps and information about tours.

Mariefred's principal attraction is **Gripsholm Slott.** Built in the 1530s by Bo Johansson Grip, the Swedish high chancellor, the castle contains fine Renaissance interiors, a superbly atmospheric theater commissioned in 1781 by the ill-fated Gustav III, and Sweden's royal portrait collection. ☎ *0159/10194 ⌗ SKr 60 ☉ May–Aug., daily 10–4; Sept., Tues.–Sun. 10–3; Oct.–Apr., weekends noon–3; guided tours only.*

An old converted barn across from Gripsholm Slott houses **Grafikens Hus** (Graphic House), a center for contemporary graphic art. Visitors can view exhibitions or take part in workshops covering all aspects of graphic art. There are also a good coffee shop and a gift shop that sells artwork. ⌗ *Mariefred, 647 21 ☎ 0159/23160 ⊕ www.grafikenshus.*

se 🛏 *SKr 50* 🕐 *May–Aug., daily 11–5; Sept.–Apr., Tues. 11–8, Wed.–Sun. 11–5.*

The **S.S. Mariefred** departs from Klara Mälarstrand, near Stadshuset, Stockholm's city hall. The journey takes 3½ hours each way, and there is a restaurant on board. ☎ *08/6698850* 🛏 *SKr 180 round-trip* 🕐 *Departures at 10: May, weekends; mid-June–late Aug., Tues.–Sun. Return trip departs from Mariefred at 4:30.*

You can also travel by narrow-gauge steam railway from Mariefred to a junction on the main line to Stockholm, returning to the capital by ordinary train. Contact the **Mariefred Tourist Office** for details.

Where to Stay & Eat

★ $$ ✕🍴 **Gripsholms Värdshus & Hotel.** At the oldest inn in Sweden (and the only one in Mariefred), guests get a sense of the real Sweden. Lovingly restored and luxuriously appointed, this yellow-wood hotel stands on the site of an old monastery. Rooms are large and airy, with wooden floors and highlights of bright yellow and sky blue. The whole hotel is full of art and artifacts, including some old Swedish-tile fireplaces. In an elegant wood-paneled dining room, the restaurant serves local dishes with an international twist, including basil-and-coriander-marinated monkfish with wasabi cream and breast of guinea fowl with caramelized turnips and a lemon and Szechuan pepper gravy. ⊠ *Kykog. 1, 647 23* ☎ *0159/34750* 🖨 *0159/34777* ⊕ *www.gripsholms-vardshus.se* 🛏 *45 rooms, 44 with bath, 10 suites* ⟂ *Restaurant, bar, no-smoking rooms, sauna* ▤ *AE, DC, MC, V* 🍴 *BP.*

Visitor Information

The **Mariefred Tourist Office** (☎ 0159/29790 ⊕ www.strangnas.se) is open only in the summer; the rest of the year, call **Mälarturism** (☎ 0152/29690) for information for all of Lake Mälaren.

Sigtuna

❸ *48 km (30 mi) northwest of Stockholm.*

An idyllic town on a northern arm of Lake Mälaren, Sigtuna was the principal trading post of the Svea, the tribe that settled Sweden after the last Ice Age; its Viking history is still apparent in the many runic stones preserved all over town. Founded in 980, Sigtuna is Sweden's oldest town, and as such it's not surprising that it has Sweden's oldest street, Stora Gatan. After it was ransacked by Estonian pirates, its merchants went on to found Stockholm sometime in the 13th century. Little remains of Sigtuna's former glory, beyond parts of the principal church. The town hall dates to the 18th century, and the main part of the town dates from the early 1800s. There are two houses said to date to the 15th century.

About 20 km (12 mi) northeast of Sigtuna and accessible by the same ferryboat from Stockholm is **Skokloster Slott**, an exquisite Baroque castle. Commissioned in 1654 by a celebrated Swedish soldier, Field Marshal Carl Gustav Wrangel, the castle is furnished with the spoils of Wrangel's successful campaigns. ⊠ *Bålsta* ☎ *018/386077* ⊕ *www.skokloster.se* 🛏 *SKr 60* 🕐 *Daily noon–6.*

Where to Stay & Eat

$ ✕🍴 **Sigtuna Stadshotell.** Near the lake shore, this beautifully restored hotel was built in 1909 and soon after became a central gathering place among locals—despite at the time being considered one of the ugliest buildings in all of Sigtuna. In its early days the hotel had Sigtuna's first cinema, and in the cellar the state liquor store operated an inn. Today's hotel rooms have hardwood floors, high ceilings, and interesting little nooks and angles. The restaurant ($–$$) offers a great view of the water. The traditional Swedish menu emphasizes herring dishes. Bread and ice cream are both made on the premises. ☒ *Stora Nyg. 3, 193 30* ☎ *08/59250100* 🖷 *08/59251587* ⊕ *www.sigtunastadshotell.se* ➪ *24 rooms* ⚲ *Restaurant, minibars, cable TV, no-smoking rooms, meeting rooms* ▤ *AE, DC, MC, V* ‖‖ *BP.*

Arriving & Departing

From June to mid-August Sigtuna can be reached by boat from the quay near Stockholm's city hall (Strömma Kanalbolaget, ☎ 08/58714000); round-trip fare is SKr 150. Another option is to take a commuter train from Stockholm's central station to Märsta, where you change to Bus 570 or 575.

Vaxholm & the Archipelago

❹ *32 km (20 mi) northeast of Stockholm.*

Skärgården (the archipelago) is Stockholm's greatest natural asset: more than 25,000 islands and skerries, many uninhabited, spread across an almost tideless sea of clean, clear water. The islands closer to Stockholm are larger and more lush, with pine tree–covered rock faces and forests. There are also more year-round residents on these islands. As you move away from the mainland, the islands become smaller and more remote, turning into rugged, rocky islets. To sail lazily among these islands aboard an old steamboat on a summer's night is a timeless delight, and all throughout the warmer months Swedes flee the chaos of the city for quiet weekends on the waters.

For the tourist with limited time, one of the simplest ways to get a taste of the archipelago is the one-hour ferry trip to Vaxholm, an extremely pleasant, though sometimes crowded, mainland seaside town of small, red-painted wooden houses. Guarding what was formerly the main sea route into Stockholm, Vaxholm's fortress now houses the small **Vaxholms Fästnings Museum** (Vaxholm Fortress Museum), which documents the defense of Stockholm over the centuries. The museum contains military memorabilia and tells how the imposing stone castle helped defend against the Danes and Russians in the 17th and 18th centuries. You can reach the fortress by taking a small boat from the town landing, which is in front of the tourist office; a discounted combination ticket includes the boat fare and entrance to the museum. ☎ *08/54172157* 🖾 *SKr 30* ☉ *Mid-May–Aug., daily noon–4. Group admission at other times by appointment.*

An even quicker trip into the archipelago is the 20-minute ferry ride to **Fjäderholmarna** (the Feather Islands), a group of four secluded islands. In the 19th-century the islands were the last chance for a refreshment stop for archipelago residents rowing into Stockholm to sell their produce. After 50 years as a military zone, the islands were opened to the public in the early 1980s. Today they are crammed with arts-and-crafts studios, shops, an aquarium, a small petting farm, a boat museum, a large cafeteria, an ingenious "shipwreck" playground, and even a smoked-fish shop.

Although it's on the mainland, **Saltsjöbaden** is far enough out into the wilds to be considered the archipelago. Construction of the seaside town started in 1891. Designed from the beginning to be a community for the affluent, Saltsjöbaden was based partly on the suburban communities springing up at the same time in the United States. By 1893 the railway had been extended to Saltsjöbaden, and the town was one of the first in Sweden to have electric street lights. The town has some of Europe's grandest 19th-century buildings, which were designed by the leading architects of the time. The best way to reach the town is by train. SJ runs a regular service from central Stockholm.

If you are interested in a longer voyage out into the islands, there are several possibilities. Contact the Sweden House and ask for the "Destination Stockholm Archipelago" catalog, which lists more than 350 holiday homes for rent. For booking accommodations, contact **Hotellcentralen** (☎ 08/7892425). The representatives at Sweden House can also help you plan a customized trip.

One of the most popular excursions is to **Sandhamn,** the main town on the island of Sandön—south of Stockholm and home to about 100 permanent residents. The journey takes about three hours by steamship, but there are faster boats available. The Royal Swedish Yacht Club was founded here at the turn of the 20th century, and sailing continues to be a popular sport. Its fine-sand beaches also make it an ideal spot for swimming. Another option is to try scuba diving—introductory lessons are available; ask at the Sweden House for details. Explore the village of Sandhamn and its narrow alleys and wooden houses, or stroll out to the graveyard outside the village, where tombstones bear the names of sailors from around the world.

The island of **Utö,** which contains Sweden's oldest iron mine (ca. AD 1100–1200), is another popular spot. A number of the miners' homes from the 18th century have been restored. About 200 people live year-round on the island, which has cafés, camping sites, and swimming areas. You can also rent bicycles from a shop near the ferry landing. The boat trip to the island takes about three hours. Utö is particularly known for its bread. *Utö limpa,* a slightly sweetened and spiced sandwich bread, is to be found only on the island and is considered a high delicacy. Many of the thousands of people who go sailing in the archipelago every year make a special detour to stock up on the bread, partly because of its exquisite taste and partly because of its long-keeping properties.

A little bit closer to Stockholm is the island of **Grinda,** long a popular recreation spot among Stockholmers. Rental cabins from the '40s have been restored to their original condition; there are about 30 of these available through **Din Skärgård** (☎08/54249072). The **Grinda Wärdshus** (☎08/54249491), a still-functioning inn from the turn of the 20th century, is one of the largest stone buildings in the archipelago. Since a number of walking paths cut through the woods and open fields, it takes just 15 minutes to walk from one end of Grinda to the other, and exploring is easy. The trip to the island takes about two hours.

At the far southern tip of Stockholm's archipelago lies **Trosa,** a town full of wooden houses that's right on the Baltic Sea. The tiny river that runs through the middle of the town is flanked by beautiful villas painted white, red, yellow, and mint green—a reflection of Trosa's heritage as a seaside retreat for stressed, wealthy Stockholmers. Around the small, cobbled town square are arts-and-crafts shops and market stalls selling fish, fruit, and vegetables.

★ Five kilometers (3 miles) to the north of Trosa is the impressive **Tullgarns Slott.** Built in the early 1700s, the palace was turned into a playful summer retreat in 1772 by King Gustaf's younger brother, Fredrik Adolf. The grounds include sculptured parks and gardens, an orangery, and a theater. The palace's interiors are full of ornate plasterwork, paintings of royals and landscapes, and much of the original French-influenced furnishings. ⊠ *Trosa* ☎ *08/55172011* ≦ *SKr 50* ☉ *May–Sept., daily 11–4.*

If you'd prefer to stay on board a boat and simply cruise around the is-lands, seek out the **Blidösund.** A coal-fired steamboat built in 1911 that has remained in almost continuous service, the *Blidösund* is now run by a small group of enthusiasts who take parties of around 250 on evening music-and-dinner cruises. The cruises depart from a berth close to the Royal Palace in Stockholm. ⊠ *Skeppsbron, Stockholm* ☎ *08/4117113* 🕾 *SKr 140* 🕓 *Departures early May–late Sept., Mon.–Thurs. 7 PM (re-turns at 10:45 PM).*

Among the finest of the archipelago steamboats is the **Saltsjön,** which leaves from Nybrokajen, close to the Strand Hotel. Tuesday through Thursday evenings you can take a jazz-and-dinner cruise for SKr 150 weekends from late June to late August. To go to Utö, an attractive is-land known for its bike paths, bakery, and restaurant, will cost you SKr 190. In December there are three daily Julbord cruises, all of which serve a Christmas smörgåsbord. ⊠ *Strömma Kanalbolaget, Skeppsbron 22, Stockholm* ☎ *08/58714000* 🕓 *Departures July–early Aug. and Dec.*

Where to Eat

$$$ ╳ **Sandhamns Värdshus.** Built in 1672 as a guest house and restaurant for tired sailors, the bright-yellow Sandhamn Inn is a delightful place to stop for meal. A terrace provides a view over the colorful seaside town below, and in the summer there's outdoor seating on a large veranda. The menu is rooted in Swedish traditions with a focus on local seafood. Try the seafood stew spiced with saffron and served with freshly baked bread and aioli. The grilled calf's liver with fried sage and apple chips is also a worthy choice. ⊠ *Sandhamn* ☎ *08/57153051* ▤ *AE, DC, MC, V.*

★ $$–$$$ ╳ **Fjäderholmarnas Krog.** A crackling fire on the hearth in the bar area welcomes the sailors who frequent this laid-back restaurant. In case you don't travel with your own sailboat, you can time your dinner to end before the last ferry returns to the mainland. The food here is self-con-sciously Swedish: fresh, light, and beautifully presented. The service is professional; it's a great choice for a special night out. ⊠ *Fjäderholmarna* ☎ *08/7183355* ▤ *AE, DC, MC, V* 🕓 *Closed Oct.–Apr.*

$$ ╳ **Dykarbaren.** The idea for this old wooden harborside restaurant came from similar cafés in Brittany, France. Simple local dishes, mostly of fish, are served up in an informal wooden-tabled dining area. Originally just catering to local divers, Dykarbaren now serves everyone. ⊠ *Strand-promenaden, Sandhamn* ☎ *08/57153554* ▤ *AE, DC, MC, V.*

¢–$ ╳ **Gröna Caféet.** A grassy garden terrace and an appealing selection of fresh open sandwiches on hearty brown bread make this small, old-fash-ioned café a hit. It's on Rådhusgatan, by the town square. ⊠ *Rådhusg. 26, Vaxholm* ☎ *08/5413151* ▤ *No credit cards.*

¢ ╳ **Tre Små Rum.** The old mint-green, red-roofed house that contains "Three Small Rooms" is a fitting place for simple light lunches. The sand-wiches (made from freshly baked bread) are delicious at this lunch-only café. There are also delicious cakes and pastries—at least 40 types daily. If you don't want to sit inside in one of the rooms, there is a small out-side seating area. ⊠ *Östra Långg., Trosa* ☎ *0156/12151* ▤ *MC, V* 🕓 *Closed dinner.*

FodorsChoice ★ (to the left of Tre Små Rum listing)

Where to Stay

Lodging options in the archipelago vary from island to island. The larger, more inhabited islands often have at least one decent hotel, if not a few, whereas some of the smaller, more deserted islands have only an inn or two or camping facilities. Hostels are available at low cost on some islands, and some private homes rent out rooms and offer B&B accommodations. It's also possible to rent small cabins. Details are available from the Sweden House.

$$$$ ✕⊠ **Radisson SAS Grand Hotel.** Many say that this is the only reason to
Fodor'sChoice come to the beautiful but quiet town of Saltsjöbaden. Next to the sea
★ and the surrounding countryside, the hotel is one of the most breathtaking in the whole archipelago. Built in 1893, it's a castlelike concoc-
tion of white stone, arched windows, and towers. The huge rooms are
filled with colorful period furniture that is set off perfectly against the
plain stone fireplaces and pastel walls. The restaurant ($$$) is a grand
gilt, pillared, and mirrored affair with crisp linens, fine crystal, and a
classic French menu. ⊠ *113 83 Saltsjöbaden* ☎ *08/50617000* 🖷 *08/
50617025* ⊕ *www.radisson.com* ⇋ *105 rooms, 85 with bath, 10 suites
⌂ Restaurant, cable TV, bar, minibars, no-smoking rooms, room ser-
vice, saltwater pool, sauna, spa, miniature golf, 2 tennis courts, jogging,
ice-skating* ⊟ *AE, DC, MC, V* ⦿� *BP.*

$$ ⊠ **Sandhamn Hotel and Conference.** Built in the "archipelago" style, the
Sandhamn overlooks the local harbor. Rooms have light-wood accents
with pale white-and-blue furnishings. The curtains are linen. The recre-
ational area has an indoor and outdoor pool as well as a gym. Live music
is often played on the grounds in summer. The hotel adjoins the Seglar-
restaurangen, also looking out over the water, which serves traditional
Swedish cuisine with a French influence. ⊠ *130 30 Sandhamn* ☎ *08/
57153170* 🖷 *08/57450450* ⊕ *www.sandhamn.com* ⇋ *81 rooms, 3 suites
⌂ Restaurant, bar, indoor-outdoor pool, sauna, gym, meeting room
⊟ AE, DC, MC, V.*

$–$$ ⊠ **Waxholms Hotell.** Perched directly on Vaxholm's harbor, Waxholms
is a stone's throw from where the ferries land. Rooms in this excellent
little hotel are bright and elegant, and most have a view of the water
and the fortress that sits in the harbor. The restaurant and bar are the
best in town, and the wraparound dining room provides great views of
the boats on the water. The varied menu concentrates on local fish and
Swedish specialties. ⊠ *Hamng. 2, 185 21* ☎ *08/54130150* 🖷 *08/
54131376* ⊕ *www.waxholmshotell.se* ⇋ *32 rooms* ⌂ *Restaurant, bar,
no-smoking rooms, meeting room* ⊟ *AE, DC, MC, V.*

★ $ ⊠ **Bomans.** Right on the water and brimming with history, this family-
run hotel dates from the early 20th century. The bedrooms are stuffed
with floral patterns, iron bedsteads, feather quilts, lace, and linen.
Downstairs there is a small bar and a very good restaurant. Lace tablecloths, chandeliers, and tangerine linens and fabrics help create a warm
mood in the restaurant ($$), where you can also dine outside in the sum-
mer months. The menu is unashamedly Swedish, with high-quality ver-
sions of such classic dishes as meatballs, salmon, and elk with
lingonberries. ⊠ *619 30 Trosa* ☎ *0156/52500* 🖷 *0156/52510* ⊕ *www.
bomans.se* ⇋ *31 rooms, 2 with bath, 2 suites* ⌂ *Restaurant, bar, no-
smoking rooms, meeting rooms* ⊟ *AE, DC, MC, V* ⦿� *BP.*

$ ⊠ **Grinda Wärdshus.** Housed in one of the archipelago's largest stone
buildings, this 19th-century villa has homey rooms and bright, comfortable
public areas. Since the hotel is right on the water, you may wish to take
a refreshing dip in the sea before tackling the sumptuous breakfast buf-
fet of Scandinavian classics. ⊠ *Södra Bryggan, 100 05 Grinda* ☎ *08/
54249491* 🖷 *08/54249497* ⊕ *www.grindawardshus.se* ⇋ *34 rooms with-
out bath* ⌂ *Restaurant, in-room VCRs* ⊟ *AE, DC, MC, V* ⦿� *BP.*

¢–$ ⊠ **Utö Värdshus.** The rooms are large and well furnished here, with tra-
ditional furniture resembling that found in a Swedish farmhouse. Choose
between a room in the sprawling white main hotel or 1 of the 30 that
are in a cabin on the grounds. The restaurant ($$) has a grand wooden
ceiling lighted with chandeliers. The food is eclectic, ranging from
salmon with dill to Cajun chicken. ⊠ *Gruvbryggan, 130 56 Utö* ☎ *08/
50420300* 🖷 *08/50420301* ⊕ *www.uto-vardshus.se* ⇋ *75 rooms with-*

out bath △ Restaurant, bar, no-smoking rooms, sauna ⊟ AE, DC, MC, V ⋈ BP.

¢ ⌑ **Rum i Backen.** This pretty, early-20th-century wooden house on Vax-
Fodor'sChoice holm's main street is a charming B&B. It's run by a family that is more
★ than happy to help you with anything you need. There's just one room,
but as it's in an annex to the house, it's a sort of self-contained apartment, with a shower, kitchen, and small veranda. The breakfast, which
you make yourself, is included. ⊠ *Kungsg. 14, 185 34 Vaxholm* ☎ *08/
314021* ⊞ *08/54133315* ⇥ *1 room* ⊟ *No credit cards* ⋈ *CP.*

Sports & the Outdoors

A visit to the islands is one of the best opportunities in Sweden you'll get
to take a bracing swim in the fresh, clean waters of the Baltic sea. Sometimes surprisingly warm, mostly heart-racingly chilly, but always memorable, a quick dip in these waters will set you up for the day. There are
literally thousands of great swimming spots, but Sandhamn and Utö have
the sandy beaches and rocky outcrops that keep them among the best.

Vaxholm & the Archipelago A to Z

*To research prices, get advice from other travelers, and book travel ar-
rangements, visit www.fodors.com.*

BOAT & FERRY Regular ferry services to the archipelago depart from Strömkajen, the
TRAVEL quayside in front of Stockholm's Grand Hotel. Boat cruises leave from
the harbor in front of the Royal Palace or from Nybrokajen, across the
road from the Royal Dramatic Theater. Ferries to the Feather Islands
run almost constantly all day long in the summer (Apr. 29–Sept. 17),
from Slussen, Strömkajen, and Nybroplan. Contact Strömma Kanalbolaget, Waxholmsbolaget, or Fjäderholmarna.

An excellent way to see the archipelago is to purchase an **Inter Skerries
Card,** which costs 250 SKr and allows unlimited boat travel throughout the islands for 16 days. Use the card for day trips from Stockholm,
or go out for longer excursions and bounce around from island to island. You can also purchase the **See Sea Card,** which costs 440 SKr and
allows unlimited travel in Stockholm, Åland, and the Åbo (Finland)
archipelago. Both cards are available at the tourist center at the Stockholm Information Service.

🚢 **Fjäderholmarna** ☎ 08/7180100. **Stockholm Information Service** ⊠ Sweden House,
Hamng. 27, Box 7542, 103 93 Stockholm ☎ 08/7892490. **Strömma Kanalbolaget** ☎ 08/
58714000. **Waxholmsbolaget** ☎ 08/6795830.

TRAIN TRAVEL There are regular train services to Saltsjöbaden from Stockholm. The
journey takes about 20 minutes. To get to Trosa, take a 1-hour train
ride from Stockholm to Vagnhärad, where there is a bus waiting to take
the 10-minute trip to Trosa.
🚆 **Train information SJ** ☎ 0771/757575 ⊕ www.sj.se.

TOURS A great way to discover the remote, less visited parts of the archipelago
is to go out with Sandhamnsguiderna, a tour group that operates out
of Sandhamn. Experienced guides will take you on tailor-made excursions, in small or large groups, to explore the outer reaches of the deserted archipelago. A tour price depends on how many people go and
for how long.
🚢 **Fees & Schedules Sandhamnsguiderna** ☎ 08/6408040.

VISITOR The Vaxholms Turistbyrå (Vaxholm Tourist Office) is in a large kiosk
INFORMATION at the bus terminal, adjacent to the marina and ferry landing. Hours are
daily 10–5. Sandhamn Turistbyrå (Sandhamn Tourist Office) is in the
town center at Sandhamns Hamnservices. The Utö Turistbyrå (Utö

Tourist Bureau) is near the ferry landing. More information on Grinda is available from the Sweden House.

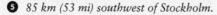 **Tourist Information Sandhamn Turistbyrå** ☎ 08/57153000 ⊕ www.varmdo.se. **Sweden House** ✉ Hamng. 27, Box 7542, 103 93 Stockholm ☎ 08/7892490. **Trosa Turistbyrå** ☎ 0156/52222 ⊕ www.trosa.com. **Utö Turistbyrå** ☎ 08/50157410. **Vaxholms Turistbyrå** ✉ Söderhamnen, 185 83 Vaxholm ☎ 08/54131480 ⊕ www.visitvaxholm.se.

Gotland

❺ *85 km (53 mi) southwest of Stockholm.*

Gotland is Sweden's main holiday island, a place of wide sandy beaches and wild cliff formations called *raukar*. Measuring 125 km (78 mi) long and 52 km (32 mi) at its widest point, Gotland is where Swedish sheep farming has its home. In its charming glades, 35 varieties of wild orchids thrive, attracting botanists from all over the world.

The first record of people living on Gotland dates from around 5000 BC. By the Iron Age it had become a leading Baltic trading center. When the German marauders arrived in the 13th century, they built most of its churches and established close trading ties with the Hanseatic League in Lübeck. They were followed by the Danes, and Gotland finally became part of Sweden in 1645.

Gotland's capital, **Visby,** is a delightful hilly town of about 20,000 people. Medieval houses, ruined fortifications, churches, and cottage-lined cobbled lanes make Visby look like a fairy-tale place. Thanks to a very gentle climate, the roses that grow along many of the town's facades bloom even in November.

In its heyday Visby was protected by a wall, of which 3 km (2 mi) survive today, along with 44 towers and numerous gateways. It is considered the best-preserved medieval city wall in Europe after that of Carcassonne, in southern France. Take a stroll to the north gate for an unsurpassed view of the wall.

Visby's cathedral, **St. Maria Kyrka,** is the only one of the town's 13 medieval churches that is still intact and in use. Built between 1190 and 1225 as a place of worship for the town's German parishioners, the church has few of its original fittings because of the extensive and sometimes clumsy restoration work done over the years. That said, the sandstone font and the unusually ugly angels decorating the pulpit are both original features worth a look.

Burmeisterska Huset, the home of the *Burmeister*—or principal German merchant—organizes exhibitions displaying the works of artists from the island and the rest of Sweden. Call the tourist office in Visby to arrange for viewing. ✉ *Strandg. 9* ☎ *No phone* 🎫 *Free.*

The **Fornsalen** (Fornsal Museum) contains examples of medieval artwork, prehistoric gravestones and skeletons, and silver hoards from Viking times. Be sure to also check out the ornate "picture stones" from AD 400–600, which depict ships, people, houses, and animals. ✉ *Mellang. 19* ☎ *0498/ 292700* 🎫 *SKr 30* 🕐 *Mid-May–Sept., daily 11–6; Oct.–mid-May, Tues.–Sun. noon–4.*

The **Visby Art Museum** has some innovative exhibitions of contemporary painting and sculpture. On the first floor is the permanent display, which is mostly uninspiring, save for a beautiful 1917 watercolor by local artist Axel Lindman showing Visby from the beach in all its splendid medieval glory. ✉ *St. Hansg. 21* 🎫 *SKr 30* 🕐 *May–Sept., daily 10–5.*

Medieval activities are re-created at **Kapitelhusgården.** Families can watch and take part in metal and woodworking skills, coin making, dressmaking, archery, and hunting. ⊠ *Drottensg. 8* ☎ *0498/292700* ☜ *SKr 40* ⊙ *June–Aug., daily noon–6.*

The 4 km (2½ mi) of stalactite caves at **Lummelunda,** about 18 km (11 mi) north of Visby on the coastal road, are unique in this part of the world and are worth visiting. The largest was discovered in 1950 by three boys out playing. ⊠ *Lummelunds Bruk* ☎ *0498/273050* ☜ *SKr 65* ⊙ *May–Sept., daily 9–5.*

A pleasant stop along the way to Lummelunda is the **Krusmyntagården** (☎ 0498/296900), a garden with more than 200 herbs, 8 km (5 mi) north of Visby.

The island has about 100 old churches dating from Gotland's great commercial era still in use. **Barlingbo,** from the 13th century, has vaulted paintings, stained-glass windows, and a remarkable 12th-century font. The exquisite **Dalhem** was constructed about 1200. **Gothem,** built during the 13th century, has a notable series of paintings of that period. **Grötlingbo** is a 14th-century church with stone sculptures and stained glass (note the 12th-century reliefs on the facade). **Öja,** a medieval church decorated with paintings, houses a famous holy rood from the late 13th century. The massive ruins of a Cistercian monastery founded in 1164 are now called the **Roma Kloster Kyrka** (Roma Cloister Church). **Tingstäde** is a mix of six buildings dating from 1169 to 1300.

Curious rock formations dot the coasts of Gotland, remnants of reefs formed more than 400 million years ago, and two **bird sanctuaries,** Stora and Lilla Karlsö, stand off the coast south of Visby. The bird population consists mainly of guillemots, which look like penguins. Visits to these sanctuaries are permitted only in the company of a recognized guide. ☎0498/241139 ☜ *SKr 180 for guided tour of both sanctuaries* ⊙ *May–Aug., daily.*

Where to Eat

$$ ╳ **Gutekällaren.** Despite the name, the Gotlander Cellar is aboveground in a 12th-century building. Mediterranean dishes, including fish and shellfish stew with coconut and lemongrass and fillet of lamb with a salad of red beets, asparagus, and Parmesan, are the draw. The striking interior includes primary-color leather chairs and coffee-color walls. ⊠ *Stora Torget 3* ☎ *0498/210043* ▤ *DC, MC.*

$–$$ ╳ **Clematis.** This campy restaurant is one of the most popular in Visby—guests are thrown back a few centuries to the Middle Ages for an authentic night of food, song, and dance. You get a flat slab of bread instead of a plate, and your only utensil is a knife. The staff dons period attire and is known to break into a tune while delivering food to tables. Traditional Swedish fare is served, with a focus on meats and island ingredients. Drinks are served in stone goblets. ⊠ *Strandg. 20* ☎ *0498/ 299690* ▤ *AE, DC, MC, V* ⊙ *No lunch.*

★ **$–$$** ╳ **Donners Brunn.** In a beautiful orange-brick house on a small square in Visby, the chef proprietor of this restaurant, Bo Nilsson, was once chef at the renowned Operakällaren in Stockholm. The menu uses excellent local ingredients to make French-influenced dishes that are reasonably priced, given their quality. The house specialty of Gotland lamb with fresh asparagus and hollandaise sauce is delicious. ⊠ *Donners Plats 3* ☎ *0498/271090* ⚭ *Reservations essential* ▤ *AE, DC, MC, V.*

$–$$ ╳ **Krusmyntagården.** This marvelous little garden-café opened in the late '70s and has been passed down through several owners. The garden now has more than 200 herbs and other plants, all of them grown organically. Most are used in such traditional Gotland dishes as tender grilled lamb (served on Tuesday and Thursday nights). ⊠ *Brissund* ☎ *0498/296900* ⊟ *AE, DC, MC, V.*

$–$$ ✕ **Björklunda Värdshuset.** This small restaurant in an old stone farmhouse is run by a husband-and-wife team. You can have an aperitif in the apple orchard before tucking into the menu of local salmon, lamb, and pork dishes, all of which come in ample proportions. ⊠ *Björklunda, Burgsvik* ☎ *0498/497190* ⊟ *AE, DC, MC, V.*

¢–$$ ✕ **Konstnärsgården.** Hans and Birgitta Belin run a wonderful establishment in the tiny village of Ala. He is an artist, she a chef. As you eat your lovingly prepared food in this old manor-house restaurant, you can view and buy works by Hans and other artists. The venison that's often on the menu comes from deer raised on the premises, and in the summer months whole lambs are spit-roasted outdoors in the orchard gardens. ⊠ *30 km (19 mi) southeast of Visby, Ala* ☎ *0498/55055* ⊟ *MC, V.*

Where to Stay

$–$$ ▦ **Strand Hotel.** An environmentally friendly hotel with efficient heating and cooling systems, the Strand may ease your conscience with its approach. In any case, the lap pool, sauna, and bright, comfortable rooms will ease your spirit. The clubby, relaxing bar has large leather sofas and a smoking area in an adjoining library. All things considered, the Strand is a good deal. ⊠ *Strandg. 34, 621 56* ☎ *0498/258800* 🖨 *0498/258811* ⊕ *www.strandhotel.net* ➷ *110 rooms, 2 with bath, 6 suites* ⌂ *Restaurant, bar, indoor lap pool, sauna* ⊟ *AE, DC, MC, V* ⍟ *BP.*

$–$$ ▦ **Wisby Hotell.** The tall, thin building that's now the Wisby dates from the 1200s and is at the junction of two narrow streets. A hotel since 1855, the ocher-color walls, light floral-patterned fabrics, dark wood, and vaulted ceilings give it old European grandeur. There are two excellent bars in the hotel, one a glassed-in courtyard that serves cocktails and the other a cozy pub with a good beer selection. ⊠ *Strandg. 6, 621 24* ☎ *0498/257500* 🖨 *0498/257550* ⊕ *www.wisbyhotell.se* ➷ *134 rooms, 94 with bath, 10 suites* ⌂ *Restaurant, 2 bars, no-smoking rooms* ⊟ *AE, DC, MC, V* ⍟ *BP.*

$ ▦ **Hotell Solhem.** A hotel that resembles a beach house, the Solhem offers wonderful views of Visby Harbor and the sea beyond. The rooms and public areas are small, but the hotel is very bright and simply furnished, making up for the lack of space. ⊠ *Solhemsg. 3, 621 58* ☎ *0498/259000* 🖨 *0498/259011* ➷ *94 rooms, 1 with bath* ⌂ *Bar, sauna* ⊟ *AE, DC, MC, V* ⍟ *BP.*

$ ▦ **Toftagården.** Nestled among the trees near the Gotland coast about 20 km (12 mi) from Visby, the placid verdant grounds here are ideal for strolling, lazing about, and reading in the shade. The long sandy beach in Tofta is also nearby, as is the Kronholmen Golf Course. Most of the brightly furnished rooms, all on the ground floor, have their own terrace. There are also a number of cottages with kitchens—a two-night minimum stay is required for these. If the seawater at the beach is too cold, take a dip in the outdoor heated pool. The restaurant serves very good regional fare. ⊠ *Toftagården, 621 98* ☎ *0498/297000* 🖨 *0498/265666* ➷ *50 rooms, 15 cottages* ⌂ *Restaurant, some kitchenettes, pool, sauna* ⊟ *AE, DC, MC, V* ⍟ *BP.*

¢ ▦ **Hotel St. Clemens.** Four buildings make up the St. Clemens, in Visby's Old Town. They range in age from a relatively young sixty-something years to about four centuries, dating to the 1600s. Rooms are simple and modern with private baths; some have small kitchens. There are two gardens on the property, one of which is shared with St. Clemens Church, one of Visby's oldest. ⊠ *Smedjeg. 3, 621 55* ☎ *0498/219000* 🖨 *0498/279443* ➷ *32 rooms* ⌂ *Breakfast room, some kitchenettes, sauna* ⊟ *AE, DC, MC, V* ⍟ *CP.*

¢ ☒ **Kronholmens Gård.** This charming little complex has its own small beach a short walk from Kronholmen's acclaimed 27-hole golf course. There are two cabins. One has four rooms, each with five small beds. Inside the other is a common kitchen and living room that all cabin guests share. For families hoping to save a little money that enjoy cooking for themselves, this is a great spot on the island. Weekly discounts are available. ☒ *Västergarn, 620 20 Klintehamn* ☎ *0498/245004* 🖷 *0498/ 245023* ☜ *1 4-bedroom cabin* ⚶ *Sauna* ⊟ *AE, DC, MC, V.*

★ ¢ ☒ **Villa Alskog.** A short drive from the sandy beaches to the south of Gotland, Villa Alskog is a delightful inn surrounded by beautiful open spaces, stone fences, and small groves of trees. The building dates to 1840 and was originally a residence for the local priest. Its 10 guest rooms are bright and simply furnished, with hardwood floors. Most have a private bath; when you reserve a room, verify that it's one that has its own bath. The location is ideal for swimming, hiking, and horseback riding. ☒ *620 16 Alskog* ☎ *0498/491188* 🖷 *0498/491120* ⊕ *www.villa-alskog.se* ☜ *10 rooms, 7 with bath* ⚶ *Restaurant, café, sauna, meeting room* ⊟ *AE, DC, MC, V* ⦿ *BP.*

Nightlife & the Arts

Medeltidsveckan (Medieval Week), celebrated in early August, is a citywide festival marking the invasion of the prosperous island by Danish king Valdemar on July 22, 1361. Celebrations begin with Valdemar's grand entrance parade and continue with jousts, an open-air market on Strandgatan, and street-theater performances re-creating the period.

In the ruins of **St. Nicolai,** the old dilapidated church in Visby, regular concerts are held throughout the summer months. Everything from folk to rock to classical is available. The tourist office has details.

There are many bars and drinking establishments on Gotland, but the best are in Visby. **Skeppet** (☒ Strandv. ☎ 0498/210710), a lively bar playing both live and recorded rock music, attracts a frantic young crowd.

Graceland (☎ 0498/215500) is on a boat moored in Visby's harbor. As the name suggests, it's a magnet for Elvis fans. The 35-and-over crowd fills its Priscilla Bar and dances to the King's finest until 2 AM.

Sports & the Outdoors

Bicycles, tents, and camping equipment can be rented from **Gotlands Cykeluthyrning** (☒Skeppsbron 2 ☎0498/214133 ⊕www.gotlandscykeluthyrning. com). **Gotlandsleden** is a 200-km (120-mi) bicycle route around the island; contact the tourist office for details.

For an aquatic adventure, **Gotlands Havskajakcenter** (☎ 0498/223012 ▨ Kr 150 for three hours) will rent you a canoe and a life jacket from its center at Valleviken, on the northeast coast of the island. From here you can explore the 15 uninhabited islands nearby. Many have beautiful rock formations.

If you do nothing else on Gotland, go for a swim. The island has miles and miles of beautiful golden beaches and unusually warm water for this part of the world. The best and least-crowded beaches are at Fårö and Själsö to the north of the island.

Shopping

Barbro Sandell (☒ Längsv. 146, Norrlanda ☎ 0498/39075) is a bright shop with one of the island's best selections of fabrics printed with local patterns.

G.A.D (Good Art and Design; ☒ Södra Kyrkog. 16 ☎ 0498/249410) sells stunningly simple modern furniture that has been designed and made on Gotland. Just as at its shop in Stockholm, the firm sells high-end pieces with a cosmopolitan flair.

Gotland A to Z

To research prices, get advice from other travelers, and book travel arrangements, visit www.fodors.com.

BOAT & FERRY TRAVEL Car ferries sail from Nynäshamn, a small port on the Baltic an hour by car or rail from Stockholm; commuter trains leave regularly from Stockholm's central station for Nynäshamn. Ferries depart at 11:30 AM year-round. From June through mid-August there's an additional ferry at 12:30 PM. A fast ferry operates from mid-April until mid-September, departing three times a day. The regular ferry takes about five hours; the fast ferry takes 2½ hours. Boats also leave from Oskarshamn, farther down the Swedish coast and closer to Gotland by about an hour. Call Gotland City Travel for more information.

🚢 **Gotland City Travel** ⊠ Kungsg. 57 ☎ 08/4061500 ⊠ Nynäshamn ☎ 08/5206400 ⊠ Visby ☎ 0498/247065.

CAR RENTAL 🚗 Agencies **Biltjänst** ⊠ Endrev. 45, Visby ☎ 0498/218790. **Budget** ⊠ Visby ☎ 0498/279396.

CONTACTS & RESOURCES 🏥 Doctors & Dentists **Visby Hospital** ☎ 0498/268009.

TOURS Guided tours of the island and Visby, the capital, are available in English by arrangement with the tourist office.

VISITOR INFORMATION The main tourist office is *Gotlands Turistförening* (Gottland Tourist Association) in Visby. Gotlands Turistservice at Österport in Visby is a private tour operator. They can help you plan trips in the region. You can also contact Gotland City Travel in Stockholm for lodging or ferry reservations.

ℹ️ Tourist Information **Gotland City Travel** ☎ 08/4061500. **Gotlands Turistförening** ⊠ Hamngatan 4 Visby ☎ 0498/201700 ⊕ www.gotland.info. **Gotlands Turistservice** ⊠ Österväg 3A Visby ☎ 0498/203300 ⊕ www.gotlandsturistservice.com.

Uppsala

❻ *67 km (41 mi) north of Stockholm.*

Sweden's principal university, Uppsala has only one rival for the title: Lund, to the south. August Strindberg, the nation's leading dramatist, studied here—and by all accounts hated the place. Ingmar Bergman, his modern heir, was born in town. It is also a historic site where pagan (and extremely gory) Viking ceremonies persisted into the 11th century. Uppsala University, one of the oldest and most highly respected institutions in Europe, was established in 1477 by Archbishop Jakob Ulfson. As late as the 16th century nationwide *tings* (early parliaments) were convened here. Today it is a quiet home for about 170,000 people. Built along the banks of the Fyris River, the town has a pleasant jumble of old buildings that is dominated by its cathedral, which dates from the early 13th century.

The last day of April never fails to make the town become one big carnival—the Feast of Valborg. To celebrate the arrival of spring (and the end of the school year), students of the university don sailorlike hats and charge down the hill from the university library (try not to get in their way). The university chorus then sings traditional spring songs on the steps of the main building. And finally the whole town slips into mayhem. Thousands descend on the city as the streets are awash in champagne and celebrations. It's an age-old custom worth seeing, but it's not for the fainthearted.

Ideally you should start your visit with a trip to **Gamla Uppsala** (Old Uppsala), 5 km (3 mi) north of the town. Here under three huge mounds lie the graves of the first Swedish kings—Aun, Egil, and Adils—of the 6th-century Ynglinga dynasty. Close by in pagan times was a sacred grove containing a legendary oak from whose branches animal and human sacrifices were hung. By the 10th century Christianity had eliminated such practices. A small church, which was the seat of Sweden's first archbishop, was built on the site of a former pagan temple.

Today the archbishopric is in Uppsala itself, and **Gamla Uppsala Kyrka,** the former seat, is largely kept up for the benefit of tourists. The whitewashed walls and simple rows of enclosed wooden pews make the church plain but calming. The tomb of Anders Celsius, the inventor of the temperature scale that bears his name, and some faded panels depicting the life of St. Erik are about the only other thing to look at inside.

need a break? To sample a mead brewed from a 14th-century recipe, stop at the **Odinsborg Restaurant** (☎ 018/323525), near the Gamla Uppsala burial mounds.

The Gamla Uppsala **Historiskt Center** (Historical Center) contains exhibits and archaeological findings from the Viking burial mounds that dominate the local area. The museum distinguishes between the myth and legends about the area and what is actually known about its history. Next to Gamla Uppsala Church, the ultramodern building made of wood and copper will change color as it ages. Its aggressive design inspires either admiration or dislike among Uppsala's populace. ☎ 018/239300 ✉ SKr 50 ☉ May–Sept., daily 11–6; Oct.–Apr., Tues.–Sun. 10–5.

★ Back in Uppsala, your first visit should be to **Uppsala Domkyrka** (Uppsala Cathedral). Its 362-foot twin towers—whose height equals the length of the nave—dominate the city. Work on the cathedral began in the early 13th century; it was consecrated in 1435 and restored between 1885 and 1893. Still the seat of Sweden's archbishop, the cathedral is also the site of the tomb of Gustav Vasa, the king who established Sweden's independence in the 16th century. Inside is a silver casket containing the relics of St. Erik, Sweden's patron saint. ☎ 018/187177 ⊕ www. uppsalacathedral.com ✉ Free ☉ Daily 8–6.

The **Domkyrka Museet,** in the north tower, has arts and crafts, church vestments, and church vessels on display. ☎ 018/187177 ✉ SKr 20 ☉ May–Aug., daily 9–5; Sept.–Apr., Sun. 12:30–3.

Gustav Vasa began work on **Uppsala Slott** (Uppsala Castle) in the 1540s. He intended the building to symbolize the dominance of the monarchy over the church. It was completed under Queen Christina nearly a century later. Students gather here every April 30 to celebrate the Feast of Valborg and optimistically greet the arrival of spring. Call the tourist center for information. ✉ Ingång C, 75310 Uppsala ⊕ www.uppsalaslott. com ✉ Castle SKr 60 ☉ Guided tours of castle mid-Apr.–Sept., daily at 11 and 2; Oct.–mid-Apr., weekdays at 11 and 2, weekends at 10, 11, 2, and 3.

In the excavated Uppsala Slott ruins, the **Vasa Vignettes,** scenes from the 16th century, are portrayed with effigies, costumes, light, and sound effects. ✉ SKr 40 ☉ Mid-Apr.–Aug., daily 11–4; Sept., weekends 10–5.

One of Uppsala's most famous sons, Carl von Linné, also known as Linnaeus, was a professor of botany at the university during the 1740s. He created the Latin nomenclature system for plants and animals. The

VALBORG EVE

THE STREETS OF THE ANCIENT UNIVERSITY TOWN OF UPPSALA are awash with humanity. Across the urban landscapes the people stream, apparently without aim. There is joy in the air and beer on the doorsteps. It is April 30, the day of Valborg Eve. Summer is on the cusp, and this is a contemporary interpretation of the traditional mass in honor of St. Valborg, the daughter of an Anglo-Saxon king and a nun who lived from 710 to 799. Near Willibald and Wunnibald in Germany she became mother superior to a monastery founded by her brothers; she was considered a spirit of God on earth.

Such noble origins are far from the minds of the masses today. Revelry is the theme. The day begins early with champagne breakfasts, and by midday the park outside one of Europe's oldest universities, founded in 1477, is crowded with picnickers. Most are adorned in their (high school) graduation caps, and all are full of whiskey and song. The chancellor gives his speech. The choirs sing. Like a shotgun spray, the people disperse to the parks. Everything feels possible today.

Although Valborg has religious roots, its meaning has evolved over the centuries. From something that centered on the village church, it has developed into an event with an agrarian theme. In these harsh climes the farmers and their families would shrug their cares away and feel the release from the long winter. The sun shone, the animals were out of their barns, and the fields were being planted. The cycle of nature had begun again. It is a moment very closely linked to the seasons, to which the Swedes, not surprisingly, are very sensitive, given their trying winters.

One of the great rituals of Valborg Eve is the night bonfire. It owes its origins not to God but to paganism and stems from the terrible otherworldly fears that people then held, surely metaphoric tales that encoded the tribulations of the human condition. The bonfire was believed to deliver protection from the spiritual realm. It was said to haunt the evil spirits themselves and chase away dangerous animals. Today it is, in a sense, a time in which people destroy the results of their spring cleaning. All the collected rubbish and pruned trees are used to build the pile, which is then torched.

Those who have shown great stamina or restraint during the day will be present at the huge bonfire that sparkles to the heavens and lights the night. It is a big social occasion, accompanied by the traditional foods herring and schnapps. Here you, too, can fly like an eagle on the wings of collective elation. Valborg in Uppsala is one of the most extraordinary events of unshackled human release that I have ever seen. It may not be the Rio carnival, but Uppsala is not Brazil, either, and the Swedish will always have their own ways.

Linné Museum is dedicated to his life and works. ⊠ *Svartbäcksg. 27* ☎ *018/136540* 🖃 *SKr 20* ☉ *Late May and early Sept., weekends noon–4; June–Aug., Tues.–Sun. 1–4.*

The botanical treasures of Linnaeus's old garden have been re-created and are now on view in **Linnéträdgården.** The garden's orangery houses a pleasant cafeteria and is used for concerts and cultural events. ⊠ *Svartbäcksg. 27* ☎ *018/109490* 🖃 *SKr 25* ☉ *May–Aug., daily 9–9; Sept.–Apr., daily 9–7.*

Uppsala Universitetet (Uppsala University; ☎ 018/4710000 ⊕ www.uu.se), founded in 1477, is known for the **Carolina Rediviva** university library, which contains a copy of every book published in Sweden, in addition to a large collection of foreign works. Two of its most interesting exhibits are the *Codex Argentus,* a Bible written in the 6th century, and Mozart's original manuscript for his 1791 opera *The Magic Flute.*

Completed in 1625, the **Gustavianum,** which served as the university's main building for two centuries, is easy to spot by its remarkable copper cupola, now green with age. The building houses the ancient anatomical theater—one of only seven in the world to function on natural light—where human anatomy lectures and public dissections took place. The Victoria Museum of Egyptian Antiquities is in the same building. ⊠ *Akademig. 3* ☎ *018/4717571* 🖃 *SKr 40* ☉ *June–Aug., daily 11–3; Anatomical Theater June–Aug., daily 11–3; Sept.–May, weekends noon–3.*

Where to Stay & Eat

$$–$$$ ✕ **Domtrappkällaren.** In a 14th-century cellar near the cathedral, Domtrappkällaren serves excellent French and Swedish cuisines. Game is the specialty, and the salmon and reindeer are delectable. ⊠ *Sankt Eriksgränd 15* ☎ *018/130955* ⚑ *Reservations essential* 🖃 *AE, DC, MC, V.*

$–$$ ✕ **Hambergs Fisk.** As the name suggests, this is a fish restaurant, the one slightly odd concession to nonfish eaters being several dishes made from goose liver. After sampling the wonderful menu you can head to the in-house deli counter to bring away fresh fish, pâtés, and other fine foods. ⊠ *Fyris Torg 8* ☎ *018/710050* 🖃 *AE, DC, MC, V.*

¢–$$ ✕ **Katalin.** You can eat and watch the trains rattle by in this converted warehouse behind the main station. Just as the interior is simple and modern, Katalin serves classic versions of such Swedish favorites as salmon and meatballs. There is often a jazz band in the evenings, and on weekends the bar is one of the most popular in town. ⊠ *Östra Station* ☎ *018/140680* 🖃 *AE, DC, MC, V.*

¢–$ ✕ **Al Harem.** Authentic cushion seating, ornate gilded arches, vibrant purples and golds, and even a belly dancer add an authentic eastern touch to the delicious Lebanese food at Al Harem. Beef and chicken dishes are a highlight, complimented by flavors of garlic, parsley, olive oil, and chickpeas. ⊠ *Kungsg. 25* ☎ *018/100903* 🖃 *AE, DC, MC, V.*

¢ ✕ **Café Alma.** A huge hit with local students, this lunch-only restaurant is in the basement of the main university building. The delicious and varied buffet (SKr 60) is overflowing with soups, salads, quiche, and bread. Everything's made in-house by the two wonderfully friendly owners. No à la carte is offered. ⊠ *Övre Slottsg.* ☎ *018/4712330* 🖃 *MC, V* ☉ *No dinner.*

$–$$$ 🏨 **Gillet.** Operated by the Radisson SAS group, Uppsala's largest hotel first opened in 1971. Rooms are bright and large, with pleasant watercolors, soft furnishings, and hardwood floors. The hotel is only a short walk from Uppsala's most famous buildings. The public areas are a little bland and standardized, but very comfortable. ⊠ *Dragarbrunnsg. 23, 751 42* ☎ *018/681800* 🖨 *018/681818* ⊕ *www.radissonsas.com* ➳ *160 rooms, 48 with bath* ♨ *2 restaurants, pool* 🖃 *AE, DC, MC, V* ⦿ *BP.*

$–$$ ⊞ **Grand Hotel Hörnan.** A castlelike creation from 1906, the Hörnan's city-center location means that it's near the train station and has views of both the castle and the cathedral. The rooms are spacious and have antique furnishings and soft lighting. ⊠ *Bandgårdsg. 1, 753 20* ☎ *018/139380* 🖨 *018/120311* ⊕ *www.eklundshof.se* 🛏 *37 rooms* ☰ *AE, DC, MC, V* ⏏ *BP.*

$ ⊞ **Scandic Hotel Uplandia.** This branch of the giant Nordic chain has the usual modern comforts and high-tech amenities expected of an international business hotel. There's also the pleasing design that's found in the best Scandinavian hotels. Blond wood accented with moss-green and aquamarine fabrics gives the decor a sophisticated edge. ⊠ *Dragarbrunnsg. 32, 751 40* ☎ *018/4952600* 🖨 *018/4952611* ⊕ *www.scandic. se* 🛏 *133 rooms, 93 with bath, 2 suites* ⚒ *Restaurant, bar, in-room data ports, no-smoking rooms, room service, sauna, meeting rooms* ☰ *AE, DC, MC, V* ⏏ *BP.*

¢ ⊞ **First Hotel Linné.** The namesake of this white-stone town-house hotel with lush gardens is the botanist Linnaeus (Carl von Linné). The hotel's interior is in harmony with the gardens outside: soft floral prints and warm reds dominate. In winter, a huge open fire is lighted. Rooms are done in a bright, modern Scandinavian design, with earth and red tones. Most of the floors and furniture are made of wood. ⊠ *Skolg. 45, 750 02* ☎ *018/102000* 🖨 *018/137597* ⊕ *www.firsthotels.com* 🛏 *116 rooms, 28 with bath, 6 suites* ⚒ *Restaurant, bar, minibars, no-smoking rooms, sauna* ☰ *AE, DC, MC, V* ⏏ *BP.*

Nightlife & the Arts

Svenssons (⊠ Sysslomansg. 15 ☎ 018/553310) is Uppsala's most popular nightspot. The two-floor building houses a bar, a restaurant, and a nightclub. The restaurant is nothing to speak of. But after 9, when food is no longer being served, on come the '80s tunes and out comes the roulette table. Downstairs are two more bars, with loads of chrome, mirrors, and people, all of them gyrating to contemporary dance music. Arrive early to avoid lines. For a relaxed evening head to **Alex Vinbar** (⊠ Skolg. 45 ☎ 018/102000), a dark, comfortable wine bar that sells many wines by the glass and plays mainly jazz. **Uppsala Stadsteater** (town theater; ⊠ Kungsg. 53 ☎ 018/160300) is a local theater known for its high-quality productions, many directly from Stockholm and a fair number in English.

Shopping

★ **Jaber** (⊠ Fyris Torg 6 ☎ 018/135050) is something of a draw for the area's wealthy elite. It is a family-run clothes shop with a line of gorgeous international designs, matched only by the personal service it provides. **Trolltyg** (⊠ Östra Åg. 25 ☎ 018/146304) has an exclusive selection of the sort of clean-line clothes and household furnishings for which Scandinavian design is known. The shop is wonderfully laid out and is a joy to explore, especially the fabrics section. Out in Old Uppsala, **Gamla Uppsala Keramik** (Gamla Uppsala Pottery; ⊠ Ulva Kvam ☎ 018/322060) makes all its own pottery and china, much of it with ancient local designs from Viking graves and stone carvings.

Uppsala A to Z

To research prices, get advice from other travelers, and book travel arrangements, visit www.fodors.com.

TRAIN TRAVEL

Trains between Stockholm and Uppsala run twice hourly throughout the day all year-round. The cost of a one-way trip is SKr 75. For timetables and train information contact SJ.

🚋 **SJ** ☎ 0771/757575 ⊕ www.sj.se.

SIGHTSEEING TOURS

You can explore Uppsala easily on your own, but English-language guided group tours can be arranged through the Uppsala Guide Service. ⓘ **Uppsala Guide Service** ☎ 018/7274818.

VISITOR
INFORMATION

The main tourist office run by the Uppsala Convention and Visitors Bureau is in the town center; in summer a small tourist information office is also open at Uppsala Castle.

ⓘ Tourist Information **Main Tourist Office** ✉ Fyris Torg 8 ☎ 018/7274800 ⊕ www. uppland.nu. **Information Office at Uppsala Castle** ☎ 018/554566.

THE BOTHNIAN COAST

3

FODOR'S CHOICE
Skellefteå Landskyrka (Skellefteå County Church), *Gävle*
Hotel Winn, *Gävle*

HIGHLY RECOMMENDED
Elite Hotel Knaust, *Gävle*
Gefle Design Forum, *Gävle*
Johansson's, *restaurant in Gävle*
Restaurang Grankotten, *restaurant in Gävle*

INDENTED WITH SHIMMERING FJORDS, peppered with pine-clad islands, and lined with sheer cliffs, the Bothnian Coast is a dramatic sliver of land on Sweden's east coast.

Its history and prosperity come from the sea and the forest. This is as true of the grand 19th-century stone houses built from the profits of international sea trading and the paper industry as it is of the ancient fishing villages, which are now used mainly as holiday homes for urban Swedes. The Bothnian Coast has both kinds of dwellings in abundance. In the north of the region you can see traces of the religious fervor that took hold in past centuries, evident in the small religious communities and the many ancient, well-preserved churches and artifacts in towns such as Umeå and Skellefteå.

Many of the original wood cottages that dotted this coastline have been destroyed by fires over the years. The worst damage, caused by Russia's many incursions through the area in the 18th century, prompted many of the towns along the coast to rebuild themselves in grand styles more befitting a capital than a local fishing town. Aided by the burgeoning shipping trade in the 1800s, port towns such as Gävle, Sundsvall, and Umeå created cities of wide boulevards, huge central squares, and monumental stone buildings partly to discourage future fires from spreading.

Exploring the Bothnian Coast

Traveling up the Bothnian Coast is a simple task, mostly involving a single road or railway track. All the major towns are on the coast and are relatively evenly spread, making it easier for you to plan your rests. The coastline is rocky and rugged in places and is bordered by the beautiful forests and lakes of Hälsingland. By car, the E4 highway quickly eats up the miles, and takes in all the major sights. By train, the coastal line that links Stockholm to the north of Sweden does the same.

About the Hotels & Restaurants

You have to pick and chose your restaurants carefully along the Bothnian Coast. Much of the remoteness that makes the area attractive has also created some rather mediocre dining spots. The region's past riches, fueled by fishing and forestry, have left many grand-looking restaurants with a much vaunted past. But looks can be deceiving and it is always a good idea to check out the menu and any independent reviews before you sit down to dinner.

Food along the Bothnian Coast is, not surprisingly, heavy on fish. Deliciously fresh and oily herrings and piquant smoked fish are a particular specialty. If you are looking for some interesting international flavors, stick to the big cities. The delight of an area such as this is the chance to sample some good local flavor. Restaurants are rarely busy along the Bothnian Coast, and most can be booked the day before or even on the day of your visit.

The rules for restaurants along Sweden's east coast can equally be applied to hotels. The many stone monoliths that dot the landscape, often christened with grand names, can all too often be just relics of the past; faded grandeur offset by tired furnishings. It is usually best to stick to the big chain hotels or the small, privately run guesthouses and B&Bs.

Outside of the major towns many of the hotels here run on a skeleton staff, so don't always expect room service or even a hotel restaurant. It is always a good idea to call ahead to check first.

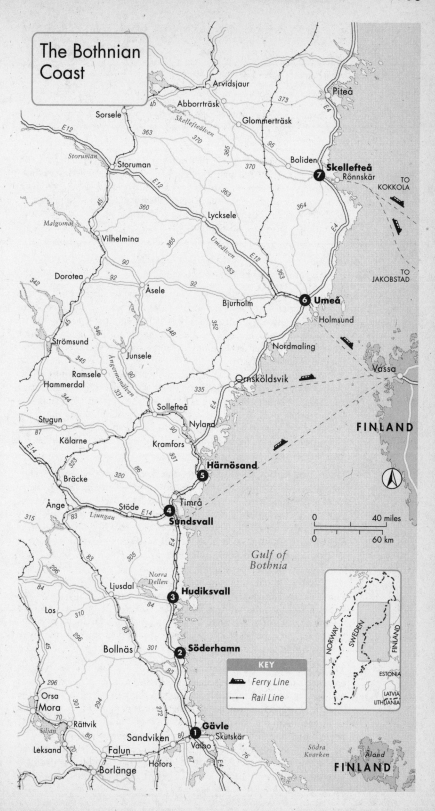

The Bothnian
Coast

Arvidsjaur

Piteå

Sorsele

Abborrträsk

45

373

E4

Glommerträsk

E12

363

Skellefteälven

370

365

95

Boliden

Skellefteå ⑦

Storuman

E12

370

Rönnskär

TO
KOKKOLA

Storuman

360

363

364

Lycksele

E4

TO
JAKOBSTAD

Vilhelmina

365

Umeälven

E12

45

Malgomaj

Dorotea

92

90

353

363

Åsele

92

Umeå ⑥

Bjurholm

Holmsund

352

Strömsund

346

348

Nordmaling

Junsele

Vassa

Ramsele

345

Ångermanälven

90

331

Örnsköldsvik

Hammerdal

344

335

Stugun

Sollefteå

FINLAND

87

90

Nyland

Kälarne

323

Kramfors

331

E14

Bräcke

320

96

Härnösand ⑤

Ånge

Stöde

Ljungan

Timrå

315

83

E14

Sundsvall ④

83

305

E4

Gulf of
Bothnia

296

84

Norra
Dellen

Ljusdal

Hudiksvall ③

0   40 miles

0   60 km

Los

310

84

45

296

83

Söderhamn ②

Bollnäs

301

296

Orsa

301

294

63

Gävle ①

Mora

70

Rättvik

Valbo

Skutskär

Siljan

80

Leksand

70

Sandviken

80

Falun

272

Hofors

67

76

E4

Borlänge

Södra
Kvarken

Åland

FINLAND

KEY

⛴ *Ferry Line*

⊢⊣ *Rail Line*

NORWAY   SWEDEN   FINLAND

ESTONIA

LATVIA
LITHUANIA

	$$$$	$$$	$$	$	¢
WHAT IT COSTS In Swedish Kronor					
RESTAURANTS	over 420	250–420	150–250	100–150	under 100
HOTELS	over 2,900	2,300–2,900	1,500–2,300	1,000–1,500	under 1,000

Restaurant prices are for a main course at dinner. Hotel prices are for two people in a standard double room in high season.

Timing

Like much of coastal Sweden, the Bothnian Coast is a harsh place to be in the winter months. This leaves the high season of mid-May to mid-September as the best time to visit. This is the time of year when most of the attractions in the region are open and when the Baltic Sea becomes approachable for boat traffic. Many museums close on Mondays and some of the shops in smaller towns have half-day closing on Saturdays.

Gävle

❶ *180 km (111 mi) north of Stockholm (via E4).*

Gävle, the capital of the county (*land* in Swedish) Gästrikland, is considered by many Swedes a gateway to the northern wildernesses. The town was granted its charter in 1446. This great age is not evident in the mix of grand 19th-century boulevards and parks and modern, bland shopping centers that make up much of the small downtown area. The original town was destroyed in a great fire in the mid-1800s, and the only part that survives today is the small enclave that lay south of the river, a watery barrier that kept the flames at bay. The grand architectural style of much of the town reflects the wealth it once enjoyed as a major trading port. Today it is better known as home of Gevalia, Sweden's largest coffee producer, which is quite evident on the days the town is filled with the delicious aroma of roasting beans drifting from the factory chimneys.

The **Joe Hill Museet,** dedicated to the Swedish emigrant who went on to become America's first well-known protest singer and union organizer, is in Hill's former home in the oldest section of Gävle. Once a poor working-class district, this is now the most highly sought-after residential part of town, with art studios and crafts workshops nearby. The museum—furnished in the same style as when Hill lived there—contains very few of his possessions but does display his prison letters. The house itself bears witness to the poor conditions that forced so many Swedes to emigrate to the United States (estimated to be between 850,000 and 1 million between 1840 and 1900). Hill, who was born Joel Hägglund, was a founder of the International Workers of the World and was executed for the murder of a Salt Lake City grocer in 1914. He maintained his innocence, an opinion shared by many, right up to the end. ⊠ *Nedre Bergsg. 28* ☎ *026/613425* 🖅 *Free* ⏰ *June–Aug., daily 11–3.*

The **Skogsmuseet Silvanum** (Silvanum Forestry Museum) is on the west end of town, by the river. Silvanum, Latin for "forest," was inaugurated in 1961; it was the first such museum in the world and is one of the largest. The museum provides an in-depth picture of the forestry industry in Sweden, still the backbone of the country's industrial wealth: trees cover more than 50% of Sweden, and forest products account for 20% of national exports. Silvanum includes a forest botanical park and an arboretum that contains an example of every tree and bush growing in Sweden. ⊠ *Kungsbäcksv. 32* ☎ *026/614100* 🖅 *Free* ⏰ *Tues. 10–2, Wed. 10–7, Thurs.–Fri. 10–4, weekends 1–5.*

For a glimpse of Gävle's past, go to the **Länsmuseet** (County Museum). Inside this impressive redbrick building is a museum celebrating the history of the town and area. On the ground floor are changing exhibits on local artists and photographers. Upstairs there are old farm implements, clothes, and re-creations of local house interiors that extend from the 12th century to the 1930s. The largest part of the museum is dedicated to the town's maritime history and includes model ships as well as trinkets and treasures brought back from sea voyages long ago. ⊠ *Strandg. 20* ☎ *026/655635* ✍ *SKr 40* ☉ *Tues.–Sun. noon–4.*

Housed in what used to be the local train storage shed, the **Sveriges Järnvägsmuseum** (Swedish Railway Museum) has many different engines and coach cars on display. The royal hunting car from 1859 is thought to be the world's oldest. ⊠ *Rälsg. 1* ☎ *026/106448* ✍ *SKr 40* ☉ *Tues.–Sun. 10–4.*

Where to Stay & Eat

★ **$–$$** ✕ **Johansson's.** Delicious local fish dishes and an extensive wine list make this restaurant in Gävle a real treat. The interior of dark wood and white tablecloths appears somewhat flat and sober at first, but the warm, friendly staff and elegant service will add a brighter dimension to your dining experience. ⊠ *Nyg. 7* ☎ *026/100734* 🚬 *AE, DC, MC, V.*

$–$$ ✕ **Söderhjelmska Gården.** This classic Swedish wooden house dates from 1773 and stands out from the rest of mostly modern Gävle. The interior, furnished in traditional white wood and blue linen, is split into the same small rooms that existed when it was still a residence. In summer you can also eat in the tree-lined garden. The traditional Swedish menu emphasizes fish. ⊠ *S. Kungsg. 23* ☎ *026/613393* ✍ *Reservations essential* 🚬 *AE, DC, MC, V.*

¢–$ ✕ **Järnvägsrestaurangen.** Very good daily lunch specials and a simple home-cooked selection in the evening are what the Railway Restaurant has to offer. The restaurant is in the old railway station building, which adjoins the current one. A large glass veranda in front is the perfect place to sit and watch Gävle go by. On weekend evenings the restaurant doubles as a lively bar and music venue. ⊠ *Stora Esplanadg.* ☎ *026/514495* 🚬 *AE, DC, MC, V.*

$ 🏨 **Hotel Winn.** What this hotel in the city center lacks in charm and design, it makes up for in facilities. Aimed at conventiongoers, the Winn has very large rooms with every convenience. The leisure facilities are also excellent. ⊠ *Norra Slottsg. 9, 801 38* ☎ *026/5958400* 🖨 *026/647009* ✍ *200 rooms, 6 suites, 20 rooms with bath* ✍ *Restaurant, bar, in-room data ports, in-room fax, in-room safes, minibars, no-smoking rooms, room service, indoor pool, sauna, gym, laundry service, concierge, meeting rooms, parking (fee)* 🚬 *AE, DC, MC, V.*

$ 🏨 **Scandic Hotel Grand.** Built in 1836, this is Gävle's best attempt to recreate the glories of yesteryear. Behind the imposing stone facade is an early-20th-century interior with some art deco features, including a sweeping lobby bar with huge chandeliers. The bedrooms are beginning to look a little worn, but they are comfortable and good-sized. ⊠ *Nyg. 45, 801 04* ☎ *026/129060* 🖨 *026/124499* ✍ *220 rooms, 95 with bath, 7 suites* ✍ *Restaurant, bar, sauna, gym, convention center* 🚬 *AE, DC, MC, V.*

Shopping

★ The beautiful furniture, clothes, and kitchenware at the **Gefle Design Forum** (⊠ Drottningg. 25 ☎ 026/188008) come from Stockholm Design House, the capital's well-known design group. It's also a good place to pick up fun gift items. For something classic, head to **Prylboden** (⊠ Norra Kungsg. 11 ☎ 026/189761) a small, friendly shop selling 19th- and 20th-century antiques, especially housewares. Drink trays, coffee cups, and large furniture pieces all vie to catch the attention of the nostalgic.

Nightlife & the Arts

In the small park between Norra Rådmansgatan and Norra Kungsgatan is the grand stone building that contains **Gävle Teatren** (Gävle Theater; ⊠ Norra Råmansg. 23 ☎ 026/129200). Its beautiful gilded auditorium was built in the late 1800s. Many of the plays it stages are in English. For a raucous night out, head to **O'Learys** (⊠ Södra Kungsg. 31 ☎ 026/652920), an Irish pub that's also a sports bar. Catch the latest soccer or baseball game while sampling some of the excellent beers available. Friday and Saturday nights the place becomes a disco and the most popular nightspot in town. **Heartbreak Hotel** (⊠ Norra Strandg. 15 ☎ 026/&183020) is a bar and nightclub with a 1950s American rock-and-roll theme. Memorabilia of Elvis and others is plastered on the walls. If you're lucky, you may catch one of the many Elvis impersonators who perform periodically.

Söderhamn

❷ *75 km (47 mi) north of Gävle (via E4).*

Söderhamn is a town with a lot of space. Besides the extensive open countryside that borders the town, the center is awash with parks, gardens, and wide boulevards. In summer Swedes come from all over to enjoy the pretty public spaces. The many trees help to remove air pollution, making sitting in an open-air café here exceptionally pleasing. The town's architecture is a mix of monumental 18th-century buildings, erected through fortunes made by fishing, and modern shopping precincts built to replace areas devastated by numerous fires. This coastal town is also close to one of the finest archipelagos in the region: more than 500 islands, islets, and skerries are near.

For stunning panoramic views of the town and the surrounding forest and sea, climb **Oscarborg**, a 75-foot tower at the edge of town. Built in 1895, the white tower and attached building resemble a Disney-esque fairy-tale castle.

Dating to the 1600s, **Smedjan** (Blacksmiths) is a living, working museum where you can watch craftsmen use traditional methods to make horseshoes and other items. ⊠ *Kungsgården* ☎ *027/035031* 🎫 *Free* ☉ *June–Aug., Mon. and Thurs. 2–8. All other times by appointment.*

Where to Stay & Eat

$–$$ ✕ **Restaurang Albertina.** This converted red wooden barn is on the water's edge, just north of Söderhamn, in the old fishing village of Skärså. Inside, scrubbed wooden walls and beamed ceilings blend with the crisp, white table linens. Fish is the specialty here. The locally caught salmon that they serve here is among the best in the region. ⊠ *Skärså* ☎ *027/032010* 🟰 *AE, MC, V.*

¢–$ ✕ **RådhusKonditoriet.** Inside an uninspiring building is a restaurant that doubles as one of the few photographic galleries in the north of Sweden. The gallery and the excellent selection of sandwiches, specialty teas, and light meals make it worth the trip. ⊠ *Kykog. 10* ☎ *027/012457* 🟰 *AE, MC, V* ☉ *Closed Sun.*

$–$$ 🏨 **First Hotell Statt.** The oldest hotel in town is also the most luxurious. All the rooms are individually furnished and have wooden floors and a comfortable mix of blond wood and pastel furnishings. The public areas have their original chandeliers, stucco-work ceilings, and large open fireplaces, giving the hotel a feel of old luxury. ⊠ *Oxtorgsg. 17, 826*

22 ☎ 027/073570 🖶 0270/13524 🛏 78 *rooms without bath* ⚿ *Restaurant, bar, sauna, nightclub, convention center* 🖃 *AE, DC, MC, V.*

¢ 🖵 **Centralhotellet.** As the name suggests, it's the central location that makes this hotel worth the stay. The rooms are quite dark and small, but are well furnished with antique-style fittings and wooden floors. ⊠ *Rådhustorget, 826 32* ☎ *027/070000* 🖶 *027/016060* 🛏 *13 rooms without bath* ⚿ *Restaurant, bar, nightclub* 🖃 *AE, DC, MC, V.*

Nightlife & the Arts

Inside the Folkets Hus (People's House), a 1950s building built for town gatherings, **Café August** (⊠ Rådhusparken ☎ 065/038450) is a lively nightspot. Although the building isn't glamorous, the interior has original paintings on the walls and a pleasingly quiet color scheme throughout. As night falls, the place comes alive with two floors of modern dance music, live bands, and an outdoor bar area for cooling off. **Pub Tre Bockar** (⊠ Bankgränd 1 ☎ 065/099994) is a traditional English pub. The dark-wood interior is jammed with people on weekend evenings. They all want to sample the live music, disco sound, and good beer.

The Outdoors

Söderhamn is the perfect place for a boat trip out to the nearby archipelago. The **MS *Sandskär*** (☎ 027/012254) is one of many boats that offer day trips with fishing and swimming. For an energetic inland-water adventure, there are myriad lakes and rivers around Söderhamn that are perfect for canoeing. For more information contact **Fritidskontoret** (leisure office; ☎ 027/075000).

Shopping

There are real bargains to be found at **Albert and Herbert** (⊠ Sannahedsv. 11 ☎ 065/017777), an outlet store that sells clothes, household items, and furniture. The range is huge, and the quality is excellent.

Hudiksvall

❸ *60 km (37 mi) north of Söderhamn via E4.*

Granted its town charter in 1582, Hudiksvall's history is bound up with the sea. Having been partially destroyed by fire 10 times, Hudiksvall is now an interesting mix of architectural styles. The small section of the old town that remains is built around a central harbor and contains some fine examples of flower-strewn courtyards and traditional wood-panel buildings built along narrow, cobbled streets.

The **Fiskarstan** (Fishertown; ☎ 065/019100 tourist office) neighborhood is tightly packed with striking streets of fishermen's huts and houses and boardwalks of wooden fish stores that hang precariously over the water. Lilla Kyrkogatan, the oldest street in town, leads to Hudiksvall's Church, which is still marked by cannonballs from a Russian invasion in 1721. Guided tours, maps, and information can be arranged through the town's tourist office.

Inside a former bank building in the middle of town, the **Hälsinglands Museum** offers insight into the development of Hudiksvall and the surrounding region. Furniture, house reconstructions, religious artifacts, local textiles, and art are all organized and displayed thoughtfully. It's a revealing picture of life in the area. ⊠ *Storg. 31* ☎ *065/019600* 🎫 *Free* 🕐 *Mon. noon–6, Tues.–Thurs. 9–4, weekends 11–3.*

Where to Stay & Eat

$–$$ ✕ **Bruns VS.** This very relaxed, informal restaurant offers a wildly diverse choice of foods, from traditional Swedish to Polynesian and beyond. There's a pub area, for those seeking only liquid refreshment, and in the summer there's a huge terrace for outside dining. ⊠ *Brunnsg. 2* ☎ *065/010402* ⊟ *AE, DC, MC, V.*

¢–$$ ✕ **Gretas Krog.** Built right by the fishing docks, this restaurant is rarely empty and seldom disappoints. The interior trades predictably on fishing history through sepia photographs of weather-beaten fishermen and old nets strung from the ceiling, but there is something undeniably cozy about it all. The menu is packed with good local specialties and traditional Swedish cuisine. ⊠ *Västra Tväkajen* ☎ *065/096600* ᴧ *Reservations essential.*

¢–$$ ▥ **First Hotell Statt.** From the outside the grand 19th-century yellow-stone facade of this hotel, with its pillars and arches, looks like a typical Swedish town hall. Once you've gone inside, the more familiar marble floor and pastel shades confirm that you have arrived at your hotel. Rooms here are nothing special; most are in need of redecoration. But the hotel is central. ⊠ *Storg. 36, SE-824 22* ☎ *065/015060* ᴧ *065/096095* ⌁ *106 rooms, 26 with bath, 8 suites* ᴧ *Restaurant, pub, pool, sauna, gym, nightclub, convention center* ⊟ *AE, DC, MC, V* ⌁◎⌁ *BP.*

Sports & the Outdoors

Hudiksvall's archipelago is centered around the peninsula of **Hornslandet**, just north of the town. As well as the usual fishing, swimming, and boating, the peninsula has Europe's second-largest system of mountain caves, which can be explored by experts and beginners alike. Call **Alf Siden** (☎065/070492), who arranges and conducts official tours of the caves.

Shopping

Slöjd i Sjöboden (⊠ Möljen ☎ 065/012041) is a series of old fishing huts now housing stalls where 15 local craftspeople sell their wares. Locally inspired textiles, jewelry, ceramics, and glassware can all be bought at very good prices.

Sundsvall

❹ *80 km (50 mi) north of Hudiksvall via E4.*

Sundsvall also goes by the name of *Stenstan* (Stone Town), and rightly so. When the town was razed by fire in 1888, it was rebuilt entirely out of stone, which is atypical for this part of Sweden. The reconstruction added more parks and widened roads to prevent later fires from spreading. Add to these Sundsvall's impressive limestone and brick buildings and it begins to resemble Sweden's largest cities, Stockholm and Göteborg.

The best place to get a feel for the city and its history is at the **Kulturmagasinet** (Culture Warehouse), a series of four 19th-century waterfront warehouses that now include a museum, library, archives, a children's culture center, art exhibitions, and street music. The museum, which traces the town's history, is built over an old street, where tram tracks and cobbles are still in place. It gives a good sense of what Sundsvall was like when it was still a busy trading port. ⊠ *Packhusg. 8* ☎ *060/191803* ⌁ *June–Aug. SKr 20, Sept.–May free* ☉ *Mon.–Thurs. 10–7, Fri. 10–6, weekends 11–4.*

Sundsvall is a good city to walk around, as most of the points of interest are woven into the streets, boulevards, and squares of **Storgatan and Stora Torget**. History comes to life here with churches, the town hall, and grand porticoed stone buildings all flexing their architectural muscles. Guided tours and maps can be arranged through the **tourist office** (☎ 060/610450).

Gustav Adolfs kyrka, at the far end of Storgatan, is Sundsvall's main church. In keeping with much of the city, it's a grand 19th-century affair that's built of red brick. There is a pleasing order about the interior, its vaults and pillars all constructed from smooth square stones that look like children's building blocks.

Where to Stay & Eat

★ **$$–$$$** ✕ **Restaurang Grankotten.** The food here, described as modern Swedish with a French influence, has won praise from all over. Dishes such as veal with truffles and anything that uses the delicious local elk are worth traveling for. The views of Sundsvall from the turn-of-the-19th-century building are stunning, especially if you dine outside in the summer. ✉ *Norra Stadsberget* ☎ *060/614222* ⌖ *Reservations essential* ⊟ *AE, DC, MC, V* ☉ *Closed Sun.*

$–$$ ✕ **Skeppsbrokällaren.** Classic Swedish design and furnishings and good Scandinavian cuisine are the main attractions at this quiet basement restaurant, on the site of the original boat entrance to the city. For a more calming dining experience book a table in the Röda Rummet (Red Room), a smaller, darkened dining area at the back of the restaurant. ✉ *Sjög. 4* ☎ *060/173660* ⌖ *Reservations essential* ⊟ *AE, DC, MC, V.*

★ **$–$$** ▥ **Elite Hotel Knaust.** The Knaust family opened this art nouveau hotel in 1860, and it has lost none of its original glory. The sweeping marble staircase and black-and-white-tile lobby is extraordinary and worth a look even if you are not staying. Comfort and luxury are watchwords in the rooms, which have warm, lush fabrics and artworks. The hotel is downtown, conveniently near Sundsvall's shops and other attractions. ✉ *Storg. 13, 85 105* ☎ *060/6080000* ▤ *060/6080010* ◁ *94 rooms, 4 suites* ⌂ *Restaurant, minibars, cable TV, in-room data ports, bar, gym, sauna, business services, convention center* ⊟ *AE, DC, MC, V* ¶Ⓞ *BP.*

$ ▥ **Comfort Hotel Sundsvall.** Grand stone arches and portals give an impression of stately luxury to this central hotel. The interior doesn't quite live up to the grand facade, but the rooms are large, comfortable, and individually furnished in earth and red tones and have wooden floors. ✉ *Sjög. 11, 852 34* ☎ *060/150720* ▤ *060/123456* ◁ *52 rooms, 3 with bath* ⌂ *Restaurant, cable TV, in-room data ports, bar, sauna, pool* ⊟ *AE, DC, MC, V.*

Nightlife & the Arts

Bars and pubs provide the best source of evening entertainment in Sundsvall. **Spegelbaren** (✉ Nybrog. 10 ☎ 060/156006), with its large mirrors, glass ceilings, and 19th-century paintings, is one of the best. If you have spare vacation money to use up, then head for **Casino Cosmopol** (✉ Södermalmsg. 7 ☎ 060/156289). Housed in the old railway station, built in 1875, it is Sweden's oldest international-style casino. The **Kulturmagasinet** (✉ Packhusg. 8 ☎ 060/191803) is a museum with art exhibitions (mostly of Swedish artists); a children's theater; and live music, readings, and debates.

Sports & the Outdoors

The nearby river of Ljungan is an excellent spot for rafting. Tours include one hour of white-water rafting, beautiful scenery, and lunch on a small island. Contact the tourist office (☎ 060/610450) for more information.

Shopping

Northern Sweden's largest shopping mall, **Ikano Huset,** is 8 km (5 mi) north of Sundsvall, along Route E4. There are shops of every type, from branches of large, internationally known companies such as IKEA to local handicraft stores. **Sköna Ting** (✉ Nybrog. 15 ☎ 060/170501), meaning "beautiful things," is a crafts store selling gifts and trinkets: dolls, linen and lace, and handblown glass. Everything is locally made and of good quality.

Härnösand

❺ *40 km (25 mi) north of Sundsvall via E4.*

Dating from 1585, Härnösand is a town rich in history. Narrow ancient streets lined with wood-panel houses contrast with 18th- and 19th-century boulevards and squares. The town has a long history as an administrative center for local government, a history hinted at in its orderly layout and infrastructure as well as in the grandness of its buildings. In the center of town is Sweden's smallest—and only—white cathedral.

With works by both Chagall and Matisse on display, **Härnösands Konsthall** is an art museum of considerable note. The museum has works by many of Sweden's prominent painters and sculptors and puts on around 20 exhibitions per year. ⊠ *Stora Torget 2* ☎ *061/1348142* ⊠ *Free* ⊙ *Tues.–Fri. 11–3, weekends noon–3.*

Länsmuseet Västernorrland is an excellent, well-thought-out history museum that covers Härnösand and the surrounding area. The museum also has one of the country's largest collections of weapons. ⊠ *Murberget* ☎ *061/188600* ⊠ *Free* ⊙ *Daily 11–5.*

Where to Stay & Eat

$–$$ ✕ **Spjutegåden.** Stark-white walls are broken up by small local paintings at this very traditional restaurant in a building from the early 1800s. The floor and ceiling are both made of white wood, and a huge, open fireplace makes the room cozy. The menu consists of very good traditional Swedish food with international touches. As in most Swedish restaurants, the fish dishes are delicious. ⊠ *Murberget* ☎ *061/1511090* ⊛ *Reservations essential* ☰ *AE, MC, V.*

¢–$ ✕ **Highlander.** At this Celtic-theme pub all the requisite details are in place—even a staff dressed in kilts. There are Irish beer and a good selection of wines. The food is hearty and filling, with lots of beef and other meat dishes on the menu. ⊠ *Nybrog. 5* ☎ *061/1511170* ☰ *AE, MC, V* ⊙ *Closed Sun.*

$–$$ ▥ **First Hotel.** Of the three hotels in Härnösand, this is the best choice. Large, functional rooms in cream, green, and purple all have wooden floors, armchairs, a desk, and generally very good views of the harbor. ⊠ *Skeppsbron 9, 871 30* ☎ *061/1554440* ⊟ *061/1554447* ⬳ *95 rooms, 7 suites* ⬧ *Restaurant, cable TV, bar, pub, sauna, gym, meeting room, no-smoking rooms* ☰ *AE, DC, MC, V.*

Nightlife & the Arts

The place to be seen in Härnösand is **Apothequet** (⊠ Köpmang. 5 ☎ 061/1511717), a nightclub and bar popular with those in their late twenties and thirties. Modern hits are mixed with classics in this darkened lounge. When you can dance no more, the bar does great cocktails.

Shopping

Hantverksboden (⊠ Järnvägsg. ☎ 061/116607) is an old wooden building next to the water where local craftsmen rent stalls to sell their wares. Silverware, jewelry, handicrafts, glassware, and pottery are all in abundance.

Umeå

❻ *225 km (140 mi) north of Härnösand (via E4).*

Built on the River Ume, Umeå is the largest city in northern Sweden. Because it's a university town with inhabitants whose average age is the youngest of anywhere in the country, there are many bars, restaurants, festivals, and cultural events to visit.

Aside from taking a walk around the city's open squares and wide boulevards, the best way to get to know Umeå is by visiting **Gammlia**, a series of museums that focus on the city and surrounding area. The open-air museum has a living village made up of farmhouses and working buildings. Actors in period costumes demonstrate how people lived hundreds of years ago. You can wander around amid farm animals of all kinds and learn about baking bread, preserving meat, and harvesting grain. There are also a church and historic gardens. The indoor museums, which have exhibitions on Umeå's history, consist of the fishing and maritime museum, the Swedish ski museum, and a modern art museum that shows work from major Swedish and international artists. A sort of intellectual theme park, it can take the better part of a day to see everything in Gammlia. ⊠ *Gammliav.* ☎ *090/171800* ⊠ *Free* ⊙ *Daily 10–5.*

off the beaten path

NORBYSKÄ – Around 1800 this island had Europe's largest sawmill, and an ambitious group of Swedes attempted to set up a utopian commune around this industry. The attempt at good living didn't work, and the commune broke up around 1830. However, much of what they built remains today as a monument to their dreams. By walking around the island you can see the remains of the houses, school, and work buildings the commune created. The island is also perfect for picnics, fishing, swimming, and safaris to view the local seal population. Norbyskä is a 15-minute boat trip from Umeå. For details and prices contact the **Umeå tourist office** (☎ 090/161616).

Where to Stay & Eat

$$ ✕ **Greta & Co.** Housed inside a somewhat indifferent hotel, Greta's is a must for those seeking out authentic regional specialties. Food from around northern Sweden is served in a dining room of simple, classic Swedish design. The reindeer, rabbit, and salmon are exceptional. ⊠ *Skolg. 62* ☎ *09/0100730* ⊟ *AE, DC, MC, V.*

$–$$ ✕ **Lottas Krog.** On the site of a former Italian bistro, this Swedish eating house has kept some of its Mediterranean feel. The food, though, is unashamedly local, with such classics as meatballs and salmon dishes. ⊠ *Nyg. 22* ☎ *090/129551* ⊟ *AE, DC, MC, V.*

¢–$ ✕ **Grottan.** This restaurant and bar is very popular with the local student population and comes alive at night. The dining room is pretty basic, with red-checked tablecloths and plain wood chairs, but the simple menu is well executed and full of café classics such as lasagna, beef bourguignonne, and steaks. ⊠ *Axtorpsv.* ☎ *090/779600* ⊟ *AE, DC, MC, V.*

$–$$ ▦ **Scandic Hotel Plaza.** A clean, modern glass-and-brick structure that dominates the city skyline, the Scandic is one of the most stylish hotels in the region. The huge open lobby has a staircase of marble and steel, copper-tone pillars, and tile floors. A lounge, restaurant, bistro, and bar all lead off from the lobby. At the very top of the hotel is a luxury health suite and spa, which has exceptional views of the city. Rooms are large, well equipped, and decorated in pastel shades. ⊠ *Storg. 40, 903 04* ☎ *090/ 2056300* 🖶 *090/2056311* 🛏 *196 rooms, 58 with bath, 1 suite* 🍴 *2 restaurants, bar, lounge, minibars, no-smoking rooms, sauna, spa, gym, convention center* ⊟ *AE, DC, MC, V.*

Fodor's Choice

$ ▦ **Hotel Winn.** The beautiful powder-blue clapboard exterior of this hotel ★ encloses a modern, officelike reception area, but one that is comfortable and welcoming nonetheless. Rooms are very stylishly furnished with paintings and lots of dark wood and asymmetrical fittings. The Mucky Duck, a classic English-style pub on the premises, serves roughly 40 types of beer and is always busy in the evening. ⊠ *Vasaplan, 901 06* ☎ *090/*

711100 🖨 090/711150 🔊 *87 rooms, 5 with bath, 5 suites* 🛎 *Bar, pub, no-smoking rooms, sauna* ⊟ *AE, DC, MC, V.*

¢ 🖭 **Strand Hotell.** Although this hotel is a severe redbrick blob from the '70s, it is right on the water and is well priced. The rooms are large and basically furnished with notably comfortable beds. ⊠ *Västra Strandg. 11, 903 26* 🖨 *090/51444* 🖨 *090/704090* 🔊 *41 rooms, 15 with bath* 🛎 *Restaurant, bar, meeting rooms* ⊟ *AE, DC, MC, V.*

Nightlife & the Arts

Being a student town, Umeå is never short of a good night out. The nightlife scene here, as in many Swedish towns, revolves around bars and pubs. The stylish **Blå** (⊠ Rådhusesplanden 🕾 090/135660) is full of chrome, glass, and people with attitude. It's the place to see and be seen in town. For an informal night out try **Rex** (⊠ Rådhustorget 🕾 090/126050), a friendly and popular haunt that attracts a young crowd. For those who prefer something a little more sedate and traditional, **Äpplet** (⊠ Vasaplan 🕾 090/156200) puts on fox-trot, cha-cha, and tango for all comers.

Shopping

Designers Guild (⊠ Kungsg. 49 🕾 090/131300), the fabric and print shop started by English designer Patricia Guild, sells beautiful English-, French-, and Italian-inspired fabrics, clothes, and household goods.

Skellefteå

❼ *140 km (87 mi) northeast of Umeå via E4.*

In 1324 King Magnus Eriksson invited anyone who believed in Jesus Christ, or anyone who wanted to convert to Christianity, to settle a town near the River Skellefte. Thus was Skellefteå born, and for hundreds of years it was a devout Christian township. Today the town makes a living from the electronics and computer industries and from nearby gold and silver mining.

Fodor'sChoice   The focus of the town's religious beliefs still stands today, in the form
★   of **Skellefteå Landskyrka.** Inside the area known as Bonnstan—a 400-room "village" built to house traveling churchgoers in the 17th century when attendance was compulsory—the striking neoclassical Skellefteå County Church has a dome roof. It has some exquisite medieval sculptures, including an 800-year-old walnut wood carving of the Virgin Mary, one of only a handful of Romanesque Maria carvings left anywhere in the world.

One of the very few art museums in the world dedicated to female artists, **Anna Nordlander Museum** displays about 80 of this Swedish painter's portraits and landscapes. Born in 1843, Nordlander found that success came quickly and increased steadily until her death from tuberculosis at the age of 36. ⊠ *Kanalg. 73* 🕾 *0910/736100* 🎟 *Free* ☉ *Daily 10–5.*

Where to Stay & Eat

$–$$ ✕ **Kriti.** An authentic Greek restaurant in the north of Sweden is not what you may expect, but you won't be disappointed. Garish yellow tablecloths with red napkins, rickety wooden chairs, white concrete walls, and a small tile roof over the bar make this the real deal. Huge portions of good meat and fish dishes are hearty and satisfying. ⊠ *Kanalg. 51* 🕾 *0910/779535* ⊟ *AE, DC, MC, V.*

$–$$ ✕ **Värdshuset Disponenten.** This beautiful green colonial-style wooden mansion has wrought-iron balconies and ivy creepers on the walls. The smörgåsbord that's offered here is generous and well prepared. Cold and hot fish, meat, and vegetable dishes are almost all made using local ingredients—some as local as the kitchen garden. ⊠ *Skelleftehamnsv. 63* ☎ *0910/30930* ⚑ *Reservations essential* ⊟ *AE, DC, MC, V* ⊘ *No dinner Sat.*

$–$$ ▦ **Scandic Hotel.** This modern building is shaped like an upturned boat, half of which is made of glass. This huge glassed portion is the Winter Garden, which houses the lobby, lounges, restaurants, and an extraordinary collection of huge trees, tropical palms, and flowers. The large rooms are furnished in blond wood and come with all the modern additions you would expect of an international hotel. ⊠ *Kanalg. 75, SE-931 78* ☎ *0910/752400* 🖷 *0910/752411* ⊕ *www.scandic.se* ⬦ *111 rooms without bath, 4 suites* ⚇ *2 restaurants, bar, indoor pool, sauna, gym, convention center* ⊟ *AE, DC, MC, V.*

$ ▦ **Rica Hotel.** Each room is individually furnished in this modern hotel. The building's low light, candles, and dark furnishings are very restful. ⊠ *Torget 2, SE-931 31* ☎ *0910/732500* 🖷 *0910/732529* ⊕ *www.rica.se* ⬦ *123 rooms, 25 with bath, 2 suites* ⚇ *Restaurant, bar, in-room data ports, sauna, 2 pools, parking (fee)* ⊟ *AE, DC, MC, V.*

Nightlife & the Arts

Underbar (⊠ Torget ☎ 0910/732530) means wonderful, and if you asked the locals, that's exactly how most would describe this dark and smoky nightclub. The three underground floors become unbelievably packed on weekends. There are two bars and dance floors, a disco, and a stage where live bands play the very popular local sound known as *Skelletepop.*

Locally sponsored and managed **Pinkerton** (⊠ Magasingränd 3 ☎ 091085060) has the promotion of Skellefteå music very much on its mind. The dark, cool club serves up cold beer, snacks, and lots of local pop, blues, jazz, and rock bands.

Shopping

The market stalls arranged under the large roof of the **Handelsgården** (⊠ Storg. 46 ☎ 09/10779924) mean that the place offers one-stop shopping for ceramics, glass, jewelry, woodwork, woven textiles, prints and artwork, and delicatessen foods.

The Bothnian Coast A to Z

To research prices, get advice from other travelers, and book travel arrangements, visit www.fodors.com.

AIR TRAVEL

CARRIERS The only carrier to Sundsvall Airport is SAS, which operates nine flights a day from Stockholm.
🛪 **SAS** ☎ 0770/727727 ⊕ www.scandinavian.net.

AIRPORTS

Sundsvall Airport (20 km [12 mi] west of Sundsvall) is the area's main airport. Local flight connections can be made to Umeå and Skellefteå. A bus service to Sundsvall runs in connection with arriving and departing SAS flights and costs SKr 80. A taxi will cost SKr 275–SKr 320.
🛪 **Sundsvall Airport** ☎ 060/6088000. **Taxi Sundsvall** ☎ 060/199000.

BUS TRAVEL

Swebus operates a twice-daily service from Stockholm to Gävle. Y-Buss operates daily from Stockholm to Hudiksvall, Sundsvall, Härnösand, and Umeå.
🛪 **Swebus** ☎ 020/0218218. **Y-Buss** ☎ 020/0334444.

CAR RENTAL

Avis and Hertz have offices in Gävle, Sundsvall, and Umeå. Europcar has offices in Gävle and Umeå.

▪ Major Agencies **Avis** ✉ Gävle ☎ 026/186880, ✉ Sundsvall ☎ 060/570210, ✉ Umeå ☎ 090/131111. **Europcar** ✉ Gävle ☎ 026/621095, ✉ Umeå ☎ 090/153960. **Hertz** ✉ Gävle ☎ 026/644938 ✉ Sundsvall ☎ 060/669080 ✉ Umeå ☎ 090/177140.

CAR TRAVEL

From Stockholm take E4 directly north 174 km (108 mi) to Gävle. From Göteborg take E20 284 km (177 mi) to Örebro, Route 60 north 164 km (102 mi) to Borlänge, and Route 80 west 70 km (43 mi) to Gävle. From Gävle the E4 runs the entire length of the Bothnian coast through every major town north to Skellefteå.

EMERGENCIES

For emergencies dial 112. There are several hospitals in the area and emergency dental care is available at Sundsvall and Umeå. There are late-night pharmacies in Gävle and Sundsvall that stay open until 11.

▪ Hospitals **Gävle Hospital** ☎ 026/154000. **Hudiksvall Hospital** ☎ 065/092000. **Söderhamn Hospital** ☎ 0270/77000. **Umeå Hospital** ☎ 090/7850000. ▪ Dental Care ✉ Sundsvall ☎ 060/613135 ✉ Umeå ☎ 070/3992480. ▪ Late-Night Pharmacies ✉ Gävle ☎ 026/149200, ✉ Sundsvall ☎ 060/181117.

TOURS

The Bothnian coast covers many miles, and tours of the entire area are not available. Individual towns and cities usually offer their own tours, either of the town or of points of interest in the surrounding area. The Umeleden Way is a waterside cycling path with many stops, including Europe's largest hydroelectric power station. Details of tours can be obtained from an individual town's tourist information offices.

▪ **Gävle City Tour** ☎ 026/147430. **Hudiksvall Town Walk** ☎ 0650/19100. **Skellefteå Countryside Tours** ☎ 091/0711210. **Umeleden Way** ☎ 090/161616.

TRAIN TRAVEL

SJ operates hourly train services from Stockholm to Gävle, Söderhamn, Hudiksvall, Sundsvall, and Härnösand. Tågkompaniet operates a night train from Stockholm to Umeå, with connections to Skellefteå.

▪ **SJ** ☎ 0771/757575. **Tågkompaniet** ☎ 020/444111.

VISITOR INFORMATION

▪ Tourist Information **Gävle** ✉ Drottningg. 37 ☎ 026/147430. **Härnösand** ✉ Järnvägsg. 2 ☎ 061/188140 ⊕ www.turism.harnosand.se. **Hudiksvall** ✉ Möljen ☎ 0650/19100 ⊕ www.hudiksvall.se. **Skellefteå** ✉ Trädgårdsg. ☎ 0910/736020 ⊕ turistinfo.skelleftea.se. **Söderhamn** ✉ Resecentrum ☎ 0270/75353 ⊕ www.turism.soderhamn.se. **Sundsvall** ✉ Stora Torget ☎ 060/610450 ⊕ www.sundsvallturism.com. **Umeå** ✉ Renmarkstorget 15 ☎ 090/161616 ⊕ www.umea.se.

GÖTEBORG

FODOR'S CHOICE

Cyrano, *restaurant in Linnéstaden*

Götaplatsen, *Göteborg*

Haga Badet (bathhouse), *Haga*

Le Village, *restaurant in Linnéstaden*

Royal Hotel, *Centrum*

Trädgårdsföreningens Park, *Centrum*

HIGHLY RECOMMENDED

RESTAURANTS 28+, *Centrum*

HOTELS Eggers, *Centrum*

Elite Plaza, *Centrum*

Europa, *Nordstan*

IF YOU ARE PASSING THROUGH GÖTEBORG (Gothenburg) on the way to your coastal vacation spot, do try to spend a day or two exploring this attractive port. Quayside cranes and warehouses attest to the city's industrial might, yet within a 10-minute walk of the waterfront is an elegant, modern city of broad avenues, green parks, and gardens. This is not to slight the harbor along both banks of the Göta Älv (river): it comprises 22 km (14 mi) of quays with warehouses and sheds covering more than 1.5 million square feet, making Göteborg Scandinavia's largest port. The harbor is also the home of Scandinavia's largest corporation, the automobile manufacturer Volvo (which means "I roll" in Latin), as well as of the roller-bearing manufacturer SKF and the world-renowned Hasselblad camera company.

Historically, Göteborg owes its existence to the sea. Tenth-century Vikings sailed from its shores, and a settlement was founded here in the 11th century. Not until 1621, however, did King Gustav II Adolf grant Göteborg a charter to establish a free-trade port on the model of others already thriving on the Continent. The west-coast harbor would also allow Swedish shipping to avoid Danish tolls exacted for passing through Öresund, the stretch of water separating the two countries. Foreigners were recruited to realize these visions: the Dutch were its builders—hence the canals that thread the city—and many Scotsmen worked and settled here, though they have left little trace.

Today Göteborg resists its second-city status by being a leader in attractions and civic structures. The Scandinavium, with a capacity of 14,000 people, is one of Europe's largest indoor arenas; the Ullevi Stadium stages some of the Nordic area's most important concerts and sporting events; Nordstan is one of Europe's biggest indoor shopping malls; and Liseberg, Scandinavia's largest amusement park in the area, attracts some 3 million visitors a year. Above the Göta River is Älvsborgsbron, at 3,060 feet the longest suspension bridge in Sweden.

EXPLORING GÖTEBORG

Göteborg is an easy city to explore: most major attractions are within walking distance of one another, and the streetcar network is excellent—in summer you can take a sightseeing trip on an open-air streetcar. The heart of Göteborg is Kungsportsavenyn (more commonly referred to as Avenyn, "the Avenue"), a 60-foot-wide, tree-lined boulevard that bisects the city along a northwest–southeast axis. Avenyn links Göteborg's cultural heart, Götaplatsen, at the southern end, with the main commercial area, now dominated by the modern Nordstan shopping center. Beyond lies the waterfront, busy with all the traffic of the port, as well as some of Göteborg's newer cultural developments.

To the west are the Haga and Linné districts. Once home to the city's dockyard, shipping, and factory workers, these areas are now alive with arts-and-crafts galleries, antiques shops, boutiques selling clothes and household goods, and street cafés and restaurants. Most of these shops are inside the original wood-and-brick cottages that line the narrow streets.

Cultural Göteborg

A pleasant stroll will take you from Götaplatsen's 1930s architecture along the Avenyn—the Boulevard Kungsportsavenyn lined with elegant shops, cafés, and restaurants—to finish at Kungsportsplats. At the square the street becomes Östra Hamngatan and slopes gently up from the canal.

A Good Walk

Start your tour in **Götaplatsen** ❶ ⌐, a square dominated by a fountain statue of Poseidon; behind him is the **Konstmuseet** ❷. Stroll downhill past the cafés and restaurants along Avenyn to the intersection with Vasagatan. A short way to the left down Vasagatan, at the junction with Teatergatan, you can visit the **Röhsska Museet** ❸, one of the few galleries dedicated to Swedish design.

Continue down Vasagatan. If the weather's good, have a look in at the Vasa Parken (Vasa Park). Then turn right to go north on Viktoriagatan, cross the canal, and make an immediate left to visit one of the city's most peculiar attractions, **Feskekörkan** ❹, whose name is an archaic spelling of *Fisk Kyrkan,* the Fish Church. It resembles a place of worship but is actually an indoor fish market.

You may now feel inspired to visit the city's principal place of worship, **Domkyrkan** ❺. Follow the canal eastward from Feskekörkan and turn left onto Västra Hamngatan; walk about four blocks to the church. Continue northward on Västra Hamngatan and cross the canal to get to Norra Hamngatan, where you'll find the **Stadsmuseet** ❻, housed in the 18th-century Swedish East India Company.

TIMING   Depending on how much time you want to spend in each museum, this walk may take anywhere from a couple of hours to the better part of a day. Note that many sites close Monday off-season.

What to See

❺ **Domkyrkan** (Göteborg Cathedral). The cathedral, in neoclassic yellow brick, dates from 1802, the two previous cathedrals on this spot having been destroyed by fire. Though disappointingly plain on the outside, the interior is impressive. Two glassed-in verandas originally used for the bishop's private conversations run the length of each side of the cathedral. The altar is impressively ornate and gilt laden. Next to it stands a post-Resurrection cross, bare of the figure of Jesus and surrounded by his gilded burial garments strewn on the floor. ⊠ *Kyrkog. 28, Centrum* ☎ *031/7316130* ⌑ *free* ⊙ *Weekdays 8–6, Sat. 9–4, Sun. 10–3.*

❹ **Feskekörkan** (Fish Church). Built in 1872, this fish market gets its nickname from its Gothic-style architectural details. The beautiful arched and vaulted wooden ceiling covers rows and rows of stalls, each offering silvery, slippery goods to the shoppers who congregate in this vast hall. ⊠ *Fisktorget, Rosenlundsg, Centrum.*

off the
beaten
path

FISKHAMNEN (Fish Docks) – An excellent view of **Älvsborgsbron** (Älvsborg Bridge), the longest suspension bridge in Sweden, is available from Fiskhamnen, west of Stigbergstorget. Built in 1967, the bridge stretches 3,060 feet across the river and was built high enough for ocean liners to pass beneath. Also look toward the sea to the large container harbors—Skarvikshamnen, Skandiahamnen, and Torshamnen—which today welcome most of the city's cargo.

⌐ ❶ **Götaplatsen** (Göta Place). This square was built in 1923 in celebration
Fodor'sChoice of the city's 300th anniversary. In the center is the Swedish-American sculp-
★   tor Carl Milles's fountain statue of Poseidon choking a codfish. Behind the statue stands the Konstmuseet, flanked by the **Konserthuset** (Concert Hall) and the **Stadsteatern** (Municipal Theater), three contemporary buildings in which the city celebrates its important contribution to Swedish cultural life. The **Stadsbiblioteket** (Municipal Library) maintains a collection of more than half a million books, many in English.

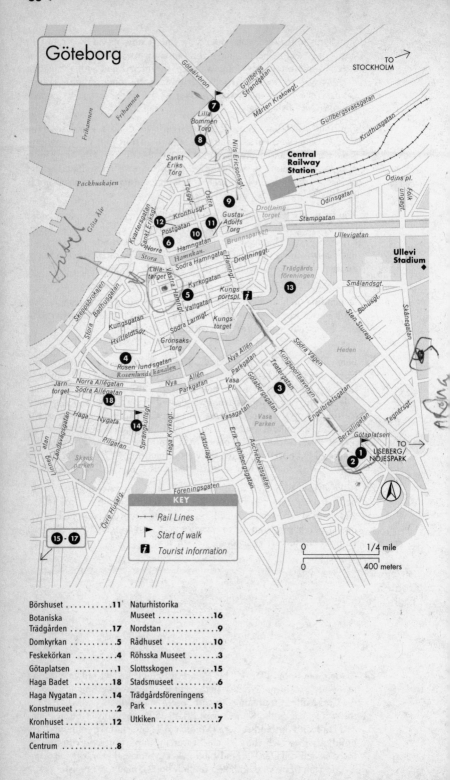

Göteborg

TO STOCKHOLM

Central Railway Station

Ullevi Stadium

KEY

↦ Rail Lines

▶ Start of walk

ℹ Tourist information

0   1/4 mile

0   400 meters

TO LISEBERG/ NÖJESPARK

❷ **Konstmuseet** (Art Museum). This impressive collection of the works of leading Scandinavian painters and sculptors encapsulates some of the moody introspection of the artistic community in this part of the world. The museum's Hasselblad Center devotes itself to showing the progress in the art of photography. The Konstmuseet's holdings include works by Swedes such as Carl Milles, Johan Tobias Sergel, impressionist Anders Zorn, Victorian idealist Carl Larsson, and Prince Eugen. The 19th- and 20th-century French art collection is the best in Sweden, and there's also a small collection of old masters. ⊠ *Götaplatsen, Götaplatsen* ☎ *031/612980* ✉ *SKr 40* ☉ *Tues. and Thurs. 11–6, Wed. 11–9, Fri.–Sun. 11–5.*

off the
beaten
path

LISEBERG NÖJESPARK – Göteborg proudly claims Scandinavia's largest amusement park. The city's pride is well earned: Liseberg is one of the best-run, most efficient parks in the world. In addition to a wide selection of carnival rides, Liseberg also has numerous restaurants and theaters, all set amid beautifully tended gardens. It's about a 30-minute walk east from the city center or a 10-minute ride by bus or tram; in summer a vintage open streetcar makes frequent runs to Liseberg from Brunnsparken, in the middle of town. ⊠ *Örgrytev. 5, Liseberg* ☎ *031/400100* ✉ *SKr 50* ☉ *mid-Apr.–mid-May, Sat. noon–9, Sun. noon–8; mid-May–July, weekdays 3–10, Sat. noon–11, Sun. noon–8; Aug., weekdays and Sun. 11–11, Fri.–Sat. 11 AM–midnight; Sept., Thurs–Fri. 4 PM–10 PM, Sat. noon–10, Sun noon–8* ⊕ *see www.liseberg.se for deviations to schedule around holidays.*

❸ **Röhsska Museet** (Museum of Arts and Crafts). This museum's fine collections of furniture, books and manuscripts, tapestries, and pottery are on view. Artifacts date back as far as 1,000 years, but it's the 20th-century gallery, with its collection of many familiar household objects, that seems to provide the most enjoyment. ⊠ *Vasag. 37–39, Vasastan* ☎ *031/613850* ✉ *SKr 40* ☉ *Year-round, Tues. noon–9, Wed.–Sun. noon–5.*

❻ **Stadsmuseet** (City Museum). Once the warehouse and auction rooms of the Swedish East India Company, a major trading firm founded in 1731, this palatial structure dates to 1750. Today it contains exhibits on the Swedish west coast, with a focus on Göteborg's nautical and trading past. One interesting exhibit deals with the East India Company and its ship the *Göteborg*. On its 1745 return from China, she sank just outside the city while crowds there to greet the returning ship watched from shore in horror. ⊠ *Norra Hamng. 12, Centrum* ☎ *031/612770* ✉ *SKr 40* ☉ *Weekdays 10–5, weekends 11–8.*

Commercial Göteborg

Explore Göteborg's port-side character, both historic and modern, at the waterfront development near the town center, where the markets and boutiques can keep you busy for hours.

A Good Walk

Begin at the harborside square known as Lilla Bommen Torg, where the **Utkiken** ❼ ▶ offers a bird's-eye view of the city and harbor. The waterfront development here includes the ship-turned-restaurant **Viking**, the Opera House, and the **Maritima Centrum** ❽.

From Lilla Bommen Torg take the pedestrian bridge across the highway to **Nordstan** ❾. Leave the mall at the opposite end, which puts you at Brunnsparken, the hub of the city's streetcar network. Turn right and cross the street to Gustav Adolfs Torg, the city's official center, dominated by **Rådhuset** ⑩. On the north side of the square is **Börshuset** ⑪, built in 1849.

Head north from the square along Östra Hamngatan and turn left onto Postgatan to visit **Kronhuset** ⑫, the city's oldest secular building, dating from 1643. Surrounding the entrance to Kronhuset are the **Kronhusbodarna,** carefully restored turn-of-the-20th-century shops and arts-and-crafts boutiques.

Return to Gustav Adolfs Torg and follow Östra Hamngatan south over the Stora Hamnkanal to Kungsportsplats, where the Saluhall (Market Hall) has stood since 1888. A number of pedestrians-only shopping streets branch out through this neighborhood on either side of Östra Hamngatan. Crossing the bridge over Vallgraven from Kungsportsplats brings you onto Kungsportsavenyn and the entrance to **Trädgårn** ⑬.

TIMING The walk itself will take about two hours; allow extra time to explore the sites and to shop. Note that the Kronhusbodarna is closed Sunday. Trädgårn is closed Monday off-season.

What to See

⑪ **Börshuset** (Stock Exchange). Completed in 1849, the former Stock Exchange building houses city administrative offices as well as facilities for large banquets. The fabric of the large, opulent banqueting halls and blue-stucco anterooms is under considerable strain through age. The building is not open to the public, but if you can get in, you won't be disappointed. ⊠ *Gustav Adolfs Torg 5, Nordstan.*

Kronhusbodarna (Historical Shopping Center). Glassblowing and watchmaking are among the arts and crafts offered in this area of shops that adjoin the Kronhuset. There is also a nice, old-fashioned café. ⊠ *Kronhusg. 1D, Nordstan* ☾ *Closed Sun.*

⑫ **Kronhuset** (Crown House). Göteborg's oldest secular building, dating from 1643, was originally the city's armory. In 1660 Sweden's Parliament met here to arrange the succession for King Karl X Gustav, who died suddenly while visiting the city. The building is now used for classical concerts and the City Museum's annual Christmas market. ⊠ *Postg. 68, Nordstan* ☎ *031/612770, City Museum.*

⑧ **Maritima Centrum** (Marine Center). In the world's largest floating maritime museum you'll find modern naval vessels, including a destroyer, submarines, lightship, cargo vessel, and various tugboats, providing insight into Göteborg's historic role as a major port. The main attraction is a huge naval destroyer, complete with a medical room in which a leg amputation operation is graphically re-created, with mannequins standing in for medical personnel. ⊠ *Packhuskajen 8, Nordstan* ☎ *031/ 105950* ☐ *SKr 60* ☾ *May–July, daily 10–6; Aug.–Apr., daily 10–4.*

⑨ **Nordstan.** Sweden's largest indoor shopping mall—open daily—is replete with a huge parking garage, pharmacy open until 10 PM, post office, several restaurants, entertainment for children, a branch of the department store Åhlens, and a tourist information kiosk. ⊠ *Entrances on Köpmansg., Nils Ericsonsg., Kanaltorgsg., and Östra Hamng., Nordstan.*

⑩ **Rådhuset.** Though the town hall dates from 1672, when it was designed by Nicodemus Tessin the Elder, its controversial modern extension by Swedish architect Gunnar Asplund is from 1937. The building therefore offers two architectural extremes. One section has the original grand chandeliers and trompe l'oeil ceilings; the other has glass elevators, mussel-shape drinking fountains, and vast expanses of laminated aspen wood. Together they make a fascinating mix. ⊠ *Gustav Adolfs Torg 1, Nordstan.*

⑬ **Trädgårdsföreningens Park** (Horticultural Society Park). Here you'll find
Fodor'sChoice beautiful open green spaces, a magnificent rose garden with 5,000 roses
★ of 2,500 varieties; the Butterfly House, with butterflies flying free, and
the Palm House, whose late-19th-century design echoes that of London's
Crystal Palace. ⊠ *Just off Kungsportsavenyn, Centrum* ☎ *031/611804*
🌐 *Park SKr 15; Palm House SKr 20; Butterfly House SKr 35* ☉ *Park
May–Aug., daily 7 AM–9 PM; Sept.–Apr., daily 7 AM–7:30 PM. Palm
House May–Aug., daily 10–5; Sept.–Aug., daily 10–4. Butterfly House
Apr., May, and Sept., daily 10–4; June–Aug., daily 10–5; Oct.–Mar., daily
10–3.*

▶ **❼** **Utkiken** (Lookout Tower). This red-and-white-stripe skyscraper towers
282 feet above the waterfront, offering an unparalleled view of the city
and skyscrapers from the viewing platform at the top. ⊠ *Lilla Bommen, Lilla Bommen* ☎ *031/609670.*

off the
beaten
path

GULLBERGSKAJEN – For an interesting tour of the docks, head
northeast from Lilla Bommen about 1½ km (1 mi) along the riverside
to the Gullbergskajen, just off Gullbergsstrandgatan. Today this is the
headquarters of a local boating association, its brightly colored
pleasure craft contrasting with the old-fashioned working barges
either anchored or being repaired at Ringön, just across the river.

NYA ELFSBORGS FÄSTNING – Boats leave regularly from Lilla
Bommen to the Elfsborg Fortress, built in 1670 on a harbor island to
protect the city from attack. ☎ *031/609660* 🌐 *SKr 85* ☉ *Early
May–Aug., 7 departures daily; Sept., weekends.*

SJÖFARTSMUSEET & AKVARIET – This museum combines maritime
history with an aquarium. The museum has model ships, cannons, a
ship's medical room, and a collection of figureheads. The adjacent
aquarium contains a good selection of Nordic marine life and a more
exotic section with, among other animals, two alligators and some
piranhas. ⊠ *Karl Johansg. 1–3, 2 km (1 mi) west of city center,
Majorna* ☎ *031/612901* 🌐 *SKr 40* ☉ *Sept.–Apr., Tues., Thurs., and
Fri. 10–4, Wed. 10–9, weekends 11–5; May–Aug., daily 10–5.*

VIKING – This four-masted schooner, built in 1907, was among the
last of Sweden's sailing cargo ships. The ship is now used as a hotel
and restaurant, with cabins for two without bath starting at SKr 650.
The restaurant serves up traditional Swedish fare starting at 79 SKr.
⊠ *Gullbergskajen, Lilla Bommen, Hamnen* ☎ *031/635800.*

Haga & Linné Districts

Just west of the main city, the Haga and Linné districts are at the fore-
front of the new cosmopolitan Göteborg. These areas once housed the
city's poor and were so run-down that they were scheduled for demolition. They now make up some of the city's most attractive areas. The
older of the two neighborhoods, the Haga district is full of cozy cafés,
secondhand stores, and artist shops along cobbled streets. The Linné
district is the trendiest neighborhood in which to live in Göteborg, and
real estate prices have shot up accordingly. Corner restaurants, expensive boutiques, and stylish cafés cater to neighborhood residents and to
Göteborg's wealthy young elite, there to see and be seen.

A Good Walk

Set off from the east end of **Haga Nygatan** ⑭ ► and stroll west past the busy cafés and boutiques selling art-deco light fixtures and antique kitchenware. Turn left onto Landsvägsgatan and walk up to join Linnégatan, the Dutch-inspired street that's now considered Göteborg's "Second Avenyn." There is an air of quiet sophistication about Linnégatan, with small antiques and jewelry shops competing for attention against secluded street cafés and high-end design and crafts shops.

Walk south along Linnégatan for five minutes to get to **Slottskogen** ⑮. If relaxing is your thing, you can spend some time lounging in this huge, tranquil expanse of parkland. Alternatively, you can make use of your time here and visit the **Naturhistorika Museet** ⑯, Göteborg's oldest museum, or the **Botaniska Trädgården** ⑰, on the south side of the park.

Depart the park the same way you came in, and wind your way north up Nordenhemsgatan. At the end of this road turn right onto Första Långgatan and then onto Södra Allégatan. Here you can find the beautiful and tranquil oasis of the **Haga Badet** ⑱, a superbly renovated bathhouse.

TIMING   At a gentle pace the walk alone will take about one hour. If you allow yourself to be tempted by the great shopping, superb cafés, and both museums, you could spend almost a whole day in this part of the city.

What to See

⑰ **Botaniska Trädgården** (Botanical Gardens). With 1,200 plant species this is Sweden's largest botanical garden. Herb gardens, bamboo groves, a Japanese valley, forest plants, and tropical greenhouses are all on display. ✉ *Carl Skottsbergs Gata 22A, Slottsskogen* ☎ *031/7411101* ✱ *Greenhouses SKr 20; Park free* ⊙ *Park daily 9–sunset; greenhouses May–Aug., daily 10–5; Sept.–Apr., daily 10–4.*

⑱ **Haga Badet.** This stunning bathhouse was built at the end of the 19th century by the Swedish philanthropist Sven Renström. Originally used by local dock- and factory workers, it now plays host to Göteborg's leisure-hungry elite. It's well worth a visit. The pretty pool is art nouveau, with wall paintings, an arched ceiling, and lamps with a diving-lady motif. The Roman baths and the massage and spa area all exude relaxation, but the architecture alone is worth a visit, even if you don't intend to take the plunge. ✉ *Södra Allég. 3, Haga* ☎ *031/600600* ✱ *SKr 320 for day pass to use facilities, otherwise free* ⊙ *Mon.–Thurs. 7 AM–9:30 PM, Fri. 7 AM–8:30 PM, Sat. 9–6, Sun. 10–6.*

Fodor'sChoice ★

► ⑭ **Haga Nygatan.** The redbrick buildings that line this street were originally poorhouses donated by the Dickson family, the city's British industrialist forefathers. ROBERT DICKSON can still be seen carved into the facades of these buildings. Like most buildings in Haga, the buildings' ground floors were made of stone in order to prevent the spread of fire (the upper floors are wood). The Dickson family's impact on the architecture of the west of Sweden can also be seen in the impressive, fanciful mansion that belonged to Robert's grandson James, in Tjolöholm, to the south of Göteborg. ✉ *Haga Nyg, Haga.*

⑯ **Naturhistoriska Museet.** Although the Natural History Museum has a collection containing more than 10 million preserved animals, you may be disappointed to discover that the majority are tiny insects that sit unnoticed in rows of drawers. It's worth a visit to see the world's only stuffed blue whale, harpooned in 1865. ✉ *Slottsskogen, Slottsskogen* ☎ *031/7752400* ⊕ *www.gnm.se* ✱ *SKr 40* ⊙ *Sept.–Apr., Tues.–Fri. 9–4, weekends 11–5; May–Aug., daily 11–5.*

<table>
<tr><td>off the beaten path</td><td>**SKANSEN KRONAN** – To the south of Haga is one of Göteborg's two surviving 17th-century fortress towers. Built on a raised mound of land, the tower houses the military museum, containing displays of weapons dating to the Middle Ages and Swedish uniforms from the 19th and 20th centuries. The museum's presentations can be a little dry at times and is probably only for the true enthusiast of military history. But the view northward across the city makes the journey worthwhile.</td></tr>
</table>

⑮ Slottsskogen. Spend some time in this stunning area of parkland containing cafés, farm animals, a seal pond, Sweden's oldest children's zoo, and many birds, in summer even pink flamingos. Slottsskogen is one of the best parts of the city in which to take a break. ✉ *South of Linnég., Slottsskogen* ☉ *Daily dawn–dusk.*

<table>
<tr><td>off the beaten path</td><td>**VOLVO MUSEUM** – In Arendal, 8 km (5 mi) west of the city center, the Volvo Museum pays homage to the car company that in one way or another helps support 25% of Göteborg's population. Not surprisingly, exhibits include most of Volvo's cars over the years as well as some prototypes, the first electric car, and an early jet engine, the first one used by the Swedish Air Force. A 20-minute film helps to put the whole history into perspective at this rather well-put-together museum. ✉ *Avd. 1670 ARU (off Rd. 155 toward Öckerö/Torslanda) Arendal* ☎ *031/664814* ⊕ *www.volvo.com* ✍ *SKr 30* ☉ *June–Aug., Tues.–Fri. 10–5, weekends 11–4; Sept.–May, Tues.–Fri. noon–5, weekends 11–4.*</td></tr>
</table>

WHERE TO EAT

You can eat well in Göteborg but expect to pay dearly for the privilege. Fish dishes are the best bet here. Call ahead to be sure restaurants are open, as many close for a month in summer.

WHAT IT COSTS In Swedish Kronor				
$$$$	**$$$**	**$$**	**$**	**¢**
AT DINNER over 420	250–420	150–250	100–150	below 100

Prices are for a main course at dinner.

$$$$ ✗ **Sjömagasinet.** Seafood is the obvious specialty at this waterfront restaurant. In a 200-year-old renovated shipping warehouse, the dining room has views of the harbor and the suspension bridge. An outdoor terrace opens up in summer. ✉ *Klippans Kulturreservat, Kiel-terminalen* ☎ *031/7755920* ✍ *Reservations essential* ⊟ *AE, DC, MC, V.*

★ **$$$–$$$$** ✗ **28+.** Step down from the street into this former wine-and-cheese cellar to find an elegant restaurant owned by two of the best chefs in Göteborg. Finely set tables, flickering candles, and country-style artwork evoke the mood of a rustic French town. Italian and American flavors blend their way into the French dishes; choose a five- or seven-course meal, or take your pick à la carte. Note that one of the best wine cellars in Sweden is at your disposal. ✉ *Götabergsg. 28, Centrum* ☎ *031/202161* ⋔ *Jacket required* ⊟ *AE, DC, MC, V* ☉ *Closed Sun.*

$$$ ✗ **Le Village.** Ever been to a restaurant with tables and chairs you liked
FodorśChoice so much you wished you could take them home? What about the lamps
★ or the paintings on the wall? Well, at Le Village that's exactly what you can do. Everything in this restaurant and the connected **antiques shop** (☎ *031/143833*) is for sale. The food is exceptional, especially the sea-

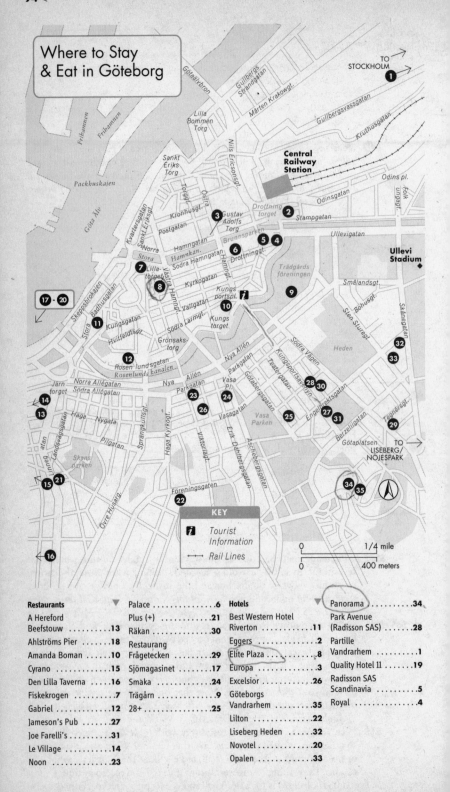

Where to Stay & Eat in Göteborg

TO STOCKHOLM ①

KEY

ℹ Tourist Information

⊢—⊣ Rail Lines

0 ———— 1/4 mile
0 ———— 400 meters

sonal meat dishes. Try the smaller dining room if you want to avoid some of the prices in the main room. ⊠ *Tredje Långgatan 13, Linnéstaden* ☎ *031/242003* ⊟ *AE, DC, MC, V* ⊗ *Closed Sun.*

$$$ ✕ **Noon.** Swedish and Asian styles fuse to produce innovative, quality seafood and noodle dishes that are served in a simple, modern dining room. Try a few of the smaller, less expensive appetizers, or go all out by ordering the flounder in lemon-ginger sauce with saffron dumplings. ⊠ *Viktoriag. 2, Vasastan* ☎ *031/138800* ⊟ *AE, DC, MC, V.*

$$$ ✕ **Räkan.** This informal and popular place makes the most of an unusual gimmick: the tables are arranged around a long tank, and if you order shrimp, the house specialty, they arrive at your table in radio-controlled boats you navigate yourself. ⊠ *Lorensbergsg. 16, Götaplatsen* ☎ *031/169839* ⌂ *Reservations essential* ⊟ *AE, DC, MC, V* ⊗ *No lunch.*

$$$ ✕ **Trägårn.** Spicy, Asian-influenced cuisine stands out against linen table-cloths in this earth-tone restaurant; the vegetarian menu is extensive. A wall of glass in the two-story dining hall affords a view of Göteborg's beautiful Trägårnpark; another wall is covered in blond-wood paneling, a contrast to the black-slate floor. ⊠ *Nya Allén, Centrum* ☎ *031/ 102080* ⊟ *AE, DC, MC, V* ⊗ *Closed Sun. No lunch fall–spring.*

$$–$$$ ✕ **A Hereford Beefstouw.** At this, an American steak house in Sweden, the chefs grill beef selections in the center of the three dining rooms, one of which is set aside for nonsmokers. The restaurant is popular in a town otherwise dominated by fish restaurants. Thick wooden tables, pine floors, and landscape paintings give the place a rustic touch. ⊠ *Linnég. 5, Linnéstaden* ☎ *031/7750441* ⊟ *AE, DC, MC, V* ⊗ *No lunch weekends and July.*

$$–$$$ ✕ **Ahlströms Pier.** Across the river from central Göteborg lies Eriksberg, where former dockyards mix with modern buildings. Perched at the end of a pier that juts out into the harbor, this restaurant has a main dining hall in an elegant triangular room on the second floor and a less expensive brasserie on the first floor; contemporary French-inspired Swedish fare is on the menu at both. In summer food is served on an outdoor patio. Finding the pier by car can prove difficult; consider taking a ferry from the city side of the river. ⊠ *Dockepiren, Eriksberg* ☎ *031/519555* ⌂ *Reservations essential* ᵯ *Jacket and tie* ⊟ *AE, DC, MC, V* ⊗ *Main dining hall closed Sun.*

$$–$$$ ✕ **Fiskekrogen.** The Fish Inn has more than 30 fish and seafood dishes from which to choose. Lunches are particularly good value, and ideal if you're coming from the Stadsmuseet across the canal. ⊠ *Lilla Torget 1, Centrum* ☎ *031/101005* ⊟ *AE, DC, MC, V* ⊗ *Closed Sun.*

$$–$$$ ✕ **Palace.** In the center of Brunnsparken, the Palace is one of Göteborg's most popular summer spots for eating, dancing, and drinking. Live bands and DJs play the '70s and '80s favorites of the well-dressed forty-somethings who frequent the restaurant and nightclub. The extensive single-malt whiskey collection is known around town: call ahead to arrange a tasting. The menu of mostly traditional Swedish cuisine is extensive. ⊠ *Brunnsparken, Brunnsparken* ☎ *031/807550* ⊟ *AE, DC, MC, V* ⊗ *Closed Sun.*

$$ ✕ **Plus (+).** This atmospheric and relaxing restaurant recalls the Sweden of the past. It's inside a beautiful early-1900s ramshackle wooden house whose foundations are attached to the original rock on which the city was built. (As you travel through town, you may see some of this rock poking up through the modern sidewalks and streets.) Eat well-prepared fish and meat dishes with a varied international flavor at polished wood tables, all the while sitting beneath antique chandeliers. ⊠ *Linnég. 32, Linnéstaden* ☎ *031/240890* ⊟ *AE, DC, MC, V.*

$–$$ ⨉ **Cyrano.** A little piece of southern France in Sweden, this superb, au-
FodorsChoice thentically Provençal bistro is an absolute must. Inside, the tables are
★ crammed close together, French art hangs on the walls, and French touches
extend throughout. Highlights include a sumptuously creamy fish soup,
sardines with garlic, and grass-fed lamb with tomatoes and sweet pep-
pers. Laid back and friendly, with helpful service, Cyrano continues to
draw in the trendier citizens of Göteborg. ⊠ *Prinsg. 7, Linnéstaden*
☎ *031/143110* ⊟ *AE, DC, MC, V.*

$–$$ ⨉ **Joe Farelli's.** Dimly lighted, with booths along the walls and black-
and-white photographs of the Big Apple, Joe Farelli's is as close to a
New York restaurant as you'll get in Göteborg. Very central, on Avenyn,
it's a good place to stop for a dish of pasta or a burger in between sights.
⊠ *Kungsportsavenyn 12, Centrum* ☎ *031/105826* ⊟ *AE, MC, V.*

$–$$ ⨉ **Restaurang Frågetecken.** With a name that translates to "Restaurant
Question Mark," this spot has attracted a good deal of curiosity. It's just
about a minute's walk from Götaplatsen, which also makes it popular
with locals and visitors alike. Eat in the busy, bright conservatory in summer or in the relaxing interior, which is decorated in neutral colors. If
you don't mind the noise and the hectic pace, dine in the open kitchen
to watch the chefs carefully preparing their Balkan-influenced food.
Anything with duck is delicious but also pricey. Pasta dishes are homey,
comforting, and are the cheaper option. ⊠ *Södra Vägen 20, Götaplatsen* ☎ *031/160030* ⟁ *Reservations not accepted* ⊟ *AE, DC, MC, V.*

$–$$ ⨉ **Smaka.** Deep-blue walls and ambient music create Smaka's mellow
mood, a perfect backdrop for sampling what the chef calls "modern-
ized" Swedish cuisine. Göteborg's younger crowd tends to stay here for
a few extra drinks after eating. ⊠ *Vasaplatsen 3, Vasastan* ☎ *031/
132247* ⊟ *AE, DC, MC, V.*

¢–$$ ⨉ **Jameson's Pub.** On Tuesday night this English pub on Avenyn comes
alive to the beat of live blues, R&B, and rock music. There's live en-
tertainment on the weekends as well; check in to find out who's per-
forming. The food, affordable and surprisingly good, is an eclectic mix
of traditional Swedish and international favorites. ⊠ *Kungsportsavenyn
32, Centrum* ☎ *031/187770* ⊟ *AE, MC, V.*

$ ⨉ **Amanda Boman.** This little restaurant in one corner of the market hall
at Kungsportsplats keeps early hours, so unless you eat an afternoon
dinner, plan on lunch instead. The cuisine is primarily Swedish, includ-
ing fish soup and gravlax. ⊠ *Saluhallen, Centrum* ☎ *031/137676*
⊟ *AE, MC, V* ☉ *Closed Sun. No dinner.*

$ ⨉ **Den Lilla Taverna.** A very good, lively, and popular place, this Greek
restaurant has paper tablecloths and Greek mythological scenes painted
on the walls. Live bouzouki music on Wednesday and Saturday evenings
gives the place an authentic feel. ⊠ *Oliver Dahlsg. 17, Linnéstaden* ☎ *031/
128805* ⊟ *AE, MC, V.*

$ ⨉ **Gabriel.** A buffet of fresh shellfish and the fish dish of the day draw
crowds to this restaurant on a balcony above the fish hall. You can watch
all the trading as you eat lunch. ⊠ *Feskekörkan, Centrum* ☎ *031/
139051* ⊟ *AE, DC, MC, V* ☉ *Closed Sun. and Mon. No dinner.*

WHERE TO STAY

Some hotels close during the winter holidays; call ahead if you expect to
travel during that time. All rooms in the hotels reviewed below are
equipped with shower or bath unless otherwise noted. Göteborg also has
some fine camping sites if you want an alternative to staying in a hotel.

WHAT IT COSTS In Swedish Kronor				
$$$$	$$$	$$	$	¢
FOR 2 PEOPLE above 2,900	2,300–2,900	1,500–2,300	1,000–1,500	under 1,000

Prices are for two people in a standard double room in high season.

$$$ ▣ **Opalen.** If you are attending an event at the Scandinavium, or if you have children and are heading for the Liseberg Amusement Park, this RESO hotel is ideally located. Rooms are bright and modern. ⊠ *Engelbrektsg. 73, Box 5106, 402 23 Liseberg* ☎ *031/7515300* 🖷 *031/ 7515311* ⊕ *www.scandic-hotels.com* ↘ *242 rooms* ⚲ *Restaurant, bar, 2 no-smoking floors, sauna* ▤ *AE, DC, MC, V* ¶⊙¶ *BP.*

$$$ ▣ **Radisson SAS Scandinavia.** Across Drottningtorget from the central train station, the Radisson SAS is Göteborg's most modern and spectacular international hotel. The attractive atrium lobby has two restaurants: Frascati, which serves international cuisine, and the Atrium piano bar, with a lighter menu. Rooms are large and luxurious and decorated in pastel shades. Hotel guests receive a discount at the health club on the premises. ⊠ *Södra Hamng. 5965, 401 24 Centrum* ☎ *031/7585000* 🖷 *031/7585001* ⊕ *www.radisson.com* ↘ *349 rooms* ⚲ *Restaurant, in-room data ports, minibars, cable TV, piano bar, no-smoking rooms, hair salon, indoor pool, health club, shops, casino, convention center, travel services* ▤ *AE, DC, MC, V* ¶⊙¶ *BP.*

$$ ▣ **Panorama.** Within reach of all downtown attractions and close to Liseberg, this Best Western hotel is a quiet, relaxing place to stay. The rooms have dark walls in reds and other earth tones, dark-wood floors, large wall mirrors, and fabrics done in light pastel colors. ⊠ *Eklandag. 5153, Box 24037, 400 22 Johanneberg* ☎ *031/7677000* 🖷 *031/7677070* ⊕ *www.bestwestern.com* ↘ *339 rooms* ⚲ *Restaurant, lounge, no-smoking floor, hot tub, sauna, meeting room, parking* ▤ *AE, DC, MC, V* ¶⊙¶ *BP.*

$$ ▣ **Park Avenue (Radisson SAS).** Though this modern luxury hotel is sorely lacking in character. It has many facilities though, including an SAS check-in counter. The well-equipped rooms are decorated in earth tones and have good views of the city. ⊠ *Kungsportsavenyn 3638, Box 53233, 400 16 Götaplatsen* ☎ *031/7584000* 🖷 *031/7584001* ⊕ *www. radisson.com* ↘ *318 rooms* ⚲ *2 restaurants, in-room data ports, cable TV, bar, gym, meeting room, no-smoking floors* ▤ *AE, DC, MC, V* ¶⊙¶ *BP.*

$$ ▣ **Best Western Hotel Riverton.** Convenient for people arriving in the city by ferry, this hotel is close to the European terminals and overlooks the harbor. Built in 1985, it has a glossy marble floor and reflective ceiling in the lobby. Rooms are decorated with abstract-pattern textiles and whimsical prints. ⊠ *Stora Badhusg. 26, 411 21 Kungshöjd* ☎ *031/7501000* 🖷 *031/7501001* ⊕ *www.bestwestern.com* ↘ *191 rooms* ⚲ *Restaurant, room service, bar, no-smoking rooms, hot tub, sauna, meeting room, free parking* ▤ *AE, DC, MC, V* ¶⊙¶ *BP.*

★ **$$** ▣ **Eggers.** Dating from 1859, Best Western's Eggers has more character and charm than any other hotel in the city. It is a minute's walk from the train station and was probably the last port of call in Sweden for many emigrants to the United States. Rooms vary in size, and all are beautifully decorated, often with antiques. A complimentary buffet breakfast is the only meal served. ⊠ *Drottningtorget, Box 323, SE-401 25 Centrum* ☎ *031/806070* 🖷 *031/154243* ⊕ *www.bestwestern.com* ↘ *65 rooms* ⚲ *Cable TV, no-smoking rooms, meeting room* ▤ *AE, DC, MC, V* ¶⊙¶ *BP.*

★ **$$** ▣ **Elite Plaza.** A five-minute walk from the central station, the Plaza is one of the smartest hotels in the city. The palatial building, an architectural attraction in itself, dates from 1889 and has been modernized with care to give it an air of grandeur, quality, and restfulness. All original features have been retained, from the stucco ceilings to the English mosaic floors, and are tastefully matched with modern art and up-to-date guest facilities. Rooms have earth tones and dark-wood furnishings. The hotel restaurant, Swea Hoff, serves delicious international cuisine, Swedish specialties, and seafood, and there is a very well-chosen wine list. ☒ *Västra Hamng. 3, Box 110 65, 404 22 Centrum* ☎ *031/7204000* 🖷 *031/7204010* 🖎 *143 rooms, 5 suites* ♻ *Restaurant, in-room data ports, minibars, in-room safes, bar, pub, gym, no-smoking rooms, convention center* ⊟ *AE, DC, MC, V* ⭘ *BP.*

★ **$$** ▦ **Europa.** Large and comfortable, this hotel is part of the Nordstan mall complex, very close to the central train station. The rooms are modern, airy, and colorful. Some rooms have data ports; ask for one of these if it's a consideration. Service throughout is efficient and friendly. ☒ *Köpmansg. 38, 411 06 Nordstan* ☎ *031/7516500* 🖷 *031/7516511* ⊕ *www.scandic-hotels.com* 🖎 *450 rooms, 5 suites* ♻ *Restaurant, cable TV, indoor pool, sauna, convention center, parking, no-smoking floor* ⊟ *AE, DC, MC, V* ⭘ *BP.*

$$ ▦ **Quality Hotel 11.** On the water's edge in Eriksberg, Hotel 11 combines the warehouse style of the old waterfront with a modern interior of multitier terraces. Commonly used by large companies for business conferences, the hotel also welcomes families that want to stay across the harbor from downtown Göteborg. The rooms are clean, bright, and modern; some offer panoramic views of the harbor. Next door is Eriksbergshallen, a theater and conference hall that hosts international performances. ☒ *Masking. 11, 417 64 Eriksberg, (from city follow signs to Norra Älvstranden)* ☎ *031/7791111* 🖷 *031/7791110* ⊕ *www.hotel11.se* 🖎 *184 rooms, 8 suites* ♻ *Restaurant, in-room data ports, bar, no-smoking rooms, sauna, meeting room* ⊟ *AE, DC, MC, V* ⭘ *BP.*

$ ▦ **Liseberg Heden.** Not far from the famous Liseberg Amusement Park, Liseberg Heden is a popular family hotel in the Sweden Hotels chain. Each of the modern rooms has light-color walls, a satellite television, a minibar, and a large desk, and most have wood floors. Perks include a sauna and a very good restaurant. ☒ *Sten Stureg., 411 38 Liseberg* ☎ *031/7506900* 🖷 *031/7506930* 🖎 *182 rooms* ♻ *Restaurant, minibars, no-smoking rooms, sauna, meeting room* ⊟ *AE, DC, MC, V* ⭘ *BP.*

$ ▦ **Excelsior.** Although a little worn around the edges, this stylish 1880 building on a road of classic Göteborg houses is the place to stay to get some character and history. The Excelsior has been in operation since 1930, and its guest rooms are full of homey comfort and faded grandeur. Greta Garbo and Ingrid Bergman both stayed here, and more recently, so did musician Sheryl Crow. Classic suites—Garbo's was number 535—with splendid 19th-century style cost no more than ordinary rooms. ☒ *Karl Gustavsg. 7, 411 25 Vasastan* ☎ *031/175435* 🖷 *031/175439* ⊕ *www.hotelexcelsior.nu* 🖎 *64 rooms, 3 suites* ♻ *Restaurant, cable TV, bar, no-smoking room* ⊟ *AE, DC, MC, V* ⭘ *BP.*

$ ▦ **Novotel.** The redbrick industrial-age architecture of this old brewery belies a mishmash of architectural styles inside. Situated just west of the city on the Göta Älv, the top floors afford spectacular views of Göteborg. There's a very big central atrium, complete with obligatory fake foliage, with an expensive restaurant, Carnegie Kay, attached. ☒ *Klippan 1, 414 51 Majorna* ☎ *031/149000* 🖷 *031/422232* ⊕ *www.novotel.se* 🖎 *148 rooms, 5 suites* ♻ *Restaurant, in-room data ports, cable TV, bar, no-smoking rooms, sauna, free parking* ⊟ *AE, DC, MC, V* ⭘ *BP.*

$ ▦ **Royal.** Göteborg's oldest hotel, built in 1852, is small, family owned, and traditional. Rooms, most with parquet floors, are individually decorated with reproductions of elegant Swedish traditional furniture. The Royal is in the city center a few blocks from the central train station.

✉ *Drottningg. 67, 411 07 Centrum* ☎ *031/7001170* 🖷 *031/7001179* ⊕ *www.hotel-royal.com* ⤳ *82 rooms* ♿ *Breakfast room, no-smoking floor* ⊟ *AE, DC, MC, V* ▮❂▮ *BP.*

¢ ⌧ **Göteborgs Vandrarhem.** This hostel is 5 km (3 mi) from the train station in a modern apartment block. Rooms are contemporary, with Swedish-designed furnishings. Breakfast (SKr 50) is not included in the rates, which are per person in a shared apartment. ✉ *Mölndalsv. 23, 412 63 Liseberg* ☎ *031/401050* 🖷 *031/401151* ⤳ *150 beds, 4- to 6-bed apartments* ⊟ *MC, V.*

¢ ⌧ **Lilton.** This unobtrusive bed-and-breakfast-style hotel is inside a small, ivy-covered brick building. Rooms are simple and comfortable, the service friendly and unfussy. ✉ *Föreningsg. 9, 411 27 Vasastan* ☎ *031/828808* 🖷 *031/822184* ⤳ *14 rooms* ♿ *Breakfast room, no-smoking* ⊟ *AE, MC, V* ▮❂▮ *CP.*

¢ ⌧ **Partille Vandrarhem.** This hostel is in a pleasant old house 15 km (9 mi) outside the city, next to a lake for swimming. Rooms have harmonious light- and dark-blue fabrics, simple wood furniture, and rich watercolors of local scenes. You can order meals or prepare them yourself in the guest kitchen. Room rates are per person based on two or more people sharing a room. ✉ *Landvetterv., 433 24, Partille* ☎ *031/446501* 🖷🖷 *031/446163* ⤳ *120 beds, 2- to 4-bed rooms* ⊟ *No credit cards.*

NIGHTLIFE & THE ARTS

Music, Opera & Theater

Home of the highly acclaimed Göteborg Symphony Orchestra, **Konserthuset** (✉ Götaplatsen, Götaplatsen ☎ 031/7265300) has a mural by Sweden's Prince Eugen in the lobby, original decor, and Swedish-designed furniture from 1935. **Operan** (✉ Christina Nilssons Gata, Packhuskajen ☎ 031/108000), where Göteborg's opera company performs, incorporates a 1,250-seat auditorium with a glassed-in dining area overlooking the harbor. **Stadsteatern** (✉ Johannebergsg. 1, Götaplatsen ☎ 031/615050 tickets, 031/615100 information) puts on high-quality productions of classics by Shakespeare, Molière, Ibsen, and other playwrights. Most of its plays are performed in Swedish.

Nightlife

Bars

As its name implies, **The Dubliner** (✉ Östra Hamng. 50, Inom Vallgraven ☎ 031/139020) is a brave attempt at re-creating what the locals imagine to be old Irish charm. If you're looking for an urbane bar, try **Nivå** (✉ Kungsportsavenyn 9, Centrum ☎ 031/7018090), a popular bar with a stylish tile interior and a crowd to match. **Avenyn 10** (✉ Kungsportsavenyn 10, Centrum ☎ 031/137565) attracts a very young, very loud crowd. **Napoleon** (✉ Vasag. 11, Vasastan ☎ 031/137550) is a dark, mellow hangout crowded with oddities. Even the exterior walls are covered in paintings.

Discos & Cabaret

One of the city's liveliest haunts is **Trädgårn** (✉ Nya Allén, Centrum ☎ 031/102080), a complex of five bars, a disco, and show bands housed in a strange building resembling a half-built sauna. **Bubbles Nightclub** (✉ Kungsportsavenyn 8, Centrum ☎ 031/105820) is big and brash, mainly attracting people in their thirties. Chrome, mirrors, and a white-tile ceiling like those found in offices make this a memorable place for a drink. At **Rondo** (✉ Örgrytev. 5, Liseberg ☎ 031/400200) you can dance the night away on Sweden's largest dance floor while surrounded by people of all ages. The crowd is always friendly, and there's a live band. The **Cabaret Lorensberg** (⊠ Park Avenue Hotel (Radisson SAS), Kungsportsavenyn 36, Centrum ☎ 031/206058) plays traditional and contemporary music and has song and dance performances by gifted artists.

Jazz Clubs

Modern jazz enthusiasts usually head for **Nefertiti** (⊠ Hvitfeldtsplatsen 6, Centrum ☎ 031/7111533), the trendy, shadowy club where the line to get in is always long. Performers at **Jazzhuset** (⊠ Eric Dahlbergsg. 3, Vasastan ☎ 031/133544) tend to play traditional, swing, and Dixieland jazz.

Film

As in all Swedish cinemas, the ones in Göteborg show mostly English-language films. The films are subtitled, never dubbed. The strangest movie theater in town is **Bio Palatset** (⊠ Kungstorget, Centrum ☎ 031/174500), a converted meat market turned into a 10-screen cinema. The walls are in various clashing fruit colors, and the floodlighted foyer has sections scooped out to reveal Göteborg's natural rock. **Hagabion** (⊠ Linnég. 21, Linnéstaden ☎ 031/428810) is a good art-house cinema housed in an old ivy-covered school.

SPORTS & THE OUTDOORS

Beaches

There are several excellent local beaches. The two most popular—though they're rarely crowded—are Askim and Näset. To reach Askim, take the Express Blå bus from the central station bus terminal. It's a 10-km (6-mi) journey south of the city center. For Näset catch Bus 19 from Brunnsparken for the 11-km (7-mi) journey southwest of Göteborg.

Diving

The water on the west coast of Sweden, although colder than that on the east coast, is a lot clearer: it's great for diving around rocks and wrecks. Wrap up warmly and bring your diving certificate. Among the many companies offering diving is **Aqua Divers** (⊠ Kungsg. 4 ☎ 031/220030).

Fishing

Mackerel fishing is popular here. The **M.S. Daisy** (☎ 031/963018), which leaves from Hjuvik on the Hisingen side of the Göta River, takes expeditions into the archipelago. With plenty of salmon, perch, and pike, the rivers and lakes in the area have much to offer. For details call Göteborg's **Sportfiskarnas fishing information line** (☎ 031/7730700).

Golf

Among the many golf courses surrounding Göteborg, **Göteborgs Golfklubb** (⊠ Golfbanevägen 17, Hovås ☎ 031/282444) is Sweden's oldest golf club. It has an 18-hole course. **Chalmers Golfklubb** (⊠ Härrydavägen 50, Landvetter ☎ 031/918433) was initially a golf club for Göteborg's Technical University but is now open to the public. It has an 18-hole course, one of the area's best. All players are welcome, but as with all Swedish courses, you must have a handicap certificate to play.

Indoor Swimming

Vatten Palatset (⊠ Häradsvägen 3, Lerum ☎ 0302/17020) is a decent indoor pool. As well as regular swimming, this huge complex offers indoor and outdoor adventure pools, water slides, water jets, wave pools, bubble pools, and saunas.

Running

Many running tracks wind their way around Göteborg, but to reach the most beautiful one, hop on Tram 8 at Gamelstadstorget and take it to Angered Centrum. Here the **Angered and Lärjeåns Dalgång** winds its way through 8 km (5 mi) of leafy forests and undulating pastures.

SHOPPING

Department Stores

Åhléns (☎ 031/3334000) is in the Nordstan mall. Try the local branch of **NK** (✉ Östra Hamng. 42, Centrum ☎ 031/7101000) for men's and women's fashions and excellent household goods.

Specialty Stores

Antiques
Antikhallarna (Antiques Halls; ✉ Västra Hamng. 6, Centrum ☎ 031/7741525) has one of Scandinavia's largest antiques selections. Sweden's leading auction house, **Bukowskis** (✉ Kungsportsavenyn 43, Centrum ☎ 031/200360), is on Avenyn. For a memorable antiques-buying experience, check out **Göteborgs Auktionsverk** (✉ Tredje Långg. 9, Linnéstaden ☎ 031/7047700). There's a large amount of very good silver, porcelain, and jewelry hidden among the more trashy items. Viewings on Friday 10–2, Saturday 10–noon, and Sunday 11–noon precede the auctions on Saturday and Sunday starting at noon.

Crafts
Excellent examples of local arts and crafts can be bought at **Bohusslöjden** (✉ Kungsportsavenyn 25, Centrum ☎ 031/160072). If you are looking to buy Swedish arts and crafts and glassware, visit the various shops in **Kronhusbodarna** (✉ Kronhusg. 1D, Nordstan ☎ 031/7110832). As they have since the 18th century, the sheds and stalls at **Crown House** (✉ Postg. 6–8, Nordstan) sell traditional, handcrafted quality goods, including silver and gold jewelry, watches, and handblown glass.

Men's Clothing
The fashions at **Gillblads** (✉ Kungsg. 44, Centrum ☎ 031/108846) suit a young and trendy customer. **Ströms** (✉ Kungsg. 2729, Centrum ☎ 031/177100) has occupied its street-corner location for two generations, offering clothing of high quality and good taste.

Women's Clothing
Gillblads (✉ Kungsg. 44, Centrum ☎ 031/108846) has the most current fashions. **H & M** (Hennes & Mauritz; ✉ Kungsg. 5557, Centrum ☎ 031/77118262) sells clothes roughly comparable to the choices at flashier Old Navy or Marks & Spencer. **Ströms** (✉ Kungsg. 27–29, Centrum ☎ 031/177100) offers clothing of high quality and mildly conservative style.

Food Markets

There are several large food markets in the city area, but the most impressive is **Salluhallen** (✉ Kungstorget, Centrum). Built in 1889, the barrel-roof, wrought-iron, glass, and brick building stands like a monument to industrial architecture. Everything is available here, from fish, meat, and bakery products to deli foods, herbs and spices, coffee, cheese, and even just people-watching.

GÖTEBORG A TO Z

To research prices, get advice from other travelers, and book travel arrangements, visit www.fodors.com.

AIR TRAVEL TO & FROM GÖTEBORG

CARRIERS Among the airlines operating to and from Göteborg are Air Botnia, Air France, British Airways, City Airline, Finnair, KLM, Lufthansa, Malmö Aviation, SAS, SN Brussels Airlines, Sterling, Swiss, and Wideroøe.
🏢 **Air Botnia** ☎ 031/7942020. **Air France** ☎ 031/946505. **British Airways** ☎ 020/781144. **City Airline** ☎ 0200/250500. **Finnair** ☎ 031/131621. **KLM** ☎ 031/942820.

Lufthansa ☎ 031/7942020. **Malmö Aviation** ☎ 020/550010. **SAS** ☎ 020/727727 or 08/7972688 from abroad. **SN Brussels Airlines** ☎ 08/58536547.**Sterling** ☎ 08/58769148. **Swiss** ☎ 031/7278132. **Wideroøe** ☎ 031/7942020.

AIRPORTS & TRANSFERS

Landvetter Airport is approximately 26 km (16 mi) from the city.
🏢 **Landvetter Airport** ☎ 031/941100 ⊕ www.lfv.se.

AIRPORT
TRANSFERS Landvetter is linked to Göteborg by freeway. Buses leave Landvetter every 15–30 minutes and arrive 30 minutes later at Nils Ericsonsplatsen by the central train station, with stops at Lisebergsstationen, Korsvägen, the Radisson SAS, and Kungsportsplatsen; weekend schedules include some nonstop departures. The price of the trip is SKr 60. For more information call Flygbussarna.

The taxi ride to the city center should cost no more than SKr 310. A shared limousine to the city costs SKr 295.
🏢 **Taxi Göteborg** ☎ 031/650000. **Scandinavian Limousine** ☎ 031/7942424.

Flygbussarna ☎ 031/272727.

BOAT & FERRY TRAVEL

Traveling the entire length of the Göta Canal by passenger boat to Stockholm takes between four and six days. For details contact the AB Göta Kanalbolaget or Rederi AB Göta Kanal.
🏢 **AB Göta Kanalbolaget** ☎ 0141/202050 ⊕ www.gotakanal.se. **Rederi AB Göta Kanal** ✉ Pusterviksgatan 13, 413 01 Göteborg ☎ 031/806315 ⊕ www.gotacanal.se.

BUS TRAVEL TO & FROM GÖTEBORG

All buses arrive in the central city area, in the bus station next to the central train station. The principal bus company is Swebus.
🏢 **Swebus** ✉ ☎ 031/103800.

CAR RENTAL

Avis, Hertz, and Europcar have offices at the airport and the central railway station. Avis has an office in town also.
🏢 **Major Agencies Avis** ☎ 031/946030 at airport, 031/805780 at central railway station. **Europcar** ☎ 031/947100.**Hertz** ☎ 031/946020.

CAR TRAVEL

Göteborg is reached by car either via the E20 or the E4 highway from Stockholm (495 km [307 mi]) and the east, or on the E6/E20 coastal highway from the south (Malmö is 290 km [180 mi] away). Markings are excellent, and roads are well sanded and plowed in winter.

CONSULATES

🏢 **United Kingdom** ✉ S. Hamngatan 23, Centrum ☎ 031/3393300.

EMERGENCIES

Dial 112 for emergencies anywhere in the country, or dial the emergency services number listed below day or night for information on medical services. Emergencies are handled by the Mölndalssjukhuset, Östra Sjukhuset, and Sahlgrenska hospitals. There is a private medical service at CityAkuten weekdays 8–6. There is a 24-hour children's emergency service at Östra Sjukhuset as well.

The national dental-service emergency number and the private dental-service number are listed below. The national service is available 8–8 on weekdays and the private service weekdays between 8 and 5; for after-hours emergencies contact a hospital.

🔢 Doctors & Dentists **Folktandvården Dental-Service Emergencies** ☎ 031/807800. **Tandakuten Private Dental Services** ☎ 031/800500.

🔢 Emergency Services **Medical Services Information (SOS Alarm)** ☎ 031/7031500.

🔢 Hospitals **After-hours emergencies** ☎ 031/7031500. **CityAkuten** ⊠ Drottningg. 45, Centrum ☎ 031/101010. **Mölndalssjukhuset** ☎ 031/3431000. **Östra Sjukhuset** ☎ 031/ 3434000. **Sahlgrenska Hospital** ☎ 031/3421000.

🔢 24-Hour Pharmacies **Vasen** ⊠ Götg. 12, in Nordstan shopping mall, Nordstan ☎ 031/802053.

ENGLISH-LANGUAGE MEDIA

BOOKS Nearly all bookshops stock English-language books. The broadest selection is at Akademibokhandeln.

🔢 Bookstores **Akademibokhandeln** ⊠ Postgatan 26-32, Nordstan ☎ 031/150284, ⊠ Norra Hamngatan 26, Nordstan ☎ 031/617030.

LODGING

CAMPING Göteborg has several fine camping sites.

🔢 **Uddevalla** ☎ 0522/644117 Hafstens Camping. **Göteborg** ☎ 031/840200 Kärralund 🏠 031/840500. **Askim** ☎ 031/286261 Askim Strand 🏠 031/681335.

TAXIS

Taxi Göteborg is the main local taxi company.

🔢 **Taxi Göteborg** ☎ 031/650000.

TOURS

BOAT TOURS For a view of the city from the water and an expert commentary on its sights and history in English and German, take one of the Paddan sightseeing boats. *Paddan* is Swedish for "toad," an apt commentary on the vessels' squat appearance. The boats pass under 20 bridges and take in both the canals and part of the Göta River.

🔢 **Paddan** ⊠ Kungsportsplatsen, Centrum ☎ 031/609670 🎫 SKr 85.

BUS TOURS A 90-minute bus tour and a two-hour combination boat-and-bus tour of the chief points of interest leave from outside the main tourist office at Kungsportsplatsen every day from mid-May through August and on Saturday in April, September, and October. Call the tourist office for schedules.

TRAIN TRAVEL

There is regular service from Stockholm to Göteborg, which takes a little over 4½ hours, as well as frequent high-speed (X2000) train service, which takes about three hours. All trains arrive at the central train station in Drottningtorget, downtown Göteborg. For schedules call SJ, the Swedish national rail company. Streetcars and buses leave from here for the suburbs, but the hub for all streetcar traffic is a block down Norra Hamngatan, at Brunnsparken.

🔢 **SJ** ☎ 0771/757575 ⊕ www.sj.se.

TRANSPORTATION AROUND GÖTEBORG

Stadstrafiken is the name of Göteborg's excellent transit service. Transit brochures, which are available in English, explain the various discount passes and procedures; you can pick one up at a TidPunkten office.

The best bet for the tourist is the Göteborg Pass, which covers free use of public transport, various sightseeing trips, and admission to Liseberg and local museums, among other benefits. The card costs SKr 175 for one day and SKr 295 for two days; there are lower rates for children younger than 18 years. You can buy the Göteborg Pass as well as regular tram and bus passes at Pressbyrån shops, camping sites, and the tourist information offices.

TidPunkten ✉ Drottningtorget, Brunnsparken, and Nils Ericsonsplatsen, Centrum ☎ 0771/414300.

TRAVEL AGENCIES

See the *Yellow Pages* under "Resor-Resebyråer."

Local Agent Referrals **Ticket Travel Agency** ✉ Östra Hamng. 35, Centrum ☎ 031/176860. **Carlson Wagonlit Travel** ✉ Kronhusg. 7, Nordstan ☎ 031/7563700

VISITOR INFORMATION

The main tourist office is Göteborg's Turistbyrå. There are also offices at the Nordstan shopping center and in front of the central train station at Drottningtorget.

A free English-language newspaper called *Metro* is available during the summer; you can pick it up at tourist offices, shopping centers, and some restaurants, as well as on the streetcars.

The Friday edition of the principal morning newspaper, *Göteborgs Posten,* includes a weekend supplement with entertainment listings—it's in Swedish but is reasonably easy to decipher.

Göteborg's Turistbyrå's Web site has a good events calendar.

The Göteborg Pass, available from the Göteborg tourist office, and on their Web site, offers discounts and savings for sights, restaurants, hotels, and other services around the city.

Tourist Information **Göteborg's Turistbyrå** ✉ Kungsportsplatsen 2, 411 10 Göteborg ☎ 031/612500 🖨 031/612501 ⊕ www.goteborg.com. **Nordstan shopping center** ✉ Nordstadstorget, 411 05 Göteborg ☎ 031/612500.

SIDE TRIPS FROM GÖTEBORG

5

BOHUSLÄN

It was from the rocky, rugged shores of Bohuslän that the 9th- and 10th-century Vikings sailed southward on their epic voyages. This coastal region north of Göteborg provides a foretaste of Norway's fjords farther north. Small towns and attractive fishing villages nestle among the distinctively rounded granite rocks and the thousands of skerries (rocky isles or reefs) and larger islands that form Sweden's western archipelago. The ideal way to explore the area is by drifting slowly north of Göteborg, taking full advantage of the uncluttered beaches and small rustic fishing villages. Painters and sailors haunt the region in summer.

Kungälv

❶ *15 km (9 mi) north of Göteborg.*

The trip from Göteborg takes you first along the Göta Älv, a wide waterway that 10,000 years ago, when the ice cap melted, was a great fjord. Some 30 minutes into the voyage the boat passes below a rocky escarpment, topped by the remains of **Bohus Fästning** (Bohus Castle), distinguished by two round towers known as Father's Hat and Mother's Bonnet. It dates from the 14th century and was once the mightiest fortress in western Scandinavia, commanding the confluence of the Göta Älv and Nordre Älv rivers. It was strengthened and enlarged in the 16th century and successfully survived 14 sieges. From 1678 onward, the castle began to lose its strategic and military importance; it fell into decay until 1838, when King Karl XIV passed by on a river journey, admired the old fortress, and ordered its preservation.

Just north of Kungälv along the Trollhätte Canal stretch is the quiet village of **Lödöse,** once a major trading settlement and a predecessor of Göteborg. From here, the countryside becomes wilder, with pines and oaks clustered thickly on either bank between cliffs of lichen-covered granite.

Though today it is something of a bedroom community for Göteborg, Kungälv was an important battleground in ancient times, strategically placed at the confluence of the two arms of the Göta River. The town's several historic sights include a white wooden church, dating from 1679, with an unusual baroque interior. Narrow cobbled streets are full of ancient, leaning, wooden houses.

For a sense of Kungälv's military past, visit the ruins of **Bohus Fästning,** a fortress built by the Norwegians in 1308; it was the site of many battles between Swedish, Norwegian, and Danish armies. ⊠ *Kungälv* ☎ *0303/99200* 🕿 *SKr 25* ⊙ *April, weekends 11–5; May–Aug., daily 10–7; Sept., daily 11–5.*

Sports & the Outdoors

The tiny village of Rönang, on the island of Tjörn, offers excellent **deep-sea fishing;** mackerel and cod are among the prized catches. There are several companies that can take you out, usually in a boat that holds 12 people. One of the best outfitters is **Havsfiske med Hajen** (⊠ Hamnen, Marstrand ☎0304/672447). Most boats leave twice daily. To get to Tjörn, drive over the road bridge from Stenungsund, just north of Kungälv on the E6.

Marstrand

❷ *17 km (11 mi) west of Kungälv (via Route 168).*

Unusually high stocks of herring used to swim in the waters around Marstrand, which is on an island of the same name. The fish made the

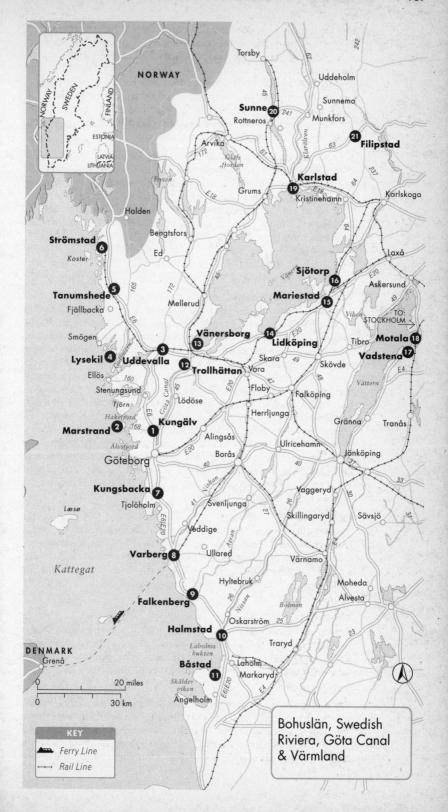

Bohuslän, Swedish Riviera, Göta Canal & Värmland

town extremely rich. But after the money came greed and corruption: in the 16th century Marstrand became known as the most immoral town in Scandinavia, a reputation that reached its lowest point with the murder of a town cleric in 1586. Soon after this the town burned down and the fish disappeared. As Göteborg and Kungälv became major trade centers, in the early 19th century, Marstrand turned to tourism. By 1820 all the town's wooden herring-salting houses had been turned into fashionable and lucrative bathhouses, and people still come to dip into the clear, blue waters and swim, sail, and fish.

Marstrand's main draw is **Carlstens Fästning,** the huge stone-wall castle that stands on the rock above the town. Tours of Carlstens Fortress are not completely in English, but most guides are more than willing to translate. The tours include a morbidly fascinating look at the castle's prison cells, where you can see drawings done in blood and hear tales of Carlstens's most famous prisoner, Lasse-Maja—he dressed up as a woman to seduce and then rob local farmers. ☎ *0303/60265* ✉ *SKr 60* ⊙ *June–mid-Aug., daily 11–6; mid-Aug.–end of Aug., daily noon–4; Sept.–May, weekends 11–4.*

Where to Stay & Eat

$$ ✕⊡ **Grand Hotell Marstrand.** History and luxury abound in this tile-roof hotel, which resembles a French château. Large balconies and verandas open onto a small park, beyond which lies the North Sea. Inside, the hotel is stylishly simple, with bold colors and clean Scandinavian furniture. The rooms are equally light and airy, and the bathrooms have white tiles and brass fittings. A windowed sauna in one of the towers looks out over the harbor. The traditional restaurant ($$) serves excellent local seafood specialties: the garlic-marinated langoustine is a standout. ✉ *Rådhusg. 2, 440 30* ☎ *0303/60322* 🖷 *0303/60053* ⊕ *www. grandmarstrand.se* ⇆ *22 rooms, 6 suites* ⚴ *Restaurant, bar, sauna, convention center* ▤ *AE, DC, MC, V* ⑩| *BP.*

$ ⊡ **Hotell Nautic.** This basic but good hotel is right on the harbor. The rooms are quite plain but functional, with wood floors and a small desk and chair. The building is a classic white-clapboard construction. ✉ *Långg. 6, 440 35* ☎ *0303/61030* 🖷 *0303/61200* ⇆ *29 rooms with shower* ▤ *AE, DC, MC, V* ⑩| *BP.*

Sports & the Outdoors

The coastline around Marstrand looks most beautiful from the water. **Franckes Marina** (✉ Södra Strandg. ☎ 0303/61584 ⊕ www.franckes.se) will rent you a boat, complete with captain, for cocktails, sightseeing, and fishing. It costs about SKr 1,500 for a two-hour excursion and SKr 650 for each additional hour. Fishing equipment is available for SKr 75 per person.

Nightlife

Among the usual peppering of provincial drinking places, **Oscars** (✉ Hamng. 11 ☎ 0303/61554) stands out as one of the best. Sweden's first disco (1964) has retained its silver-and-wood glamour and serves up good music on weekends and great beer all the time.

Shopping

The center of Marstrand is full of ancient cobbled streets, pastel-painted wooden houses, and arts-and-crafts shops selling locally inspired paintings, handicrafts, and ceramics. Worth a visit is **Mary Carlsson** (✉ Kungsg. 2–4 ☎ 0303/60459). Else Langkilde of **Konstnärsateljé Langkilde** (✉ Myren 29 ☎ 070/3965131 or 0303/60144) paints intriguingly with vivid colors.

<table>
<tr><td>

off the
beaten
path

</td><td>

GULLHOLMEN – A frequent ferry from Ellös, on the island of Orust, will take you on the short ride to the windswept, rugged cliff tops of the small island of Gullholmen. In its 13th-century fishing village, tiny, red-painted wooden houses huddle together around a large church. The rest of Gullholmen is set aside as a nature reserve that supports bird life of all kinds. The island of Orust can be reached via Route 160 off E6.

</td></tr>
</table>

Uddevalla

❸ *64 km (40 mi) north of Kungälv, 79 km (49 mi) north of Göteborg.*

A former shipbuilding town located at the head of a fjord, Uddevalla is best known for a 1657 battle between the Danes and the Swedes. Heavy rains doused the musketeers' tinderboxes, effectively ending hostilities.

The history of the entire Bohuslän region can be seen at the **Bohusläns Museum.** Exhibitions reflect the local culture, countryside, and industries, including, of course, fishing. The museum also traces the history of local inhabitants over the 10,000 years since people first settled this part of Sweden. ⊠ *Museeg. 1* ☎ *0522/656500* ⊡ *Free* ☉ *Mon.–Thurs. 10–8, Fri.–Sun. 10–4.*

Ten thousand years ago receding land ice formed the unique shell banks, the world's largest, just outside Uddevalla. When the 1-km-thick (0.66-mi-thick) ice melted, huge masses of water mixed with saltwater from the sea and left behind fossils from more than 100 species. **Skall-banksmuseet,** the Shell Bank Museum, organizes guided walks in the shell banks every Monday. ⊠ *Kurödsvägen 1* ☎ *0522/656571* ⊡ *Museum free; guided tours SKr 30* ☉ *Apr.–May, weekends 11–5; June–Aug., daily 11–5; Sept., weekends 11–5. Monday tour time varies.*

<table>
<tr><td>

off the
beaten
path

</td><td>

GUSTAFSBERG – Adjoining Uddevalla to the west, Gustafberg lays claim to being Sweden's oldest seaside resort, having been mentioned by the botanist Linnaeus in a book he wrote in 1746. There is little left to see of the resort now, save the richly ornamented wooden Society House and a few 18th-century villas, but there is a beautiful little park that leads down to the water's edge, a perfect place for a refreshing swim.

</td></tr>
</table>

Where to Stay

$ ⊡ **Bohusgården.** From its cliff-top location, this modern concrete-block hotel has stunning views of the sea. But even though the rooms are comfortable, they're not that inspiring. The plain, cold, and basic furnishings make them livable but not very welcoming. It is the spa that attracts guests. Pampering treatments include facials, mineral-water baths, massages, and more opulent services. ⊠ *Nordens Väg 6, 451 43* ☎ *0522/ 36420* 🖷 *0522/34472* ⊕ *www.bohusgarden.se* ⇄ *97 rooms* ⌂ *Restaurant, bar, pool, spa* ⊟ *AE, DC, MC, V* ⦿ *BP.*

$ ⊡ **Carlia.** A hotel by this name has been in Uddevalla for more than 100 years in one form or another. In its latest guise it has large comfortable rooms with furnishings and fabrics that are a touch on the floral side; a homey bar; and a well-equipped reading area with books, newspapers, and periodicals. All the suites have Jacuzzis. ⊠ *N. Drottningg. 26, 451 31* ☎ *0522/14140* 🖷 *0522/17081* ⊕ *www.carlia.com* ⇄ *114 rooms, 7 suites* ⌂ *Bar, breakfast room, sauna, library* ⊟ *AE, DC, MC, V* ⦿ *BP.*

Lysekil

❹ *30 km (19 mi) west of Uddevalla via E6 and Route 161.*

Perched on a peninsula at the head of Gullmarn Fjord, Lysekil has been one of Sweden's most popular summer resorts since the 19th century, when the wealthiest citizens of Sweden would come to take the therapeutic waters. Back then, the small resort was made up mainly of fancy villas painted mustard and brown. Today you can still see the original houses, but among them now are amusement arcades and cotton-candy stalls.

The surrounding coastline has great, rugged walking trails. These trails offer stunning views of the undulating skerries and islets that dot the water below. Guided botanical and marine walks can be organized by the **tourist office** (☎ 0523/13050).

Take any of the many flights of steps that start from Lysekil's main seafront road to get to **Lysekils Kyrka** (Lysekil Church). Probably the town's most impressive landmark, Lysekil Church was carved from the pink granite of the area and has beaten-copper doors. Its windows were painted by Albert Eldh, the early-20th-century artist. ⊠ *Stora Kyrkog.*

Havets Hus. (House of the Sea) concentrates on the fish and other sea life found in local waters. The giant aquariums contain everything from near-microscopic life-forms to giant cod and even a small but menacing shark. The tour ends with a walk with a stunning view of the fish through a 26-ft glass tunnel. The in-house café has a hole in the floor that looks down into the water above the tunnel. As you sip your coffee, you can watch with amusement as slightly befuddled people wander below you and parents try to stop their children from throwing their cakes in to feed the fish. ⊠ *Strandv.* ☎ *0523/19670* ☒ *SKr 10* ☉ *Daily 10–6.*

Twenty minutes north of Lysekil on Route 162 is **Nordens Ark.** A cut above the usual safari parks, Nordens Ark is a sanctuary for endangered animals. This haven of tranquillity is home to red pandas, lynxes, snow leopards, and arctic foxes. The best way to see the elusive wild animals is to follow the small truck that delivers their food at feeding times. ⊠ *Åby Säteri, Hunnebostrand* ☎ *0523/79590* ☒ *SKr 105* ☉ *Mar.–mid-June, daily 10–5; mid-June–mid-Aug., daily 10–7; mid-Aug.–Oct., daily 10–5; Nov.–Mar., daily 10–4.*

off the
beaten
path

SMÖGEN – At the very tip of a westerly outcrop of land, Smögen is an ideal point for a quick stop-off. To get here, head north on Route 162 and then west on Route 171 until it stops. The small village's red fishing huts, crystal-blue water, and pretty scrubbed boardwalks appear on many postcards of Bohuslän. Down on the main boardwalk, a stop at the **Bageri Skäret** (⊠ Hamnen 1 ☎ 0523/32317) is a must. As well as having a great ocean view from the upstairs veranda, this small café and bar makes exquisite cakes and bread.

FJÄLLBACKA – Twenty-seven kilometers (16 miles) north of Lysekil, directly along the coast route, is this village with pastel wooden houses nestled in the rock. Fjällbacka, part of an archipelago, was home to actress Ingrid Bergman's summerhouse. In the square named after her, you can see her statue peering out over the water where her ashes were scattered, to the distant island Dannholmen, where her house was. Behind the square is a dramatic ravine known as Kungskliftan (King's Cliff), where, among many others added since, you can find King Oscar II's name, which he etched into the rock in 1887.

Where to Stay & Eat

$–$$ ✕ **Brygghuset.** A short boat ride and a walk through a breathtaking hill-top fishing village on the island of Fiskebäckskil will bring you to this lovely little restaurant. The interior is rustic, with wooden beams and plain wooden tables. Watch the chefs in the open kitchen as they prepare excellent local fish dishes. In the summer there is outdoor eating, or you can just choose a glass of wine from the excellent wine list and watch the boats sail by. The ferry *Carl Wilhelmsson* leaves from outside the tourist office in Lysekil every half hour, bringing you to the restaurant 20 minutes later. ⊠ *Lyckans Slip Fiskebäckskil* ☎ *0523/22222* ⌂ *Reservations essential* ▤ *AE, DC, MC, V.*

$–$$ ✕ **Pråmen.** This modern-looking restaurant has large windows and is propped on legs that allow it to jut out over the water. The view is great; with the windows open you can smell the sea. You can feast on good portions of simply cooked local fish and wash it down with cold beer. ⊠ *Södra Hamng.* ☎ *0523/13452* ▤ *AE, DC, MC, V.*

$ ⊡ **Lysekil Havshotell.** This tall, narrow hotel has great views from atop a cliff. Stripped-wood floors and a miscellany of furnishings and fabrics create relaxed surroundings. Many rooms have sofas and provide bathrobes. Only breakfast is served, and there's a stocked bar (done on the honor system) in each room. For the best view across the water, reserve Room 18, which costs SKr 200 extra. ⊠ *Turistg. 13, 453 30* ☎ *0523/79750* ⎙ *0523/14204* ⇌ *15 rooms, 2 suites* ⌂ *Breakfast room, minibars, conference room* ▤ *AE, MC, V* ⅠⓄⅠ *BP.*

¢ ⊡ **Strand Vandrarhem.** This hostel on the seafront offers simple, friendly accommodations. Unless you stipulate otherwise and pay an additional fee, you may find yourself sharing the room with another guest (the rooms are outfitted with bunk beds). The welcome here is warm, and the breakfast (SKr 50 extra) is excellent. ⊠ *Strandv. 1, 453 30* ☎ *0523/79751* ⎙ *0523/12202* ⊕ *www.strandflickorna.se* ⇌ *20 rooms without bath* ⌂ *Breakfast room* ▤ *MC, V.*

Nightlife & the Arts

During July Lysekil comes alive to the sounds of the annual **Lysekil Jazz Festival.** Big-name Swedish, and some international, jazz musicians play in open-air concerts and in bars and restaurants. Contact **Lysekils Turistbyrå** (tourist office; ☎ 0523/13050) for details of events.

Sports & the Outdoors

For a taste of the sea air and a great look at some local nature, take one of the regular seal safaris. Boat trips to view these fascinating, wallowing, slippery mammals leave from the main harbor three times daily between June and August, cost SKr 120, and take about two hours. Details and times are available from **Lysekils Turistbyrå** (☎ 0523/13050).

Tanumshede

❺ *45 km (28 mi) north of Lysekil (via Routes 161 and E6).*

From roughly 4000 to 3000 BC, Tanumshede was a coastal settlement. Now it's 5 km (3 mi) from the sea, since sea level is now 50 ft lower than it was then. Although the town itself is not extraordinary, it does hold the largest single collection of **Bronze Age rock carvings** (*hällristningar*) in Europe. People from all over the world flock to this UNESCO World Heritage Site to see the rudimentary scrapings that depict battles, hunting, and fishing.

Most of the carvings are within a short distance of the road, etched onto the weather-worn rocks that were picked up and deposited around the countryside by retreating Ice Age glaciers; the ones that are farther out, carved onto the largest rocks, are best reached by bicycle. Bikes can be rented from **Tanum Strand** (⊠ Tanums Strand Grebbestad ☎ 0525/ 19000), for SKr 50 per hour or Skr 200 per day.

Heralded for its fantastic architecture, the **Vitlycke Museet** tells the story of the area's famous rock carvings and conveys what life was like between 1500 and 500 BC. It also makes some amusing and seemingly random attempts at decoding the messages held in the stones. ⊠ *Vitlycke 2 Tanumshede* ☎ *0525/20950* 🖃 *SKr 50* ☉ *Apr.–Sept., daily 10–6; Oct.–Mar., by appointment only.*

Strömstad

❻ *90 km (56 mi) northwest of Uddevalla, 169 km (105 mi) north of Göteborg.*

This popular Swedish resort claims to have more summer sunshine than any other town north of the Alps. Formerly Norwegian, it has been the site of many battles between warring Danes, Norwegians, and Swedes. A short trip over the Norwegian border takes you to Halden, where Sweden's warrior king, Karl XII, died in 1718.

The **Strömstad Museum,** housed in a beautiful, 18th-century redbrick mansion, has thoughtful, informative displays on the town's history and the importance of fishing as a local industry. Attached to the museum is a good town archive that includes old pictures showing how life was lived here. ⊠ *Södra Hamng. 26* ☎ *0526/10275* 🖃 *SKr 20* ☉ *Mid-June–mid-Aug., Mon. 11–6, Tues.–Fri. 11–4, Sat. 11–2; mid-Aug.–mid-June, weekdays 11–4, Sat. 11–2.*

Although it is of no particular historical importance, **Strömstads Kyrka** is well worth a visit just to marvel at its interior design. The Strömstad Church's seemingly free-form decoration policy throws together wonderfully detailed, crowded frescoes; overly ornate gilt chandeliers; brass lamps from the 1970s; and model ships hanging from the roof. In the graveyard you can find the stone of Adolf Fritiof Cavalli-Holmgren, the eccentric jeweler's son who went on to become a financier and Sweden's richest man for a brief period around 1900. He was responsible for the design of the grand, copper-roof town hall in the middle of Strömstad. He never actually got to see it or to live in its specially created penthouse apartment, since he fell out with the local council over the design. ⊠ *S. Kyrkog. 10* ☎ *0526/10029.*

> **off the beaten path**

KOSTER ISLANDS – There are regular ferryboats from Strömstad to the Koster Islands, Sweden's two most westerly inhabited islands. With no motorized vehicles allowed, the two islands are a perfect place for tranquil bike riding. Bikes can be rented for SKr 50 where you disembark from the boat. Most of the island is a sanctuary for wildlife, so the only sounds you'll hear through the meadows are bird calls. Small, red wooden houses occasionally hold a café or coffee shop. The prawn sandwiches are always superb.

Where to Stay & Eat

$–$$$ ✕ **Göstases.** Somewhat resembling the interior of a wooden boat, this restaurant on the quayside specializes in locally caught fish and seafood. Knots, ropes, life preservers, stuffed fish, and similar paraphernalia abound. But it all pales when you see the low prices for fresh lobster, crab, prawns, and fish, all of which can be washed down with equally affordable cold beer. Sit outside in summer and watch the fishing boats bring in your catch and the pleasure boats float by. ⊠ *Strandpromenaden* ☎ *0526/10812* ⊟ *MC, V.*

$ ✕⊡ **Laholmen.** This huge, sprawling hotel and restaurant offers good-quality food and excellent accommodations on a grand scale. The rooms are a bit garish, with overly vivid color schemes, but they are large and well equipped. The restaurant ($) has a good buffet and an interesting menu of local dishes, including exquisite prawn sandwiches at lunch. The restaurant as well as most guest rooms have views across the pretty harbor and the water beyond, which is scattered with skerries. ⊠ *Laholmen, 452 30* ☎ *0526/197000* ⊟ *0526/10036* ⊕ *www.laholmen.se* ⟲ *150 rooms, 4 suites* ⌂ *Restaurant, bar, lounge, sauna, convention center* ⊟ *AE, DC, MC, V* ⍥ *BP.*

Bohuslän A to Z

To research prices, get advice from other travelers, and book travel arrangements, visit www.fodors.com.

BUS TRAVEL

Buses to the region leave from behind the central train station in Göteborg; the main bus company is Västtrafik. The trip to Strömstad takes between two and three hours.

⁊ Bus Information **Västtrafik** ☎ 0771/414300.

CAR TRAVEL

The best way to explore Bohuslän is by car. The E6 Highway runs the length of the coast from Göteborg north to Strömstad, close to the Norwegian border, and for campers there are numerous well-equipped and uncluttered camping sites along the coast's entire length.

TRAIN TRAVEL

Regular service along the coast connects all the major towns of Bohuslän. The trip from Göteborg to Strömstad takes about two hours, and there are several trains each day. For schedules call SJ.

⁊ Train Information **SJ** ⊠ Göteborg ☎ 0771/757575.

VISITOR INFORMATION

⁊ Tourist Information **Göteborg Turistbyrå** ⊠ Kungsportsplatsen 2, 411 10 Göteborg ☎ 031/612500 ⎙ 031/612501 ⊕ www.goteborg.com. **Kungälv** ⊠ Fästningsholmen ☎ 0303/99200 ⊕ www.kungalv.se/turism. **Kungshamn** ⊠ Hamng. 6 ☎ 0523/665550 ⊕ www.kungshamn.com. **Lysekil** ⊠ Södra Hamng. 6 ☎ 0523/13050. **Marstrand** ⊠ Hamng. ☎ 0303/60087. **Strömstad** ⊠ Torget, Norra Hamnen ☎ 0526/62330 ⊕ www.stromstadtourist.se. **Tanumshede** ⊠ Bygdegårdsplan ☎ 0525/18380. **Uddevalla** ⊠ Kungstorget 4 ☎ 0522/99720 ⊕ www.uddevallaforum.se.

SWEDISH RIVIERA

The coastal region south of Göteborg, Halland—locally dubbed the Swedish Riviera—is the closest that mainland Sweden comes to having a resort area. Fine beaches abound, and there are plenty of sporting activities. But Halland's history is dark, since it was the frontline in the fighting between Swedes and Danes. Evidence of such conflicts can be found in its many medieval villages and fortifications. The region stretches down to Båstad, in the country's southernmost province, Skåne.

Kungsbacka

❼ *25 km (15 mi) south of Göteborg.*

This bedroom community of Göteborg holds a market for all sorts of goods on the first Thursday of every month—a 600-year-old tradition.

A break in a high ridge to the west, the **Fjärås Crack,** offers a fine view of the coast. Formed by melting ice 13,000 years ago, the ridge made a perfect transport route for nomadic tribes of 10,000 years ago, who used it to track the retreating ice northward to settle their new communities. Some important archaeological discoveries have been made here, and much of the information learned is on display on signs dotted along the ridge. The signs act as a sort of self-guided outdoor museum, dealing with the geological and anthropological history of the ridge.

FodorsChoice At Tjolöholm, 12 km (7 mi) down the E6/E20 highway from Kungs-
★   backa, is **Tjolöholms Slott** (Tjolöholm Castle), a manor house built by James Dickson, a Scottish merchant and horse breeder. (He was also the grandson of Robert Dickson, the philanthropist and founder of the Swedish East India Trade Company.) The English Tudor–style house, constructed at the beginning of the 20th century, contains many fascinating elements. By and large, they have become a tribute to Dickson's passion for all things modern, including an early version of a pressurized shower and a horse-drawn vacuum cleaner with a very long hose to reach up through the house windows. Dickson died of lead poisoning before the house was completed—he cut his finger while opening a bottle of champagne and wrapped the lead-foil wrapper around the cut. The house he left behind offers much insight into one man's dream. ⊠ *Fjärås* ☎ *0300/ 544200* ✉ *SKr 60* ☉ *Apr.–mid-June, weekends 11–4; mid-June–Aug., daily 11–4; Sept., weekends 11–4, Oct., Sun. 11–4.*

Near Tjolöholm is the tiny 18th-century village of Äskhult, the site of an open-air museum, the **Äskhults 1700-tals by** (Äskhult's 18th-Century Village). When land reforms forced farmers to combine patches of land into large estates, the four farmers living in Äskhult refused and kept their land separate. This refusal left the village unable to expand while both of the neighboring areas became towns. And so it stayed that way, until the last inhabitants moved away in the mid-19th century. Today you can wander through the houses and farm buildings to get a glimpse of what life was like for 18th-century peasant farmers. ☎ *0300/542159* ✉ *SKr 25* ☉ *May–Aug., daily 10–6; Sept., weekends 10–6.*

en route Forty kilometers (25 miles) southeast of Kungsbacka (on E6 and Route 153) is the shopping mecca of **Ullared,** once a single discount store, now a whole town of huge outlet stores and malls visited by 3 million Swedes each year. It's overwhelming, but even the most resolute nonshoppers may find it difficult to resist the selection and the prices.

Varberg

❽ *40 km (25 mi) south of Kungsbacka, 65 km (40 mi) south of Göteborg.*

Varberg is a busy port with connections to Grenå, in Denmark. Although the town has some good beaches, it's best known for a suit of medieval clothing preserved in the museum inside the 13th-century **Varbergs Fästning** (Varberg Fortress). The suit belonged to a man who was murdered and thrown into a peat bog. The peat preserved his body, and his clothes are the only known suit of ordinary medieval clothing. The museum also contains a silver bullet said to be the one that killed Karl XII. ☎ *0340/18520* 🖼 *SKr 40* ☉ *Fortress open yr-round; guided fortress tours June 15–Aug. 9, daily 11–4 every hr on the hr; museum mid-June–mid-Aug., daily 10–6; mid-Aug.–mid-June, weekdays 10–4, weekends noon–4.*

Where to Stay & Eat

$$ ✕ **Societen.** Housed in the cream-and-green carved-wood confection that is the 19th-century Society House, this restaurant presents dining on a grand scale. Two huge, high-windowed dining rooms offer French-influenced dishes such as mussels with eggplant and garlic. There's fox-trot dancing on Friday and live bands and DJs on Saturday. Two separate lively bar areas are on hand if you need to increase your intake of courage before taking to the dance floor. ⊠ *Societetsparken* ☎ *0340/676500* ⚓ *Reservations essential* 🖃 *AE, DC, MC, V.*

$$ 🖼 **Kust Hotellet.** A former sanatorium on the beachfront, the grandiose Kust Hotellet stuffs curly pieces of art-nouveau furniture into every room. Guest rooms are a little small but comfortable. There is a large and well-equipped spa and sauna area with hot tubs, a heated seawater pool, a regular pool and a Turkish steam bath. Experienced instructors offer spinning, aerobics, and yoga classes. ⊠ *Nils Kreugers Väg 5, 432 24* ☎ *0340/629800* 🖷 *0340/629850* ➹ *106 rooms, 38 suites* ⚴ *Restaurant, bar, indoor pools, heath club, sauna, spa* 🖃 *AE, DC, MC, V* ⦿*BP.*

Falkenberg

❾ *30 km (20 mi) south of Varberg, 100 km (60 mi) south of Göteborg.*

With its attractive beaches and the plentiful salmon that swim in the Ätran River, Falkenberg is one of Sweden's most attractive resorts. Its Gamla Stan (Old Town) is full of narrow cobblestone streets and quaint, old wooden houses.

In the middle of Gamla Stan stands the 12th-century **St. Laurentii Kyrka** (St. Laurentii Church). After the construction of a new church at the end of the 19th century, St. Laurentii was deconsecrated and used as a shooting range, a cinema, and a gymnasium, among other things. It was reconsecrated in the 1920s and is now fully restored with its 16th-century font and silver, as well as some awe-inspiring 17th- and 18th-century wall paintings.

Although it does have the usual archaeological and historical artifacts depicting its town's growth and development, the **Falkenberg Museum** also has an unusual and refreshing obsession with the 1950s. The curator here thinks that is the most interesting period of history, and you can make up your own mind once you've learned about the local dance-band scene, visited the interior of a shoe repair shop, and seen a collection of old jukeboxes. ⊠ *Skepparesträtet 2* ☎ *0346/86125* 🖼 *Free* ☉ *June–Aug., Tues.–Sun. noon–4, Sept.–May, Tues.–Fri. and Sun. noon–4.*

Falkenberg's first movie theater is now home to **Fotomuseum Olympia,** a fascinating display of cameras, camera equipment, and photographs dating to the 1840s. ⊠ *Sandg. 13* ☎ *0346/87928* 🖼 *SKr 30* ☉ *Mid-June–Aug., Tues.–Thurs. 1–7, Sun. 1–6; Sept.–May, Tues.–Thurs. 5–7, Sun. 2–6.*

When the weather gets hot, what better way to quench that raging thirst than a stroll around a cool brewery, followed by a glass of ice cold beer? At the **Brewery in Falkenberg** groups can do just that. The beer Falcon has been brewed on the premises since 1869, and a tour of the facility takes in both old brewing traditions and modern beer-making technology. The tour ends with dinner and refreshing glasses of the house brew.

⊠ *Åstadv.* ☎ *0346/721000 (brewery), 0706/977380 (to book a group tour)* 🖂 *Four-hour tour, including dinner and beer tasting, SKr 350 per person in groups of minimum 15* ⊕ *www.alltommalt.se.*

Doktorspromenaden, on the south side of the river in the town center, is a beautiful walk set against a backdrop of heathland and shade trees. The walk was set up in 1861 by a local doctor in an effort to encourage the townsfolk to get more fresh air. ⊠ *Doktorspromenaden.*

Where to Stay & Eat

$–$$ ✕ **Restaurant Hertigen.** This beautiful white villa is in wooded grounds on an island just outside the center of town. Dining takes place on a large veranda and garden during the summer. The classic French dishes are prepared with a nod in the direction of local cooking styles. ⊠ *Hertings Gård* ☎ *0346/10018* 🗠 *Reservations essential* 🖃 *AE, DC, MC, V.*

$$ 🏨 **Elite Hotel Strandbaden.** A sprawling, white wood-and-glass building, Elite Hotel Strandbaden sits right on the beach at the south end of town. The rooms here are quite small but well equipped, with amenities and modern, comfortable furnishings. Most have a view of the sea. There is a state-of-the-art spa and health club in the hotel, and a very good restaurant decked out in startling blue and orange. ⊠ *Havsbadsallén, 311 42* ☎ *0346/714900* 🖷 *0346/16111* 🖙 *135 rooms, 5 suites* ♨ *Restaurant, bar, brasserie, cable TV, in-room data ports, minibars, sauna, health club* 🖃 *AE, DC, MC, V* ⫚⃝ *BP.*

$ 🏨 **Grand Hotel Falkenberg.** Not as imposing as the name suggests, this pretty, yellow, 19th-century hotel is comfortable and friendly, with very large rooms. The interior is a jumble of furnishings from the last 30 years, with the odd antique thrown in for good measure. Cherrywood and dark rich fabrics are used throughout. ⊠ *Hotellg. 1, 311 31* ☎ *0346/14450* 🖷 *0346/14459* ⊕ *www.grandhotelfalkenberg.se* 🖙 *70 rooms, 3 suites* ♨ *2 restaurants, 2 bars, lounge, sauna* 🖃 *AE, DC, MC, V* ⫚⃝ *BP.*

Sports & the Outdoors

BEACHES A 15-minute walk south from the town center is **Skrea Strand,** a 2-mi stretch of sandy beach. At the northern end of the beach is the huge swimming complex **Klitterbadet** (⊠ Klitterv. ☎ 0346/86330 ☒ SKr 35 ⊙ June–Aug., Sun.–Mon. 9–4, Tues. 6 AM–7 PM, Wed. 9–7, Thurs. 6 AM–7 PM, Fri. 9–7, Sat. 9–5; Sept.–May, Mon. 4 PM–8 PM, Tues. 6–9 and noon–8, Wed. noon–8, Thurs. 6–9 and noon–8, Fri. noon–7, Sat. 9–5, Sun. 9–3), with pools (including one just for children), water slides, a sauna, a whirlpool, a 50-meter-long pool with heated seawater, and steam rooms. Farther south the beach opens out onto some secluded coves and grasslands.

FISHING In the 1800s Falkenberg had some of the best fly-fishing in Europe. This prompted a frenzy of fishermen, including many English aristocrats, to plunder its waters. But despite the overfishing, the Ätran is one of few remaining rivers in Europe inhabited by wild salmon. Fishing permits and rod rentals can be arranged through the local **tourist office** (☎0346/86100).

Shopping

Törngrens (⊠ Krukmakareg. 4 ☎ 0346/10354 ⊙ weekdays 9–5) is probably the oldest pottery shop in Scandinavia, and is now owned by the seventh generation of the founding family. Call ahead to make sure the shop is open.

Halmstad

➓ *40 km (25 mi) south of Falkenberg, 143 km (89 mi) south of Göteborg.*

With a population of 55,000, Halmstad is the largest seaside resort on the west coast. The Norre Port town gate, all that remains of the town's original fortifications, dates from 1605. The modern town hall has interior decorations by the so-called Halmstad Group of painters, which formed here in 1929.

Most of Halmstad's architectural highlights are in and around **Stora Torg**, the large town square. In the middle is the fountain *Europa and the Bull*, by the sculptor Carl Milles. Around the square are many buildings and merchants' houses dating from Halmstad's more prosperous days, in the last half of the 19th century.

At the top of Stora Torg is the grand **St. Nikolai Kyrka,** a huge church from the 14th century containing fragments of medieval murals and a 17th-century pulpit.

The **Tropic Centre,** just a few minutes' walk from the center of Halmstad, holds flora and fauna that come from outside Sweden. Tropical plants, birds, snakes, monkeys, spiders, and crocodiles are all safely tucked away behind glass, ready both to amuse and to, perhaps, horrify you. ⊠ *Tullhuset, Strandg.* ☎ *035/123333* ⊡ *SKr 60* ☽ *July, daily 10–6; Aug.–June, daily 10–4.*

No Swedish town would be complete without its local museum, and the **Halmstad Länsmuseet** is more accomplished than most. Everything from archaeological finds to musical instruments to dollhouses is on display. There's also a haunting display of large figureheads taken from ships that sank off the local coastline. ⊠ *Tollsg.* ☎ *035/162300* ⊡ *SKr 20* ☽ *Tues., Thurs., and Sun. noon–4, Wed. noon–9.*

★ The bizarre **Martin Luther Kyrka** is unique among churches. Built entirely out of steel in the 1970s, its exterior resembles that of a shiny tin can. The interior is just as striking, as the gleaming outside gives way to rust-orange steel and art-deco furnishings that contrast with the outside. To some, Martin Luther Church may seem more like a temple to design, not deity. ⊠ *Långg.* ☎ *035/151961* ☽ *Weekdays 9–3, Sun. services at 10.*

In the 1930s the Halmstad Group, made up of six local artists, caused some consternation with their surrealist and cubist painting styles, influenced strongly by artists such as René Magritte and Salvador Dalí. The **Mjellby Konstgård** (Mjellby Arts Center) contains some of the most important works created over the group's 50-year alliance. ⊠ *Mjellby (4 km [2½ mi] from Halmstad)* ☎ *035/31619* ⊡ *SKr 40* ☽ *Hrs vary with exhibits; call for details.*

Where to Stay & Eat

$$–$$$ ✕ **Pio & Co.** Half informal bar and half bistro, this restaurant offers something for all. It's a bright and airy place with good service and excellent Swedish classics on the menu—the steak and mashed potatoes is wonderful. The list of drinks is extensive. ⊠ *Storg. 37* ☎ *035/210669* ⊟ *AE, DC, MC, V.*

$$ ⊞ **Scandic Hotel Grand.** A shiny white-tile floor, white ceiling tiles, and a circular podlike lobby create a strange first impression. But don't be alarmed. Rooms here come with all the space, comfort, modernity, and up-to-date technology you would expect from a Scandinavian hotel. ⊠ *Rådhusg. 4, 302 43* ☎ *035/2958600* 🖷 *035/2958611* ⟶ *130 rooms, 1 suite* ♨ *Restaurant, bar, in-room data ports, sauna, spa, convention center* ⊟ *AE, DC, MC, V* ⠿⏐ *BP.*

$ ⊞ **Hotel Continental.** Built in 1904 in the national romantic style, the interior of this hotel has been nicely preserved. The sophisticated design includes exposed-brick walls, subtle spotlighting, and light wood fittings. The rooms are bright, modern, and spacious. Five rooms have whirlpool baths. ⊠ *Kungsg. 5, 302 45* ☎ *035/176300* 🖶 *035/128604* 📠 *46 rooms, 3 suites* ♤ *Bar* ☰ *AE, DC, MC, V* ○| *BP.*

Nightlife & the Arts

The nightlife in Halmstad centers around the bars in Storgatan, the main street that runs into Storatorg. **Harry's** (☎ 035/105595) is worth a visit, if only to see its bizarre English phone box with a life-size model of Charlie Chaplin inside. **Pio & Co.** (☎ 035/210669) has a cozy "cognac corner" in the lounge area of the restaurant.

Sports & the Outdoors

There are many good beaches around Halmstad. **Tjuvahålan,** extending west of Halmstad, has an interesting old smugglers' cove that provides pleasant walking. For details contact the **tourist office** (☎ 035/132320).

Båstad

❶ *35 km (22 mi) south of Halmstad, 178 km (111 mi) south of Göteborg.*

In the southernmost province of Skåne, Båstad is regarded by locals as Sweden's most fashionable resort, where ambassadors and local captains of industry have their summerhouses. Aside from this, it is best known for its tennis. In addition to the **Båstad Open,** a grand prix tournament in late summer, there is the annual **Donald Duck Cup** in July, for children from ages 11 to 15; it was the very first trophy won by Björn Borg, who later took the Wimbledon men's singles title an unprecedented five times in a row. Spurred on by Borg and other Swedish champions, such as Stefan Edberg and Mats Wilander, thousands of youngsters take part in the Donald Duck Cup each year. For details contact the **Svenska Tennisförbundet** (Swedish Tennis Association; ⊠ Lidingövägen 75, Stockholm ☎ 08/4504310).

The low-rise shuttered buildings in the center of Båstad give it an almost French provincial feel. In the main square is **St. Maria Kyrka** (St. Maria's Church), which looks much more solidly Swedish. Dating from the 15th century, the plain exterior hides a haven of tranquillity within the cool thick walls. The unusual altar painting depicts Christ on the cross with human skulls and bones strewn beneath him.

Norrviken Gardens, 3 km (2 mi) northwest of Båstad, are beautifully laid out in different styles, including a Japanese garden and a lovely walkway lined with rhododendrons. The creator of the gardens, Rudolf Abelin, is buried on the grounds. A restaurant, shop, and pottery studio are also on the premises. ⊠ *Båstad* ☎ *0431/369040* ⊕ *www. norrvikenstradgardar.se* 🎫 *May–Aug., SKr 60; Sept.–Apr., free* ⊙ *May–Aug., daily 10–6; Sept.–Apr., daily dawn–dusk.*

Where to Stay & Eat

$$ ✕ **G. Swenson's Krog.** Well worth the 3-km (2-mi) journey out of Båstad, this harbor-front restaurant was originally a fisherman's hut and has been converted into a magnificent dining room with cornflower-blue walls, wooden floors, and a glass roof. The menu is full of Swedish classics such as white asparagus with lemon-butter sauce and the most delicious homemade meatballs. The service is friendly, with the family atmosphere really shining through. ⊠ *Pål Romaresg. 2, Torekov* ☎ *0431/ 364590* ♤ *Reservations essential* ☰ *AE, DC, MC, V.*

¢ ✕ **The Wooden Hut.** Actually, this restaurant has no name: it's just a wooden hut on the harbor side. It has no tables either. It has no wine list, no waiters, no interior design, no telephone, and it doesn't accept credit cards. What this restaurant does have is simple and delicious smoked mackerel with potato salad, which will magically take you away from all the pomp and wealth that sometimes bogs Båstad down. Walk past all the hotels and restaurants, smell the fresh sea air, and get ready for a great meal. ⊠ *Strandpromenaden* ☎ *No phone* ⚲ *Reservations not accepted* ⊟ *No credit cards.*

$$ ╳⊡ **Hotel Skansen.** Set in a century-old bathhouse, Skansen's interior reflects the best of modern design. Wonderfully simple earth, cream, and moss green tones create a sense of comfort, simplicity, and relaxation. The rooms are bright, many with glass roof or wall features. Restaurant Sand ($–$$), with a sea view, serves stylish and well-prepared Swedish fare, with fish as a specialty. The bar is well stocked, but the nightclub is nothing special. ⊠ *Kyrkog. 2, 269 21* ☎ *0431/558100* ᵬ *0431/558110* ⊕ *www.hotelskansen.se* ⤶ *112 rooms, 1 suite* ⚘ *Restaurant, bar, spa, steam room, sauna, nightclub* ⊟ *AE, DC, MC, V* ⦿⃝ *BP.*

$ ⊡ **Hjortens Pensionat.** A classic summer resort hotel, Hjortens Pensionat is Båstad's oldest inn. The antiques-filled rooms are light and the common areas cozy. Right in the center of Båstad, the hotel is close to shops, beaches, and tennis courts. ⊠ *Roxmansvägen 23, 269 36* ☎ *0431/ 70109* ᵬ *0431/70180* ⊕ *www.hjorten.net* ⤶ *42 rooms, 37 with bath* ⚘ *Restaurant, bar* ⊟ *DC, MC, V* ⦿⃝ *BP.*

Swedish Riviera A to Z

To research prices, get advice from other travelers, and book travel arrangements, visit www.fodors.com.

BUS TRAVEL

Buses to Kungsbacka, Varberg, Falkenberg, Halmstad, and Båstad leave from behind Göteborg's central train station.

⛊ **Hallandstrafiken** ☎ 0346/48600. **Västtrafik** ☎ 0771/414300.

CAR TRAVEL

Simply follow the E6/E20 highway south from Göteborg toward Malmö. It runs parallel to the coast.

TRAIN TRAVEL

Regular train services connect Göteborg's central station with Kungsbacka, Varberg, Falkenberg, Halmstad, and Båstad.

⛊ SJ ⊠ Göteborg ☎ 0771/757575.

VISITOR INFORMATION

⛊ Tourist Information **Båstad** ⊠ Stortorget 1 ☎ 0431/75045. **Falkenberg** ⊠ Holgersgatan 9 ☎ 0346/86100. **Halmstad** ⊠ Halmstad Slott ☎ 035/132320. **Kungsbacka** ⊠ Storg. 41 ☎ 0300/834595. **Laholm** ⊠ Rådhuset ☎ 0430/15450. **Varberg** ⊠ Brunnsparken ☎ 0340/88770.

GÖTA CANAL

Stretching 614 km (382 mi) between Stockholm and Göteborg, the Göta Canal is actually a series of interconnected canals, rivers, lakes, and even a stretch of sea. Bishop Hans Brask of Linköping in the 16th century was the first to suggest linking the bodies of water; in 1718 King Karl XII ordered the canal to be built, but work was abandoned when he was killed in battle the same year. Not until 1810 was the idea again taken up in earnest. The driving force was a Swedish nobleman, Count Baltzar Bogislaus von Platen (1766–1829), and his motive was commercial. Von Platen saw the canal as a way of beating Danish tolls on ships that passed through the Öresund. He also sought to enhance Göteborg's standing by linking the port with Stockholm, on the east coast. At a time when

Swedish fortunes were at a low ebb, the canal was also viewed as a way to reestablish faith in the future and boost national morale.

The building of the canal took 22 years and involved 58,000 men. Linking the various stretches of water required 87 km (54 mi) of man-made cuts through soil and rock and building 58 locks, 47 bridges, 27 culverts, and 3 dry docks. Unfortunately, the canal never achieved the financial success that von Platen sought. By 1857 the Danes had removed shipping tolls, and in the following decade the linking of Göteborg with Stockholm by rail effectively ended the canal's commercial potential. The canal has nevertheless come into its own as a modern-day tourist attraction.

You may have trouble conceiving of the canal's industrial origins as your boat drifts lazily down this lovely series of waterways; across the enormous lakes, Vänern and Vättern; and through a microcosm of all that is best about Sweden: abundant fresh air; clear, clean water; pristine nature; well-tended farmland. A bicycle path runs parallel to the canal, offering another means of touring the country. You can bike faster than the boats travel, so it's easy to jump off and on as you please.

Trollhättan

⑫ *70 km (43 mi) north of Göteborg.*

In this pleasant industrial town of about 53,000 inhabitants, a spectacular waterfall was rechanneled in 1906 to become Sweden's first hydroelectric plant. On specific days in the summer the waters are allowed to follow their natural course, a fall of 106 feet in six torrents. This sight is well worth seeing. The other main point of interest is the 82-km-long (51-mi-long) Trollhätte Canal, of which a 10-km (6-mi) stretch runs through the city. The canal's six locks date from 1916. Along the canal are also disused locks from 1800 and 1844, beautiful walking trails, and *The King's Cave,* a rock formation on which visiting monarchs have carved their names since 1754. Trollhättan also has a fine, wide marketplace and waterside parks. The city has become somewhat of a center of the Swedish film industry, earning it the nickname "Trollywood." Lukas Moodyson (*Show Me Love, Together,* and *Lilya 4-Ever*) is just one of the directors who have chosen Trollhättan production studios.

In the summer months the **Trollhättans Turistbyrå** (Tourist Office; ⊠ Åkerssjövägen 10 ☎ 0520/488472 ⊕ www.visittrollhattan.se) offers the *Sommarkort* (Summer Pass), with free entrance to the Innovatum, the Innovatum Cableway, Saab Bilmuseum, and the Canal Museum. It costs SKr 100 per day, and accompanying children under 16 are free.

The best way to see the town's spectacular waterfalls and locks is on the **walking trail** that winds its way through the massive system. The walk takes in the hydroelectric power station and the canal museum. Part of the walk is through wooded cliffs that overlook the spectacular cascades of water. The falls flow freely May–June, weekends at 3, and July–August, Wednesday and weekends at 3. In July the falls are also illuminated at 11 PM on Wednesday, Saturday, and Sunday. Details and directions can be found at the tourist office, which will also tell you the best places to watch the waterfall when the waters are allowed to follow their natural course.

The canal and the locks gave Trollhättan its life, and a visit to the **Kanalmuseet** (Canal Museum) tells as full a history of this as you can find. Housed in a redbrick 1893 waterside building, the museum covers the history of the canal and the locks and displays model ships, old tools, and fishing gear. ⊠ *Åkersbergsvägen, Övre Slussen* ☎ *0520/472251* ⊠ *SKr 10* ☉ *May, weekends noon–5; June–Aug., daily 11–7.*

Kids at the **Innovatum–Kunskapens Hus** (Innovatum–Technology Center) get to touch, examine, and poke at objects illustrating technology, energy, media, design, and industrial history. In the film studio you can edit yourself into contemporary Swedish movies. A big hit are the two robots, Max and Gerda, that spend their days vacuum-cleaning their futuristic apartment. As a reward for their hard work, the staff at Innovatum feeds the robots trash at set times. ✉ *Åkerssjövägen 10* ☎ *0520/488480* ⊕ *www.innovatum.se* ✆ *SKr 50* ☉ *Tues.–Sun. 11–4.*

The **Innovatum Cableway** will take you 400 meters (.25 mi) across the canal at a height of nearly 30 meters (98 feet), with spectacular views of the canal, the town, and the waterfall area. ✉ *Åkerssjövägen 10* ☎ *0520/488480* ✆ *SKr 40* ☉ *June–Aug., daily 10–6.*

The **Saab Bilmuseum** (Saab Car Museum) surveys Saab's automotive output from 1946 to the present. Since the exhibition consists primarily of row upon row of cars, fenced off by rope, there's little here for any but true car enthusiasts. ✉ *Åkerssjövägen 10* ☎ *0520/84344* ✆ *SKr 40* ☉ *Tues.–Fri. 11–4.*

Culture abounds at **Folkets Hus** (People's House), in the pedestrianized downtown area. Part of the building is given over to dramatic, ever-changing displays of contemporary art and art installations. ✉ *Kungsg. 25* ☎ *0520/422500* ✆ *Free* ☉ *Kulturhallen (Culture Hall) at Folkets Hus, Sun.–Mon. noon–4, Tues.–Thurs. noon–7, Sat. 11–2.*

en route
Soon after leaving Trollhättan, the Göta Canal takes you past Halleberg and Hunneberg, two flat-top hills that are each more than 500 ft high; the woods surrounding them are extraordinarily rich in elk, legend, and Viking burial mounds. The canal then proceeds through **Karls Grav**, the oldest part of the canal, begun early in the 18th century. It was built to bypass the Ronnum Falls, on the Göta River, which have been harnessed to power a hydroelectric project.

Where to Stay & Eat

¢–$ ✕ **Shangri La.** The large, elegant dining room is decorated in deep brown and gold shades to go along with the restaurant's mixed Asian theme. In summer you can sup on the outdoor terrace against a backdrop of humming waterfalls. ✉ *Storg. 36* ☎ *0520/10222* ☰ *AC, MC, V.*

¢–$ ✕ **Strandgatan.** This popular, relaxed café is in an 1867 building that once housed canal workers. There's always a good crowd, especially in summer. Locals come to while away the hours over coffee, bagels, home-cooked international cuisine, and beer and wine. ✉ *Föerningsgatan 1* ☎ *0520/83717* ☰ *AE, DC, MC, V.*

$ 🏨 **Hotel Scandic Swania.** Stunning views over the waterfalls and locks on up to the hills above town are what distinguish this comfortable hotel near Trollhättan's center. Ask for a top-floor room at the front of the hotel and enjoy the sights. If you're up for a party, one of Trollhättan's few clubs is in the basement. ✉ *Storg. 49, 461 23* ☎ *0520/89000* 🖶 *0520/89001* ⊕ *www.hotel-scandic.com* ⇆ *296 rooms, 10 suites* ⚴ *Restaurant, bar, lounge, nightclub, no-smoking rooms* ☰ *AE, DC, MC, V* ¶◎¶ *BP.*

The Outdoors

Daily boat trips from the center of town take you right into the heart of the lock system and waterfalls. The **MS Strömkarlen** (☎ *0520/32100* ✆ *SKr 162*) leaves two times daily (at 10 and 1:30) June 29–August 10.

Nightlife

Trollhättan's nightlife mostly revolves around the excellent **KK's Bar & Nightclub** (✉ Torgg. 3 ☎ 0520/481049), which is always crowded, mostly with those under 25. The bar is comfortable and fun and has a good cocktail selection. On Friday those who are slightly older hit the dance floor.

Vänersborg

⑬ *15 km (9 mi) north of Trollhättan, 85 km (53 mi) north of Göteborg.*

Eventually, the canal enters **Vänern**, Sweden's largest and Europe's third-largest lake: 3,424 square km (1,322 square mi) of water, 145 km (90 mi) long and 81 km (50 mi) wide at one point.

At the southern tip of the lake is Vänersborg, a town of about 30,000 inhabitants that was founded in the mid-17th century. The church and the governor's residence date from the 18th century, but the rest of the town was destroyed by fire in 1834. Vänersborg is distinguished by its fine lakeside park, the trees of which act as a windbreak for the gusts that sweep in from Vänern.

Fans of the esoteric may find the **Vänersborgs Museum** worth a visit. The oldest museum in Sweden outside Stockholm, it has been restored to its 1888 appearance, and as such it has become an unintentional museum of museums. A gloomy apartment in which the museum's janitor once lived is now part of an exhibit—one that preserves the space in all its 1950s glory. The museum's most eccentric collection is one of birds from southwestern Africa—Namibia, Botswana, and Angola. This collection is the most extensive in the world and is the base of an exchange between the museum and the National Museum of Namibia. ✉ Östra Plantaget ☎ 0521/264100 ⊕ www.alvlanmus.se/museer/vbg/vbgstart.htm ✉ SKr 20 ۞ June–Aug., Tues–Thurs. and weekends, noon–4; Sept.–May, Tues., Thurs., and weekends, noon–4.

A few minutes' walk from the center of town, **Skracklan Park** is a good place to relax. Take a break in the 1930s coffeehouse after walking along the park's promenade. A lake, parkland, and trees are set around the park's centerpiece, a statue of Frida, the muse of a famous local poet named Birger Sjöberg (1885–1929). Frida always has fresh flowers stuffed into her bronze hand.

> **off the beaten path**
>
> **HALLEBERG AND HUNNEBERG –** Five kilometers (3 miles) east of Vänersborg are the twin plateaus of Halleberg and Hunneberg. Thought to be 500 million years old, these geological wonders are the site of early Viking forts and the resting place of early humans. But they are best known for their stunning natural beauty and the fauna they support: the county's biggest herd of elk. As tradition dictates, the king of Sweden still comes here every October for the royal hunt. To see the animals yourself, head for the walking trail that winds around Halleberg. At dawn or dusk the leggy, long-faced giant elk, inquisitive by nature, will be more than comfortable eating apples from your hand. Whether you'll be so comfortable, once you see the size of them, is another matter. Those less daring can hide behind a guide from the **Älgens Berg & Kungajaktsmuseum** (Elk Mountain & Royal Hunt Museum) – ✉ Vargön ☎ 0521/277991 ✉ Museum SKr 60; private guide 1 hr SKr 795, 30 mins SKr 530 ۞ May–Aug., daily 10–6; Sept.–Apr., Tues.–Sun. 11–4.

Where to Stay & Eat

¢–$ ✕ **Pizzeria Roma.** Directly across the road from the hotel Ronnums Herrgård, this small restaurant is perfect for informal meals. The very good and very cheap pizza and pasta served here are worth suffering the somewhat stark and brightly lighted interior. ⊠ *Stora Gårdsvägen 2* ☎ *0521/221070* ▤ *MC, V.*

$ ▥ **Ronnums Herrgård.** A mile outside town, this old manor house has been converted into a hotel of some local repute. Some rooms are a little shabby, so try to get one in the main building. What you do get here is peace, natural beauty, and a very good hotel restaurant. The breakfast offered with the room is worthy of a king. ⊠ *Parkvägen, Vargön, 468 30* ☎ *0521/260000* 🖷 *0521/260009* 🛏 *60 rooms, 10 suites* ⟁ *Restaurant, bar, no-smoking rooms* ▤ *AE, DC, MC, V* �‖ *BP.*

¢ ▥ **Hotell Strand.** Lodging choices are limited in Vänersborg, but the Hotell Strand's welcoming staff make it the best in town. ⊠ *Hamng. 7, 462 33* ☎ *0521/13850* 🖷 *0521/15900* ⊕ *www.strandhotell.com* 🛏 *28 rooms* ⟁ *No-smoking rooms* ▤ *AE, DC, MC, V* �‖ *BP.*

Nightlife

Nightlife is limited here, but at **Club Roccad** (⊠ Kungsg. 23 ☎0521/61200) there's always good, modern dance music, and the cool, dark interior attracts a young, good-looking crowd that's serious about dancing.

Lidköping

⑭ *55 km (34 mi) east of Vänersborg, 140 km (87 mi) northeast of Göteborg.*

On an inlet at the southernmost point of Vänern's eastern arm lies the town of Lidköping, which received its charter in 1446 and is said to have the largest town square in Sweden. Nya Stadens Torg (New Town Square) is dominated by the old courthouse building, a replica of the original that burned down in 1960. Lidköping had been razed by fire several times before that, leaving a lot of the old town gone. However, the 17th-century houses around the square Limtorget survived, and are still worth seeing today.

A pleasant enough town, Lidköping's villagelike layout comes from an old rule forbidding buildings from being taller than the street it stands on is wide. The only exception seems to be the ugly industrial park on the northern edge of town, which obscures an otherwise perfect view of Lake Vänern.

The **Rörstrands Porslins Museum** has on display a wealth of pieces that trace the history of china. Rörstrands, Europe's second-oldest porcelain company, also offers tours of its adjoining factory. The factory shop carries a large range of beautiful china at very reasonable prices. ⊠ *Fabriksg. 4* ☎ *0510/82300* ⊡ *Free* ⊙ *Weekdays 10–6, Sat. 10–2, Sun. noon–4. Factory tours on Thurs. and Fri. for groups; call 0510/82348 for details.*

Väner Museet is dedicated to Lake Vänern's history, the life it supports, and the ways in which it has helped the surrounding area develop. What could be a slightly dull subject is vividly brought to life in this well-planned, modern museum, which has exhibits of meteorites and fossils as well as model ships and maritime photographs. ⊠ *Framnäsvägen 2* ☎ *0510/770065* ⊡ *SKr 20* ⊙ *Tues.–Fri. 10–5, Thurs. 10–7, weekends noon–5.*

off the beaten path

HUSABY HYRKA – This church, 15 km (9 mi) east of Lidköping, is a site of great religious and historical significance. The church itself, dating from the 12th century, houses some fine 13th-century furniture, 15th-century murals, and carved floor stones. But the biggest draw is outside the church, at St. Sigfrid's Well. Here, in 1008, King Olof Skötkonung converted to Christianity—the first Swedish king to do so—and was baptized by the English missionary Sigfrid. Since that time many Swedish kings have come to carve their names in the rock. Most signatures can still be clearly read today.

LÄCKÖ SLOTT – One of Sweden's finest 17th-century Renaissance palaces is 24 km (15 mi) to the north of Lidköping. It's on a peninsula off the site where the eastern arm of Vänern divides from the western. Läckö Castle's 250 rooms were once the home of Magnus Gabriel de la Gardie, a great favorite of Queen Christina. Only the Royal Palace in Stockholm is larger. In 1681 Karl XI confiscated it to curtail the power of the nobility, and in 1830 all its furnishings were auctioned off. Many have since been restored to the palace. ⊠ *Kållandsö* ☎ *0510/10320* ✉ *June–Aug. SKr 70, May and Sept. SKr 50* ☉ *May–Sept., daily 10–6.*

Where to Stay & Eat

$–$$ ✕ **Götes Festvåning.** Anything with pike (*gädda*) is particularly worth trying at this typical Swedish dining room serving good regional specialties. ⊠ *Östra Hamnen 5* ☎ *0510/21700* ▤ *DC, MC, V.*

$ 🏨 **Stadtshotellet.** Like most town-hotels in Sweden, the Stadtshotel offers a faded grandeur with a lot of character. Rooms are a little on the small side but comfortable, with the best ones overlooking the river and the main town square. ⊠ *Gamla Stadens Torg 1, 531 02* ☎ *0510/22085* 🖶 *0510/21532* ⊕ *www.stadtlidkoping.se* ➥ *67 rooms, 2 suites* ♿ *Restaurant, bar, no-smoking rooms* ▤ *AE, DC, MC, V* ⦿ *BP.*

¢ 🏨 **Hotell Rådhuset.** This basic hotel is somewhat oddly located inside a former office building. The rooms are large and have cable TV. There are several computers on which you can access the Internet. ⊠ *Nya Stadens Torg 8, 531 31* ☎ *0510/22236* 🖶 *0510/22214* ➥ *24 rooms* ♿ *Breakfast room, cable TV, Internet* ▤ *AE, DC, MC, V* ⦿ *BP.*

---

en route On a peninsula 20 km (12½ mi) to the east of Lidköping, the landscape is dominated by the great hill of **Kinnekulle**, towering 900 feet above Lake Vänern. The hill is rich in colorful vegetation and wildlife and was a favorite hike for the botanist Linnaeus.

Mariestad

⓯ *40 km (25 mi) northeast of Lidköping.*

This town on the eastern shore of Lake Vänern is an architectural gem and an excellent base for some aquatic exploring. The town's center has a fine medieval quarter, a pretty harbor, and houses built in styles ranging from Gustavian (a baroque style named after King Gustav Vasa of the 1500s) to art nouveau. Others resemble Swiss chalets.

Domkyrkan, the late-Gothic cathedral on the edge of the old part of town, stands as a monument to one man's competitiveness. Commissioned at the end of the 16th century by Duke Karl—who named the town after his wife, Maria—it was built to resemble and rival Klara Kyrka in Stockholm, the church of his brother King Johan III, of whom he was insanely jealous. Karl made sure the church was endowed with some wonderfully excessive features, which can still be seen today. The stained-glass windows have real insects (bees, dragonflies, etc.) sandwiched within them, and the silver-and-gold cherubs are especially roly-poly and cute.

Vadsbo Museum is a museum of the local area's industry, which centers not surprisingly around the lake. The museum is just off the old town, on a small island in the River Tidan, which flows off Vänern. Named after the old jurisdiction of Vadsbo, the museum—housed in the medieval judge's residence—has displays on the region from the prehistoric age to the 20th century. ⊠ *Residensö, Marieholmn* ☎ *0501/63214* 🖾 *SKr 20* ☺ *June–Aug., Tues.–Sun. 1–4, Wed. 1–7; Sept.–May, weekends 1–3.*

off the
beaten
path

GULLSPÅNG – Forty kilometers (25 miles) north of Mariestad, this town is the starting place for 20 km (12 mi) of railway track, originally built to improve Sweden's rail links in the 1960s but now used for leisure purposes. The tracks run through some beautiful countryside and along the Gullspångälv (Gullspång River), which has great swimming. You get to travel the tracks in handcars, which aren't often seen outside cartoons and cowboy movies. The small cars are operated by having two people push a lever up and down. If you've got the energy, it's a great trip.

Where to Stay & Eat

$–$$ ✕ **St. Michel.** The outdoor patio of this old-style restaurant shoots out into Lake Vänern on stilts. Both the indoor and outdoor seating options offer beautiful views of the lake. The traditional Swedish dishes are heavily meat-based, and most come with a side of *rösti* (hash potatoes mixed with grated cheese and chopped onions and shaped to a pancake). ⊠ *Kungsgatan 1* ☎ *0501/19900* ⊟ *MC, V* ☺ *Closed Sun. No lunch Sat.*

$ 🏨 **Stadtshotellet.** This is the best choice in a town full of below-average hotels. The building is unobtrusive, but the rooms are comfortable, if a little bland in their furnishings. ⊠ *Nygatan 10, 542 30* ☎ *0501/13800* 🖷 *0501/77640* 🛏 *29 rooms* ⚬ *Bar, no-smoking rooms* ⊟ *AE, MC, V* ⓧ *BP.*

Nightlife & the Arts

Evenings can be fairly quiet and relaxing in Mariestad, but the bar at **Restaurang Björnes Magasin** (⊠ Karlagatan 2 ☎ 0501/18050) can be a lively spot for the young adults in town.

The Outdoors

The nearby island of **Torsö** is perfect for fishing and lying out on the beach. It's reachable by a 1-km-long (½-mi-long) bridge, that makes for a good jog or bike ride. For information on hiring equipment for fishing, contact the **tourist office** (⊠ Hamnplan ☎ 0501/10001).

Sjötorp

⑯ *27 km (17 mi) northeast of Mariestad, 207 km (129 mi) northeast of Göteborg.*

At the lakeside port of Sjötorp, the Göta Canal proper begins. A series of locks raises steamers to the village of Lanthöjden—at 304 ft above sea level it's the highest point on the canal. The boats next enter the narrow, twisting lakes of Viken and Bottensjön and continue to Forsvik through the canal's oldest lock, built in 1813. Boats then sail out into **Vättern**, Sweden's second-largest lake, nearly 129 km (80 mi) from north to south and 31 km (19 mi) across at its widest point. Its waters are so clear that in some parts the bottom is visible at a depth of 50 feet. The lake is subject to sudden storms that can whip its normally placid waters into choppy waves.

Vadstena

⑰ *249 km (155 mi) northeast of Göteborg (via Jönköping).*

This little-known gem of a town grew up around the monastery founded by St. Birgitta, or Bridget (1303–1373), who wrote in her *Revelations* that she had a vision of Christ in which he revealed the rules of the religious order she went on to establish. These rules seem to have been a precursor for the Swedish ideal of sexual equality, with both nuns and monks sharing a common church. Her order spread rapidly after her death, and at one time there were 80 Bridgetine monasteries in Europe. Little remains of the Vadstena monastery; in 1545 King Gustav Vasa ordered its demolition, and its stones were used to build **Vadstena Slott** (Vadstena Castle), a huge fortress created to defend against Danish attack. It was later refurbished and used as a home for Gustav's mentally ill son. Many of the original decorations were lost in a fire in the early 1600s. Unable to afford replacement decorations, the royal family had decorations and fittings painted with three-dimensional effect directly onto the walls. Many of the "curtains" that can be seen today come from this period. Swedish royalty held court at Vadstena Slott until 1715. It then fell into decay and was used as a granary. Recent efforts have returned the castle to something approaching its former glory. Today it houses part of the National Archives, the tourist bureau, and is also the site of an annual summer opera festival. ☎ *0143/31570* ✆ *SKr 50 (in winter SKr 30)* ☉ *Mid-May–end of May, daily 11–4; June and Aug., daily 10–6; July, daily 10–7; Sept. 1–Sept. 15, daily 10–4; mid-Sept.–mid-May, daily 11–2; guided tours on the hr in summertime.*

The triptych altarpiece on the south wall of the **Vadstena Kyrka** (Vadstena Church) shows St. Birgitta presenting her book of revelations to a group of kneeling cardinals. In a cherub-covered tomb are the remains of Gustav Vasa's son. St. Birgitta's bones are here as well, but less grandly stored in a red-velvet box inside a glass case.

Housed in what was once Sweden's oldest mental hospital, the **Hospital Museet** is a fascinating, moving reminder of centuries of misguided treatments and "cures" for the mentally ill. Devices on display include a chair into which patients were strapped and spun until they were sick and a bath in which unruly patients were scalded. Perhaps the most moving display includes photographs of inmates from the 19th century and the drawings they made of the tortures inflicted upon them. The tour also includes **Mårten Skinnares Hus,** a very well-preserved private medieval residence once inhabited by the hospital priest. ⊠ *Lastköpingsg.* ☎ *0143/31570* ✆ *SKr 40* ☉ *June and Aug., daily 2–3; July, daily 1–3; 1 guided tour in June and Aug. (2 PM) and 2 in July (1 PM and 2 PM).*

A donation of a private doll collection was the start of the **Leksaksmuseet** (Toy Museum). Private donations have now expanded the museum's holdings into one of the largest in Sweden. The museum also has an interesting collection of clocks from the 17th century on. ⊠ *Lilla Hamnarmen* ☎ *0143/29275* ✆ *SKr 40* ☉ *May and Sept., daily 8–6; June–Aug., 8–8; Oct.–Apr., 8–4.*

> **off the beaten path**

VÄVERSUNDA – This scenic hamlet, 15 km (9 mi) southeast of Vadstena, contains a pretty 12th-century limestone church. Inside there are some fine, restored wall paintings from the 13th century. Next to the church is a very popular bird-watching tower that overlooks a bird sanctuary.

$$ ⊞ **Vadstena Klosterhotel.** Sweden's oldest secular building, parts of which date from the 13th century, is now a hotel. Rooms are modern and well appointed, and there are three comfortable lounges. You can choose a view of either Lake Vättern or the hotel's courtyard. The former is infinitely more preferable and only SKr 100 extra. ⊠ *Klosterområdet, off Lasarettsg., 592 24 Vadstena* ☎ *0143/31530* 🖷 *0143/13648* 🛏 *31 rooms* ⚭ *Restaurant, lounge, meeting room, no-smoking rooms* ⊟ *AE, DC, MC, V* |◎| *BP.*

$ ⊞ **Kungs-Starby Wärdshus.** This functional guest house, reached via Route 50, is next to a renovated manor house and restaurant. The rooms use light wood throughout and have earth-tone carpets and green, blue, and brown color schemes. The complex is surrounded by a park on the outskirts of town. ⊠ *Ödeshögsv., 592 21 Vadstena* ☎ *0143/75100* 🖷 *0143/75170* 🛏 *61 rooms* ⚭ *Restaurant, indoor pool, hot tub, sauna, spa, meeting room* ⊟ *AE, DC, MC, V* |◎| *CP.*

Motala

⑱ *13 km (8 mi) north of Vadstena, 262 km (163 mi) northeast of Göteborg.*

Before reaching Stockholm, the canal passes through Motala, where Baltzar von Platen is buried. He had hoped that four new towns would be established along the waterway, but only Motala rose according to plan. He designed the town himself, and his statue is in the main square. Motala itself is not an essential sight. Instead, it's the activities along the canal and lake, along with a few very good museums, that make Motala worth a stop.

★ Stop at the **Motala Motormuseum** even if you are not in the slightest bit interested in cars. All the cars and motorcycles on display—from 1920s Rolls Royces, through 1950s Cadillacs and modern racing cars—are presented in their appropriate context, with music of the day playing on contemporary radios; mannequins dressed in fashions of the time; and newspapers, magazines, televisions, and everyday household objects all helping to set the stage. More a museum of 20th-century technology and life than one solely of cars, it makes for a fascinating look back at the last century. ⊠ *Hamnen* ☎ *0141/58888* ⊕ *www.motala-motormuseum. se* 🎟 *SKr 50* ◷ *June–Aug., daily 10–8; May and Sept., daily 10–6; Oct.–Apr., weekdays 8–5, weekends 11–5.*

Europe's most powerful radio transmitter was built in Motala in 1927. In later years radio became an important industry for this little town. The **Rundradiomuseet** uses interactive displays to present the history of radio's birth as well as a glimpse into its future. ⊠ *Radiovägen* ☎ *0141/ 225100* 🎟 *SKr 25* ◷ *May, daily noon–4; June–mid-Aug., daily 10–6; mid-Aug.–Oct., weekends noon–4.*

$ ⊞ **Palace Hotel.** Ship models decorate the lobby windows of this hotel with a nautical theme. The rooms are designed to look like cabins, though fortunately larger and more comfortable. Paintings of sea motifs and round windows in the bathrooms add to the charm. Just a five-minute walk from the train station, this hotel is close to most of Motala's sights. ⊠ *Kungsgatan 1, 591 30, Motala* ☎ *0141/216660* 🖷 *0141/ 57221* 🛏 *55 rooms, 1 suite* ⚭ *Breakfast room, bar, sauna, free parking* ⊟ *AE, MC, V* |◎| *BP.*

en route

At Borenshult a series of locks takes the boat down to **Boren,** a lake in the province of Östergötland. On the southern shore of the next lake, Roxen, lies the city of **Linköping,** capital of the province and home of Saab, the aircraft and automotive company. Once out of the lake, you follow a different stretch of canal past the sleepy town of **Söderköping.** A few miles east, at the hamlet of Mem, the canal's last lock lowers the boat into Slätbaken, a Baltic fjord presided over by the **Stegeborg Slottsruin,** the ancient ruins of the Stegeborg Fortress. The boat then steams north along the coastline until it enters **Mälaren** through the Södertälje Canal and finally anchors in the capital at Riddarholmen.

Göta Canal A to Z

To research prices, get advice from other travelers, and book travel arrangements, visit www.fodors.com.

BIKE TOURS

For two-day bike tours along the canal from Sjötorp to Tåtorp and back, contact Resespecialisten utmed Göta Kanal. The price is 1000 SKr for adults and 500 SKr for children under 13. The price includes lodging in a youth hostel in Töreboda, a breakfast, lunch, and dinner, as well as a bike rental for an adult. The same company also has four-day combined bike and boat tours along the canal for 2,500 SKr (all inclusive) for adults.

🚩 **Resespecialisten utmed Göta Kanal** ⊠ Kungsgatan 10 545 30 Töreboda ☎ 0506/12500 ⊕ www.gotakanalturer.com.

CAR TRAVEL

From Stockholm follow E18 west; from Göteborg take Route 45 north to E18.

CRUISE TRAVEL

Rolfs Flyg och Buss has one-day cruises along the canal originating in Gothenburg (with bus service to the canal) for 675 SKr (dinner included). The day trip takes 12 hours (7–7). For more details about cruises along the Göta Canal, *see* Göteborg A to Z.

🚩 **Rolfs Flyg och Buss** ⊠ Hjalmar Brantingsg. 1 417 06 Göteborg ☎ 031/511290 🖷 031/515060 ⊕ www.rolfsbuss.se.

TRAIN TRAVEL

Call SJ Göteborg for information about service.

🚩 Train Information **SJ** ⊠ Göteborg ☎ 0771/757575.

VISITOR INFORMATION

🚩 Tourist Information **Karlsborg** ⊠ Ankarvägen 2 ☎ 0505/17350. **Lidköping** Götene-Lidköping Turistbyrå ⊠ Bangatan 3 ☎ 0510/770500 **Mariestad** ⊠ Hamnplan ☎ 0501/10001 ⊕ www.turism.mariestad.se. **Motala** ⊠ Göta Kanalbolagsmuseet, Hamnen ☎ 0141/225254. **Skövde** ⊠ Sandtorget ☎ 0500/446688. **Uddevalla** ⊠ Kungstorget 4 ☎ 0522/99720 ⊕ www.uddevallaforum.se. **Vadstena** ⊠ Slottet ☎ 0143/31572. **Vänersborg** Vänersborgs Turist ⊠ Järnvägsstationen ☎ 0521/271400 ⊕ www.vanersborg.se/turist.

VÄRMLAND

Close to the Norwegian border on the north shores of Vänern, the province of Värmland is rich in folklore. It was also the home of Alfred Nobel and the birthplace of other famous Swedes, among them Nobel Prize–winning novelist Selma Lagerlöf, poet Gustaf Fröding, former prime minister Tage Erlander, and present-day opera star Håkan Hagegård. Värmland's forested, lake-dotted landscape attracts artists seeking refuge and Swedes on holiday.

Karlstad

19 *255 km (158 mi) northeast of Göteborg.*

Värmland's principal city (population 80,000) is on Klarälven (Klara River) at the point where it empties into Vänern. Karlstad received its charter in 1684, and the city, then known as Tingvalla, changed its name to Karlstad, meaning Karl's Town, to honor King Karl IX who had extended the charter. In **Residenstorget,** the square in front of the county governor's residence, there is a statue of Karl IX by the local sculptor Christian Eriksson.

Only eleven buildings survived a devastating fire in 1865, but as through a miracle, the fire did not claim a single life. The tourist office organizes free guided walks, in English upon request, during the summer months. The city makes bicycles available for free at Stora Torget in the summertime.

Northeast of Stora Torget, the main square, is **Östra Bron** (East Bridge). Completed in 1811, it is Sweden's longest arched stone bridge, its 12 arches spanning 510 feet across the water. Anders Jacobsson, the bridge's builder, carved his name on a stone in the bridge's center.

Consecrated in 1730, **Karlstads Katedral** (Karlstad's Cathedral; ⊠ Kungsg.) fared fairly well in the great fire of 1865. Only one tower was destroyed, and a new, pointier tower was subsequently added. Particular features worth looking for are the angels by the altar, made by sculptor Tobias Sergel, and the altar itself, made of limestone and with a crystal cross, and the font, also made of crystal.

One of the buildings that survived the 1865 fire, the **Biskopsgården** (Bishop's Residence) is a beautiful, two-story, cream-color wooden building with red window trims that was built in 1781. The row of huge elm trees that surrounds the building acted as a natural firebreak and saved it from the flames. The building is now a private home.

The original building of the **Värmlands Museum** has been connected by a glass walkway to a new, red, seven-pointed wing by architect Carl Nyrén. Värmland's history and local notables like sculptor Christian Eriksson and poet Gustaf Fröding make up the base of the exhibits. ⊠ *Sandgrun, Karlstad* ☎ *054/143100* ⊠ *SKr 40* ◷ *Tues.–Fri. 8:30–5, Wed. 8:30 AM–9 PM, weekends 11–5.*

☼ In 1920 ten farm buildings were moved to **Marieberg Skogspark** (Marieberg Forest Park) to create an open-air museum. A delight for the whole family, the park has nature trails, a minizoo, a beach, walking trails, minigolf, restaurants, and an outdoor theater. In the middle of the forest there is a "nature room," giving a glimpse of Värmland's flora and fauna. ☎ *0550/86543* ◷ *Dawn–dusk.*

Karlstad is the site of the **Emigrant Registret** (Emigrant Registry), which maintains detailed records of the Swedes' emigration to America. Those of Swedish extraction can trace their ancestors at the center's research facility. ⊠ *Hööksgatan 2, Karlstad* ☎ *054/617720* ⊠ *Free* ◷ *June–Aug., daily 8:30–3; Sept.–May, Mon. 8:30–8, Tues.–Fri. 8:30–4.*

Where to Stay & Eat

\$\$–\$\$\$ ✕ **Inn Alstern.** Overlooking Lake Alstern, this elegant restaurant offers Swedish and Continental cuisine, with fish dishes the specialty. ⊠ *Morgonv. 4* ☎ *054/834900* ▭ *AE, MC, V.*

$$–$$$ ✕ **Restaurang Munken.** Walking down the steps into this cellar restaurant is like stepping into a *Three Musketeers* set. Low, arched stone ceilings, long wooden benches, and dim candlelight make this a cozy, informal spot. The food is warming, filling Swedish fare with a heavy Continental hand. Anything with veal is worth trying here. ⊠ *Västra Torgg. 17* ☎ *054/185150* ▤ *AE, DC, MC, V* ☾ *Closed Sun.*

¢–$$ ✕ **Ristorante Alfie.** The three dining rooms are dimly lighted, and the dark-wood tables are close together, making Alfie a very sociable dining experience. The menu includes pizzas and pasta and a huge and varied steak menu. The entrecôte steaks, served extremely rare with béarnaise sauce, are some of the best around. ⊠ *Västra Torgg. 19* ☎ *054/216262* ▤ *AE, DC, MC, V.*

$$ ⊡ **First Hotel Plaza.** The very large rooms here are in soothing neutral tones and come with excellent amenities. There is a sauna and relaxation area on the top floor, which offers great views across the city. ⊠ *Västra Torgg. 2, 652 25* ☎ *054/100200* ⌨ *054/100224* ⌇ *131 rooms, 5 suites* ♿ *Restaurant, bar, lounge, in-room data ports, minibars, dance club* ▤ *AE, DC, MC, V* ⑩ *BP.*

$ ⊡ **Comfort Hotel Bilan.** Security will be the least of your worries here since the hotel is in a converted old county jail. Not surprisingly, the outside is a little imposing and uninviting, but once inside, public areas and rooms all have cheery furnishings and fabrics. In the basement there is a museum where you can look at the original cells and see letters and some of the objects—including a hacksaw—once sent to prisoners. ⊠ *Karlbergsg. 3, 652 24* ☎ *054/100300* ⌨ *054/219214* ⌇ *68 rooms* ♿ *Restaurant, sauna, indoor pool, conference room, non-smoking rooms* ▤ *AE, DC, MC, V* ⑩ *BP.*

$ ⊡ **Elite Stadshotellet.** On the banks of the Klarälven, this hotel from 1870 is steeped in tradition. All the rooms are decorated differently, some in modern Swedish style, others in ways that evoke their original look. You can dine at the fancy Matsalen or in the more casual atmosphere of the Bishop's Arms, an English pub offering 50 types of beer. ⊠ *Kungsg. 22, 651 08* ☎ *054/293000* ⌨ *054/293031* ⌇ *139 rooms* ♿ *Restaurant, lounge, pub, sauna, meeting room, no-smoking rooms* ▤ *AE, DC, MC, V* ⑩ *BP.*

$ ⊡ **Stay Hotel Karlstad.** In the town center, this small hotel offers nondescript common areas and rather blandly decorated rooms. The hotel's studio apartments, however, are a great deal for visitors staying a week or more. ⊠ *Drottningg. 1, 652 24* ☎ *054/150190* ⌨ *054/154826* ⌇ *38 rooms, 11 studios* ♿ *Breakfast room, kitchenettes, sauna, meeting room, no-smoking rooms* ▤ *AE, DC, MC, V* ⑩ *BP.*

Sports & the Outdoors

The Klarälven River runs for 500 km (312 mi) through Scandinavia. The rapid waters used since the 18th century for floating logs downstream to sawmills now offer great opportunities for rafting trips. On the way you can swim, fish, and contemplate the beautiful scenery and wildlife (elk, beavers, wolverines, and bears). At night you camp in tents on the water's edge. Two companies, **Sverigeflottan** (☎ 0564/40227) and **Vildmark i Värmland** (☎ 0560/14040) operate trips along the river on two-person rafts.

You can canoe or boat on Lake Vänern in the center of the city. **Vänerkajak HB** (⊠ Östra Rosenlundsvägen 54 Hammarö ☎ 054/521627 ⊕ www.vanerkajak.se) rent boats and offer introductory courses.

Nightlife & the Arts

The choice of bars and pubs in Karlstad is good for a town of this size. **Harry's** (⊠ Kungsg. 16 ☎ 054/102020) is an American-style bar with a large wooden interior and good beer on tap. The English-style pub, the **Woolpack Inn** (✉ Järnsvägsg. 1 ☎ 054/158016), is a perennial favorite with the locals.

For late-night dancing try **Plaza Nightclub** (✉ Västra Torgg. 2 ☎ 054/100200), in the basement of the First Hotel Plaza. This is the place to be seen in Karlstad. Those in their mid-20s and beyond dance the night away to the latest club tunes, fueled by lavishly over-the-top cocktails and lots of beer.

Shopping

Stores selling clothes, jewelry, furniture, antiques, and crafts are all concentrated on the streets of **Drotninggatan** and **Östra Torggatan.** All the main national retail brands are here, as are individual boutiques.

en route Värmland is, above all, a rural experience. Drive along the **Klarälven,** through the beautiful Fryken Valley, to Ransater, where author Erik Gustaf Geijer was born in 1783 and where Tage Erlander, the former prime minister, also grew up. The rural idyll ends in **Munkfors,** where some of the best-quality steel in Europe is manufactured.

Sunne

⑳ *63 km (39 mi) north of Karlstad, 318 km (198 mi) northeast of Göteborg.*

A small village more than a town, Sunne is mainly known for two things. First, the famed Swedish author Selma Lagerlöf has many connections here. Sunne is also known for the prominent spa that dominates the entrance road to the village. It's a haven for stressed executives from all over Sweden.

In the middle of town, **Sundsbergs Gård** is a beautiful building said to have inspired one of the settings in Selma Lagerlöf's novel, *Gösta Berling*. Sundsberg's Manor House (built in 1780) is now a museum charting the last three centuries of Swedish history. ✉ *Ekebyv* ☎ *0565/10363* ✉ *SKr 30* ☉ *Museum mid-June–mid-Aug., Tues.–Thurs. and weekends noon–4; art exhibition hall and café year-round, Tues.–Thurs. and weekends noon–4.*

A small collection of old buildings makes up **Sunne Hembygdsgård,** a museum showing how life was lived in the 1800s. The well-preserved buildings include a manor house, school, general store, and courthouse. ✉ *Hembygdsvägen 7* ☎ *0565/12958* ✉ *Free* ☉ *By appointment.*

off the beaten path **MÅRBACKA –** The estate on which Nobel Prize winner Selma Lagerlöf was born in 1858 can be found in this town, 10 km (7 mi) southeast of Sunne. Lagerlöf is considered the best Swedish author of her generation and is known and avidly read by Swedes young and old. The house can be seen by guided tour. Her furnishings, including her study desk and beautiful wood-panel library, have been kept much as she left them at the time of her death in 1940. ✉ *Östra Ämtervik, 686 26* ☎ *0565/31027* ✉ *SKr 60* ☉ *Mid-May–Aug., daily 10–4, tours every hr; July, daily 10–5, tours every ½ hr; Sept., weekends 11–2.*

ROTTNEROS HERRGÅRDS PARK – On the western shore of Fryken Lake, 5 km (3 mi) south of Sunne, is Rottneros Manor, the inspiration for Ekeby, the fictional estate in Lagerlöf's *Gösta Berlings Saga* (*The Tale of Gösta Berling*). The house is privately owned, but you can go to the park, with its fine collection of Scandinavian sculpture. Here there are works by Carl Milles, Norwegian artist Gustav Vigeland, and Wäinö Aaltonen of Finland. The entrance fee covers both the sculpture park and the Nils Holgerssons Adventure Park, an elaborate playground for children. ⊠ *Rottneros* ☎ *0565/ 60295* ⛿ *SKr 100* ⊙ *May, weekdays 10–4, weekends 10–5; June, daily 10–5; July, daily 10–6; Aug., daily 10–4.*

Where to Stay & Eat

¢–$ ✗ **Köpmangården.** If you blink, you may miss this tiny bar and restau-
Fodor'sChoice rant that's on a road of private residences. Looking like a derelict old
★ house from the outside, the faded carpet, chipped and frayed furniture, and dingy restrooms on the inside aren't much better. But the food is some of the best around. Everything is homemade. The tomato soup with crème fraîche, huge prawn sandwiches, and inch-thick steaks are all delicious. The warm welcome from the little old lady who runs the place is as good as the food. ⊠ *Ekebyv. 40* ☎ *0565/10121* ⊟ *AE, MC, V.*

$$ ✗⊡ **Quality Hotel and Spa Selma Lagerlöf.** This huge complex of a hotel is split onto two sides of the road leading into Sunne. Each side has large rooms furnished in a simple Scandinavian design, public rooms and lobbies, a bar, a restaurant, and a nightclub. The main hotel has a very well-equipped spa and fitness center. Guests can use most of the facilities for free, with a nominal charge for treatments. The restaurants ($$) in each hotel serve good Swedish classics, and French-influenced food. Be sure to try the reindeer if it's available. The extensive grounds of the hotel has many wooded walking and jogging paths. Ask for a room at the front of the hotel, as these have stunning views over the lake. ⊠ *Eke-byvägen, Lagerlöf 686 28 Sunne* ☎ *0565/688810* ⊟ *0565/16631* ⊕ *www.selmaspa.se* ⇆ *156 rooms, 10 suites* ⚅ *2 restaurants, 2 bars, 2 nightclubs, lounge, 2 pools, sauna, spa, health club, convention center* ⊟ *AE, DC, MC, V* ❙⊚❙ *BP.*

Shopping

If you're passing through Sunne and feeling a little ravaged by life, you can pick up some pick-me-ups at the local spa resort. **Quality Hotel and Spa Selma Lagerlöf** (⊠ Sundsberget, ☎ 0565/688810) offers all manner of wonderful herb, spice, mud, and clay concoctions.

The Outdoors

You're almost guaranteed to see an elk on an **elk safari** (Gräsmarks turistbyrå; ☎ 0565/40016). Departures are every Wednesday and Friday in July and cost SKr 150.

Filipstad

➋ *63 km (39 mi) northeast of Karlstad via Route 63.*

For hundreds of years Filipstad was the center of the area's mineral mining and metalworking. You can still see many of the ancient mining and stonecutting methods and lifestyles in various working museums and villages such as Nykroppa and Långban. Persberg has the Värmland's only surviving underground mine still producing limestone. Details of mine tours can be obtained from **Filipstad Turistbyrå** (tourist office; ⊠ Stora Torget 3D ☎ 0590/61354). Authorized city guides can also be hired through the tourist office, or directly at ☎ 070/2409939.

Visitors to **Hornkullens Silver Mine** (⊠Nykroppa ☎0590/41000 Kroppgårdens Vandrarhem) in Nykroppa can pan for gold after the mine tour, although the finds are not likely to finance any Sweden vacations. A hostel takes care of the tour bookings. Guided tours of the limestone mine

Gåsgruvan (✉ Persberg ☎ 0590/21377), in Persberg, are arranged through Yngens Café.

Långban is interesting not just for its **Långbans Museum** for mining and minerals, but also as the birthplace of inventor John Ericsson. Ericsson left Sweden for England in 1826 at the age of 23, and emigrated from there to America. During the U.S. Civil War the Union asked him to construct an armored ship. His *Monitor* would ultimately defeat the Confederate ship *Merrimack* at Hampton Roads, Virginia. Tours are available in Swedish, English, and German. Groups of five can call ahead to visit during the off-season. ☎ *0590/22181 or 0590/22115* ✆ *20 SKr, with tour 30 SKr* ☉ *early June–late Aug., weekdays 10–5, weekends noon–4. Guided tours at 11, noon, 2, 3 and 4.*

Filipstad's other mainstay is **Wasa** (✉ Konsul Lundströms väg 11 ☎ 0590/18100 ⊕ www.wasa.com), Scandinavia's largest producer of crispbread. The factory runs guided tours, showing the history of the company and how crispbread is produced. Call to arrange a tour.

Where to Stay & Eat

¢ ✕⊡ **Hennickehammars Gård.** Big windows, original wooden floors, and antique furniture define the large and airy guest rooms at this old Swedish manor house. The restaurant ($$$) serves traditional Swedish food in a fresh white-and-blue antique dining room with open fire. After you're full from dinner, a stroll around the peaceful grounds is a delight. ✉ *Rte 64, 6.5 km/4 mi south of Filipstad, Box 52 682 22* ☎ *0590/608500* ⊟ *0590/608505* ⊕ *www.hennickehammar.se* ✎ *54 rooms, 3 suites* ☓ *Restaurant, bar* ⊟ *AE, DC, MC, V* ⊠ *BP.*

Värmland A to Z

To research prices, get advice from other travelers, and book travel arrangements, visit www.fodors.com.

CAR TRAVEL

From Stockholm follow E18 west; from Göteborg take Route 45 north to E18.

TRAIN TRAVEL

There is regular service to Karlstad from Stockholm and Göteborg on SJ. 🚆 SJ ✉ Göteborg ☎ 0771/757575.

VISITOR INFORMATION

🅸 Tourist Information **Karlstad** ✉ Tage Erlandergatan 10 ☎ 054/222140 ⊕ www.karlstad. se. **Filipstad** ✉ Stora Torget 3D ☎ 0590/61354 ⊕ www.filipstad.se/main.html. **Sunne** Turistbyrå ✉ Kolsnäsv. 41 ☎ 0565/16460

THE SOUTH &
THE KINGDOM
OF GLASS

6

SOUTHERN SWEDEN IS CONSIDERED, even by many Swedes, to be a world of its own, clearly distinguished from the rest of the country by its geography, culture, and history. Skåne (pronounced *skoh*-neh), the southernmost province, is known as the granary of Sweden. It is a comparatively small province of beautifully fertile plains, sand beaches, thriving farms, bustling, historic towns and villages, medieval churches, and summer resorts. These gently rolling hills, extensive forests, and fields are broken every few miles by lovely castles, chronologically and architecturally diverse, that have given this part of Sweden the name Château Country. A significant number of the estates, often surrounded by beautiful grounds and moats, have remained in the hands of the original families, and many are still inhabited.

The two other southern provinces, Blekinge and Halland, are also fertile and rolling and edged by seashores. Historically, these three provinces are distinct from the rest of Sweden: they were the last to be incorporated into the country, having been ruled by Denmark until 1658. They retain the influences of the Continental culture in their architecture, language, and cuisine, viewing the rest of Sweden—especially Stockholm—with some disdain. Skåne even has its own independence movement, and the dialect is so akin to Danish that many Swedes from other regions have trouble understanding it.

Småland, to the north, is larger than the other provinces, with a harsh countryside of stone and woods. A poorer, bleaker way of life here led thousands of peasants to emigrate to the United States in the 19th century. Those who stayed behind developed a reputation for their inventiveness in setting up small industries and are also notorious for being extremely careful—if not downright mean—with money. The area has many small glassblowing firms, and it is these glassworks, such as the world-renowned Kosta Boda and Orrefors, that have given the area the nickname the Kingdom of Glass.

Perhaps the most significant recent event for the South has been the bridge that opened over the Öresund, linking Malmö to Copenhagen in Denmark. At 3 mi (5 km), the bridge is the longest in the world that carries both road and rail traffic. It opened on July 1, 2000, amid hopes that it would bring a windfall to the South. As a tourist, your travel alternatives have improved.

Your itinerary should follow a route that sweeps from the western coastal town of Mölle around the southern loop and along the eastern shore, taking a side trip to the Baltic island province of Öland before heading inland to the finish at Växjö. The entire route can be done by train, with the exception of Mölle, Öland, and most of the glassworks in Småland—the Orrefors factory is the only one on the railway line. Continue your journey in any direction from Växjö.

Exploring the South & the Kingdom of Glass

Since it covers a fairly large area of the country, this region is best explored by car. The coastal road is a pleasure to travel on, with scenic views of long, sandy beaches and the welcoming blue sea. Inland, the hills, fertile plains, and thickly wooded forests are interconnected by winding country roads. The southern peninsula around the province of Skåne has the most urban settlements and, thanks to the spectacular Oresund bridge, fast connections to Denmark and mainland Europe. The rest of the area is more picturesque and slow-paced, inviting you to take your time exploring the pretty fishing villages and ancient castles that dot the landscape.

About the Hotels & Restaurants

The south is Sweden's bread basket, cashing in on its relatively mild climate to produce top quality fruit, vegetables, meat, and fish. Like in all good food-producing areas, southerners keep the best for themselves. Everything from modern restaurants serving international cuisines to small local eating spots abounds in the region. The emphasis is on high-quality ingredients.

WHAT IT COSTS In Swedish Kronor				
$$$$	**$$$**	**$$**	**$**	**¢**
RESTAURANTS over 420	250–420	150–250	100–150	under 100
HOTELS over 2,900	2,300–2,900	1,500–2,300	1,000–1,500	under 1,000

Restaurant prices are for a main course at dinner. Hotel prices are for two people in a standard double room in high season.

Timing

The south of Sweden had a relatively mild climate compared to the rest of the country, making it possible to visit any time of year. Like much of Sweden, though, it really comes alive in the summer months, when you will find many more outdoor activities, restaurants and cafés that close during the winter. The region's large tracts of agricultural land are at their most spectacular when in full bloom, during July and August. Kivik, Sweden's cider capital on the east coast, is best appreciated during early autumn when the trees are heavily laden with apples and pears.

July is the best time to visit the classic Skåne markets in the very south of the region; they are reminiscent of old trading days when traveling tinkers used to ply their wares. You'll find everything from horses to handwoven baskets, and clogs and sweets to ducks and geese.

Mölle

 35 km (21 mi) northwest of Helsingborg, 220 km (132 mi) south of Göteborg, 235 km (141 mi) southwest of Växjö, 95 km (57 mi) northwest of Malmö.

Mölle, in the far northwest of Skåne, is a small town set in spectacular isolation on the dramatic headland of the Kulla Peninsula. It is an old fishing village with a beautiful harbor that sweeps up to the Kullaberg Range. You will find beech forests, stupefying views, and rugged shores and beaches, surrounded on three sides by sea.

For those who love nature or want a break from cities and touring, Mölle is perfect. Not only is it a good base from which to explore, but the town itself has a charm that has never been tarnished by an overabundance of tourists or a relentless drive to modernize at all costs.

But Mölle's past isn't all quaintness and tradition. In the late 19th century the town was notorious throughout the country and the rest of Europe as a hotbed of liberal hedonism. This reputation was based on the penchant of locals to enjoy mixed-sex bathing, a scandalous practice at the time. Berliners loved it, and until World War I there was a weekly train that went all the way to Mölle. But as soon as war broke out, the Germans disappeared.

Today it is a relatively wealthy place, as the elaborate residences and the upmarket cars crowding the narrow streets show. Much of this wealth supposedly arrived when the more fortunate men of the sea returned to build mansions. Many of the mansions have local, although perhaps distorted, legends about them.

The **Villa Italienborg** (✉ Harastolsv. 6) was completed in 1910 by a scrap dealer inspired by a trip to the Italian Riviera. The exterior is covered in striking red-and-white tiles that form a checked pattern, which was quite stylish at the time.

The verandas, balconies, and sliding windows all make the two-story **Villa Africa** (✉ N. Brunnsv.) stand out. It was built in a South African colonial style by a local captain to please his South African wife. Legend also has it that while wooing her, he would claim that Mölle's climate was the equal of that of her homeland!

The **Kullaberg** nature reserve is just outside Mölle and covers more than 35 square km (13½ square mi). You can walk, bike, or drive in. This natural playground includes excellent trails through beech forests and along coastal routes. There's a lighthouse here set in stark land that resembles that of the Scottish Highlands—it even has longhaired Highland cattle. The park contains cafés, a restaurant, safe swimming beaches, and a golf course that's one of Sweden's most spectacular. Rock climbers consider the rock structure here to be similar to that of the Himalayas—many climbers planning to travel to that range first train here. ▣ *SKr 25 per car.*

Krapperup Castle was built in 1570 over the ruins of a medieval stronghold dating to the 13th century. The present building was extensively renovated in the late 18th century, although remnants of the stronghold still exist. The garden is among Sweden's best-preserved parks. There's an art gallery and museum inside, and concerts and performance theater are held here in the summer. It is 4 km (2½ mi) from Mölle on the main road to Helsingborg. ☎ *042/344190* ▣ *Castle tours for groups of 10 minimum SKr 70; gallery and museum SKr 30* ☉ *Call to book castle tour for group; gallery and museum May and Sept., weekends 1–6; June–Aug., daily 1–6.*

Just a few kilometers from town, the **Mölle Kapell** is a quaint white church that stands in fields under the Kullaberg. Despite its ancient appearance, the church was built in 1937. Much of the interior—the pulpit, the altar painting, and the pews—was done by local artist Gunnar Wallentin.

The haunting **Nimis** and **Arx** artworks are built of scrap wood and stone and stand on a rugged beach that can be reached only on foot. The artist Lars Vilks has been working on the weird, highly controversial structures since the 1970s. They are the most visited sight in Kullaberg. Vilks has been under constant legal threat because he didn't apply for permission from the local government, which owns the land. ⊕ *Head 2 km (1¼ mi) east out of Mölle to a road sign directing you to Himmelstorps Hembygdsgård. Following this sign you will reach a parking lot and an old farmhouse. From here it is a 1-km (½-mi) walk marked by small blue N symbols* ⊕ *www.turism.hoganas.se.*

off the beaten path

ARILD – This beautiful fishing village of bright fishermen's and sailors' cottages has been important since the Middle Ages. It is 6 km (4 mi) east of Mölle. The nicest place to stay is **Hotel Rusthållargården** (✉ Utsikten 1 ☎ 042/346530), which costs SKr 740 per person. It has an excellent restaurant. If you're looking for a break, continue east from Arild for 2 km (1 mi) to reach the village of **Skäret**. Head for the copper sign shaped like a coffeepot, which marks **Flickorna Lundgren** (☎ 042/346044 ☉ Mid-Apr.–mid-Sept.), one of Sweden's most famous cafés. The outstanding gardens look out onto the sea, and the café's regular visitors have included King Gustav IV as well as Gustav V.

Where to Stay & Eat

Most cafés and restaurants in town are in hotels.

$$ ✕▥ **Turisthotellet.** The rooms at this hotel are well appointed, and some have a view of the harbor. The breakfast, included in room rates, is generous and could see you through to dinner. The restaurant ($$$$) serves good food with a Continental flavor, focusing on meat entrées with Swedish side dishes such as lingonberries. The lamb, cooked medium rare with mint sauce, is outstanding. ⊠ *Kullabergsv. 32* ☎ *042/347084* 🖷 *042/347100 (to Hotel Kullaberg)* ⊕ *www.molleturisthotell.se* ➥ *14 rooms* ☖ *Restaurant, bar* ▤ *AE, DC, MC, V* ⱺ *BP* ⊘ *Restaurant closed Sept.–May.*

★ $$ ✕▥ **Grand Hôtel.** The spectacular Grand Hôtel—a turreted building set high up on in town—has an unrivaled setting, great views, and a helpful staff. The best rooms are those with a sea view, but they are all pleasant. For dining you have a choice of two restaurants, the one in the hotel and the attached Captain's Room. The more expensive ($$) and adventurous meals are from the hotel dining room. ⊠ *Bökebolsvägen 11 260 42* ☎ *042/362230* 🖷 *042/362231* ⊕ *www.grand-molle.se* ➥ *44 rooms* ☖ *2 restaurants, bar, sauna, library, meeting rooms* ▤ *AE, D, MC, V* ⱺ *BP.*

$$$ ▥ **Hotel Kullaberg.** At this luxurious place all the rooms are plush and decorated in themes. One room suggests *Out of Africa,* and another has a large biplane hanging from the ceiling. You may or may not love it, depending on your feelings about kitsch. But the Kullaberg is lush, with views of the sea and the harbor and ornate reading rooms. ⊠ *Gyllenstiernas Allé 16* ☎ *042/347000* 🖷 *042/347100* ⊕ *www.hotelkullaberg. se* ➥ *18 rooms* ☖ *Breakfast room, library* ▤ *AE, DC, MC, V* ⱺ *BP.*

Shopping

In the otherwise unremarkable town of Höganäs (south of Mölle) is a good factory outlet store for ceramics and glassware. **Höganäs Keramik** (⊠ Norregatan 4, Höganäs ☎ 042/361100 ⊘ Sept.–Apr., weekdays 10–6, Sat. 10–4, Sun. 11–4; May–June and Aug., weekdays 9–6, weekends 10–5; July, weekdays 9–7, weekends 10–5 ⊠ Free guided tours in summer) sells brands such as BodaNova at discounts of up to 40%.

Sports

The Skola Mölle Hamn (⊠ Special Sports School, Södra Strandvägen 6B ☎ 042/347705, 070/3771210) caters to most outdoor activities. It organizes trips and provides gear and training for mountaineers, scuba divers, and kayakers of all skill levels.

Kullens Hästskjutsar and Turridning (⊠ Himmelstorp 765 ☎ 042/346358) organizes horseback riding.

Mölle Golfklubb (⊠ Kullahalvön ☎ 042/347520 ⊠ Greens fee June–Aug. SKr 320, Sept.–May SKr 220), one of the most spectacular 18-hole courses in Sweden, will slake the most fanatic golfers' thirst for their sport.

en route Viken and Lerberget are two small villages on the way from Mölle to Helsingborg. Viken is a preserved fishing village with narrow stone-walled streets, traditional cottages, and a well-kept example of the old windmills once used in Skåne. If you are here between late spring and fall, you can combine dinner at the Gula Boden seafood restaurant in Viken with a stay at the quaint Pensionat Solgården guest house, in nearby Lerberget (a drive of two minutes).

$$ ✕ **Gula Boden.** With a local reputation for excellent fish meals and great views of the boat harbor and sunsets, Gula Boden is quite popular. Reservations are essential in July. ⊠ *Vikens Hamn* ☎ *042/238300* ▤ *AE, DC, MC, V* ⊘ *Closed Oct.–Apr.*

$ ⊞ **Pensionat Solgården.** Run by an artistic woman who spends six months of each year at a B&B in Tonga in the South Pacific, this quaint pension hosts poetry readings outside in the summer. ⊠ *Byav. 102 Lerberget* ☎ *042/330430* ⊘ *Closed mid-Sept.–mid-Apr.* ⫣⊘ *BP.*

Helsingborg

❷ *221 km (137 mi) south of Göteborg, 186 km (116 mi) southwest of Växjö, 64 km (40 mi) north of Malmö.*

Helsingborg, with a population of 120,000, may seem to the first-time visitor little more than a small town with a modern ferry terminal (there are about 125 daily ferry connections to Denmark and one a day to Norway). The town sees itself differently, claiming titles as Sweden's "gateway to the Continent," and the "pearl of the Öresund" region. Helsingborg was first mentioned in a letter written by Canute, the king of Denmark, in 1085; later it was the site of many battles between the Danes and the Swedes. Together with its twin town, Helsingør (Elsinore in William Shakespeare's *Hamlet*), across the Öresund, it controlled shipping traffic in and out of the Baltic for centuries. Helsingborg was officially incorporated into Sweden in 1658 and totally destroyed in a battle with the Danes in 1710. It was then rebuilt, and Jean-Baptiste Bernadotte, founder of the present Swedish royal dynasty, landed here in 1810.

Built in 1897, the turreted **Rådhuset** (City Hall) has a richly adorned facade and window paintings by artist Gustav Cederström that depict important dates in Helsingborg's history. Five times a day (at 9 AM, noon, 3, 6, and 9 PM) songs ring from the 216-foot-tall bell tower. ⊠ *Drottninggatan 2* ☎ *042/105000.*

All that remains of Helsingborg's castle is **Kärnan** (the Keep), which was built in the late 14th century. It has walls 15 ft thick. This surviving center tower, built to provide living quarters and defend the medieval castle, is one of the most remarkable relics of its kind in the north. It fell into disuse after the Swedish defeated the Danes in 1658 but was restored in 1893–94. The interior is divided into several floors, which contain a chapel, an exhibition of kitchen implements, old castle fittings, and some weaponry. ⊠ *Slottshagen* ☎ *042/105991* ⊠ *SKr 15* ⊘ *Jan.–Mar., Tues.–Sun. 11–3; Apr.–May, Tues.–Fri. 9–4, weekends 11–4; June–Aug., daily 11–7; Sept., Tues.–Fri. 9–4, weekends 11–4; Oct–Dec., Tues.–Sun. 11–3.*

Fodor'sChoice
★ In 1865 **Sofiero Slott** (Sofiero Palace) was built in Dutch Renaissance style by Prince Oscar and his wife, Sofia, as a summer home. Half a century later Oscar II gave the palace to his grandson, Gustav Adolf, and his wife, Margareta, as a wedding gift. Since the estate is now owned by the city of Helsingborg, you can gain access to Sofiero's park, a haven for more than 10,000 samples of 300 kinds of rhododendron, various statues donated by international artists, and a large English garden; nearby greenhouses have plant exhibits. A café and fine restaurant are on the grounds. ⊠ *Sofierovägen (on the road to Laröd)* ☎ *042/137400* ⊠ *SKr 60* ⊘ *Apr., daily 10–5; May–Aug., 10–6; guided tours only. Park, restaurant, and café open year-round.*

Maria Kyrkan (St. Mary's), constructed in the beginning of the 14th century and finished 100 years later, is a fine example of Danish Gothic architecture. St. Mary's has several highlights: the 15th-century reredos, the silver treasure in the sacristy, and a memorial plaque to Dietrich Buxtehude (1637–1707), a prominent German composer as well as the church's organist. ⊠ *Mariatorget, Södra Storgatan 20* ☎ *042/372830* ⊘ *Aug.–June, daily 8–4, July, daily 8–6.*

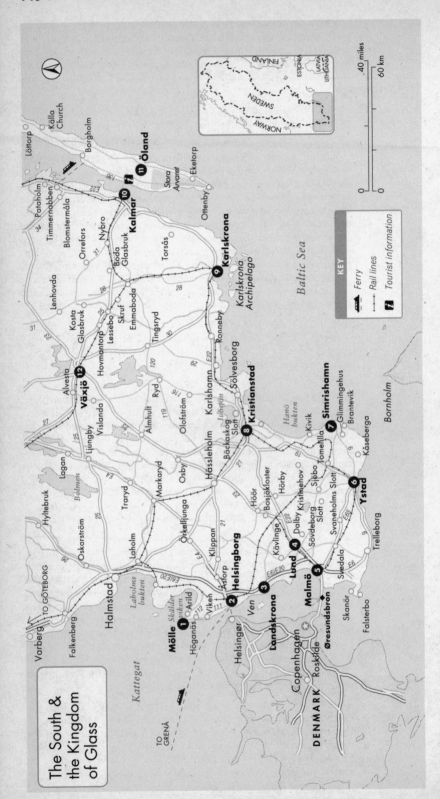

The **Dunkers Kulturhus** (Henry Dunker Culture Center) includes a theater, the city museum, a music school, a concert hall, an art museum, a cultural center for children and youth, a multimedia center, a bar, and a restaurant. It was designed by Kim Utzon, the son of the controversial architect Jørn Utzon, the Dane who designed the Sydney Opera House. ⊠ *Kungsgatan 11* ☎ *042/107400* ⊠ *SKr 60* ☼ *Mon., Wed., and Fri.–Sun. 11–6, Tues. and Thurs. 11–10* ⊕ *www.dunkerskultuhus.com.*

Helsingborg's refurbished harborside area, **Norra Hamnen** (Northern Harbor), has a pleasant marina with a string of architecturally impressive cafés and restaurants.

Where to Eat

$$$ ✕ **Gastro.** A long leather booth divides this dining room into two halves: one is packed with small tables for groups of two or three, the other with tables for five or six. Larger parties sit in the more formal back of the restaurant, but everyone orders from the same menu of Swedish-based international fare. Fish and seafood are the stars. ⊠ *Södra Storg. 11–13* ☎ *042/243470* ⊟ *AE, DC, MC, V* ☼ *Closed Sun.*

★ $$ ✕ **Pålsjö Krog.** Beside the pier that leads out to the Pålsjö Bath House, this restaurant offers a beautiful view of the Öresund. The owners have partially restored the restaurant to its original 1930s style—note the antique sofa in the lounge and the art on the walls. Seafood is the specialty in summer months, game in winter. Reservations are essential in summer. ⊠ *Drottningg. 151* ☎ *042/149730* ⊟ *AE, DC, MC, V.*

$$ ✕ **SS *Swea.*** Those with a nautical bent or nostalgia for past traveling days will be well served at this restaurant ship modeled after cruise liners of old. The docked boat specializes in fresh seafood and international menus. Enjoy the wide-ranging menu but don't forget to disembark—there are no cabin bunks here. ⊠ *Kungstorget* ☎ *042/131516* ⊟ *AE, DC, MC, V.*

$-$$ ✕ **Restaurang La Petite.** If you are yearning for the delicacy of French cuisine and the genuine look and feel of a French restaurant, then look no farther. La Petite has been here since 1975, suggesting success, and can also indulge the diner in Spanish and international meals. ⊠ *Bruksg. 19* ☎ *042/219727* ⊟ *AE, DC, MC, V* ☼ *Closed Sun.*

Where to Stay

$$ ▥ **Elite Hotel Marina Plaza.** This relaxing and stylish modern hotel, with its enormous central glass atrium, is right next to the Knutpunkten ferry, rail, and bus terminal. Rooms are spacious and elegantly decorated. ⊠ *Kungstorget 6, 251 10* ☎ *042/192100* ⊟ *042/149616* ☎ *190 rooms* ♢ *Restaurant, bar, minibars, sauna, meeting rooms, parking, no-smoking rooms* ⊟ *AE, DC, MC, V* ⬦ *BP.*

$$ ▥ **Elite Hotel Mollberg.** Only a short walk from the central station, the Mollberg has spacious rooms with hardwood floors and large windows. Corner rooms have balconies that overlook a cobblestone square. The restaurant offers dining at reasonable prices. ⊠ *Stortorget 18, 251 14* ☎ *042/373700* ⊟ *042/373737* ☎ *104 rooms* ♢ *Restaurant, bar, minibars, sauna, meeting room, parking, no-smoking rooms* ⊟ *AE, DC, MC, V* ⬦ *BP.*

$$ ▥ **Hotel Högvakten.** This hotel on the main square has bright, fresh rooms with a mix of modern and antique furniture. Rooms can be a bit small, but the hotel is close to the main shopping street and the central station. ⊠ *Stortorget 14, 251 10* ☎ *042/380490* ⊟ *042/380499* ☎ *40 rooms* ♢ *Breakfast room, sauna, meeting rooms* ⊟ *AE, DC, MC, V* ⬦ *BP.*

★ $$ ▥ **Radisson SAS Grand Hotel.** One of Sweden's oldest hotels has been completely renovated, maintaining its long-standing reputation for excellence. Antiques and fresh flowers fill the hotel, and the well-equipped guest rooms have cable TV, a hair dryer, minibar, and trouser press. The hotel is close to the railway station and ferry terminals. ✉ *Stortorget 8–12, 251 11* ☎ *042/380400* 📠 *042/380404* *117 rooms* *Restaurant, bar, sauna, gym, meeting rooms, no-smoking rooms* 💳 *AE, DC, MC, V.*

$ **Villa Thalassa.** This youth hostel 3 km (1.9 mi) from the city center has fine views over Öresund. In the main building and in bungalow-style buildings, all with private patios, there are 172 bunks in two-, four-, and six-bunk rooms. The SKr 45 breakfast is not included. ✉ *Dag Hammarskjölds väg, 254 33* ☎ *042/380660* 📠 *042/128792* *172 beds in 64 rooms (24 rooms with private shower facilities)* *Breakfast room, meeting rooms* 💳 *No credit cards.*

Nightlife & the Arts

The plush culture and art center, **Dunkers Kulturhus** (✉ Kungsgatan 11 ☎ 042/107400), stages an array of events in the fields of music, drama, visual arts, and cultural heritage.

Open weekends only, the **Tivoli** (✉ Kungsgatan 1, Hamntorget ☎ 042/187171 🌐 www.thetivoli.nu) concentrates on live rock bands, attracting major Swedish and international acts. The moderate-size dance floor has good lighting. If you're looking for a nightclub feel but want to be out of the razzmatazz, check out the vinyl bar. It has a restaurant, too.

Jazz in Helsingborg stages some of its events at a cozy club on Nedre Långvinkelsgatan and some in the culture and arts center Dunkers Kulturhus. If you strike on the right night, you may well find yourself in jazz heaven, since the organizers attract jazz musicians from all over. Admission varies and goes as high as SKr 225. ✉ *Nedre Långvinkelsg 22* ☎ *042/184900* ✉ *Dunkers Kulturhus, Kungsgatan 11, Sundstorget* ☎ *042/107400.*

The old-world **Charles Dickens** (✉ Söderg 43 ☎ 042/135100) is the oldest pub in town.

Sports & the Outdoors

Consider taking a relaxing dip in the sound at the late 19th-century **Pålsjö Baden** (Pålsjö Bath House) just north of town. It's a Helsingborg tradition to sweat in a sauna and then jump into the cool waters of the channel—even in the winter months. After an evening sauna, nearby Pålsjö Krog is a good dinner option. ✉ *Drottninggatan 151* ☎ *042/149707* *Single visit SKr 25.*

Ramlösa Brunnspark (☎ 042/105888) is the source of the famous Ramlösa mineral water, which is served in restaurants and cafés throughout the world. Since it opened in 1707, the park has attracted summertime croquet players and those eager to taste the water (an outdoor café also serves beer and wine). Nearby is the **Ramlösa Wärdshus** (☎ 042/296257), which has been serving authentic Swedish cuisine since 1830. To reach the park by bus, take Bus 2 or 8 going south from the central station (Knutpunkten).

If your bones are weary, visit **Öresundsmassage.** The professionally trained staff offers various massage services and can deal with problems such as cramping or poor blood circulation. ✉ *Roskildeg. 4* ☎ *042/127042* *20 min SKr 200, 40 min SKr 350, 55 min SKr 450* ⏲ *Mon. and Wed. noon–7; Tues. and Thurs. 10–6.*

Skåne (☎ 042/104350 Helsingborg Tourist Information) is a golfers' delight. There are more than 60 golf courses in the region in total; within an hour's drive of Helsingborg you can find more than 20.

Shopping

Helsingborg has convenient shopping, and it's a good place to run errands. The best place to head is **Kullagatan,** which was the first pedestrians-only street in Sweden. It's a convenient collection of most of the sorts of shops you might need (e.g., a pharmacy, a photo shop, and a stationery store). If it's cheaper, medium-quality skins, furs, or leathers you want, try the **Skin and Fur Centre** at Kullagatan 7.

Landskrona

❸ *26 km (16 mi) south of Helsingborg (via E6/E20), 41 km (25 mi) north of Malmö, 204 km (127 mi) southwest of Växjö.*

The 17th-century Dutch-style fortifications of Landskrona are among the best preserved in Europe. Though it appears to be a modern town, Landskrona dates from 1413, when it received its charter.

The eclectic **Landskrona Museum** has temporary exhibits as well as permanent coverage of Landskrona history and the Swedish contributions to art, medicine, aviation, and architecture. ⊠ *Slottsg.* ☎ *0418/473123* ⊕ *www.landskrona.se/kultur* ☟ *Free* ☉ *Mon.–Sun. noon–5.*

Landskrona's **Citadellet** (castle) was built under orders of the Danish king Christian III in 1549 and is all that remains of the original town, which was razed in 1747 by decree of the Swedish Parliament to make way for extended fortifications. The new town was built on land reclaimed from the sea. ⊠ *Slottsg.* ☎ *0418/448250* ☟ *SKr 40* ☉ *Early June–late Aug., Tues.–Sun. 11–4; guided tours Tues.–Fri. noon, 2, and 4, weekends noon and 2.*

> **off the beaten path**
>
> **VEN –** From Landskrona Harbor there are regular 25-minute boat trips to the island of Ven (☟ SKr 70 round-trip; boats depart every 90 mins 6 AM–9 PM). It's an ideal place for camping; check with **Landskrona's tourist office** (☎ 0418/473000). There are special paths across Ven for bicycling; rentals are available from Bäckviken, the small harbor.
>
> The Danish astronomer Tycho Brahe conducted his pioneering research here from 1576 to 1597. The foundations of his Renaissance castle, **Uranienborg,** can be visited, as can **Stjärneborg,** his reconstructed observatory. The small **Tycho Brahe Museet** is dedicated to Brahe and his work. ⊠ *Landsv. 182, Ven* ☎ *0418/72530* ☟ *SKr 35* ☉ *Apr.–June, daily 10–4, July–mid-Aug., 10–5; mid-Aug.–mid-Sept., 11–4.*

Sports & the Outdoors

Three kilometers (2 miles) north of Landskrona lies the **Borstahusen** (⊠261 61 Landskrona ☎ 0418/10837) recreation area, with long stretches of beach, a marina, and a group of 74 small cabinlike chalets.

Lund

❹ *34 km (21 mi) southeast of Landskrona via E6/E20 and Route 16, 25 km (15 mi) northeast of Malmö, 183 km (113 mi) southwest of Växjö.*

One of the oldest towns in Europe, Lund was founded in 990. In 1103 Lund became the religious capital of Scandinavia and at one time had 27 churches and eight monasteries—until King Christian III of Denmark ordered most of them razed to use their stones for the construction of Malmöhus Castle. Lund lost its importance until 1666, when its university was established—the second-oldest university in Sweden after Uppsala.

FodorsChoice Lund's **Domkyrkan** (Cathedral), consecrated in 1145, is a monumental ★ gray-stone Romanesque cathedral, the oldest in Scandinavia. Since the

Reformation it has been Lutheran. Its crypt has 23 finely carved pillars, but its main attraction is an astrological clock, Horologum Mirabile Lundense, dating from 1380 and restored in 1923. The "Miraculous Clock of Lund" depicts an amazing pageant of knights jousting on horseback, trumpets blowing a medieval fanfare, and the Magi walking in procession past the Virgin and Child as the organ plays *In Dulci Jubilo*. The clock plays at noon and at 3 Monday–Saturday and at 1 and 3 on Sunday. The oldest parts of the cathedral are considered the finest Romanesque constructions in Sweden. English and Swedish tours are available, and there are concerts at 10 AM on Sundays. ⌧ *Free.*

Historiska museet med Domkyrkomuseet (The Cathedral Museum and the Museum of History) are just north of the cathedral. The Cathedral Museum has exhibitions and a slide show about the Domkyrkan's history. The Museum of History has Sweden's second-largest collection of treasures from the Stone, Bronze, and Iron ages. It also houses one of the oldest human skeletal finds, dated to 5000 BC. ⌧ *Kraftstorg Sq. 1* ☎ *046/2227944* ⌧ *SKr 30* ⊙ *mid-June–mid-Aug., Tues.–Sat. 11–4.*

One block east of the cathedral is the **Botaniska Trädgården** (Botanical Gardens), which contains more than 7,000 specimens of plants from all over the world, including such exotics as the paper mulberry tree, from the islands of the South Pacific. ⌧ *Östra Vallg. 20* ☎ *046/2227320* ⌧ *Free* ⊙ *Daily 6 AM–8 PM, greenhouses daily noon–3.*

The Lundagård park separates the Domkyrkan from the oldest parts of **Lund University.** The main building is crisp white and easily spotted among the cobbled streets and traditional cottages. The university was founded in 1666 and today has 30,000 students. Its **History Museum** (☎ 046/350400), part of the **Kulturen** group of museums, exhibits old texts, university regalia, and other items used in the university long ago. ⌧ *Kyrkog.*

need a
break?

Just across from the university is a Lund institution—**Conditori Lund** (⌧ Kyrkog. 17), a bakery and coffeehouse. It's easy to imagine the rooms filled with the smoke and loud opinions of intellectuals of the past.

Founded in 1934 in connection with Lund University, **Skissernas Museum** (Sketches Museum) houses more than 20,000 sketches in addition to models and first drafts by major artists. It is scheduled to reopen in 2004 after a major renovation. The international collection contains the early ideas of artists such as Henri Matisse, Pablo Picasso, Fernand Léger, and many others. ⌧ *Finng. 2* ☎ *046/2227283* ⌧ *SKr 30* ⊙ *Tues. and Thurs.–Sat. noon–4, Wed. 6:30–8:30, Sun. 1–5.*

Esaias Tegnér, a Swedish poet, lived from 1813 to 1826 in a little house immediately behind the cathedral. The house has since been turned into the **Tegnér Museet,** providing insight into his life and works. ⌧ *Stora Gråbrödersg. 11* ☎ *046/291319* ⌧ *SKr 5* ⊙ *July–Aug., Sun. noon–3; Sept.–June, 1st weekend each month noon–3.*

On the southern side of Stortorget, the main square, is **Drottens Kyrko-ruin** (Church Ruins of Drotten), an underground museum showing life as it was in Lund during the Middle Ages. The foundations of three Catholic churches are here: the first was built of wood around AD 1000. It was torn down to make room for one of stone around 1100; this was replaced by a second stone church, built around 1300. ⌧ *Kattensund 6* ☎ *046/141328* ⌧ *SKr 10* ⊙ *Tues.–Fri. noon–4, weekends 10–2.*

☕ **Kulturen** (The Museum of Cultural History) is both an outdoor and an indoor museum; it includes 20 old cottages, farms, and manor houses from southern Sweden, plus an excellent collection of ceramics, textiles, weapons, and furniture. Kulturen's **gardens** have free admission on summer nights, and on many of those nights there is live music and dancing. Call the museum for further details. ✉ *Tegnérsplatsen* ☎ *046/ 350400* ☎ *SKr 50* ☉ *Mid-Apr.–Sept., Fri.–Wed. 11–5, Thurs. 11–9; Oct.–mid-Apr., Tues.–Sun. noon–4.*

The all-brick **Lund Konsthallen** (Lund Art Gallery) may have a rather foreboding iron entrance and few windows, but skylights allow ample sunlight into the large exhibit room full of modern art. ✉ *Måtenstorget 3* ☎ *046/355000* ☎ *Free* ☉ *Mon.–Wed. and Fri. noon–5, Thurs. noon–8, Sat. 10–5, Sun. noon–6.*

Fodor'sChoice ★ The **Heligkorskyrkan i Dalby** (Holy Cross Church of Dalby) was founded in 1060, making it the oldest stone church in Scandinavia. It was for a short time the archbishop's seat until this was moved to Lund. Among the hidden treasures is a renowned baptismal font, brought here in 1150. The exposed brick within the church is original and many figures and icons date from medieval times, including a wooden relief at the front of the church called *Veronica's Napkin*, which shows the face of Jesus. The church is on a hill and less than 10 km (8 mi) from Lund. ✉ *Head east on Rte. 16 and follow signs* ☎ *046/208600* ☎ *Free* ☉ *May–Aug., daily 9–6; Sept.–Apr., daily 9–4.*

> off the
> beaten
> path

BOSJÖKLOSTER – About 30 km (19 mi) northeast of Lund via E22 and Route 23, Bosjökloster is an 11th-century, white Gothic castle with lovely grounds on Ringsjön, the second-largest lake in southern Skåne. The castle's original owner donated the estate to the church, which turned it over to the Benedictine order of nuns. They founded a convent school (no longer in operation) for the daughters of Scandinavian nobility and built the convent church with its tower made of sandstone. The 300-acre castle grounds, with a 1,000-year-old oak tree, also have a network of pathways, a children's park, a rose garden, and an indoor-outdoor restaurant. ✉ *Höör* ☎ *0413/ 25048* ☎ *SKr 45* ☉ *Castle grounds, Apr.–Sept., daily 8–sunset; restaurant and exhibition halls Apr.–Sept., daily 10–6.*

Where to Eat

★ $$ ✕ **Bantorget 9.** The restaurant-bar inside this 18th-century building is true to the past, with restored woodwork and paintings on the ceilings, antique flowerpots and candleholders, and classical statues in the corners of the room. The menu offers traditional Swedish dishes plus some more intriguing entrées such as duck breast with pickled red cabbage in apple honey. Bantorget 9 is a short walk from Lund's central train station. ✉ *Bantorget 9* ☎ *046/320200* ▭ *AE, DC, MC, V* ☉ *Closed Sun.*

$$ ✕ **Godset.** Inside an old railroad warehouse right on the tracks near central station, Godset's modern tables and chairs stand on rustic wooden floors between brick walls. On one wall hangs a large 1950s clock taken from Mariakyrkan (Maria Church) in nearby Ystad. The menu is mostly seafood and meat dishes. Try the roasted venison poached in a cream sauce with raspberry vinaigrette. ✉ *Bang. 3* ☎ *046/121610* ▭ *AE, DC, MC, V* ☉ *Closed Sun.*

$–$$ ✕ **Dalby Gästgifveri.** This is one of Skåne's oldest inns and a gastronomic delight. The many red-meat dishes on the menu follow a tradition of history and quality, but innovative Swedish fare is served, too. Entrées such as the rich, somewhat gamey deer fillet with mushroom spring rolls and cranberry sauce are not for the faint of heart. Be sure to make reservations in the summer. ✉ *Tengsg. 6* ☎ *046/200006* ▭ *AE, MC, V.*

★ $$ ✕ **Restaurang Café Finn.** Connected to the Lund Konsthallen, Café Finn is an excellent option for lunch or dinner. The creamy lobster soup with mussels is perfect if you're not overly hungry, but for a more substantial meal go for the veal fillet with creamy red-onion sauce and grape jelly. The walls have an extensive collection of museum exhibit posters from the '60s, '70s, and '80s. Just outside is the Krognoshuset; built in the 1300s, it is Lund's best-kept medieval residence. ⊠ *Mårtenstorget 3* ☎ *046/130565* ☰ *AE, DC, MC, V.*

$ ✕ **Ebbas Skafferi.** Just across the central station, Ebbas Pantry serves a number of excellent sandwiches on bagels, baguettes, or *ciabattas* (a flat Italian bread). ⊠ *Bytaregatan 5* ☎ *046/127127* ☰ *MC, V.*

Where to Stay

$–$$ 🏨 **Djingis Khan.** This English colonial–style Best Western hotel caters to business travelers but is also a great place for families or couples seeking a quiet location. The hotel's unusual name comes from a comedy show that has been performed at Lund University since 1954. With squash, tennis, and badminton courts nearby, along with a large swimming pool, it's ideal if you're looking to keep in shape. ⊠ *Margaretav. 7, 222 40* ☎ *046/333600* 🖨 *046/333610* 🛏 *55 rooms* ♨ *Hot tub, sauna, gym, bicycles, meeting room, no-smoking rooms,* ☰ *AE, DC, MC, V* ⊘ *Closed July.*

$$ 🏨 **Concordia.** Formerly a private residence, this elegant city-center property was built in 1890. Rooms have a modern, clean look but are without much character. ⊠ *Stålbrog. 1, 222 24* ☎ *046/135050* 🖨 *046/137422* 🛏 *65 rooms* ♨ *Sauna, meeting room, no-smoking rooms* ☰ *AE, DC, MC, V.*

$$ 🏨 **Grand Hotel.** This elegant red-stone hotel is in the heart of the city on a pleasant square close to the railway station. Rooms have turn-of-the-20th-century decor and charm. The fine restaurant serves an alternative vegetarian menu. ⊠ *Bantorget 1, 221 04* ☎ *046/2806100* 🖨 *046/2806150* 🛏 *84 rooms* ♨ *Restaurant, hot tub, sauna, meeting room, no-smoking rooms* ☰ *AE, DC, MC, V.*

$$ 🏨 **Hotel Lundia.** Only a few hundred feet from the train station, Hotel Lundia is ideal for those who want to be near the city center. Built in 1968, the modern, four-story square building has transparent glass walls on the ground floor. Rooms are decorated with Scandinavian fabrics and lithographs. ⊠ *Knut den Stores torg 2, 221 04* ☎ *046/2806500* 🖨 *046/2806510* 🛏 *97 rooms* ♨ *Restaurant, lounge, nightclub, meeting room, no-smoking rooms* ☰ *AE, DC, MC, V.*

$ 🏨 **STF Vandrarhem Tåget.** So named because of its proximity to the train station (*tåget* means "train"), this youth hostel faces a park in central Lund. ⊠ *Bjerredsparken, Vävareg. 22, 222 37* ☎ *046/142820* 🛏 *108 beds without bath* ☰ *No credit cards.*

Nightlife & the Arts

The **Lundia** (⊠ Knut den Stores Torg 2 ☎ 046/2806500) nightclub is in the Hotel Lundia, near the Burger King. Women must be 23 or older to enter, men over 25, and not many attendees are much over 35. It costs SKr 50 to dance to the electronic sounds.

★ **Basilika** (⊠ Stora Söderg. 13 ☎ 046/2116660) has a smallish dance floor and also hosts live bands. On Friday and Saturday things don't get going until 11 and rage on until 3. Basilika draws young hipsters and will cost at least SKr 50 to get in.

The hot spot in town **Stortorget** (⊠ Stortorget 1 ☎ 046/139290) has live music as well as a DJ night and is popular with students. You won't get in here unless you are over 22.

Shopping

About 200,000 secondhand books are stacked in crazy piles in the **Åkards Antikvariat** (✉ Klosterg. ☎ 046/2112499), making it full of the smells of aged literature. The oldest book dates to about 1500, around the time the printing press was developed. Any sort of book can be found, even an airport thriller.

The oldest coins in Europe date to between 500 and 600 BC, and the coin shop **Lunds Mynthandel** (✉ Klosterg. 5 ☎ 046/14436) often has specimens going back that far. Lunds Mynthandel also carries books on numismatics.

Saluhalen (✉ Corner of Mårtenstorget and Botulfsg.), known as Foodhall, is an adventure in itself, an excellent example of the traditional Swedish food house but also one that stocks delicacies from Italy, Japan, and beyond. Cheese, meats, fresh and pickled fish, and pastries are all in great supply. It is the perfect place to get some food for a picnic in one of Lund's many squares and parks. The cheese selection at **Bengsons Ost** (✉ Klosterg. 9) is hard to surpass. The people are friendly, and it's a great spot to fill your picnic hamper. Bring your own wine and have a tasting session.

Skånae–kraft (✉ Östra Mårtensg. 5 ☎ 046/144777) carries a wide range of ceramics, crafts, and designer goods that changes frequently. **Teahuset Java** (✉ Västra Mårtensg.), a well-known tea-and-coffee shop, sells leaves and beans from all over the world. You can also get all the paraphernalia that goes with brewing.

Malmö

❺ *25 km (15 mi) southwest of Lund (via E22), 198 km (123 mi) southwest of Växjö.*

Capital of the province of Skåne, with a population of about 265,000, Malmö is Sweden's third-largest city. It was founded at the end of the 13th century. The remarkable 8-km (5-mi) bridge and tunnel from Malmö to Copenhagen has transformed travel and trade in the area, cutting both time and costs, and replacing the ferries that used to shuttle between the two towns. Eight years in the making, the $3 billion Öresund Bridge has proved to be a success, both environmentally and commercially.

The city's castle, **Malmöhus,** completed in 1542, was for many years used as a prison (James Bothwell, husband of Mary, Queen of Scots, was one of its notable inmates). Today Malmöhus houses a variety of **museums,** including the City Museum, the Museum of Natural History, and the Art Museum, which has a collection of Nordic art. Across the street is the Science and Technology Museum, the Maritime Museum, and a toy museum. ✉ *Malmöhusvägen* ☎ *040/344437* 💰 *SKr 40 for all museums* ⊙ *June–Aug., daily 10–4; Sept.–May, daily noon–4.*

In the same park as Malmöhus is the **Malmö Stadsbibliotek** (Malmö City Library), designed by the famous Danish architect Henning Larsen. Take a walk through the colossal main room—there's a four-story wall of glass that brings seasonal changes of colors inside. ✉ *Kung Oscars Väg* ☎ *040/6608500.*

On the far side of the castle grounds from Malmöhus, the **Aq-va-kul** water park offers a variety of bathing experiences, from water slides to bubble baths. ✉ *Regementsg. 24* ☎ *040/300540* 💰 *SKr 65* ⊙ *Weekdays 9–8:30, weekends 9–5:30; Mon. and Wed. adult sessions 7 PM–9:30 PM.*

SWEET TOOTH

THE SWEDES, LIKE EVERY PEOPLE OF THE EARTH, have developed an intricate web of storytelling and fairy tales. These are the realms of trolls and elves, of witches and spirits. The myths interweave the good and the bad and reinterpret the experience of life as lived by people with few other ways to explain the apparently inexplicable.

With these thoughts in mind I was on my way to the town of Gränna, on the mystical island Visingsö, which is said to have been created by a giant called Vist. Gränna is home to a great Swedish confectionery tradition: the making of the peppermint stick, which in Swedish is called polkagris and is exported around the world.

I walked into the factory of the oldest stick maker in the land, as the public is welcome to do, to watch the production process. Here the widow Amalia Erikson made the first red-and-white sweets in 1859. As a woman, she had to seek government permission to do so. Behind the glass window the craftsmen ply their trade: brewing, coloring, twisting, and turning something that looked like dough into fluorescent candy sticks. Some 2,000 a day are made in this factory alone. With so much tooth-rotting sugar—about 75% of the product—it made sense of the elfin image: those wicked, toothless grins. Was evil afoot?

Oh, yes. Like the bright-eyed child drawn to Grandma's candy drawer, I marveled at the colors as I watched the candy sticks roll out. It was inevitable that I would take the sugar hit that would take me to Mars. The first bite was pure pleasure, a crunching and splintering of the stick, and then the rush. But it was as if this event was written in the stars, foretold by a wise old troll. There was more crunch than I would have liked and, as if by magic, my tooth bounced onto the floor. The shopkeeper didn't know where to look. This adventure had extracted its price.

I beat an embarrassed retreat, beset with my own toothless grin. It was as if I had known not the facts of the future, but the sense of it. I took the ferry to Visingsö,

with its timeless villages, eccentric art history, its rugged coast and people with their own enchanted look. In moments of mindless drift, I cast my eyes toward the woods, the trees, and the toadstools. Would I see one of these underworld creatures? Did they have something to teach?

But the island, as magical as it seemed, proved to be a temporal place. The locals told me the elves mostly come out at night. I, however, saw Visingsö and its origins through the eyes of legend. The giant Vist, returning from a feast with his wife, discovered that, full of food, she could not take Lake Vättern in a step. With great might he lifted a piece of turf and placed it in the lake for her to step on. This is Visingsö's creation story.

As for me? Well, the lesson I had to learn, as I could best understand it, was one of the seven deadly sins, according to the Bible: that of avarice, or greed. From then on Sweden could be seen only in a cautious supernatural light. I never found a troll, but I believe they exist. My dental work is irrefutable and permanent proof.

A clutch of tiny red-painted shacks called the **Fiskehodderna** (Fish Shacks) is next to a dock where the fishing boats come in every morning to unload their catch. The piers, dock, and huts have been restored and are now a government-protected district. You can buy fresh fish directly from the fishermen Tuesday through Saturday mornings.

★ In Gamla Staden, the Old Town, look for the **St. Petri Church**, on Kalendegatan; dating from the 14th century, it is an impressive example of the Baltic Gothic style, with distinctive stepped gables. Inside there is a fine Renaissance altar.

★ You can learn about Scandinavian art and design at the **Form/Design Center.** The center is run by SvenskForm, a nonprofit association that promotes top-quality design in Sweden; Swedish and other Scandinavian artworks are on display throughout the center. ⊠ *9 Lilla Torg* ☎ *040/664510* ☒ *Free admission.* ☉ *Tues.–Fri. 11–5, Thurs. 11–6, weekends 11–4.*

The **Rådhuset** (Town Hall), dating from 1546, dominates Stortorget, a huge, cobbled market square in Gamla Staden, and makes an impressive spectacle when illuminated at night. In the center of the square stands an equestrian statue of Karl X, the king who united this part of the country with Sweden in 1658. Off the southeast corner of Stortorget is the square Lilla Torg.

The **Idrottsmuseum** (Museum of Sport) occupies Baltiska Hallen (the Baltic Building), next to Malmö Stadium. It traces the history of sports, including soccer and wrestling, from antiquity to the present. ☎ *040/342688* ☒ *Free* ☉ *Weekdays 8–4.*

One of Sweden's most outstanding art museums, **Rooseum,** is in a turn-of-the-20th-century brick building that was once a power plant. It has exhibitions of contemporary art and a quality selection of Nordic art. ⊠ *Gasverksg. 22* ☎ *040/121716* ☒ *SKr 40* ☉ *Wed.–Fri. 2–8; weekends noon–6. Guided tours in Swedish and English weekends at 2 and Thurs. at 6:30.*

Founded in 1975, the **Malmö Konsthall** (Malmö Art Gallery) is one of the largest contemporary art museums in Europe, with a huge single room that's more than 20,000 square feet. It arranges about 10 exhibitions a year, from the classics of modern art to present-day experiments. Other activities include theater performances, film presentations, and poetry readings. ⊠ *St. Johannesg. 7* ☎ *040/341293* ☒ *Free* ☉ *Mon.–Tues. and Thurs.–Sun. 11–5, Wed. 11–9.*

Lilla Torg is a cobblestone square with some of the city's oldest buildings, which date to the 17th and 18th centuries. It is clustered with cafés, restaurants, and bars and is a great place to wander or watch the world go by. Walk into the side streets and see the traditional buildings, which were originally used mainly to store grain and produce. Check out the *Saluhallen* (food hall), which contains one of Sweden's best coffee purveyors.

★ The **Öresundbron** (Öresund Bridge) is an engineering miracle. Its train tracks and four car lanes stretch 8 km (5 mi) from the southern coastal suburbs of Malmö to Copenhagen. Designed under the auspices of Öresund Konsortiet, the bridge is a minimalist beauty. ⊠ *Lookout at Öresund Utställningen at the end of Utställningen Rd. Approach on E20 Hwy.* ⊕ *www.oeresundsbron.com* ☒ *SKr 275 each way for car.*

The houses and business buildings designed and erected for the 2001 **European Housing Expo** show 58 different types of housing. Wander around the development around the Ribersborgsstranden waterfront, where the expo was held, in order to see the exteriors of more than 500 homes. They were sold as residences after the expo was over. ⊠ *Ribersborgsstranden waterfront.*

off the
beaten
path

FALSTERBO AND SKANÖR – The idyllic towns of Falsterbo and Skanör are two popular summer resorts on a tiny peninsula, 32 km (20 mi) southwest of Malmö. Falsterbo is popular among ornithologists, who flock there every fall to watch the spectacular migration of hundreds of birds, especially swallows, geese, hawks, and eagles.

TORUPS SLOTT – Built around 1550 near a beautiful beech forest, Torup Castle is a great example of the classic, square fortified stronghold. From Malmö drive 10 km (6 mi) southeast on E65, then head north for another 6 km (4 mi) to Torup. ⊠ *Torup* 🖼 *SKr 60* ☉ *Sun. tours at 1, 2, and 3* 🖼 *040/447050.*

Where to Eat

★ **$$-$$$** ✕ **Årstiderna i Kockska Huset.** Formed by merging two discrete restaurants that were in different locations, the combination is housed in a 16th-century building with beautiful interiors. Several of the dining areas are in an underground cellar. Traditional Swedish dishes, often centered on beef, game, and seafood, are given a contemporary twist. The fried halibut, for example, is served with a crab mousse and a rich shellfish sauce flavored with curry. Like the food, the wine list is excellent. ⊠ *Frans Suellsgatan 3* 🖼 *040/230910* 🖃 *AE, DC, MC, V.*

$$-$$$ ✕ **Johan P.** This extremely popular restaurant specializes in seafood and shellfish prepared in Swedish and Continental styles. White walls and crisp white tablecloths give it an elegant air, which contrasts with the generally casual dress of the customers. An outdoor section is open in the summer. ⊠ *Saluhallen, Lilla Torg* 🖼 *040/971818* 🖃 *AE, DC, MC, V* ☉ *Closed Sun.*

$$ ✕ **Hipp.** Distinguishing this bar-restaurant that dates to 1899 are ornate columns that support a high ceiling painted with flower patterns. Heavy chandeliers hang over the dark-wood bar in the center of the restaurant. Hipp's hearty fare is the perfect cap to a night at the city theater, next door. The finely sliced raw salmon with black roe is a standout, as is the vegetable stir-fry. Dry martinis are the specialty of the bar. ⊠ *Kalendeg. 12* 🖼 *040/974030* 🖃 *AE, DC, MC, V* ☉ *Closed Sun. and Mon.*

$-$$ ✕ **Anno 1900.** This charming little restaurant sits in a former working-class area of Malmö. It is a popular local luncheon place with a cheerful outdoor garden terrace. Head here for such light dishes as salads and fish, as well as for traditional Swedish lunches built around the potato. The bread is outstanding. ⊠ *Norra Bulltoftav. 7* 🖼 *040184747* 🗪 *Reservations essential* 🖃 *AE, DC, MC, V.*

$-$$ ✕ **Glorias.** This friendly restaurant and sports bar offers a good value. The food is Tex-Mex, with a few international appetizers thrown in. ⊠ *Södra Förstadsgatan 23B* 🖼 *040/70200* 🖃 *AE, DC, MC, V.*

$-$$ ✕ **Salt & Brygga.** The traditional Swedish kitchen has found some inspiration in the Mediterranean at this quayside restaurant. Endive and Gorgonzola toast, and smoked saithe (coalfish) and horseradish *fromage* (cheese) appetizers are followed by rich shellfish casseroles. The restaurant not only uses only organic produce, but also uses ecologically friendly alternatives for everything from the wall paint to the table linens and the staff's clothes. The restaurant's selection of organic wines and beers is unique for the region. ⊠ *Sundspromenaden 7* 🖼 *040/6115940* 🖃 *AE, DC, MC, V.*

FodorsChoice ★

¢-$ ✕ **B & B.** It stands for *Butik och Bar* (Shop and Bar) and is named as such because of its location in the market hall in central Malmö. There's always good home cooking, with dishes like grilled salmon and beef fillet with potatoes. Sometimes there's even entertainment at the piano. ⊠ *Saluhallen, Lilla Torg* ☎ *040/127120* ▤ *AE, DC, MC, V.*

¢ ✕ **Spot.** Reasonable prices and unpretentious food draw a lively group of regulars to this Italian eatery for lunch. ⊠ *Stora Nygatan 33* ☎ *040/120203* ▤ *AE, DC, MC, V* ⊘ *Closed Sun. No dinner.*

Where to Stay

$$ 🏨 **Hilton Malmö City.** Ultramodern in steel and glass, the Hilton is the city's only skyscraper—at a modest 20 floors. It provides excellent views all the way to Copenhagen on a clear day. Rooms are plain but comfortable. ⊠ *Triangeln 2, 200 10* ☎ *040/6934700* 🖷 *040/6934711* ⇖ *216 rooms* ⚇ *Restaurant, bar, cable TV, in-room data ports, sauna, gym, meeting room, no-smoking rooms* ▤ *AE, DC, MC, V.*

★ $$ 🏨 **Mäster Johan Hotel.** The plain exterior of this Best Western hotel disguises a plush and meticulously crafted interior. A top-to-bottom redesign of a 19th-century building, with the focal point an Italianate atrium breakfast room, the Mäster Johan is unusually personal for a chain hotel. The rooms are impressive, with exposed plaster-and-stone walls, recessed lighting, oak floors, Oriental carpets, and French cherry-wood furnishings. ⊠ *Mäster Johansg. 13, 211 21* ☎ *040/6646400* 🖷 *040/6646401* ⇖ *69 rooms* ⚇ *Breakfast room, room service, sauna, meeting room, no-smoking rooms* ▤ *AE, DC, MC, V.*

$$ 🏨 **Radisson SAS Hotel.** Only a five-minute walk from the train station, this modern luxury hotel has rooms decorated in several styles: Scandinavian, Asian, and Italian. There are even special rooms for guests with pets. Service is impeccable. The restaurant serves Scandinavian and Continental cuisine, and there's a cafeteria. ⊠ *Österg. 10, S211 25* ☎ *040/6984000* 🖷 *040/6984001* ⇖ *229 rooms* ⚇ *Restaurant, cafeteria, sauna, gym, spa, meeting room, no-smoking rooms* ▤ *AE, DC, MC, V.*

★ $ 🏨 **Baltzar.** This turn-of-the-20th-century house in central Malmö makes a small, comfortable hotel. Rooms are modern, with the original hardwood floors. ⊠ *Söderg. 20, 211 34,* ☎ *040/6655700* 🖷 *040/236375* ⇖ *41 rooms* ⚇ *No-smoking rooms* ▤ *AE, DC, MC, V.*

$ 🏨 **Comfort Hotel.** In a rejuvenated part of Malmö Harbor, this low-overhead, minimal-service hotel has small but comfortable rooms equipped with satellite TV, telephone, and radio. The large front entrance and lobby atrium are inventively created out of a narrow strip between two buildings. Though the hotel doesn't add a surcharge to the telephone bill, breakfast does cost extra (SKr 65). ⊠ *Carlsg. 10C, 211 20* ☎ *040/330440* 🖷 *040/330450* ⇖ *109 rooms* ⚇ *Breakfast room, cable TV, parking* ▤ *AE, DC, MC, V.*

Nightlife & the Arts

The Bishop's Arms (⊠ Savoy Hotel, Nora Vallg. 62 ☎ 040/6644888) is a classic and busy English pub. It is in the former grill room of the Savoy Hotel and can hardly fail to impress the pub connoisseur. There's an excellent assortment of old whiskeys.

Étage (⊠ Stortorget 6 ☎ 040/232060 ⊴ SKr 50 or more ⊘ Mon., Thurs., Fri., and Sat. 11 PM–5 AM) is a centrally located nightclub for hipsters, with two dance floors. It also has a piano bar for relaxing, as well as a restaurant. Dancing begins late under psychedelic lights Thursday, Friday, and Saturday. Karaoke, roulette, and blackjack tables are available.

Five rooms of an old patrician apartment make up **Klubb Plysch** (⊠ Lilla Torg 1 ☎ 040/127670 ⊴ SKr 60 ⊘ Weekends 10 PM–3 AM). Lounge about in the superb velvet chairs with champagne and cigars in the early evening, and join the dance floor around 11.

Wallmans Salonger (⊠ Generalsg. 1 ☎ 040/74945 ⊴ SKr 100–Skr 180) has an artistic, bohemian staff that is part of the entertainment. They may burst into song or start juggling. A dance show with terrific lighting begins at 7, and the nightclub proper begins at 11. There are also a casino and a restaurant.

The Malmö Symfoni Orkester (☎ 040/343500 ⊕ www.mso.se) is a symphony orchestra that has a reputation across Europe as a class act. Each concert is a finely tuned event. Performances are held at many venues, including outdoors; some are at the impressive Malmö Konserthus.

Sports & the Outdoors

From Ribersborg Beach you can walk on a pier to the **Kallbadhuset Ribersborgsstranden,** which are old baths (the name translates as "cold bathhouses Ribersborg Beach"). Built in 1898, they are a popular place to swim, since a man-made harbor of boulders offers protection from the sea's turbulence. It also hosts cultural events such as poetry readings and has a bar and a café. To get to the beach, follow Citadellsvägen to the west from the central railway station. Walk alongside Öresunds Parken and turn right at the sign for Ribersborg. ⊠ *Ribersborg Beach* ☎ *040/ 260366* ⊠ *SKr 40.*

Paddle boating on the canals is a great way to see the city. Each boat takes up to four people. Start paddling from Raoul Wallenberg Park, just southeast of Gustav Adolfs Square along Lilla Nygatan. ⊠ *Raoul Wallenberg Park* ☎ *0704/710067* ⊠ *SKr 100 per hr, SKr 70 for 30 mins* ⊙ *June–Sept., daily 11–7.*

Shopping

Malmö has many quality housewares and design stores. **Duka** (⊠ Hansacompagniet Centre, Malmborgsg. 6 ☎ 040/121141) is a high-quality housewares shop specializing in glass, crockery, and glass art. Special tables are set up with Swedish products on display, and hand-carved and hand-painted wood Dala horses are for sale. **Cervera** (⊠ Södra Förstadsgatan 24 ☎ 040/971230) carries big-name glassware brands such as Kosta and Orrefors. There's an excellent selection of glass art as well as porcelain and china—and almost everything you might need as far as housewares.

The **Form/Design Centre** (⊠ Lilla Torg 9 ☎ 040/6645150) sells products related to its changing exhibitions on everything from ceramics to books. Also look here for the very latest in Scandinavian interior design. **Formagruppen** (⊠ Engelbrektsg. 8 ☎ 040/4078060) is an arts-and-crafts cooperative owned and operated by its 22 members. It sells high-quality woodwork, including cabinets. Quality ceramics, textiles, metalwork, and jewelry are also for sale. An arts-and-crafts shop with a Nordic twist, **Älgamark** (⊠ Östra Rönneholmsvägen 4 ☎ 040/974960) sells many antiques dating from Viking and medieval times up to the 1600s. The shop also sells gold, silver, and bronze jewelry, much of which is also quite old.

Duxiana (⊠ Södra Promenaden 63 ☎ 040/305977) sells the world-famous Dux beds, which have elaborate spring systems and are built into wooden frames. Shipping can be arranged. Beds range in price from SKr 25,000 to SKr 57,000. **Outside** (⊠ Kyrkog. 3, Stortorget ☎ 040/300910) specializes in high-quality outdoor gear. Everything from sleeping bags, boots, and tents to gas canisters and waterproofing products is stocked here. In addition to such brands as North Face and Patagonia, Outside is the only Scandinavian store to carry products from Mac Pac of New Zealand. At the summer market called **Möllevångstorget,** on the square of the same name, there is usually a wonderful array of flowers, fruit, and vegetables. It is an old working-class area and a nice place to stroll. The market is open Monday–Saturday.

One of Skåne's outstanding Renaissance strongholds, **Svaneholms Slott** lies 30 km (19 mi) east of Malmö, on E65. First built in 1530 and rebuilt in 1694, the castle today features a museum occupying four floors with sections depicting the nobility and peasants. On the grounds are **Gästgiveri** (☎ 0411/40540), a notable restaurant, walking paths, and a lake for fishing and rowing. ⊠ *Skurup* ☎ *0411/40012* ✍ *SKr 25* ⊙ *May–Aug., daily 11–5; Apr. and Sept., Wed.–Sun. 11–4.*

Ystad

❻ *64 km (40 mi) southeast of Malmö (via E65), 205 km (127 mi) south-west of Växjö.*

A smuggling center during the Napoleonic Wars, Ystad has preserved its medieval character with winding narrow streets and hundreds of half-timber houses built over a span of five centuries. A good place to begin exploring is the main square, Stortorget.

The principal ancient monument, **St. Maria Kyrka** (St. Mary's Church; ⊠ Lilla Norregatan) was built shortly after 1220 as a basilica in the Romanesque style, though there have been later additions. The watchman's copper horn sounds from the church tower beginning at 9:15 PM and repeating every 15 minutes until 1 AM. It's to proclaim that "all is well." The church lies behind Stortorget on Lilla Norregatan. The 16th-century Latinskolan (Latin School) is adjacent to the church—it's said to be the oldest schoolhouse in Scandinavia.

Charlotte Berlin's Museum is a well-preserved burgher's home from the 19th century. Charlotte Berlin left the home and the contents to the city upon her death in 1916. It has a variety of displays, including one that shows many antique clocks and watches. ⊠ *Dammg. 23* ☎ *0411/18866* ✍ *SKr 20* ⊙ *June–Aug., weekdays noon–5, weekends noon–4.*

The Franciscan monastery **Gråbrödraklostret** adjoins St. Peter's church and is one of the best-preserved cloisters in Sweden. The oldest parts date to 1267. Together, the church and monastery are considered the most important historical site in Ystad. ⊠ *Sankt Petri Kyrkoplan* ☎ *0411/577590* ✍ *SKr 20* ⊙ *Weekdays noon–5, weekends noon–4.*

Sweden's best-preserved theater from the late 1800s, **Ystads Teater** (⊠ Sjö-mansg. 13 ☎ 0411/577199) is a beautiful, ornate building. The dramatic interior adds a great deal to any performance seen here. Outside is a battery of cannons first used in 1712 to defend the harbor from its many marauders, especially the Danes.

Ystads Konstmuseum houses a collection of important Swedish and Danish 20th-century art, as well as a photographic collection that includes a daguerreotype from 1845. ⊠ *St. Knuts Torg* ☎ *0411/577285* ⊕ *www.konstmuseet.ystad.se* ✍ *SKr 20* ⊙ *Tues.–Fri. noon–5, weekends noon–4.*

SÖVDEBORGS SLOTT – Twenty-one kilometers (thirteen miles) north of Ystad on Route 13 is Sövdeborgs Slott. Built in the 16th century and restored in the mid-1840s, the castle, now a private home, consists of three two-story brick buildings and a four-story-high crenellated corner tower. The main attraction is the Stensal (Stone Hall), with its impressive stuccowork ceiling. It's open for tours if booked in advance for groups of at least 10. Otherwise, the grounds are open. ⊠ *Sjöbo* ☎ *0416/16012.*

★ **ALES STENAR** – Eighteen kilometers (11 miles) east of Ystad, on the coastal road off Route 9, is the charming fishing village of Kåseberga. On the hill behind it stands the impressive Ales Stones, an intriguing 230-foot-long arrangement of 58 Viking stones in the shape of a ship. Believed to be between 1,000 and 1,500 years old, the stones and their purpose still puzzle anthropologists.

GLIMMINGEHUS – About 10 km (6 mi) east of Ales Stenar and 10 km (6 mi) southwest of Simrishamn just off Route 9 lies Glimminge House, Scandinavia's best-preserved medieval stronghold. Built between 1499 and 1505 to defend the region against invaders, the late-Gothic castle was lived in only briefly. The walls are 8 feet thick at the base, tapering to 6½ feet at the top of the 85-foot-high building. On the grounds are a small museum and a theater. There are concerts and lectures in summer and a medieval festival at the end of August. ⊠ *Hammenhög* ☎ *0414/18620* ◻ *SKr 50* ☉ *Easter–May, daily 11–5; June–mid-Sept., daily 10–6; mid-Sept.–end of Sept., daily 11–5.*

Where to Stay & Eat

$–$$ ✕ **Bryggeriet.** A lovely cross-timbered inn, this restaurant brews its own beer—there are two large copper boilers near the bar. It has a pleasant garden, and the dimly lighted interior is made out of bricks in the curved shape of an underground cavern. Hearty traditional fare, including reindeer and other game, is Bryggeriet's specialty. Try the duck, which is prepared in an elegant port sauce with an herb garnishing. ⊠ *Långg. 20* ☎ *0411/69999.*

$–$$ ✕ **Lottas.** This restaurant is in an interesting two-story building on the main square in the heart of town. The food includes several lighter fish dishes, including scallops in season. As is typical in Sweden, there are many red-meat options; the steaks are cooked and presented with care. ⊠ *Stortorget 11* ☎ *0411/78800.*

$$
FodorsChoice
★
✕▦ **Hotel Continental.** The Continental opened in 1829 and is a truly stunning building, both inside and out. Take a good look at the lobby with its marble stairs, crystal chandelier, stained-glass windows, and marble pillars. No two guest rooms are alike. The restaurant ($$) gives each dish its own flair. The meat dishes are served with a selection of root vegetables, including fresh potatoes, carrots, and what the British call *swedes* (rutabagas), when they're in season. ⊠ *Hamng. 13* ☎*0411/13700* 🖷*0411/12570* ⊕*www.hotelcontinental-ystad.se* ⇌ *52 rooms* ♨ *Restaurant* ⊟ *AE, MC, V* ❀❙ *BP.*

$ ▦ **Anno 1793 Sekelgården Hotell.** Centered around a cobblestone courtyard, this small and comfortable family-owned hotel is in the heart of Ystad, a short walk from St. Maria's Church and the main square. The half-timber buildings that make up the hotel date from the late 18th century, and in the summer breakfast is served in the courtyard. ⊠ *Låggatan 18* ☎. *0411/739 00* 🖷 *0411/189 97* ⇌ *18 rooms* ♨ *Restaurant, sauna, meeting room* ⊟ *AE, DC, MC, V* ❀❙ *BP.*

$ ▦ **Bäckagården.** This homey small hotel is centrally located. It dates from the 17th century, has a secluded garden, and serves breakfast. ⊠*Dammg. 36* ☎ *0411/19848* 🖷 *0411/65715* ⇌ *8 rooms* ⊟ *AE, MC, V* ❀❙ *BP.*

Shopping

Gifts, souvenirs, clothes, and various household items are sold at **Tidlöst** (⊠ Bökareg. 12 ☎ 0411/73029). The items are a mix of old and new. Head to **Sjögrens–Butikerna** (⊠ The Mall, Stora Österg. 6 ☎ 0411/17200) for an excellent selection of well-priced design ware, including crystal, jewelry, glassware, china, and pottery.

Simrishamn

❼ *41 km (25 mi) northeast of Ystad via Route 9, 105 km (65 mi) east of Malmö, 190 km (118 mi) southwest of Växjö.*

This fishing village of 20,000 swells to many times that number during the summer, though for most, Simrishamn doesn't warrant an overnight stay. Built in the mid-1100s, the town has cobblestone streets lined with tiny brick houses covered with white stucco. The medieval St. Nicolia Kyrka, which was once a landmark for local sailors, dominates the town's skyline.

The **Frasses Musikmuseum** contains an eclectic collection of music oddities, such as self-playing barrel organs, antique accordions, children's gramophones, and what may be the world's most complete collection of Edison phonographs. ⊠ *Peder Mörks Väg 5* ☎ *0414/14520* ☑ *SKr 20* ⊙ *Early June–late June and Aug., Sun. 2–6; July, Mon.–Wed. and Sun. 2–6.*

The construction of **St. Nicolai Kyrka** (St. Nicolai's Church) began around 1161. Inside are models of sailing ships given to the church by sailors as a token of gratitude for their safe return from the Baltic Sea. The two sculptures outside the church are by the famous Swedish sculptor Carl Milles. In July there is a lunchtime concert starting at noon. ⊠ *Stortorget* ☎ *0414/412480* ⊙ *Mar.–June 10 and mid-Sept.–Dec., weekdays noon–3, Sat. 10–1, Sun. after service; June 11–mid-Sept., weekdays 10:30–6:30, Sat. 9:30–4, Sun. 11–4.*

off the beaten path

BRANTEVIK – Less than 10 km (6 mi) south of Simrishamn on the coastal road is this classic but tiny southern fishing village. It has a marvelous harbor, and the homes are small, brightly colored fishermen's cottages. A hundred years ago only 1,100 people lived here, but the village had Sweden's then-largest sailing fleet with 124 ships. The village hasn't changed much since then. A good place for lunch is **Bronterögen,** a café that serves excellent meals and is right beside the harbor. It will cost between SKr 45 and SKr 125 for an entrée. For something a little more formal or even a night's stay, try the old inn **Brantevik's Bykrog and Hotel** (⊠ Mästergränd 2 ☎ 0414/22069). There are seven rooms here, along with a restaurant.

en route

About 20 km (12 mi) north of Simrishamn is the tiny village of **Kivik.** You are now firmly in the heart of Sweden's apple country, a spectacular place to be when the trees are blooming in early to late May. From Kivik follow the signs to the **Äpplets Hus** (the House of Apples; ☎ 0414/71900), a museum that tells the history of apple orcharding. Alongside is the cider brewery and a gift shop full of apple paraphernalia. On the way back from the Äpplets Hus is a small café—and a huge pile of boulders. This is the **Kivik grave,** one of the most remarkable Bronze Age monuments in Sweden. Dating from before 3000 BC, the tomb consists of a cairn nearly 250 feet across. Walk into the tomb and find the cist with eight tombstones engraved with symbols.

If you're in the area between June and August, you might want to stop off at **Kronovall Castle** (☎ 0417/19710), about 20 km (13 mi) northwest of Simrishamn for a tour that features local wines. The castle is now a restaurant run by restaurateur Petri Pumpa. Guided tours of the castle are organized three times a day in the summer. The 18th-century castle was given its baroque appearance through a remodeling in 1890 by architect Isak Gustaf Clason, best known for the Nordic Museum in Stockholm. Surrounding the castle is a beautiful park with a magnificent hedge labyrinth.

Kristianstad

❽ *73 km (45 mi) north of Simrishamn via Routes 9/19 and E22, 95 km (59 mi) northeast of Malmö (via E22), 126 km (78 mi) southwest of Växjö.*

Kristianstad was founded in 1614 by Danish king Christian IV as a fortified town to keep the Swedes at bay. Today its former ramparts and moats are wide tree-lined boulevards. For most, there isn't much of great interest in the town itself.

About 17 km (11 mi) east of Kristianstad and just north of the E22 highway is **Bäckaskog Slott.** Standing on a strip of land between two lakes, Bäckaskog Castle was originally founded as a monastery by a French religious order in the 13th century. Danish noblemen turned it into a fortified castle during the 16th century. It was later appropriated by the Swedish government and used as a residence for the cavalry. The castle was a favorite of the Swedish royalty until 1900. Today the castle is a hotel and restaurant. ⊠ *Fjälkinge* ☎ *044/53250* 🎫 *Free* ☉ *Year-round.*

> **off the beaten path**
>
> **ÅHUS –** Ten kilometers (7 miles) southeast of Kristianstad is this seaside resort. The town has a medieval center and sandy beaches stretching for 60 km (40 mi) down Hanöbukten. The best-known feature of Åhus is the **Absolut Vodka distillery.** Every drop of Absolut Vodka, the world's third-largest vodka brand, consumed in the world is still made in this little town. The distillery gives 1½-hour guided tours, which must be booked ahead by telephone; tickets must be picked up and paid for at the tourist office by 6 PM the day before the tour. ☎ *044/240106 for reservations* 🎫 *30 SKr* ☉ *Tour mid-June–mid-Aug., Tues. 12:45.*

> **en route**
>
> Six kilometers (4 miles) east of Kristianstad on E22, take a left turn to Fjälkinge and follow brown signs marked with a white flower. The route, **Humlesingan,** is a scenic drive of 48 km (30 mi) around Skåne's largest lake, Lake Ivösjö. The geology dates from millions of years ago and is rich in minerals. It was a famed hops region until 1959. The old hop houses can still be seen—one is a café. The big mountainous island is Ivö, 440 feet high.

Karlskrona

❾ *111 km (69 mi) east of Kristianstad via E22, 201 km (125 mi) northeast of Malmö, 107 km (66 mi) southeast of Växjö.*

A small city built on the mainland and on 33 nearby islands, Karlskrona achieved great notoriety in 1981, when a Soviet submarine ran aground a short distance from its naval base. The town dates from 1680, when it was laid out in baroque style on the orders of Karl XI. Two churches around the main square, **Trefaldighetskyrkan** and **Frederikskyrkan,** date from this period and were both designed by the architect Nicodemus Tessin the Younger. Because of the excellent state of preservation of the naval museum and other buildings in town, Karlskrona has been designated a World Heritage Site by UNESCO.

Although the archipelago is not as large or as full of dramatic scenery as Stockholm's islands, Karlskrona is still worth the boat trip. One can be arranged through **Skärgårdstrafiken** (☎ 0455/78330).

★ The **Admiralitetskyrkan** (Admiralty Church) is Sweden's oldest wooden church, built in 1685. It is an unusual variant of the Swedish style of churches, which are generally made of stone. Although it was supposed to be temporary, the stone replacement was never built. The wooden statue of constable Matts Rosenborn, who froze to death here one New Year's Eve in the 18th century, stands outside tipping his hat to those who give alms. The church is on Bastionsgatan on the naval island. Walk east a few minutes from Stortorget, the main square to get to the bridge.

★ The **Marinmuseum** (Naval Museum), in a building dating from 1752, is one of the oldest museums in Sweden and has a superb collection perfect for those with a nautical bent. The shed for making rope is ancient (1692) and huge—nearly 1,000 ft long. In the museum are old maps and charts, old navigating equipment, ship designs, and relics from actual ships, as well as weaponry. The museum can also provide you with brochures of the port area, perfect for a pleasant walk. ✉ *Stumholmen* ☎ *0455/53902* 🎫 *SKr 50* ⊘ *June–Aug., daily 10–6; Sept.–May, daily noon–5.*

Stunning **Kungsholm Fort,** on the island of Kungsholmen, was built in 1680 to defend the town's important naval port. The fortress was on full alert when the Russians blockaded Karlskrona in the 1780s and when the English were cruising the Baltic in 1801. Perhaps the most impressive aspect of the fort is the round harbor, built into the fort itself with only a narrow exit to the sea. The fort is accessible only by a boat booked through the **tourist office** (✉ Stortorget ☎ 0455/303439) on the main island of Trossö.

The **archipelago** is made up of dozens of islands scattered off the coast of Karlskrona's mainland. They are stunning low-lying islands that make excellent places to walk and picnic. Although some are accessible by road, the best way to take it all in is to go by ferry. The cruises take half a day. Contact **Affärsverken Båttrafik** (✉ N. Kungsgatan 36 ☎ 0455/78300 🎫 SKr 40–SKr 110), the ferry operators, with offices at the ferry terminal.

Where to Stay & Eat

¢–$$ ✕ **Lisas Sjökrog.** Floating on the sea, this docked ship is a great place to see a sunset and look out over the archipelago. The emphasis here is on seafood, including herring, halibut, and shellfish in season. You can also try well-prepared meat dishes and the popular summer salads. ✉ *Fisktorget* ☎ *0455/23465* 🍽 *AE, MC, V* ⊘ *Closed Sept.–April.*

¢ ✕ **Eat—The Home Company.** If you like to mix your dining with design, then Eat (placed within a home-design store) is a good choice for lunch. The menu is vaguely nouvelle, with beautiful presentations of small portions. The soups are terrific, ranging from mushroom to pumpkin. Try the lamb, cooked medium rare and served with mint. Trains were once repaired inside the 18th-century building. ✉ *Bleklingeg 3 Lokstallarna* ☎ *0455/300003* 🍽 *AE, DC, MC, V* ⊘ *No dinner.*

$ 🏨 **First Hotel Statt.** The rooms are well appointed, the decor classic, and the style Swedish traditional. Built around 1900, this immaculate hotel with an ornate stairwell and candelabras in the lobby is in the heart of the city and is fully renovated. ✉ *Ronnebygatan 37–39* ☎ *0455/19250* 📠 *0455/169 09* ⊕ *www.firsthotels.com* 🛏 *107 rooms* ♨ *Restaurant, bar, nightclub, hot tub, sauna, no-smoking rooms* 🍽 *AE, DC, MC, V.*

$ 🏨 **Hotel Carlscrona.** From this seaside hotel, the beach is a 10-minute walk. The town center and the naval museum are even closer. Though the rooms are nothing special, many have good views. ✉ *Skeppsbrokajen* ☎ *0455/361500* 📠 *0455/361509* 🛏 *80 rooms* ♨ *Dining room, in-room data ports, sauna, parking, no-smoking rooms* 🍽 *AE, MC, V* 🍴 *BP.*

¢ ⊡ **Hotel Conrad.** For simple but functional accommodations at a reasonable price, the Hotel Conrad is a good choice. It is a short walk from shopping, restaurants, and entertainment. ⊠ *V. Köpmansg. 12* ☎ *0455/ 363200* 🖷 *0455/363205* ⊕ *www.hotelconrad.se* 🛏 *58 rooms* 🛁 *Sauna, free parking* ▭ *AE, MC, V* ⦿I *BP.*

Nightlife & the Arts

In a renovated old theater **Bio Bar och Matsalar** (⊠ Borgmästareg. 17 ☎ 0455/311100) is an ornate setting with crystal chandeliers. The scene varies greatly, but you're more likely to hear Top 40 hits than the latest dance music. Playing on the town's seafaring heritage with its name, **Piraten Nattklubb** (⊠ Ronnebyg. 50 ☎ 0455/81853) serves up good cocktails, but amid a decor that suggests the Middle Ages.

The Outdoors

Karlskrona has a reputation for both saltwater and freshwater fishing. **Senoren's Sportfishing Tours** (☎ 0455/44010) will take you to the outermost archipelago to fish by boat or from cliffs. Kurt Ola Oftedal of **Hasslö Island Tourist and Fishing Service** (☎ 0455/332492 or 0708/332492) organizes fishing in the ocean and in freshwater streams and lakes.

Kalmar

🔟 *91 km (57 mi) northeast of Karlskrona via E22, 292 km (181 mi) northeast of Malmö, 109 km (68 mi) southeast of Växjö.*

Fodor'sChoice ★ The attractive coastal town of Kalmar, opposite the Baltic island of Öland, is dominated by the imposing **Kalmar Slott**, Sweden's best-preserved Renaissance castle. Part of it dates from the 12th century. The living rooms, chapel, and dungeon can be visited. ⊠ *Slottsvägen* ☎ *0480/451490* 🎫 *SKr 75* ⊙ *Apr.–May and Sept., daily 10–4; June and Aug., daily 10–5; July, daily 10–6; Oct.–Mar., 2nd weekend every month 11–3:30.*

The **Kalmar Läns Museum** (Kalmar District Museum), with good archaeological and ethnographic collections, contains the remains of the royal ship *Kronan,* which sank in 1676. Cannons, wood sculptures, and old coins were all raised from the seabed in 1980. Another exhibit focuses on Jenny Nystrom, a painter famous for popularizing the *tomte,* a rustic Christmas elf. ⊠ *Skeppsbrog. 51* ☎ *0480/451300* 🎫 *SKr 50* ⊙ *Mid-June–mid-Aug., daily 10–6; mid-Aug.–mid-June, Tues.–Fri. 10–4, weekends 11–4.*

Kalmar Domkyrkan is a highly impressive building designed by Nicodemus Tessin the Elder in 1660 in the Italian baroque style. Inside, the massive open spaces create stunning light effects. Strangely, the cathedral is the only one in Sweden without a bishop. Music is played at noon during the week. ⊠ *Stortorget* ☎ *0480/12300* 🎫 *Free* ⊙ *Daily 10–6.*

off the beaten path

PATAHOLM AND TIMMERNABBEN – Numerous seaside towns dot the coastline along E22, opposite Öland. **Pataholm** has a cobblestone main square, and **Timmernabben** is famous for its caramel factory. Miles of clean, attractive, and easily accessible—if windy—beaches line this coastal strip.

Where to Stay & Eat

★ $$ ✕ **Byttan.** In fine weather this restaurant's large outdoor eating area and beautiful gardens are the perfect place for a leisurely meal. Served with a vast range of freshly baked breads, the summer salads, especially the chicken salad with limes, are terrific. You can also choose a heartier entrée of traditional herring with mashed potatoes. ⊠ *Slottsallén* ☎ *0480/ 16360* ▭ *MC, V* ⊙ *Closed Oct.–Apr.*

$$ ✕ **Källaren Kronan.** Given the quality of the eclectic international dishes here, the meals are surprisingly cheap. Try the pheasant breast with Calvados sauce or the fillet of venison with black currant sauce. The building dates to the 1660s and has been preserved as a cultural heritage site. ✉ *Ölandsg. 7* ☎ *0480/411400* 🚫 *AE, DC, MC, V.*

¢–$$ ✕ **Ernesto Salonger.** This outdoor Italian restaurant serves everything from pizza to pasta. On Friday and Saturday nights a nightclub and casino are in action. ✉ *Larmtorget* ☎ *0480/20050* 🚫 *AE, DC, MC, V.*

$$ 🏨 **Slottshotellet.** On a quiet street, this gracious old house faces a waterfront park that's a few minutes' walk from both the train station and Kalmar Castle. Guest rooms are charmingly individual, with carved-wood bedsteads, old-fashioned chandeliers, pretty wallpaper, wooden floors, and antique furniture. The bathrooms are spotlessly clean. Breakfast is served year-round, and full restaurant service is available in the summer. ✉ *Slottsv. 7, 392 33* ☎ *0480/88260* 🖨 *0480/88266* ⌨ *44 rooms* ⚴ *Restaurant, sauna, meeting room, no-smoking rooms* 🚫 *AE, DC, V* 🍴 *BP.*

$$ 🏨 **Stadshotellet.** In the city center, Scandic's Stadshotellet is a fairly large hotel with traditional English decor. The main building dates from 1907. Guest rooms are freshly decorated and have hair dryers and radios, among other amenities. There's also a fine restaurant. ✉ *Stortorget 14, 392 32* ☎ *0480/496900* 🖨 *0480/496910* ⌨ *138 rooms* ⚴ *Restaurant, bar, hot tub, sauna, meeting room, no-smoking rooms* 🚫 *AE, DC, MC, V.*

$–$$ 🏨 **Frimurare.** Set inside a spacious park, the attractive Frimurare radiates calm and peacefulness. Both the rooms and the hotel itself have old-time touches. It's a short walk from here to the castle. ✉ *Lamtorget 2* ☎ *0480/15230* 🖨 *0480/85887* ⊕ *www.frimurarehotellet.gs2.com* ⌨ *34 rooms, 31 with bath* ⚴ *Meeting rooms* 🚫 *MC, V.*

Öland

★ ⑪ *8 km (5 mi) east of Kalmar via the Ölandsbron Bridge.*

The island of Öland is a magical and ancient place—and the smallest province in Sweden. The area was first settled some 4,000 years ago and is fringed with fine sandy beaches and dotted with old windmills, churches, and archaeological remains. In the 16th century King Gustav Vasa used land he had confiscated from the church to establish farms around the country. These farms were meant to foster the country's agricultural development and supply the court and the army with grain, meat, butter, and wool. The king founded five farms on Öland: Borgholm, Halltorp, Horn, Gärdslösa, and Ottenby. Of these, Ottenby, Bogholm and Horn are still operating farms.

The island also has spectacular bird life—swallows, cranes, geese, and birds of prey. Many migrate to Öland from Siberia. The southern part of the island, known as Stora Alvaret, is a UNESCO World Heritage Site due partly to its stark beauty and unique flora and fauna. Private car travel is prohibited, so let the public bus shuttle you around the island.

To get to Öland, take the 6-km (4-mi) bridge from Kalmar. Be sure to pick up a tourist information map (follow the signs as soon as you get on the island). Most of the scattered sights have no address. Close to the bridge is the popular **Historium**, where slide shows, wax figures, and constructed dioramas illustrate what Öland was like 10,000 years ago.

Head clockwise around the island. **Borgholms Slott**, the largest castle ruin in northern Europe, is just outside the island's principal town, Borgholm (25 km [16 mi] north of the bridge). Nearby is the royal family's summer home at **Solliden.** If you get hungry, try Pappa Blå, a restaurant on Borgholm's pleasant square. It serves a variety of food, from pizzas to sandwiches to steaks, which run about SKr 60–SKr 150. From Borgholm follow the signs north to **Knisa Mosse,** a marshland area that's home to many bird species.

Heading farther north brings you to Löttorp. From here drive west to **Horns Kungsgård,** a nature preserve on a lake that has a bird-watching tower and walking trails. Horns Kungsgård is also a royal estate, meaning "king's farm" or "king's estate." The government maintains its appearance to look as it did in 1900.

Some 5 km (3 mi) north along the coast from Horns Kungsgård is **Byrum,** a nature preserve with striking, wind-carved limestone cliffs. The botanist Linnaeus (Carl von Linné) discussed this area in his writings. Just a few more kilometers on is **Skäftekärr,** which has a culture museum, a café, an Iron Age farm with an arboretum, and walking trails. At the northernmost tip is the Långe Erik lighthouse.

Turning back you will find one of the island's three nature centers, **Trollskogen.** On its trails are some majestic old oaks, prehistoric barrow graves, and pines. A little to the south is northern Europe's longest beach, a great swimming spot with sparkling white sand.

Pass back through **Löttorp,** heading south. Keep an eye out for the signs leading east off the main road for the intriguing **Källa** church ruins, some of the best on the island. Return to the main road and head south to **Kappelludden,** one of the island's best year-round bird sites. A medieval chapel's ruins and a lighthouse make this coastal spot very scenic.

Gärdslösa, to the southwest of Kappelludden, has an excellently preserved medieval church. Look for the Viking inscriptions on its wall.

Continuing south, turn right at Långlöt for the **Himmelsberga Museum** (☎ 0485/561022 or 0485/561011 ☎ SKr 50 ☉ May–Aug., daily 10–6), a farm museum dating from the end of the 18th century. The buildings and furnishings include horse buggies and horse sleds. The old stables were home to the small, swift Öland horses, which were extinct by the beginning of the 19th century. Old documents claim that they could dance to horns and drums and jump through hoops.

Gråborg, a 6th-century fortress with massive stone walls 625 feet in diameter, is a must-see. To get here, turn right at Norra Möckleby.

Return and head south. About 2 km [1 mi] north of Seby are some strings of **rune stones:** engraved gravestones dating from 500 BC to AD 1050, stone circles, and cists and cairns. Continue south to come to the southeastern edge of Stora Alvaret. This bleak and eerie area has been farmed for 1,000 years.

Just before you reach the 5th-century fortified village of **Eketorp,** you'll reach a turnoff for the **Gräsgård,** an important fishing village. Eketorp's castle is partially renovated; the area includes small tenants' fields from the Iron and Middle ages. Admission to the castle and its grounds is SKr 50.

Ottenby is the southernmost tip of Öland and was a hunting area as long as 5,000 years ago. It's now a popular site for bird-watching. The entrance fee to the burial fields is SKr 50 per car or SKr 10 per person arriving by bus.

Now drive north up the west coastal road. Shortly after **Södra Möckleby** you'll come across the impressive burial grounds of **Gettlinge.** More than

200 graves lie across a distance of 2 km (1 mi). The site was in use from the time of Christ into the Viking era, which lasted until 1050. Beginning in late spring, the land north of here blooms with many different wild orchids.

Farther on is **Mysinge Tunukus,** a Bronze Age site. A group of rune stones here is placed in a shape resembling a ship: it's beautiful at sunset. From here continue on back to the bridge and mainland Sweden.

Where to Stay

$ ⊞ **Halltorps Gästgiveri.** This 17th-century manor house has modernized duplex rooms decorated in Swedish landscape tones and an excellent restaurant. Driving north from Ölandsbron, it's on the left side of the road. ⊠ *387 92 Borgholm* ☎ *0485/85000* ⊟ *0485/85001* ⇌ *36 rooms* ⚭ *Restaurant, 2 saunas, meeting room, no-smoking rooms* ⊟ *AE, DC, MC, V.*

¢ ⊞ **Eksgården Värdshus.** The red cottages at this hotel resemble farmhouses. The pleasant dining room often hosts cultural performances. There's even a museum with farm and domestic implements and footwear, and an arts and crafts shop. ⊠ *Gårdby 386 93 Färjestaden* ☎ *0485/33450* ⊟ *0485/33434* ⇌ *13 rooms* ⚭ *Dining room, shop* ◷ *Closed Sept.–Jan.*

¢ ✕⊞ **Guntorps Herrgård.** Spacious parkland surrounds this manor house, which is 2,500 ft from the center of Borgholm. Outside, there's a heated pool. The restaurant has hardwood floors, a grandfather clock along one wall, and copper pots hanging on an other. ⊠ *387 36 Borgholm* ☎ *0485/13000* ⊟ *0485/13319* ⊕ *www.guntorp.oland.com* ⇌ *32 rooms* ⚭ *Restaurant, sauna, whirlpool* ⊟ *AE, DC, MC, V.*

¢ ⊞ **Värdshuset Briggen Tre Liljor.** Large trees stand alongside this lovely, old stone-clad hotel, which is 25 km (16 mi) north of Borgholm. The rooms are spacious and old-fashioned, making you feel as if you've stepped into the past. The restaurant serves good traditional food. ⊠ *Lofta, 387 91 Borgholm* ☎ *0485/26400* ⊟ *0485/26420* ⇌ *17 rooms* ⚭ *Restaurant* ⊟ *AE, MC, V.*

The Kingdom of Glass

Stretching roughly 109 km (68 mi) between Kalmar and Växjö.

Småland is home to the world-famous Swedish glass industry. Scattered among the rocky woodlands of Småland province are isolated villages whose names are synonymous with high-quality crystal glassware. This spectacular creative art was at its height in the late 19th century. The conditions were perfect: large quantities of wood to fuel the furnaces and plenty of water from the streams and rivers. At the time demand was such that the furnaces burned 24 hours a day.

The region is still home to 16 major glassworks, many of them created through the merging of the smaller firms. You can still see glass being blown and crystal being etched by craftspeople. You may also be interested in attending a *Hyttsill* evening, a revival of an old tradition in which Baltic herring (*sill*) is cooked in the glass furnaces of the *hytt* (literally "hut," but meaning "the works"). Most glassworks also have shops selling quality firsts and not-so-perfect seconds at a discount.

Though the glass factories generally prospered before and during the 1900s, this wealth didn't filter down to many of their workers or to Småland's other inhabitants. Poverty became so widespread that the area lost vast numbers of people to the United States from the late 19th through the 20th century. If you're an American with Swedish roots, chances are your ancestors are from this area. The Utvandrarnas Hus (Emigrants' House), in Växjö, tells the story of this exodus.

The Kingdom of Glass's oldest works is **Kosta Glasbruk.** Dating from 1742, it was named for the two former generals who founded it, Anders Koskull and Georg Bogislaus Stael von Holstein. Faced with a dearth of local talent, they initially imported glassblowers from Bohemia. The Kosta works pioneered the production of crystal (to qualify for that label, glass must contain at least 24% lead oxide). You can see glass-blowing off-season (mid-August–early June) between 9 and 3. To get to the village of Kosta from Kalmar, drive 49 km (30 mi) west on Route 25, then 14 km (9 mi) north on Route 28. ⊠ *Kosta* ☎ *0478/34500* ⊙ *May–June and Aug–mid-Sept., weekdays 9–10 and 11–3, Sat. 10–3; July, daily 10–4; mid-Sept–Apr., weekdays 9–10 and 11–3.*

Orrefors is one of the best-known glass companies. Orrefors arrived on the scene late—in 1898—but set particularly high artistic standards. The skilled workers in Orrefors dance a slow, delicate minuet as they carry the pieces of red-hot glass back and forth, passing them on rods from hand to hand, blowing and shaping them. The basic procedures and tools are ancient, and the finished product is the result of unusual teamwork, from designer to craftsman to finisher. One of Orrefors's special attractions is a magnificent display of pieces made during the 19th century; you can appease bored children in the cafeteria and playground. From early June to mid-August you can watch glass being blown. ⊠ *On Rte. 31, about 18 km (11 mi) east of Kosta Glasbruk* ☎ *0481/34189* ⊕ *www.orrefors. se* ⊙ *July–mid-Aug., weekdays 9–6, Sat. 10–5, Sun. 11–5; mid-Aug.–June, weekdays 10–6, Sat. 10–4, Sun. noon–4.*

Mystical animal reliefs and female figures play a big role in the work at **Målerås,** which was founded in 1890. The glass workers are great to watch; they use classic techniques with names such as "the grail." Overlooking the factory is a pleasant restaurant with panoramic views. ⊠ *12 km (7 mi) north of Orrefors* ☎ *0481/31401* ⊙ *June–Aug., weekdays 9–6, Sat. 10–5, Sun. 11–5; Sept.–May, weekdays 10–6, Sat. 10–4, Sun. 11–4.*

Boda Glasbruk, part of the Kosta Boda Company, is the second-oldest glass-works, founded in 1864. The work here has an ethereal theme, with the designers drawing on cosmic bodies such as the sun and the moon. Much of the work has veils of violet and blue suspended in the crystal. ⊠ *Just off Rte. 25, 42 km (26 mi) west of Kalmar* ☎ *0481/42410* ⊙ *July–mid-Aug., weekdays 9–6, Sat. 10–5, Sun. 11–5; mid-Aug.–June, weekdays 9–6, Sat. 10–4, Sun. noon–4.*

Continue west from Boda Glasbruk for 20 km (12 mi) to the town of Lessebo. From mid-June to mid-August you can visit the 300-year-old **Lessebo Handpappersbruk,** which is the only handmade-paper factory in Sweden. Since the 18th century the craftsmen have been using much the same techniques to produce fine paper, which is available from the shop. Guided tours take place on weekdays at 9:30, 10:30, 2, and 2:15. ⊠ *Storgatan, Lessebo* ☎ *0478/47691* 🎫 *Tours free.* ⊙ *Jan.–Dec., weekdays 7–4; June–Aug., guided tours at 9:30, 10:30, 1, and 2:15.*

Skruf Glasbruk began in 1896. Today it's a purveyor to the king of Sweden. The royal family, the ministry of foreign affairs, and the parliament have all commissioned work from Skruf. Local farmers encouraged the development of the glassworks because they wanted a market for their wood. The museum takes you through the historic eras of fine glass craft in Småland. The factory specializes in lead-free crystal, which has a unique iridescence and form. ⊠ *10 km (6 mi) south of Lessebo. Turn left at Åkerby* ☎ *0478/20133* ⊙ *Weekdays 9–5, weekends 10–4.*

★ ⓒ Founded in 1889, **Bergadala Glasbruk** is one of the most traditional glassworks. Alongside the main road are the former workers' homes, now used mainly as long-term rentals. Note the impressive circular furnace that stands in the middle of the wooden floor. Bergadala is often called the blue glassworks, since many of its pieces have a rich cobalt hue. A stone's throw from the smelter is a children's playground and a glass-painting workshop that will keep them occupied for hours. From here you are 10 km (6 mi) from Växjö. ⊠ *About 15 km (9 mi) northwest of Lessebo, toward Växjö* ☎ *0478/31650* ⊙ *Weekdays 9–5, weekends 10–4.*

Where to Stay

¢ ⚇ **Hotell Björkäng.** Set in a park that will give you plenty of opportunity to take evening strolls, the Björkäng has well-kept rooms. They have some rustic decorations, such as traditional ornaments, wood carved by nature, and glass pieces. You also have the opportunity to spend an evening in the glassblowing room. The dining room offers a range of good traditional Swedish food. ⊠ *Stora Vägen 2, Kosta* ☎ *0478/50000* 🖷 *0478/50437* ⇆ *24 double and 2 single rooms* ◊ *Dining room, sauna, billiards* ▤ *MC, V* � ️◉ *BP.*

¢ ⚇ **Orrefors.** The rooms are cozy, and the hotel is set in the authentic center of the Kingdom of Glass. The restaurant and bar offer good dining and a pleasant atmosphere. ⊠ *Kantav. 29, Orrefors* ☎ *0481/30035* 🖷 *0481/30056* ⇆ *10 rooms* ◊ *Restaurant, bar* ▤ *MC, V* ◉ *BP.*

¢ ⚇ **Wärdhusset Flustret.** With a big garden, trees, and a forest surrounding you, this countryside inn can't help but be relaxing. It's a great place from which to head out for a walk. ⊠ *Storg. 83, Lessebo* ☎ *0478/10100* 🖷 *0478/10103* ⇆ *13 rooms, 5 with bath* ▤ *MC, V.*

Växjö

⑫ *109 km (68 mi) northwest of Kalmar via Route 25, 198 km (123 mi) northeast of Malmö, 228 km (142 mi) southeast of Göteborg, 446 km (277 mi) southwest of Stockholm.*

Some 10,000 Americans visit this town every year, for it was from this area that their Swedish ancestors departed in the 19th century. A large proportion of those emigrants went to Minnesota, attracted by the affordable farmland and a geography reminiscent of parts of Sweden. On the second Sunday of every August, Växjö celebrates Minnesota Day: Swedes and Swedish-Americans come together to commemorate their common heritage with American-style square dancing and other festivities. Beyond this, the city is really just a stopover.

The **Utvandrarnas Hus** (Emigrants' House), in the town center, tells the story of the migration, when more than a million Swedes—one quarter of the population—departed for the promised land. The museum exhibits provide a vivid sense of the rigorous journey, and an archive room and a research center allow Americans with Swedish blood to trace their ancestry. The archives are not open for genealogy research on weekends. ⊠ *Vilhelm Mobergsg. 4* ☎ *0470/20120* ⊕ *www.svenskaemigrantinstitutet.g.se* 🖾 *SKr 40* ⊙ *June–Aug., weekdays 9–6, Sat. 11–4; Sept.–May, weekdays 9–4, weekends 11–4.*

★ The **Smålands Museum** is famous for its presentation of the development of glass and has the largest glass collection in northern Europe. Its excellent display puts the area's unique industry into perspective and explains the different styles of the various glass companies. ⊠ *Södra Jarnvägsg. 2* ☎ *0470/704200* ⊕ *www.smalandsmuseum.se* 🖾 *SKr 40* ⊙ *Jun.–Aug., weekdays 10–5, weekends 11–5; Sept.–May, Tues.–Fri. 10–5, weekends 11–5.*

KRONOBERGS SLOTTSRUIN – About 5 km (3 mi) north of Växjö, this 14th-century castle ruin lies on the edge of the Helgasjön (Holy Lake). The Småland freedom fighter Nils Dacke used the castle as a base for his attacks against the Danish occupiers during the mid-1500s; now it's an idyllic getaway. In summer you can eat waffles under the shade of birch trees by the café, or take a dinner or sightseeing cruise around the lake on the small toylike *Thor*, Sweden's oldest steamboat. ☎ *0470/63000 Café Ryttmästargården, 0470/704200 boat tours ☒ Castle ruins SKr 10; dinner cruise SKr 400; 2½-hr canal trip to Årby and back SKr 125; 1-hr lake trip SKr 100 incl. coffee ☉ Castle tours offered late June–late Aug.; Dinner cruise Sun.*

Where to Stay

$$ 🏨 **Hotel Statt.** Now a Best Western hotel, the Statt is popular with tourist groups. It has a convenient, central location. The building dates from 1853, but the rooms are up to modern standards. The hotel has a cozy pub, bistro, and café. ☒ *Kungsg. 6, 351 04* ☎ *0470/13400* 🖷 *0470/ 44837* 🛏 *124 rooms 🗱 Restaurant, café, pub, sauna, gym, meeting room, no-smoking rooms* 🟰 *AE, DC, MC, V.*

$ 🏨 **Esplanad.** In the town center, the Esplanad is a small family-run hotel with basic amenities. ☒ *Norra Esplanaden 21A, 352 31* ☎ *0470/22580* 🖷 *0470/26226* 🛏 *23 rooms, 20 with bath 🗱 No-smoking rooms* 🟰 *MC, V* 🍽 *BP.*

The South & the Kingdom of Glass A to Z

To research prices, get advice from other travelers, and book travel arrangements, visit www.fodors.com.

AIR TRAVEL

CARRIERS Five airlines serve the Malmö airport (Sturup).
🛪 **Direktflyg** ☎ 021/800645. **KLM** ☎ 040/500530. **Malmö Aviation** ☎ 020/550010. **RyanAir** ☎ 0900/2020240 in Sweden ⊕ www.ryanair.com when booking from abroad. **SAS** ☎ 0770-727727.

CUTTING COSTS SAS offers discounts on trips to Malmö year-round; ask for the "Jackpot" discount package.

AIRPORTS

Malmö's airport, Sturup (MMX), is approximately 30 km (19 mi) from Malmö and 25 km (15 mi) from Lund. Buses for Malmö and Lund meet all flights at Sturup Airport. The price of the trip is SKr 90 to either destination. A taxi from the airport to Malmö or Lund costs about SKr 470.
🛪 **Bus Information** ☎ 040/6131100. **Taxi and Limousine Service** ☎ 020/979797 in Sweden, (46)8/797-5025 from abroad. **Sturup** ☎ 040/6131100.

BOAT & FERRY TRAVEL

Since the inauguration of the Öresund bridge, between Malmö and Copenhagen, it is no longer possible to travel by ferry between the two cities, but there is still regular ferry service between Helsingborg in Sweden and Helsingøor in Denmark (by Scandlines, HH-Ferries, and Sundsbussarna). From Ystad there is ferry service to Swinoujscie in Poland (by Polferries), and from Trelleborg ferries run to Sassnitz and Rostock in Germany (by Scandlines). Stena Line ferries run between Karlskrona and Gdynia in Poland.
🛪 **HH-Ferries** ☎ 042/198000. **Polferries** ☎ 08/52018101. **Scandlines** ☎ 0410/65000. **Sundsbussarna** ☎ 042/216060. **Stena Line** ☒ Danmarksterminalen, Masthuggskajen, Göteborg ☎ 031-7040300 in Göteborg and 0455/366300 in Karlskrona.

CUTTING COSTS The Malmökortet (Malmö Card) entitles the holder to, among other benefits, free travel on the city buses, free parking, discounts on tours, and free admission or discounts to most museums, concert halls, nightclubs, and theaters; the Royal Cab company; and many shops and restaurants. A one-day card costs SKr 120, a two-day card SKr 150, and a three-day card SKr 180. Cards are available from the tourist office in Malmö.

CAR RENTAL

If you are coming from Denmark and want to rent a car as soon as you arrive, several rental companies have locations at Malmö Harbor, including Avis, Hertz, and Europcar. Hertz car rentals are available for less than SKr 600 a day on weekends (less during the summer) if you book an SAS flight.

🚗 Major Agencies **Avis** ☎ 040/77830. **Europcar** ☎ 040/71640. **Hertz** ☎ 040/330770.

CAR TRAVEL

Copenhagen and Malmö are connected by the Öresund bridge. It costs SKR 275 one-way.

Malmö is 620 km (386 mi) from Stockholm. Take the E4 Highway to Helsingborg, then the E6/E20 to Malmö and Lund. From Göteborg take the E6/E20.

Roads are well marked and well maintained. Traveling around the coast counterclockwise from Helsingborg, you take the E6/E20 to Landskrona, Malmö, and Lund, then the E6/E22 to Trelleborg; Route 9 goes along the south coast from there all the way to Simrishamn and then heads north until just before Kristianstad. It's there that you can pick up E22 all the way through Karlshamn, Ronneby, Karlskrona, and on across the east coast to Kalmar. From Kalmar, Route 25 goes almost directly west through Växjö to Halmstad, on the west coast between Helsingborg and Göteborg.

EMERGENCIES

As elsewhere in Sweden, call 112 for emergencies.

TRAIN TRAVEL

The major towns of the south are all connected by rail.

There is regular service from Stockholm to Helsingborg, Lund, and Malmö. Each trip takes about 6½ hours, and about 4½ hours by high-speed (X2000) train. All three railway stations are centrally located in their respective towns.

Trains between Malmö and Copenhagen take 35 minutes and run three times an hour during the day and once an hour at night. A one-way ticket is SKr 80.

🚆 Train Companies **Skånetrafiken** ☎ 0771/777777.

TRANSPORTATION AROUND THE SOUTH

A special 48-hour Öresund Runt (Around Öresund) pass is available from the Malmö Tourist Office or any train station in Skåne. Costing between SKr 199 and SKr 249, depending on where you start your trip, the ticket covers a train ticket from the Skåne province to Malmö, a train from Malmö to Helsingborg, a ferry to Helsingør; a train to Copenhagen, and a ferry back to Malmö (or if you so prefer, the same trip clockwise).

VISITOR INFORMATION

🛈 Tourist Information **Helsingborg** ✉ Södra Storgatan 1 ☎ 042/104350 🌐 www. helsingborgsguiden.com. **Jönköping** ✉ Järnvägsstationen (central train station) ☎ 036/105050. **Kalmar** ✉ Ölandskajen 9 ☎ 0480/417700 🌐 www.kalmar.se/turism/index2.

html. **Karlskrona** ✉ Stortorget 2 ☎ 0455/303490. **Kristianstad** ✉ Stora Torg ☎ 044/121988 ⊕ www.kristianstad.se. **Landskrona** ✉ Storgatan 36 ☎ 0418/473000 ⊕ www.tourism.landskrona.se. **Lund** ✉ Kyrkog. 11 ☎ 046/355040 ⊕ www.lund.se. **Malmö** ✉ Centralstationen (Central Train Station) ☎ 040/341200 ⊕ www.malmo.se. **Öland** ✉ Träffpunkt Öland, Färjestaden ☎ 0485/560600. **Ronneby** ✉ Västra Torggatan 1 ☎ 0457/18090. **Simrishamn** ✉ Tullhusgatan 2 ☎ 0414/819800 **Växjö** ✉ Stationen, Norra Järnvägsgatan 3 ☎ 0470/41410. **Ystad** ✉ St. Knuts Torg ☎ 0411/577681 ⊕ www.visitystad.com.

DALARNA: THE FOLKLORE DISTRICT

7

FODOR'S CHOICE

Hotel Dalecarlia, *Tällberg*

Hotel Winn, *Falun*

Leksands Kyrka (Leksands Church), *Leksand*

HIGHLY RECOMMENDED

SIGHTS   Åkerblads, *Rättvik*

Carl Larsson Gården, *Sundborn*

Dalhalla, *Rättvik*

Jernet Bar & Matsal, *Mora*

Storamuseum, *Falun*

Zorn Museet, *Mora*

A PLACE OF FORESTS, MOUNTAINS, AND RED-PAINTED wooden farmhouses and cottages by pristine, sun-dappled lakes, Dalarna is considered the most traditional of all the country's 24 provinces. It is the favorite sight for celebrations on Midsummer Day, when Swedes don folk costumes and dance to fiddle and accordion music around maypoles covered with wildflower garlands.

Dalarna played a key role in the history of the nation. It was from here that Gustav Vasa recruited the army that freed the country from Danish domination during the 16th century. The region is also important artistically, both for its tradition of naive religious decoration and for producing two of the nation's best-loved painters, Anders Zorn (1860–1920) and Carl Larsson (1853–1915), and one of its favorite poets, the melancholy, mystical Dan Andersson (1888–1920). He sought inspiration in the remote forest camps of the old charcoal burners, who spent their days slowly burning wood to make the charcoal for factory furnaces.

Dalarna offers very little in the way of restaurants and accommodation. Visitors to the area—many from elsewhere in Scandinavia or from Germany—make use either of the region's many well-equipped campsites or of *stugbyar* (small villages of log cabins, with cooking facilities), usually set near lakesides or in forest clearings.

Our itinerary circles Siljan, the largest of the 6,000 lakes in the province and the center of Dalarna's folklore. The main points can all be reached by train, except for the southern side of Lake Siljan.

Exploring Dalarna

Dalarna is a gloriously compact region, mostly consisting of a single road that rings Lake Siljan, the area's main attraction. A drive round the lake will take in most of the highlights, leaving you only to decide whether to travel clockwise or counterclockwise. The lake itself provides a focal point for the region, providing fish to eat, and swimming and boating to entertain. The tiny villages and towns strung around the lake each have their own particular attraction to offer, making Dalarna a well-ordered, neat little package of a region to explore.

About the Hotels & Restaurants

The shores of Lake Siljan are dotted with delightful hotels, some dating back hundreds of years. Many are painted in classic Swedish red, and all are rustic and welcoming. It's difficult to find a region in Sweden where it is easier to relax than in Dalarna.

WHAT IT COSTS In Swedish Kronor				
$$$$	**$$$**	**$$**	**$**	**¢**
RESTAURANTS over 420	250–420	150–250	100–150	under 100
HOTELS over 2,900	2,300–2,900	1,500–2,300	1,000–1,500	under 1,000

Restaurant prices are for a main course at dinner. Hotel prices are for two people in a standard double room in high season.

Timing

Dalarna is truly a region for all seasons. In June and July it is where every Swede wants to be, an idyllic reflection of everything that is good about Swedish summer. In the winter months, Dalarna offers some very fine skiing, skating, and winter sports. And spring and autumn bring changing colors and fine fishing in Lake Siljan.

Falun

❶ *230 km (143 mi) northwest of Stockholm via E18 and Route 70.*

Falun is the traditional capital of Dalarna, though the adjacent nonde-script railway town of Borlänge has grown in importance as a business center. Falun's history has always been very much bound to its copper mine, worked since 1230 by Stora Kopparbergs Bergslags AB (today just Stora), which claims to be the oldest limited company in the world. During its great period of prosperity in the 17th century, it financed Sweden's "Age of Greatness," when the country became the dominant Baltic power. In 1650, Stora produced a record 3,067 tons of copper; probably as a result of such rapid extraction, 37 years later its mineshafts caved in. The collapse was on Midsummer Day, when most miners were off duty, and as a result no one was killed. The mine eventually closed in 1992.

★ Today the major part of the mine is an enormous hole in the ground that, in combination with the adjoining **Storamuseum,** has become Falun's principal tourist attraction. The one-hour tour through a network of old shafts and tunnels begins with a hair-raising 150-foot descent in an old elevator. Wear old shoes and warm clothing, since the copper-tinged mud can stain footwear and it's cold down there. The Stora Museum puts into perspective the lives of the men who worked the mines and has eye-opening displays on just how bad working conditions were below ground. ☎ *023/711475* ✉ *Mine SKr 90, museum free with mine tour* ◷ *Mine May–Aug., daily 10–5; Sept.–mid-Nov. and Mar.–Apr., weekdays 11–5, weekends 11–4; museum May–Aug., daily 10–5; Sept.–Apr., weekdays 11–5, weekends 11–4.*

The folk art, folklore, clothing, and music of the area are all well covered at **Dalarnasmuseet** (the Dalarnas Museum). There is also a grand reconstruction of the study in which Selma Lagerlöf (1858-1940), the celebrated Swedish author, worked after she moved to Falun in 1897. ✉ *Stigareg. 2–4* ☎ *023/765500* ✉ *SKr 40* ◷ *May–Aug., Mon.–Thurs. 10–5, Fri.–Sun. noon–5; Sept.–May, Mon.–Tues. and Thurs. 10–5, Wed. 10–9, Fri.–Sun. noon–5.*

Where to Stay & Eat

$$ ✕ **MS Slussbruden.** This restaurant on a boat offers "prawn cruises." For a set price you can feast on as many prawns as you can shell during the three-hour cruise. Live music acts serenade you all the while. Limitless bread and butter, cheese, fruits, and coffee are included. Wine and drinks are extra, and the choice is a little limited but good nonetheless. Combined with the beautiful scenery, the dinner cruise is a great hit. ✉ *Strandv.* ☎ *023/63850* 🍴 *Reservations essential* ▤ *AE, DC, MC, V* ◷ *Closed Nov.–Apr.*

$–$$ ✕ **Blå Apelsinen.** The Blue Orange serves up what's known as *husman-skost* (homey) Swedish food. Simple, hearty pork, beef, and fish dishes are all offered here in straightforward surroundings at reasonable prices. ✉ *Bergskolegränd 8A* ☎ *023/29111* ▤ *AE, MC, V.*

$$ ▥ **Scandic.** Outside Falun, the ultramodern Scandic was built for the 1993 World Skiing Championships that took place in the Lungnet sports and recreation center. The building itself looks like a giant ski jump made of Legos. The comfortable rooms have good views of the giant ski jump that's still used for competitions. ✉ *Svärdsjög. 51, 791 31 Falun* ☎ *023/6692200* 🖷 *023/669211* 🛏 *153 rooms* 🍴 *Restaurant, pub, indoor pool, sauna, meeting room, no-smoking rooms* ▤ *AE, DC, MC, V.*

$ ▥ **Grand.** Part of the First Hotel chain, this conventional modern hotel is close to the town center. The bright rooms are decorated with Chip-

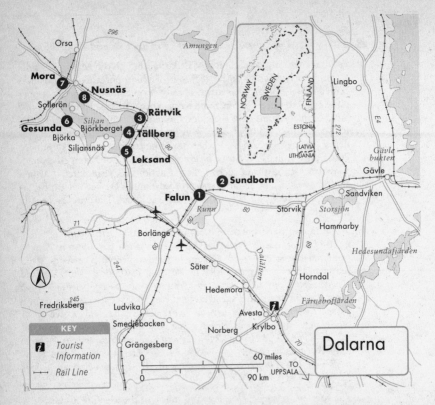

pendale-style furniture. ✉ *Trotzg. 9–11, 791 71* ☎ *023/794880* 🖨 *023/14143* 🛏 *153 rooms* ⚒ *Restaurant, bar, minibars, indoor pool, sauna, gym, convention center, no-smoking rooms* ⊟ *AE, DC, MC, V.*

$ 🏨 **Hotel Winn.** This small, cozy hotel in the town center is built in rustic Dalarna style and filled with antique furnishings. There is a pleasant relaxation area where the hot tub and sauna will let you unwind from the day's stresses. ✉ *Bergskolegränd 7, 791 12* ☎ *023/701700* 🖨 *023/701709* 🛏 *88 rooms, 84 with bath* ⚒ *Restaurant, hot tub, sauna, meeting room, no-smoking rooms* ⊟ *AE, DC, MC, V.*

Fodor'sChoice ★

¢–$ 🏨 **Hotel Falun.** Margaretha Eriksson runs this small, friendly, but bland-looking hotel just 1,300 feet from the railway station. The five rooms that share baths are offered at a lower rate. The front desk closes at 9 PM. ✉ *Centrumhuset, Trotzg. 16, 791 30* ☎ *023/29180* 🖨 *023/13006* 🛏 *22 rooms, 17 with bath* ⚒ *No-smoking rooms* ⊟ *AE, DC, MC, V.*

¢ 🏨 **Birgittagården.** The Dalarna Sisters of Birgitta religious order runs this small hotel, 8 km (5 mi) outside town. It's smoke- and alcohol-free and set in a fine park. ✉ *Uddnäsv. 58, 791 46* ☎ *023/32147* 🖨 *023/32471* 🛏 *20 rooms* ⚒ *Meeting room, no-smoking; no room phones, no room TVs* ⊟ *No credit cards.*

Sports & the Outdoors

A 25-minute walk from the center of Falun, east on Svärdsjögatan, takes you to **Lungnet** (☎ 023/83500), Falun's sports complex and national ski stadium. Horseback riding, swimming, bowling, an indoor sports center, and running tracks are all available. The ski stadium is home to the 260-foot ski jump (used only in competitions). In the winter you can watch the daredevil jumpers fly through the air, and in the summer, when the snow has gone, you can go to the top yourself and admire the view across Falun and beyond.

A SWEDISH BATH

T IS AUTUMN ON THE STOCKHOLM ARCHIPELAGO ISLAND OF FINNHAMN TODAY, but you could be forgiven for thinking it is winter as an arctic wind scythes bitterly across the landscape. To the north, clouds that are surely laden with snow creep south and the people shiver. You need heat, and lots of it.

There is a solution, one forged in defense against the cold for eons of time by the people who have populated these frozen lands. And it is as traditionally Swedish as Absolut vodka and just as warming. The bastu (sauna) has been the answer to frozen Nordic bones since long before medieval times, although its true date of origin has not been determined.

The bastu takes many different shapes and forms, but the classic model is little more than a small wooden shed, parked beside a freezing lake or the sea. The one on Finnhamn looks like something from the fairy-tale writings of Hans Christian Anderson (admittedly Danish). It is painted a traditional rust red and is no more than 16 feet long. It sits on a creaky wooden pier under bleak, leafless trees, plumb against the sea.

This evening it is a welcome sight, and there is no alternative but to take the plunge into a dry heat that will soar to 80°C or 90°C. The snow clouds have arrived, and snowflakes the size of golf balls are swirling and drifting. The sea is churning and the wind is coaxing the trees into an eerie dance. Through a small glass window you can see the storm.

Taking a sauna has reached a fine art in Sweden. It is often a social event. Some men do business here (a last bastion of gender exclusion), and there is a definite ritual. The practice is about heat and cleansing. In fact, the bastu has historically been the primary cleansing place in times when running water was scarce. Nordic people came here for their weekly (or less often) bathing routine. It was also used as the place for medical treatment, due to its hygienic setting. Babies were born here. Corpses were brought to lie here. The sauna was once a sacred place.

A visit begins with showering off the wrath of the day. Completely dry yourself, allowing the heat to properly open your pores for a clean, sweat. Take a seat, buck naked, on a towel—a must for hygienic protocol.

Now the work begins. And it is work, although it may not feel like it at first. It will take a while, but the sweat will trickle, then flood. Put some water on the coals to wet the air. When you reach near-fission, the next and most daring step awaits: the big freeze. On Finnhamn I stepped unadorned out into the snow, down the frozen steel ladder. Sha-la-la! By the powers, it was cold, head-splitting cold.

Back on terra firma within microseconds, your skin begins to tingle and your head spins in dizziness and shock. Absolute elation. Make haste to the bastu. The next rule is to dry off in the warming room. This is one full cycle. Keep going until you can take no more. At the end an ocean of warmth and exhaustion will engulf you.

The Swedish believe in the practice of sauna as an elixir and proclaim it aids good health, vigor, and life. But do beware: some of those with a heart condition or who are otherwise in ill health have come to grief in the bastu. Everything in moderation, the saying goes. Proceed with caution.

SKIING At the **Bjursås Ski Center** (☎ 023/774177 ⊕ www.bjursas.com), 25 km (15 mi) northwest of Falun on Route 80, you can make use of the resort's seven lift systems and 18 varied pistes. It's open between December and April and has numerous hotels, restaurants, and cafés.

Sundborn

❷ *10 km (6 mi) northeast of Falun off Route 80.*

★ In this small village you can visit **Carl Larsson Gården,** the lakeside home of the Swedish artist (1833–1915). Larsson was an excellent textile designer and draftsman who painted scenes from his family's busy domestic life. The house itself was creatively painted and decorated by Larsson's wife, Karin, also trained as an artist. Their home's turn-of-the-20th-century fittings and furnishings have been carefully preserved; their great-grandchildren still use the house on occasion. Waits for guided tours in summer can take two hours. You'll receive a timed ticket and can visit the café or stroll around the garden or lake while you wait. ☎ 023/60053 ⊠ *Guided tours only, SKr 80* ⊙ *May–Sept., daily 10–5; Oct.–Apr., guided tour every Tues.; call for details.* ⊕ *www.clg.se.*

Rättvik

❸ *48 km (30 mi) northwest of Falun via Route 80.*

On the eastern tip of Lake Siljan, Rättvik is a pleasant town of timbered houses surrounded by wooded slopes. A center for local folklore, the town has several shops that sell handmade articles and produce from the region.

Every year in June, dozens of people wearing traditional costumes arrive in longboats to attend midsummer services at the town's 13th-century church, **Rättviks Kyrka,** which stands on a promontory stretching into the lake. Its interior contains some fine examples of local religious art. Next to the church are 90 stables, the oldest from the 1400s, where churchgoers once rested their horses.

The open-air museum **Rättvik Gammelgård,** a 20-minute walk along the banks of the lake north of Rättvik, reconstructs peasant life of bygone days. More than 3,500 pieces of art, clothing, ceramics, tools, and furniture are on display in the old buildings. Tours in English can be arranged through the Rättvik tourist office. ⊠ *Free; guided tour SKr 20* ⊙ *Mid-June–mid-Aug., daily 11–6; tours at 1 and 2:30.*

Just to the west of Rättvik in the forest is **Vidablick.** The top of this tall wooden tower, more than 100 years old, will give you some of the most stunning views across Lake Siljan that you can find.

★ Once a lucrative open chalk mine, the huge multitier quarry left at **Dalhalla** (7 km [4½] mi north of Rättvik) has become one of the world's most beautiful outdoor stages. One side is banked with seats, and the stage, surrounded with water and supported on pillars, appears to float on the cobalt-blue lake at the quarry's bottom. Opera, rock concerts, and amazing light shows are all presented here, where the sound is enhanced by the quarry's incredible acoustics. There is also a museum covering the meteor crash that formed Lake Siljan 360 million years ago, the chalk mining that still takes place, and the history of mining. Guided tours of the more remote parts of the quarry can be booked year-round. ⊠ *Stationshuset, Rättvik* ☎ 0248/797950 ⊠ *SKr 45 for museum and tour* ⊙ *Museum mid-May–Sept., daily 10–5; July, daily 10–6.*

Where to Stay & Eat

¢ ✕ **Strandrestaurangen.** A family-style restaurant with a huge outdoor seating area by the lake, Strandrestaurangen serves such standard Swedish fare as meatballs, sausages, and pork chops. It's all well cooked and filling. Kids enjoy the beach, miniature golf, the ice cream bar, and the swimming pool. For the adults, there's a pub attached, which has live music in the evening. ⊠ *Rättvik* ☎ *0248/13400* ⊟ *AE, MC, V* ☉ *Summer months only.*

¢ 🏨 **Hotell Vidablick.** Set on its own grounds, with a pleasant view of the lake from the veranda, this small hotel makes a welcome, relaxing stop. Rooms are modern and sparsely furnished, and there's a small private beach where you can take to the water, if it's warm enough. ⊠ *Hantverks-byn, 795 36* ☎ *0248/30250* 🖷 *0248/30660* ⌕ *50 rooms* ♨ *Bar, beach* ⊟ *AE, DC, MC, V* ⍾ *BP.*

Tällberg

❹ *9 km (5 mi) south of Rättvik via Route 70 57 km (35 mi) northwest of Falun via Route 80.*

Tällberg is considered by many to be the real Dalarna. Once a sleepy town that few knew about, an 1850 visit from Hans Christian Andersen put an end to all that. He extolled its virtues—tiny flower-strewn cottages, sweet-smelling grass meadows, stunning lake views—to such an extent that Tällberg quickly became a major tourist stop. This tiny village, one of the smallest in the region with only about 200 permanent residents, is packed with crowds in summer.

The farm buildings that make up **Klockargården** have become a living museum of handicrafts and local industry. Artists and craftsmen work in the old buildings, performing such skills as blacksmithing, baking flat bread, making lace, and weaving textiles. ⊠ *Tällberg* ☎ *0247/50265* 🖷 *Free* ☉ *June–Aug., daily 10–7.*

Where to Stay & Eat

★ $ ✕🏨 **Åkerblads.** A sprawling, low-built hotel, with parts dating from the 1400s, Åkerblads is known primarily for its gourmet achievements. The restaurant ($$) serves an interesting blend of Swedish and French cuisine, including such dishes as pork roasted with eggplants and blueberries, and salmon with asparagus, truffle, and burgundy wine sauce. The hotel rooms are comfortable, and most have very good views of Lake Siljan. ⊠ *Sjögattu 2, 793 70* ☎ *0247/50800* 🖷 *0247/50652* ⊕ *www.akerblads-tallberg.se* ⌕ *67 rooms, 25 suites* ♨ *Restaurant, bar, pool, sauna, spa* ⊟ *AE, DC, MC, V* ⍾ *BP.*

$ 🏨 **Tällbergsgården.** A classic Dalarna red-wood building, this one claiming to be the oldest in the village, is home to a small hotel with lake views. The guest rooms are light and airy, with neutral shades and wooden floors. ⊠ *Holgattu 1, 793 70* ☎ *0247/50850* 🖷 *0247/50200* ⊕ *www.tallbergsgarden.se* ⌕ *38 rooms, 6 suites* ♨ *Restaurant, bar, sauna, meeting rooms* ⊟ *AE, DC, MC, V* ⍾ *BP.*

¢ ✕🏨 **Hotel Dalecarlia.** There's a homey feel to this first-class hotel, which has exacting standards and good lake views. The lobby's comfy sofas and darkened corners are welcoming spots to sink into. Rooms are large and done in soft colors, and there is a spa and fitness center with pool, sauna, and beauty treatments. The restaurant ($$) is candlelighted and reminiscent of a farmhouse. It has oak beams, crisp white linen, and a large open fireplace perfect for warming your after-dinner brandy. The food is well presented and emphasizes local and regional specialties. The game is especially good. ⊠ *Tällberg, 793 70* ☎ *0247/89100* 🖷 *0247/*

FodorsChoice ★

50240 ⊕ *www.dalecarlia.se* 🛏 *80 rooms, 5 suites* ⚲ *Restaurant, bar, pool, sauna, spa, gym, convention center* ☰ *AE, DC, MC, V* ⦿ *BP.*

Leksand

❺ *9 km (5½ mi) south of Tällberg via Route 70, 66 km (41 mi) northwest of Falun via Rättvik.*

Thousands of tourists converge on Leksand every June for the Midsummer celebrations; they also come in July for *Himlaspelet* (*The Play of the Way that Leads to Heaven*), a traditional musical with a local cast that's staged outdoors near the town's church. It is easy to get seats; ask the local tourist office for details.

Leksand is also an excellent vantage point from which to watch the "church-boat" races on Siljan. These vessels are supposedly the successors to the Viking longboats. They were used in the 13th and 14th centuries to take peasants from outlying regions to church on Sunday. On Midsummer Eve the longboats, crewed by people in folk costumes, skim the lake once more.

In the hills around Leksand and elsewhere near Siljan are many *fäbodar,* small settlements in the forest where cattle were taken to graze during the summer. Less idyllic memories of bygone days are conjured up by **Käringberget,** a 720-foot-high mountain north of town where alleged witches were burned to death during the 17th century.

Fodor'sChoice The oldest parts of **Leksands Kyrka** date from the 13th century, and the
★ current exterior dates from 1715. The Leksand Church's interior contains some interesting touches: a German font from the 1500s, a crucifix from 1400, and Dalarna's oldest organ. But what makes this church really shine is its location, perhaps one of the prettiest in the country. The peaceful tree-lined churchyard and the view across the entire lake are both breathtaking. ⊠ *Kyrkudden* 🕾 *0247/80700.*

At the **Leksands Hembygdsgårdar,** the site of the oldest farm buildings in Dalarna, you can find out more about the famous red structures that dot the region's landscape. Other displays look at building techniques that arose in the Middle Ages as well as the history of country living in Dalarna. ⊠ *Kyrkallén* 🕾 *070/4095044* 🖙 *SKr 20* ⦿ *June–Aug., daily noon–4.*

Famous local doctor and author Axel Munthe built **Munthes Hildasholm** as a present for his English wife in 1910. The house and gardens, filled with exquisite antiques, paintings, and furniture from across Europe, can now be visited and seen exactly as they were left. You can have coffee and cake in the café, set in beautifully manicured gardens and lawns. ⊠ *Klockaregatan 5, Kyrkudden* 🕾 *0247/10062* 🖙 *SKr 60* ⦿ *June–Sept., Mon.–Sat. 11–6, Sun. 1–6.*

Where to Stay & Eat

¢–$$ ✕ **Bosporen Restaurang.** The large terrace outside this restaurant is a great place to dine in summer. The menu is long and interesting, with some great Swedish classics. The best bet is the selection of pizzas, which make use of such ingredients as arugula, pine nuts, Gorgonzola, and pears. Wine by the glass is of good quality, and the beers are wide-ranging and cheap. ⊠ *Stortorget 1* 🕾 *0247/13280* ☰ *AE, MC, V.*

¢ 🖭 **Hotell Korstäppan.** The beautiful rooms, many with traditional tile fireplaces and all with wooden floors, are the main attraction at this large, yellow wooden hotel. All the rooms are spacious and simply furnished with stylish antiques and beautiful old rugs. ⊠ *Hjortnäsv. 33, 793 31* 🕾 *0247/12310* 🖴 *0247/14178* 🛏 *30 rooms* ⚲ *Breakfast room, convention center* ☰ *AE, MC, V* ⦿ *BP.*

¢ 🏠 **Leksands Gästhem.** Simplicity bordering on minimalism is the theme at this converted old school near a farmyard just outside Leksand. The bedrooms have plain, scrubbed wooden floors, large windows, and pale-blue chairs. Each bathroom is shared by several rooms. In the hallway—where you can still see the low coat hooks for the schoolchildren— is a sweeping wood staircase that leads to a TV and lounge area. Wonderful breakfasts are included in the rate; everything is homemade. ⊠ *Krökbacken 5, 793 90* ☎ *0247/13700* 🖷 *0247/13737* ⊕ *www. leksandsguesth.nu* 🗩 *13 rooms* 🛆 *Breakfast room, lounge* 🖃 *AE, DC, MC, V* ◉ *BP.*

Sports & the Outdoors

Leksand is the perfect base for a bike ride around Lake Siljan. There are many paths and tracks to choose from, and maps and rental bikes are available from the **tourist office** (☎ 0247/796130).

Gesunda

❻ *38 km (24 mi) northwest of Leksand*

A chairlift from Gesunda, a pleasant little village, will take you to the top of a mountain for unbeatable views over the lake. The large island of **Sollerön** is connected to the mainland by a bridge at Gesunda. The island has fine views of the mountains surrounding Siljan. Several excellent beaches and an interesting Viking gravesite are also here. The church dates from 1775.

⟳ **Tomteland** (Santa World), on Gesundaberget, claims to be the home of Santa Claus, or Father Christmas. Toys are for sale at Santa's workshop and at kiosks. There are rides in horse-drawn carriages in summer and sleighs in winter. ⊠ *Gesundaberget, Sollerön* ☎ *0250/21200* 🖾 *SKr 125* ⊙ *Mid-June–late Aug., daily 10–5; late Nov.–early Jan., daily 10–4* ⊕ *www.santaworld.se.*

Mora

❼ *50 km (31 mi) northwest of Leksand, 40 km (25 mi) northwest of Rättvik via Rte. 70.*

To get to this relaxed lakeside town of 20,000, you can follow the northern shore of Lake Silja (there is a bridge at Färnäs, or follow the lake's southern shore through Leksand and Gesunda to get a good sense of Dalarna.

Mora is best known as the finishing point for the world's longest cross-country ski race, the Vasalopp, which begins 90 km (56 mi) away at Sälen, a ski resort close to the Norwegian border. The race commemorates a fundamental piece of Swedish history: the successful attempt by Gustav Vasa in 1521 to rally local peasants to the cause of ridding Sweden of Danish occupation. Vasa, only 21 years old, had fled the capital and described to the Mora locals in graphic detail a massacre of Swedish noblemen ordered by Danish king Christian in Stockholm's Stortorget. Unfortunately, no one believed him, and the dispirited Vasa was forced to abandon his attempts at insurrection and take off on either skis or snowshoes for Norway, where he hoped to evade King Christian and go into exile.

Just after he left, confirmation of the Stockholm bloodbath reached Mora, and the peasants, already discontented with Danish rule, sent two skiers after Vasa to tell him they would join his cause. The two men caught up with the young nobleman at Sälen. They returned with him to Mora, where an army was recruited. Vasa marched south, defeated the Danes, and became king and the founder of modern Sweden.

The commemorative race, held on the first Sunday in March, attracts thousands of competitors from all over the world, including the Swedish king. There is a spectacular mass start at Sälen before the field thins out. The finish is eagerly awaited in Mora, though since the start of live television broadcasts the number of spectators has fallen.

You can get a comfortable glimpse of the Vasalopp's history in the **Vasaloppets Hus,** which contains a collection of the ski gear and photos of competitors, news clippings, and a short film detailing some of the race's finer moments. ✉ *Vasag.* ☎ *0250/39225* ✉ *SKr 20* ⊙ *Mid-June–mid-Aug., daily 10–5; mid-Aug.–mid-June, weekdays 10–5.*

Mora is also known as the home of Anders Zorn (1860–1920), Sweden's leading impressionist painter, who lived in Stockholm and Paris before returning to his roots here and painting the local scenes for which he is now known. His former private residence—**Zorngården**— a large, sumptuous house designed with great originality and taste by the painter himself, has retained the same exquisite furnishings, paintings, and decor it had when he lived there with his wife. Next door, the ★ **Zorn Museet** (Zorn Museum), built 19 years after the painter's death, contains many of his best works. ✉ *Vasag. 36* ☎ *0250/16560* ✉ *Museum SKr 35, home SKr 45* ⊙ *Museum mid-May–mid-Sept., Mon.–Sat. 9–5, Sun. 11–5; mid-Sept.–mid-May, Mon.–Sat. noon–5, Sun. 1–5; home (guided tours only) mid-May–mid-Sept., Mon.–Sat. 10–4, Sun. 11–4; mid-Sept.–mid-May, Mon.–Sat. noon–4, Sun. 1–4.*

On the south side of town is **Zorns Gammalgård,** a fine collection of old wooden houses from local farms, brought here and donated to Mora by Anders Zorn. One of them holds the **Textil Kammare** (Textile Chamber), a collection of textiles and period clothing. ✉ *Yvradsv.* ☎ *0250/ 16560 (June–Aug. only)* ✉ *SKr 20* ⊙ *June–Aug., daily 11–5.*

off the beaten path

SILJANSFORS SKOGSMUSEUM – (Siljansfors Forest Musuem) – Partly because there's always been a lot of wood available for firing furnaces, the area around Mora is well known for its metalworking. This outdoor museum shows the smithies' many connections to local forestry, in particular with the art of charcoal burning. A track through the forest will take you to smithies, ironworks, woodcutting sheds, and charcoal-burning towers. The walks are all linked together at the information center near the entrance. ✉ *12 mi southwest of Mora on Rte. 45* ☎ *0250/20331.*

ORSA – Fifteen kilometers (9 miles) north of Mora on Route 45 is a small sleepy town that becomes a big chaotic symphony every Wednesday in July. It's then that the **Orsa Spelmän,** groups of traditional folklore music players, take part in what's called the Orsayran (Orsa rush). The musicians take over the streets of the town, wandering and playing their instruments. This soon becomes a free-for-all in which all the people in town, whether accomplished or not, bring out their instruments and play. It's great fun.

ORSA GRÖNKLITTS BJÖRNPARK – Just outside Orsa is the wildlife reserve inhabited by Sweden's native brown bears and other animals, including wolves. There's a limited chance of spotting one of these shy creatures, but if you do, it is an unforgettable sight. (Be sure to follow common sense safety rules, being sure not to approach the bears too closely. It's important to not make them feel threatened— that's when bears tend to attack).

Where to Stay & Eat

★ **$$** ✕ **Jernet Bar & Matsal.** In one of Mora's oldest industrial buildings (1879), Jernet serves high-quality Swedish and international dishes, which may include roast elk with mustard potatoes and lingonberries and breast of chicken stuffed with Brie and apricots. The tables are bare antique oak, the wooden chairs are of a traditional Leksand style, and the crisp linen napkins are woven locally. In the bar area, furnished in birch and stainless steel, the large windows allow for great views over the lake. ⊠ *Strandg. 6* ☎ *0250/15020* ▭ *AE, DC, MC, V.*

$ ▣ **Kung Gösta.** This modern, reasonably sized hotel is 2 km (1 mi) from the town center and only 330 feet from the Mora train station. The small rooms are brightly furnished, with wood floors and large windows. ⊠*Kristinebergsg. 1, S792 32* ☎*0250/15070* 🖷*0250/17078* 🖅*47 rooms* ⚘ *Restaurant, indoor pool, sauna, gym, meeting room, no-smoking rooms* ▭ *AE, DC, MC, V* ⫧ *BP.*

$ ▣ **Mora.** This pleasant little hotel, a part of the First Hotel group, is in the town center 5 km (3 mi) from the airport. Its comfortable rooms are brightly decorated. ⊠*Strandg. 12, S792 30* ☎*0250/592650* 🖷*0250/18981* 🖅 *135 rooms* ⚘ *Restaurant, bar, indoor pool, sauna, meeting room, no-smoking rooms* ▭ *AE, DC, MC, V* ⫧ *BP.*

$ ▣ **Mora Parken.** This modern hotel sits in a park by the banks of the Dala River, not far from the town center. Rooms are small and simply furnished with pastel fabrics and plain wood furniture and floors. ⊠ *Parkgatan 1, 792 37* ☎ *0250/27600* 🖷 *0250/27615* 🖅 *75 rooms* ⚘ *Restaurant, sauna, convention center, no-smoking rooms* ▭ *AE, DC, MC, V* ⫧ *BP.*

$ ▣ **Siljan.** Part of the Sweden Hotel group, this small modern hotel has views over the lake. Rooms are standard, with radio and television. ⊠*Morag. 6, 792 22* ☎*0250/13000* 🖷*0250/13098* ⊕*www.swedenhotels. se* 🖅*44 rooms* ⚘ *Restaurant, bar, no-smoking floor, sauna, dance club, meeting room* ▭ *AE, DC, MC, V* ⫧ *BP.*

Sports & the Outdoors

SKIING Dalarna's principal ski resort is **Sälen,** starting point for the Vasalopp, about 80 km (50 mi) west of Mora. Snow here is pretty much guaranteed from November to May, and there are more than 100 pistes from which to choose, from simple slopes for the beginner to challenging black runs that weave through tightly forested slopes. For more information contact any of the tourist offices in Dalarna.

WALKING For the energetic traveler it's possible to walk the 90-km (56-mi) **track from Sälen to Mora** that's used for the Vasalopp ski race in March. Along the way you may very well see some elk wandering through the forest. Day shelters, basic night shelters, fireplaces, tables, signposts, and restrooms are set up along the trail. Facilities are free, but a donation of SKr 25 is suggested for the night shelters. Maps and other details can be obtained from the **Mora tourist office** (⊠ Stationsvägen ☎ 0250/592020).

Nusnäs

❽ *6 km (4 mi) southeast of Mora via Route 70, 28 km (17 mi) northwest of Falun.*

The lakeside village of Nusnäs is where the small, brightly red-painted, wooden Dala horses are made. These were originally carved by the peasants of Dalarna as toys for their children, but their popularity rapidly spread with the advent of tourism in the 20th century. Mass production of the little horses started at Nusnäs in 1928. In 1939 they achieved international popularity after being shown at the New York World's Fair, and since then they have become a Swedish symbol (although today some of the smaller versions available in Stockholm's tourists shops are actually made in East Asia). At Nusnäs you can watch the genuine article being made, now with the aid of modern machinery but still painted by hand.

Shopping

Shops in the area are generally open every day except Sunday. The best place to buy painted horses is **Nils Olsson** (✉ Edåkersvågen 17 ☎ 0250/ 37200).

Dalarna A to Z

To research prices, get advice from other travelers, and book travel arrangements, visit www.fodors.com.

AIRPORTS

There are six flights daily from Stockholm to Dala Airport, which is 8 km (5 mi) south of Borlänge. Flights also arrive from Gothenburg. There are half-hourly bus connections on weekdays between Dala Airport and Falun, 26 km (16 mi) away. Bus 601 runs every half hour from Dala Airport to Borlänge; the trip costs SKr 15. Mora Airport has three Skyways flights daily from Stockholm on weekdays, fewer on the weekends. The airport is 6 km (4 mi) from Mora; no buses serve the airport.

A taxi from Dala Airport to Borlänge costs around SKr 125, to Falun approximately SKr 275. A taxi into Mora from Mora Airport costs SKr 100. Order taxis in advance through your travel agent or when you make an airline reservation. Book a cab by calling the Borlänge taxi service.
🛪 **Dala Airport** ☎ 0243/64510 ⊕ www.dalaairport.se. **Borlänge Taxi** ☎ 0243/13100. **Mora Airport** ☎ 0250/30175.

BUS TRAVEL

Swebus runs tour buses to the area from Stockholm on weekends. The trip takes about four hours one-way.
🛪 **Swebus Express** ☎ 020/218218, from outside Sweden 8/50309400 ⊕ www. swebusexpress.se.

CAR RENTAL

Avis has offices in Borlänge and Mora. Europcar has an office in Borlänge. Hertz has an office in Falun, and independent company Bilkompaniet, formerly a part of Hertz, rents cars in Mora.
🛪 **Major Agencies Avis** ✉ Borlänge ☎ 0243/87080 ✉ Mora ☎ 0250/16711. **Europcar** ✉ Borlänge ☎ 0243/19050. **Hertz** ✉ Falun ☎ 023/58872. **Bilkompaniet** ✉ Mora ☎ 0250/28800.

CAR TRAVEL

From Stockholm take E18 to Enköping and follow Route 70 northwest. From Göteborg take E20 to Örebro and Route 60 north from there. Villages are well sign-posted.

EMERGENCIES

For emergencies dial 112. There are no late-night pharmacies in the area. Vasen Pharmacy, in Falun, is open 9–7 weekdays and 9–noon on Saturday.
🛪 **Falun Hospital** ☎ 023/492000. **Mora Hospital** ☎ 023/493000. **24-hour medical advisory service** ☎ 023/492900. **Vasen Pharmacy** ✉ Åsg. 25 Falun ☎ 023/20000.

TOURS

Call the Falun tourist office for English-speaking guides to Falun and the region around Lake Siljan; guides cost about SKr 900 per day.

BOAT TOURS Just next to the Falun train station, on the quay in the center of town, is the MS *Gustaf Wasa*, a beautiful old steamship that's used for sightseeing tours of Lake Siljan. Trips can take from two to four hours and range in price from SKr 80 to SKr 120. It's a good way to see the stunning countryside from another perspective.

🚢 **MS *Gustaf Wasa*,** ☎ 010/2523292.

TRAIN TRAVEL

There is regular daily train service from Stockholm to both Mora and Falun.

VISITOR INFORMATION

On the approach to the area from the south via Route 70, a 43-ft, bright orange-red Dala horse marks a rest stop just south of Avesta. It has a spacious cafeteria and a helpful tourist information center.

🚺 Tourist Information **Falun**. ✉ Trotzgatan 10-12 ☎ 023/83050 ⊕ www.visitfalun.se. **Leksand** ✉ Stationsgatan 14 ☎ 0247/796130. **Ludvika** ✉ Fredsgatan 10 ☎ 0240/86050. **Mora** ✉ Stationsvägen ☎ 0250/592020 ⊕ www.siljan.se. **Rättvik** ✉ Riksvägen 40 ☎ 0248/797210. **Sälen** ✉ Sälen Centrum ☎ 0280/18700.

NORRLAND & NORRBOTTEN

8

FODOR'S CHOICE

Hotel Jokkmokk, *Jokkmokk*

Jukkasjärvi Wärdshus, *restaurant in Jukkasjärvi*

HIGHLY RECOMMENDED

HOTELS   Arctic hotel restaurant, *Luleå*

Ice Hotel, *Jukkasjärvi*

THE NORTH OF SWEDEN, Norrland, is a place of wide-open spaces where the silence is almost audible. Golden eagles soar above snow-capped crags; huge salmon fight their way up wild, tumbling rivers; rare orchids bloom in Arctic heathland; and wild rhododendrons splash the land with color.

In the summer the sun shines at midnight above the Arctic Circle. In the winter it hardly shines at all. The weather can change with bewildering speed: a June day can dawn sunny and bright; then the skies may darken and the temperature drops to around zero as a snow squall blows in. Just as suddenly, the sun comes out again and the temperature starts to rise.

Here live the once-nomadic Lapps, or Sámi, as they prefer to be known. They carefully guard what remains of their identity while doing their best to inform the public of their culture. Many of the 17,000 Sámi who live in Sweden still earn their living herding reindeer, but as open space shrinks, the younger generation is turning in greater numbers toward the allure of the cities. As the modern world makes its incursions, the Sámi often exhibit a sad resignation to the gradual disappearance of their way of life. A Sámi folk poem says it best: "Our memory, the memory of us vanishes/We forget and we are forgotten."

Yet there is a growing struggle, especially among younger Sámi, to maintain their identity, and, thanks to their traditional closeness to nature, they are now finding allies in Sweden's Green movement. They refer to the north of Scandinavia as *Sapmi,* their spiritual and physical home, making no allowance for the different countries that now rule it.

Nearly all Swedish Sámi now live in ordinary houses, having abandoned the *kåta* (Lapp wigwam), and some even herd their reindeer with helicopters. Efforts are now being made to protect and preserve their language, which is totally unlike Swedish and bears a far greater resemblance to Finnish. The language reflects their closeness to nature. The word *goadnil,* for example, means "a quiet part of the river, free of current, near the bank or beside a rock."

Nowadays many Sámi depend on the tourist industry for their living, selling their artifacts, such as expertly carved bone-handle knives, wooden cups and bowls, bark bags, silver jewelry, and leather straps embroidered with pewter thread.

The land that the Sámi inhabit is vast. Norrland stretches 1,000 km (625 mi) from south to north, making up more than half of Sweden; it's roughly the same size as Great Britain. In the west there are mountain ranges, to the east a wild and rocky coastline, and in between boundless forests and moorland. Its towns are often little more than a group of houses along a street, built around a local industry such as mining, forestry, or hydropower utilities. Thanks to Sweden's excellent transportation infrastructure, however, Norrland and the northernmost region of Norrbotten are no longer inaccessible. Even travelers with limited time can get at least a taste of the area. Its wild spaces are ideal for open-air vacations. Hiking, climbing, canoeing, river rafting, and fishing are all popular in summer; skiing, ice-skating, and dogsledding are winter activities.

A word of warning: in summer mosquitoes are a constant nuisance, even worse than in other parts of Sweden, so be sure to bring plenty of repellent (you won't find anything effective in Sweden). Fall is perhaps the best season to visit Norrland. Roads are well maintained, but be careful of *gupp* (holes) following thaws. Highways are generally traffic free, but keep an eye out for the occasional reindeer.

Dining and lodging are on the primitive side in this region. Standards of cuisine and service are not nearly as high as prices—but hotels are usually exceptionally clean and staff scrupulously honest. Accommodations are limited, but the various local tourist offices can supply details of bed-and-breakfasts and holiday villages equipped with housekeeping cabins. The area is also rich in campsites—but with the highly unpredictable climate, this may appeal only to the very hardy.

Norrbotten is best discovered from a base in Kiruna, in the center of the alpine region that has been described as Europe's last wilderness. You can tour south and west to the mountains and national parks, east and south to Sámi villages, and farther south still to Baltic coastal settlements.

Exploring Norrland & Norrbotten

Exploring the vast wilderness of Norrland and Norbotten can be extremely rewarding, but it must be done with care. The harsh plains and rugged mountains of this region are best taken under advisement, with someone who has experience in these matters. Having said that, by using one of the larger towns as your base, it is perfectly possible to explore the extreme beauties that the region has to offer without having to make any additional arrangements for your overnight accommodations.

About the Hotels & Restaurants

Adventurous eaters should prepare themselves for a lot of fun in Norrland and Norbotten. The harsh living conditions have historically driven the locals to resort to some unusual ingredients and combinations. On menus in this region, you might see, among other things, whale meat, seal, and coffee with cheese.

WHAT IT COSTS In Swedish Kronor				
	$$$$	**$$$**	**$$**	**$**	**¢**
RESTAURANTS	over 420	250–420	150–250	100–150	under 100
HOTELS	over 2,900	2,300–2,900	1,500–2,300	1,000–1,500	under 1,000

Restaurant prices are for a main course at dinner. Hotel prices are for two people in a standard double room in high season.

Timing

Unless you are interested in winter sports and extreme weather conditions, summer is probably the best time to visit Norland and Norbotten. Days are long, sometimes never ending, and there are many more restaurants and shops open. But winter has its advantages up here too. If you can stand the cold, there is skiing and sledding, reindeer sleigh rides, and the wonderful northern lights. And if you want to visit the world-famous Ice Hotel in Jukkasjärvi, you have to go in the winter—between December and April to be precise.

Kiruna

❶ *1,352 km (840 mi) north of Stockholm.*

About 250 km (155 mi) north of the Arctic Circle, and 1,804 feet above sea level, Kiruna is Sweden's northernmost municipality. Although its inhabitants number only around 26,000, Kiruna is Sweden's largest city geographically—it spreads over the equivalent of half the area of Switzerland. Until an Australian community took the claim, Kiruna was often called "the world's biggest city." With 20,000 square km (7,722 square mi) within the municipal limits, Kiruna boasts that it

Darkness & Lights

In a world gone crazy with 24-hour services that are always on hand, it is novel and refreshing to experience the vast spaces and uninhabited landscape of the north of Sweden. You can drive for hours in Norrland and Norrbotten and find nothing to do except marvel at the dramatic beauty surrounding you. Summer brings the midnight sun to the north of Sweden, bathing the country in sunlight around the clock. For a period of about three weeks (it can last as long as fifty days) it doesn't get dark at all. It's an amazing thing to see the sun shining all the time, even if it does do strange things to your body clock—drinking beer and fishing at 4 AM has never seemed so natural. If you can stand the cold, winter in the north also holds distinctive pleasures. From November to March, instead of days of light, you can immerse yourself in darkness—not pitch black, but rather a kind of twilight during the day. If you're visiting around the Winter Solstice in December, you really will be in darkness all the time. And if it's a dark and clear night sky, look out for the Northern Lights, there's a good chance you might see them.

8

---

could accommodate the entire world population with 43 square ft of space per person.

Kiruna lies at the eastern end of Lake Luossajärvi, spread over a wide area between two mountains, Luossavaara and Kirunavaara, that are largely composed of iron ore—Kiruna's raison d'être. Here is the world's largest underground iron mine, with reserves estimated at 420 million tons. Automated mining technology has largely replaced the traditional miner in the Kirunavaara mine, which is some 500 km (280 mi) long and has an underground network of 400 km (249 mi) trafficable roads. Of the city's inhabitants, an estimated fifth are Finnish immigrants who came to work in the mine in the 1950s.

The city was established in 1900 as a mining town, but true prosperity came only with the building of the railway to the Baltic port of Luleå and the northern Norwegian port of Narvik in 1902.

Like most of Norrland, Kiruna is full of remarkable contrasts, from the seemingly pitch-black, months-long winter to the summer, when the sun never sets and it is actually possible to play golf round-the-clock for 50 days at a stretch. Here, too, the ancient Sámi culture exists side by side with the high-tech culture of cutting-edge satellite research. Since the 1960s the city has supported the Esrange Space Range, about 40 km (24 mi) east, which sends sounding rockets and stratospheric balloons to probe the upper reaches of the earth's atmosphere, and the Swedish Institute of Space Physics, which has pioneered the investigation of the phenomenon of the northern lights. The city received a boost in 1984 with the opening of Nordkalottvägen, a 170-km-long (106-mi-long) road to Narvik.

One of Kiruna's few buildings of interest is **Kiruna Kyrka** (Kiruna Church; ⊠ Gruvvägen), near the center of the city. It was built in 1921, its inspiration a blending of a Sámi kåta with a Swedish stave church. The altarpiece is by Prince Eugen (1863–1947), Sweden's painter prince.

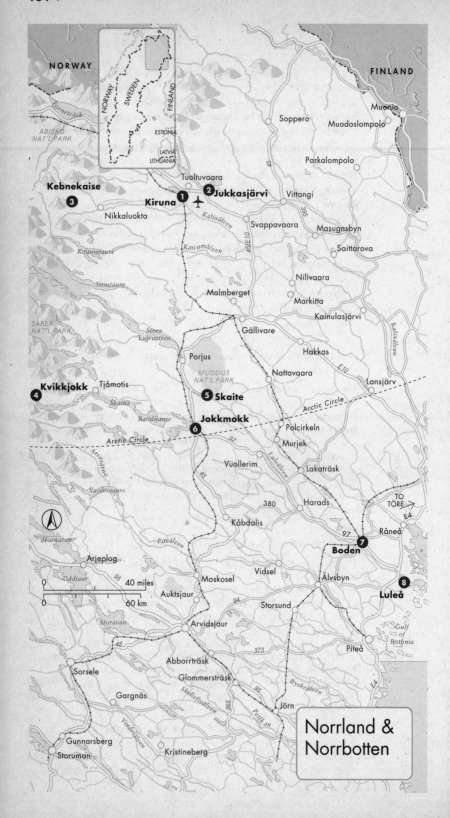

NORWAY

FINLAND

ABISKO
NAT'L PARK

Torneträsk

Muonio

Soppero

Muodoslompolo

Parkalompolo

Kebnekaise **3**

Nikkaluokta

Tuoltuvaara

Kiruna **1**

2 Jukkasjärvi

Vittangi

Kajtumjaure

Kalixälven

Svappavaara

Masugnsbyn

Kaitumälven

Saittarova

Sitasjaure

Nilivaara

Malmberget

Markitta

SAREK
NAT'L PARK

Stora
Lulevatten

Gällivare

Kainulasjärvi

Porjus

MUDDUS
NAT'L PARK

Hakkas

Nattavaara

E10

Lansjärv

Kvikkjokk **4**

Tjåmotis

5 Skaite

Arctic Circle

Skalka

Raudijaure

6 Jokkmokk

Polcirkeln

Arctic Circle

Murjek

Arjesjaure

Vuollerim

Lakaträsk

Luleälven

Vuolvojaure

97

TO
TÖRE

E4

Hornavan

380

Harads

Kåbdalis

97

Råneå

Arjeplog

Boden **7**

Uddjaur

40 miles

Moskosel

Vidsel

Älvsbyn

8
Luleå

60 km

Auktsjaur

94

Storavan

Arvidsjaur

Storsund

Gulf
of
Bothnia

45

Piteälven

373

Piteå

Sorsele

Abborrträsk

Glommersträsk

95

Byskeälven

E4

Gargnäs

Skellefteälven

365

Jörn

Petikån

Vindelälven

Gunnarsberg

Storuman

Kristineberg

Norrland &
Norrbotten

Where to Stay & Eat

$ ✕🛏 **Kebne och Kaisa.** These twin modern hotels—named after the local mountain, Kebnekaise—are close to the railway station and the airport bus stop. Rooms are bland but modern and comfortable. The restaurant is one of the best in Kiruna; it's open for breakfast and dinner. ⊠ *Konduktörsg. 3, 981 34* ☎ *0980/12380* 🖷 *0980/68181* ⊕ *www.hotellkebne. com* 🛏 *54 rooms* ⚓ *Restaurant, 2 saunas, no-smoking rooms* 🖃 *AE, DC, MC, V.*

$$ 🛏 **Ferrum.** Part of the Scandic Hotels chain, this late-1960s-vintage hotel is near the railway station. Rooms have wood floors and modern standard furniture. ⊠ *Lars Janssonsg. 15, 981 31* ☎ *0980/398600* 🖷 *0980/398611* ⊕ *www.scandic-hotels.com* 🛏 *171 rooms* ⚓ *3 restaurants, 2 bars, sauna, gym, dance club, meeting room, no-smoking rooms* 🖃 *AE, DC, MC, V.*

¢ 🛏 **Järnvägshotellet.** Dating from 1903, this small hotel has the advantage of being close to the railway station. ⊠ *Bangårdsv. 7, 981 34* ☎ *0980/84444* ⊕ *www.jarnvagshotellet.com* 🛏 *20 rooms* ⚓ *Restaurant, breakfast room, no-smoking rooms* 🖃 *DC, MC, V* 🍴 *BP.*

en route   Driving south from Kiruna toward Muddus National Park, you'll pass several small former mining villages before coming into the **Kalixälv** (Kalix River) Valley, where the countryside becomes more settled, with small farms and fertile meadows replacing the wilder northern landscape.

Jukkasjärvi

❷ *16 km (10 mi) east of Kiruna.*

The history of Jukkasjärvi, a Sámi village by the shores of the fast-flowing Torneälven (Torne River), dates from the early 16th century, when a market was already here. There is a wooden church from the 17th century and a small open-air museum that evokes a sense of Sámi life in times gone by.

If you are gastronomically adventuresome, you may want to sample one of the most unusual of all Sámi delicacies: a cup of thick black coffee with *kaffeost*, small lumps of goat cheese. After the cheese sits in the coffee for a bit, you fish it out with a spoon and eat it, then drink the coffee.

Where to Stay & Eat

¢ ✕🛏 **Jukkasjärvi Wärdshus.** The restaurant specializes in Norrland cuisine—characterized by reindeer, wild berries, mushrooms, dried and smoked meats, salted fish, fermented herring, and rich sauces using thick creams—and is the lifework of its manager, Yngve Bergqvist. The manor has one large honeymoon suite with wood floors and antique furniture; there are 45 cabins around it, 30 with bathroom, kitchen, and two bedrooms with bunk beds. Breakfast is not included. River-rafting and canoeing trips can be arranged. ⊠ *Marknadsv. 63, 981 91* ☎ *0980/66800* 🖷 *0980/66890* 🛏 *1 suite, 30 cabins* ⚓ *Restaurant, sauna, meeting room* 🖃 *AE, DC, MC, V.*

FodorśChoice ★

★ $ 🛏 **Ice Hotel.** At the peak of winter, tourists are drawn by the annual construction of the world's largest igloo, which opens for business as a hotel in mid-December continuing through April, after which it melts away, until being revised and built again nine months later. Made of snow, ice, and sheet metal, the Ice Hotel offers rooms for 40 guests, who spend the night in specially insulated sleeping bags on top of layers of reindeer skins and spruce boughs. At the Absolute Icebar, colored electric lights liven up the solid-ice walls. Breakfast is served in the sauna, with a view of the (nonelectric) northern lights. The entire hotel is designated nonsmoking, as it takes only a few puffs to tarnish the snow-white interiors. ☒ *Marknadsv. 63, 981 91 Jukkasjärvi* ☎ *0980/66800* 🖷 *0980/ 66890* ⊕ *www.icehotel.com* 🛏 *120 beds without bath, 18 suites* ♨ *Restaurant, bar, sauna, cross-country skiing, snowmobiling, chapel, meeting room, no smoking* 🖃 *AE, DC, MC, V* ☉ *Closed May–Nov.*

Sports & the Outdoors

A challenging local activity is riding the rapids of the Torne River in an inflatable boat. In winter Jukkasjärvi also offers dogsled rides and snow-mobile safaris. For more information call the **Ice Hotel** (☎ 0980/66800) or the Kiruna Lappland Tourist Office.

Kebnekaise

❸ *85 km (53 mi) west of Kiruna.*

At 7,000 feet above sea level, Kebnekaise is Sweden's highest mountain, but you'll need to be in good physical shape just to get to it. From Kiruna you travel about 66 km (41 mi) west to the Sámi village of Nikkalu-okta (there are two buses a day from Kiruna in the summer). From Nikkaluokta it is a hike of 19 km (12 mi) to the Kebnekaise Fjällsta-tion (mountain station), at the foot of Kebnekaise, though you can take a boat 5 km (3 mi) across Lake Ladtjojaure. Kebnekaise itself is rela-tively easy to climb, provided there's good weather and you're in shape; extensive mountaineering equipment is not necessary. If you feel up to more walking, the track continues past the Kebnekaise Fjällstation to become part of what is known as Kungsleden (the Royal Trail), a 500-km (280-mi) trail through the mountains from Abisko National Park, in the north, to Hemavan, in southern Lappland.

Where to Stay

$ 🏠 **Kebnekaise Fjällstation.** This rustic, wooden mountain station consists of six buildings. Choose between the main building, with its heavy wood beams, wood floors, and wood bunk beds—five per room—and the newer annexes, where more modern rooms each contain two or four beds. All guests share the use of a service house, with toilets, showers, and sauna. Though the main lodge is closed in fall and winter, one annex stays open year-round. The facility is 19 km (12 mi) from Nikkaluokta and can be reached by footpath, a combination of boat and hiking, or helicopter. Guided mountain tours are available. ☒ *981 29 Kiruna* ☎ *0980/55000, off-season, contact Abisko tourist office* 🖷 *0980/55048* 🛏 *196 beds without bath* ♨ *Restaurant, bar, sauna* 🖃 *AE, V* ☉ *Closed mid-Aug.–mid-Mar.*

Sports & the Outdoors

All the regional tourist offices can supply details of skiing holidays, but never forget the extreme temperatures and weather conditions. For the really adventuresome, the **Kebnekaise mountain station** (☎ 0980/55000) offers combined skiing and climbing weeks at around SKr 8,700, including lodging and all meals. It also offers weeklong combined dogsledding, skiing, and climbing holidays in the mountains. Because of the extreme cold and the danger involved, be sure to have proper equipment. Con-sult the mountain station well in advance for advice.

Kvikkjokk & Sarek National Park

❹ *310 km (193 mi) southwest of Kiruna via Route 45.*

Sarek is Sweden's largest high-mountain area and was molded by the last ice age. The mountains have been sculpted by glaciers, of which there are about 100 in the park. The mountain area totals 487,000 acres, a small portion of which is forest, bogs, and waterways. The remainder is bare mountain that is either totally vegetation free or is covered by low-growing alpine vegetation. The park has 90 peaks some 6,000 feet above sea level.

The Rapaätno River, which drains the park, runs through the lovely, desolate Rapadalen (Rapa Valley). The area is marked by a surprising variety of landscapes—luxuriant green meadows contrast with the snowy peaks of the mountains. Moose, bears, wolverines, lynx, ermines, hares, arctic foxes, red foxes, and mountain lemmings inhabit the terrain. Bird life includes ptarmigan, willow grouse, teals, wigeon, tufted ducks, blue-throats, and warblers. Golden eagles, rough-legged buzzards, and merlins have also been spotted here.

Visiting Sarek demands a good knowledge of mountains and a familiarity with the outdoors. The park can be dangerous in winter because of avalanches and snowstorms. In summer, however, despite its unpredictable, often inhospitable climate, it attracts large numbers of experienced hikers. At Kvikkjokk, a major overnight base for visitors, hikers can choose between a trail through the Tarradalen (Tarra Valley), which divides the Sarek from Padjelanta National Park, to the west, or part of the Kungsleden Trail, which crosses about 15 km (9 mi) of Sarek's southeastern corner.

Skaite & Muddus National Park

❺ *225 km (140 mi) south of Kiruna via E10 and Route 45.*

Established in 1942, Muddus National Park is less mountainous and spectacular than Sarek. Its 121,770 acres are mainly taken up by virgin coniferous forest, some of whose trees may be as much as 600 years old. The park's 3,680 acres of water is composed primarily of two huge lakes at the center of the park and the Muddusjåkkå River, which tumbles spectacularly through a gorge with 330-foot-high sheer rock walls and includes a waterfall crashing 140 feet down. The highest point of Muddus is Sör-Stubba Mountain, 2,158 feet above sea level. From Skaite, where you enter the park, a series of well-marked trails begins. There are four well-equipped, overnight, communal rest huts and two tourist cabins. The park is home to bears, lynx, wolverines, moose, ermines, weasels, otters, and many bird species. A popular pastime is picking cloudberries (a member of the raspberry family) in autumn.

Jokkmokk

❻ *225 km (140 mi) south of Kiruna via E10 and Route 45.*

Jokkmokk is an important center of Sámi culture. Each February it is the scene of the region's largest market, where everything from frozen reindeer meat to Sámi handcrafted wooden utensils is sold. If you're an outdoor enthusiast, Jokkmokk may be the best base in Norrland for you. The village has good campsites and is surrounded by wilderness. The local tourist office sells fishing permits, which cost SKr 50 for 24 hours, SKr 100 for three days, SKr 175 for one week, and SKr 350 for the entire year. The office can also supply lists of camping and housekeeping cabins.

Where to Stay

$ ⊡ **Hotel Jokkmokk.** A modern hotel this luxurious seems incongruous in this remote region but is welcome nevertheless. The hotel is in the town center, but the staff can arrange dogsled rides and helicopter trips to the Sarek and Muddus national parks; there is excellent fishing

FodorśChoice
★

nearby. ✉ *Solg. 45, S962 23* ☎ *0971/77700* 🖨 *0971/77790* 🌐 *www. hoteljokkmokk.se* 🛏 *75 rooms* ♨ *Restaurant, sauna, meeting room, no-smoking rooms* 🍴 *AE, DC, MC, V.*

¢ 🏠 **Gästis.** This small hotel in central Jokkmokk opened in 1915. Rooms are standard, with television, shower, and either carpeted or vinyl floors. ✉ *Herrev. 1, S962 31* ☎ *0971/10012* 🖨 *0971/10044* 🛏 *30 rooms* ♨ *Restaurant, room TVs, sauna, meeting room, no-smoking rooms* 🍴 *AE, DC, MC, V.*

¢ 🏠 **Jokkmokks Turistcenter.** This complex is in a pleasant forest area near Luleälven, 3 km (2 mi) from the railway station. ✉ *Nortudden, Box 75, S962 22* ☎ *0971/12370* 🖨 *0971/12476* 🛏 *59 cabins with bath* ♨ *4 pools, sauna, meeting room* 🍴 *DC, MC, V.*

Boden

❼ *290 km (180 mi) southeast of Kiruna, 130 km (81 mi) southeast of Jokkmokk on Route 97.*

Boden, the nation's largest garrison town, dates from 1809, when Sweden lost Finland to Russia and feared an invasion of its own territory. The **Garrisonsmuseet** (Garrison Museum) contains exhibits from Swedish military history, with an extensive collection of weapons and uniforms. ✉ *Sveav. 10* ☎ *0921/68399* 🎫 *Free* ⊙ *Mid-June–late Aug., Mon.–Sat. 11–4, Sun. noon–4.*

Luleå

❽ *340 km (211 mi) southeast of Kiruna via E10 and E4.*

The northernmost major town in Sweden, Luleå is an important port at the top of the Gulf of Bothnia, at the mouth of the Luleälv (Lule River). The town was some 10 km (6 mi) farther inland when it was first granted its charter in 1621, but by 1649 trade had grown so much that it was moved closer to the sea. Gammelstad Church Town, at the site of the original city, is now protected by the UNESCO World Heritage list. The development of Kiruna and the iron trade is linked, literally, by a railway, with the fortunes of Luleå, where a steelworks was set up in the 1940s. Like its fellow port towns farther south—Piteå, Skellefteå, Umeå, and Sundsvall—Luleå is a very modern and nondescript city, but it has some reasonable hotels. A beautiful archipelago of hundreds of islands hugs the coastline. Many of these islands can be reached by car in the wintertime through a 250-km (166-mi) network of roads on the frozen sea. Wintertime visitors with kids shouldn't miss the iceslide in the city park: each year it's in the shape of a different indigenous animal.

The **Norrbottens Museum** has one of the best collections of Sámi ethnography in the world. ✉ *Hermelinsparken 2* ☎ *0920/243502* 🎫 *Free* ⊙ *Weekdays 10–4, weekends noon–4.*

Where to Stay & Eat

★ $–$$ ✕🏠 **Arctic.** Right in the town center, the Arctic is known locally for its restaurant, which serves local specialties. The hotel is warm and cozy, with tastefully decorated rustic rooms. ✉ *Sandviksg. 80, 972 34* ☎ *0920/ 10980* 🖨 *0920/60787* 🌐 *www.arctichotel.se* 🛏 *94 rooms* ♨ *Restaurant, hot tub, sauna, meeting room, no-smoking rooms* 🍴 *AE, DC, MC, V.*

$$$ 🏠 **Elite Stads Hotellet.** This large, central Best Western hotel has nightly—sometimes boisterous—dancing. Rooms in the building dating to 1903 are spacious and carpeted, with turn-of-the-20th-century furnishings. ✉ *Storg. 15, 97128* ☎ *0920/67000* 🖨 *0920/67092* 🛏 *135 rooms, 3 suites* ♨ *Restaurant, café, lounge, minibars, sauna, dance club, meeting room, no-smoking rooms* 🍴 *AE, DC, MC, V* 🍴 *BP.*

$$ 🖵 **Scandic.** This hotel on a small tarn has an extremely pleasant setting and is 2 km (1 mi) from the railway station. ⊠ *Banv. 3, 973 46* ☎ *0920/ 276400* 🖶 *0920/276411* ⊕ *www.scandic-hotels.com* 🛏 *160 rooms* 🍴 *Restaurant, no-smoking rooms, indoor pool, sauna, gym, meeting room* 🖃 *AE, DC, MC, V.*

$ 🖵 **Aveny.** Rooms are of varying sizes and colors, but all are spotless and fresh. It's close to the railway station. ⊠ *Hermelinsg. 10, 973 46* ☎ *0920/221820* 🖶 *0920/220122* 🛏 *24 rooms* 🍴 *No-smoking rooms* 🖃 *AE, DC, MC, V.*

¢ 🖵 **Amber.** A particularly fine old building listed on the Historic Register, this hotel is close to the railway station. Rooms are modern. ⊠ *Stationsg. 67, 972 34* ☎ *0920/10200* 🖶 *0920/87906* 🛏 *16 rooms* 🍴 *Cable TV, minibars, no-smoking rooms* 🖃 *AE, DC, MC, V.*

Norrland & Norrbotten A to Z

To research prices, get advice from other travelers, and book travel arrangements, visit www.fodors.com.

AIR TRAVEL

CARRIERS There are two nonstop SAS flights a day from Stockholm to Kiruna Airport and three additional flights via Luleå. Check SAS for specific times. 🔢 **SAS** ☎ 0770/727727, from outside Sweden: 8/7972688.

AIRPORTS

In summer buses connect Kiruna Airport, which is 5 km (3 mi) from Kiruna, to the city center; the fare is about SKr 50. A taxi from the airport to the center of Kiruna costs about SKr 200; book through the airline or call the taxi directly. 🔢 **Kiruna Airport** ☎ 0980/68001 ⊕ www.lfv.se. **Taxi Kiruna** ☎ 0980/12020.

CAR RENTAL

🔢 **Major Agencies Avis** ⊠ Kiruna Airport, Kiruna ☎ 0980/13080. **Europcar** ⊠ Forv. 33, Kiruna ☎ 0980/80759. **Hertz** ⊠ Industriv. 5, Kiruna ☎ 0980/19000.

CAR TRAVEL

Since public transportation is nonexistent in this part of the country, having a car is essential. The few roads are well built and maintained, although spring thaws can present potholes. Keep in mind that habitations are few and far between in this wilderness region.

EMERGENCIES

For emergencies dial 112. A medical advisory service in Luleå is available 24 hours a day.

There are no late-night pharmacies in Norrbotten. The pharmacy at the Gallerian shopping center in Kiruna is open weekdays 9:30–6 and Saturday 9:30–1. 🔢 **Gallerian Pharmacy** ⊠ Föreningsg. 6, Kiruna ☎ 0980/18775. **Jokkmokk Health Center** ⊠ Lappstav. 9, Jokkmokk ☎ 0971/44444. **Kiruna Health Center** ⊠ Thuleg. 29, Kiruna ☎ 0980/73000. **Sunderbu Hospital Luleå** ⊠ Luleå ☎ 0920/282000.

TOURS

Local tourist offices have information on guided tours involving dogsledding, snowmobiling, and ice fishing. Samelands Resor arranges tours to points of interest in Lappland. Call the Swedish Sámi Association for Sámi tours. 🔢 **Samelands Resor** ⊠ Hermelinsg. 20, 962 33, Jokkmokk ☎ 0971/10606 ⊕ www. samelandsresor.com. **Swedish Sámi Association** ⊠ Brog. 5, 903 25, Umeå ☎ 090/141180.

TRAIN TRAVEL
The best and cheapest way to get to Kiruna is to take the evening sleeper from Stockholm on Tuesday, Wednesday, or Saturday, when the fare is reduced to SKr 595 for a single. The regular one-way price is SKr 600 when sharing a cabin with six people and SKr 700 when sharing a cabin with three people, twice that for round-trip. You'll arrive at around lunchtime the next day. To book a train, call Tåg Kompaniet, the rail company that handles northern Sweden.

🚆 **Tåg Kompaniet** ☎ 020/444111, from outside Sweden: 690/691017.

VISITOR INFORMATION
Norrbottens Turistråd is the regional tourist office. Local tourist offices are listed below by town.

🚆 Tourist Information **Abisko** ✉ 980 24 Abisko ☎ 0980/40200. **Gällivare** ✉ Centralplan 3 ☎ 0970/16660. **Jokkmokk** ✉ Stortorget 4 ☎ 0971/22250. **Kiruna** ✉ Folkets Hus ☎ 0980/18880. **Luleå** ✉ Storgatan 43B ☎ 0920/293500.

UNDERSTANDING SWEDEN

CHRONOLOGY

ca. 12000 BC	The first migrations into Sweden.
ca. 2000	Tribes from southern Europe, mostly Germanic peoples, migrate toward Denmark.
ca. 770	The Viking Age begins. For the next 250 years Scandinavians set sail on frequent expeditions to areas stretching from the Baltic to the Irish seas, and even to the Mediterranean as far as Constantinople and to North America, employing superior ships and weapons and efficient military organization.
ca. 800– ca. 1000	Swedes control river trade routes between the Baltic and Black seas; establish Novgorod, Kiev, and other cities.
830	Frankish monk Ansgar makes one of the first attempts to Christianize Sweden and builds the first church in Slesvig, Denmark. Sweden is not successfully Christianized until the end of the 11th century, when the temple at Uppsala, a center for pagan resistance, is destroyed.
1000	King Olof Skötkonung becomes the first Swedish king to be baptized and becomes the country's first Christian king.
1100	Christianity is spread throughout Sweden as a result of German missionaries in the 800s and English missionaries in the 1000s.
1248	Erik Eriksson appoints Birger as jarl, in charge of military affairs and expeditions abroad. Birger improves women's rights, makes laws establishing peace in the home and church, and begins building Stockholm.
1250	Stockholm is officially founded.
1319	Sweden and Norway form a union that lasts until 1335.
1370	The Treaty of Stralsund gives the north German trading centers of the Hanseatic League free passage through Danish waters and full control of Danish herring fisheries for 15 years. German power increases throughout Scandinavia.
1397	The Kalmar Union is formed as a result of the dynastic ties between Sweden, Denmark, and Norway, the geographical position of the Scandinavian states, and the growing influence of Germans in the Baltic. Erik of Pomerania is crowned king of the Kalmar Union.
1477	University of Uppsala, Sweden's oldest university, is founded.
1520	Christian II, ruler of the Kalmar Union, executes 82 people who oppose the Scandinavian union, an event known as the Stockholm Bloodbath. Sweden secedes from the union three years later. Norway remains tied to Denmark and becomes a Danish province in 1536.
1527	A Swedish national church is created by parliamentary decree at the Swedish Riksdag in Västerås.
1523	Gustav Ericsson founds Swedish Vasa dynasty as King Gustav I Vasa.
1534	Count Christoffer of Oldenburg and his army demand the restoration of Christian II as king of Denmark, initiating a civil war between supporters of Christian II and supporters of Prince Christian (later King Christian III).
1541	The Bible is published in Swedish.

1593 The Lutheran Church is adopted as the national church of Sweden.

1611–16 The Kalmar War: Denmark wages war against Sweden in hopes of restoring the Kalmar Union.

1611–60 This crucial era is initiated by the actions of Gustav II Adolphus, the great warrior king (he dies in 1632). During this time Sweden defeats Denmark in the Thirty Years' War and becomes the greatest power in Scandinavia as well as in northern and central Europe.

1632–54 Queen Christina reigns. In 1654 she abdicates the throne, converts to Catholicism, leaves for Rome, and is accepted by the pope.

1660 The Peace of Copenhagen establishes the modern boundaries of Denmark, Sweden, and Norway.

1666 Lund University, Scandinavia's largest university, is founded in Lund, Sweden.

1668 The Bank of Sweden, now the world's oldest central bank, is founded.

1700–21 In the Great Northern War, Sweden, now led by Karl XII, first broadens its position, then loses it to Russia, to which it is forced to cede southeastern Finland and the Baltic provinces of Livonia, Estonia, and Ingria.

1773 Gustavo III creates the Swedish Opera Institution, which is still functioning today.

1782 The Royal Opera House in Stockholm, designed by architect C. F. Adelcrantz, is inaugurated.

1801–14 The Napoleonic Wars are catastrophic for Denmark economically and politically: its policy of armed neutrality fails, the English destroy the Danish fleet in 1801, Copenhagen is devastated during the bombardment of 1807, and Sweden, after Napoléon's defeat at the Battle of Leipzig, attacks Denmark and forces the Danish surrender of Norway. The Treaty of Kiel, in 1814, calls for a union between Norway and Sweden despite Norway's desire for independence. The Danish monarchy is left with three parts: the Kingdom of Denmark and the duchies of Schleswig and Holstein.

1807 During the Napoleonic Wars, Swedish king Gustav III joins the coalition against France, reluctantly agreeing to war against it and Russia.

1809 Sweden surrenders the Åland Islands and Finland to Russia, Finland becomes a grand duchy of the Russian Empire, and the Instrument of Government, Sweden's constitution, is adopted.

1818 Sweden takes a Frenchman as king, Karl XIV Johann, who establishes the Bernadotte dynasty.

ca. 1850 The building of railroads begins in Scandinavia.

1889 The Swedish Social Democratic Party is founded.

1896 The first moving picture film is shown in Sweden.

1901 Alfred Nobel, the Swedish millionaire chemist and industrialist, initiates the Nobel prizes.

1905 Norway's union with Sweden is dissolved.

1911–1960 Jussi Björling lives to become Sweden's most renowned tenor singer and is said to be the world's second best in history, after Caruso.

1914   At the outbreak of World War I Sweden declares neutrality but is effectively blockaded.

1918   Swedish women gain the right to vote, with some restrictions.

1918   Birgit Nilsson, who would become Sweden's best-known and most acclaimed woman opera singer, is born. In 1958 she became the first non-Italian to open the season at famed La Scala opera house in Milan.

1920   The Scandinavian countries join the League of Nations.

1921   Restrictions on women's suffrage are lifted.

1932   The Social Democrat Party wins the parliamentary elections and Per Albin Hansson becomes prime minister. The Social Democrats will hang on to power for the next 44 years.

1939   Sweden declares its neutrality in World War II.

1945   Swedish diplomat Raoul Wallenberg disappears into the Soviet gulag. Two years later Soviet officials report that Wallenberg has died in captivity, but evidence remains inconclusive.

1946   Sweden joins the United Nations.

1949   Sweden declines membership in NATO.

1952   The Nordic Council, which promotes cooperation among the Nordic parliaments, is founded.

1957   A Swedish referendum votes yes to a compulsory state pension for people age 67 and over.

1972   Sweden, on the basis of its neutral foreign policy, declines membership in the European Union (EU).

1974   The pop group ABBA wins the European song contest in Brighton, England, with the song *Waterloo*.

1975   Sweden's Instrument of Government of 1809 is revised and replaced with a new Instrument of Government. This constitution reduces the voting age to 18 and removes many of the king's powers and responsibilities.

1976   At only 20 years old, Björn Borg wins the first of five Wimbledon titles. King Carl XIV Gustaf marries Silvia Sommerlath of Germany. A right-wing coalition wrings power from Sweden's Social Democrats, ending the latter's uninterrupted 44-year reign.

1980   Fifty-eight percent of Sweden's voters advocate minimizing the use of nuclear reactors at Sweden's four power plants.

1980   Björn Borg wins his fifth consecutive Wimbledon tennis title.

1981   Björn Borg wins the French Tennis Open for the sixth time.

1982   Swedish actress Ingrid Bergman, the winner of three Oscar awards, dies at the age of 67. She was best known for the films *Casablanca* and *Spellbound*.

1986   Sweden's prime minister, Olof Palme, is assassinated for unknown reasons. Ingvar Carlsson succeeds him.

1986   Sweden is the first country to detect nuclear fallout from the Soviet power plant in Chernobyl, unknown to the West at the time.

1987   The Swedish national ice hockey team, Tre Kronor, wins the world ice hockey championship in Vienna for the first time in 25 years.

1991   The Social Democrats are voted out of office, and the new government launches a privatization policy.

1992   Sweden's Riksbank (National Bank) overnight raises interest rates to a world record of 500% in an effort to defend the Swedish krona against speculation.

1994   The ferry *Estonia,* en route from Tallinn to Stockholm, sinks in the worst maritime disaster in Europe since World War II. Eight hundred fifty-two people die. The right-wing coalition government loses the parliamentary elections to the Social Democrats, and Ingvar Carlsson steps up as prime minister.

1995   Finland and Sweden join the EU in January.

1998   Stockholm is named the 1998 Cultural Capital of Europe, hosting arts, culture, and nature events throughout the year. The Social Democrats, led by Göran Persson, win the parliamentary elections.

2000   The Öresund road and rail bridge linking Sweden with Denmark is opened, effectively connecting Sweden to continental Europe.

2001   Sweden holds the presidency of the EU for six months.

2002   As most of Europe adopts the euro currency, Sweden, Denmark and Britain opt to keep their respective currencies. Prime Minister Göran Persson wins a second term in the parliamentary elections.

2003   Sweden's foreign minister, Anna Lindh, is assasinated in Stockholm. The Swedish people again reject adopting the Euro as their national currency in a referendum in September.

SWEDISH SPECTACULAR

SWEDEN REQUIRES THE VISITOR to travel far, in both distance and attitude. Approximately the size of California, Sweden reaches as far north as the Arctic fringes of Europe, where glacier-top mountains and thousands of acres of pine, spruce, and birch forests are broken here and there by wild rivers, countless pristine lakes, and desolate moorland. In the more populous south, roads meander through mile after mile of softly undulating countryside, skirting lakes and passing small villages with sharp-pointed church spires. Here the lush forests that dominate Sweden's northern landscape have largely fallen to the plow.

Once the dominant power of the region, Sweden has traditionally looked mostly inward, seeking to find its own Nordic solutions. During the cold war it tried with considerable success to steer its famous "middle way" between the two superpowers, both economically and politically. Its citizens were in effect subjected to a giant social experiment aimed at creating a perfectly just society, one that adopted the best aspects of both socialism and capitalism.

In the late 1980s, as it slipped into the worst economic recession since the 1930s, Sweden made adjustments that lessened the role of its all-embracing welfare state in the lives of its citizens. Although fragile, the conservative coalition, which defeated the long-incumbent Social Democrats in the fall of 1991, attempted to make further cutbacks in welfare spending as the country faced one of the largest budget deficits in Europe. In a kind of nostalgic backlash, the populace voted the Social Democrats back into power in 1994, hoping to recapture the party's policy of cradle-to-grave protection. The world economy didn't exactly cooperate; although Sweden appeared to be crawling toward stability in the mid-1990s, the struggle to balance the budget intensified again by the end of the decade. The Social Democrats won a further victory in 2002, but the social safety net once so heavily relied upon by the Swedes remains somewhat incomplete; a reflection perhaps of modern economics rather than any temporary budgetary hiccup.

Sweden took off with the rest of the globe with the explosion of the Internet and new technology and watched with it as the bubble burst at the start of the new millennium. It continues to be one of the world's dominant players in the information-based economy. Although many start-up companies (and well-established giants such as Ericsson) have taken their share of economic bumps and bruises, as a whole there remains a lively entrepreneurial spirit and an intense interest in the business possibilities of the Internet and wireless communications. During the past few years Sweden has received substantial international press coverage for its innovative technological solutions, new management philosophies, and unique Web design.

New technology is widely used and accepted throughout Sweden. The country has the highest Internet penetration in the world, and more than 50% of the population uses cell phones. If there's an expensive new gadget out on the market, chances are you'll see a stylish Stockholmer using it.

On the social front, an influx of immigrants, particularly from countries outside Europe, is reshaping what was once a homogeneous society. Sweden continues to face political and social difficulties in the areas of immigration and integration, although the tension appears to be fading slightly as more and more artists, musicians, actors, directors, and writers with immigrant backgrounds are receiving national recognition for their work. As considerable public debate about these issues sweeps the country, a society known for its blue-eyed blondes is considering what it means to be a Swede.

Another sign that Swedes seem more willing than ever to refashion their image was Sweden's decision to join the European Union (EU) in January 1995, a move that represented a radical break with its traditional independent stance on international issues. Thus far, the domestic benefits of membership are still debated heavily, but the country's exporting industries have made considerable gains. During its relatively short membership Sweden has held the presidency of the Union and hosted the first ever visit by a sitting U.S. president, when George W. Bush visited Göteborg for a meeting with EU member states. Despite these landmark moments and perhaps partly because of the lack of concrete results in being part of the EU, the first years of the millennium have seen citizens undecided about the value of membership and politicians struggling to demonstrate its importance.

The country possesses stunning natural assets. In the forests, moose, deer, bears, and lynx roam, coexisting with the whine of power saws and the rumble of automatic logging machines. Logging remains the country's economic backbone. Environmental awareness, however, is high. Fish abound in sparkling lakes and tumbling rivers, and sea eagles and ospreys soar over myriad pine-clad islands in the archipelagoes off the east and west coasts.

The country is Europe's fourth largest, 449,963 square km (173,731 square mi) in area, and its population of 8.8 million is thinly spread. If, like Greta Garbo—one of its most famous exports—you enjoy being alone, you've come to the right place. A law called Allemansrätt guarantees public access to the countryside; NO TRESPASSING signs are seldom seen.

Sweden stretches 1,563 km (977 mi) from the barren Arctic north to the fertile plains of the south. Contrasts abound, but they are neatly tied together by a superbly efficient infrastructure, embracing air, road, and rail. You can catch salmon in the far north and, thanks to the excellent domestic air network, have it cooked by the chef of your luxury hotel in Stockholm later the same day.

The seasons contrast savagely: Sweden is usually warm and exceedingly light in summer, then cold and dark in winter, when the sea may freeze and northern iron railway lines may snap. Spring and fall tend to make brief appearances, if any.

Sweden is also an arresting mixture of ancient and modern. The countryside is dotted with runic stones recalling its Viking past: trade beginning in the 8th century went as far east as Kiev and as far south as Constantinople and the Mediterranean, expanded to the British Isles in the 9th through 11th centuries, and settled in Normandy in the 10th century. Small timbered farmhouses and maypoles—around which villagers still dance at Midsummer in their traditional costumes—evoke both their pagan early history and more recent agrarian culture.

Many of the country's cities are sci-fi modern, their shop windows filled with the latest in consumer goods and fashions, but Swedes are reluctant urbanites: their hearts and souls are in the forests and the archipelagoes, and to there they faithfully retreat in the summer and on weekends to take their holidays, pick berries, or just listen to the silence. The skills of the woodcarver, the weaver, the leather worker, and the glassblower are highly prized. Similarly, Swedish humor is earthy and slapstick. Despite the praise lavished abroad on introspective dramatic artists such as August Strindberg and Ingmar Bergman, it is the simple trouser-dropping farce that will fill Stockholm's theaters, the scatological joke that will get the most laughs.

Although it isn't unusual to see gray-haired men in pastel sweaters playing saxophones on TV, or to warp back to the 1950s in modern concert halls and discos, Sweden's cultural tenor also incorporates a host of global trends. Most radio stations play a mix of Swedish, American, and British hits, and a number of Swedish television programs track international music, art, and culture. Films from all over the world can be seen at the box office, although it's Hollywood that dominates. And when it comes to fashion and design, Stockholm is certainly among the trendiest cities in the world. Glossy magazines like *Wallpaper* seem to be in constant discussion about "cool Stockholm" and the like.

Despite the much-publicized sexual liberation of Swedes, the joys of hearth and home are most prized in what remains in many ways a conservative society. Conformity, not liberty, is the real key to the Swedish character; however, the good of the collective is slowly being replaced by that of the individual as socialism begins to lose its past appeal.

At the same time, Swedes remain devoted royalists and patriots, avidly following the fortunes of King Carl XVI Gustaf,

Queen Silvia, and their children in the media and raising the blue-and-yellow national flag each morning on the flagpoles of their country cottages. Few nations, in fact, make as much of an effort to preserve and defend their natural heritage.

It is sometimes difficult in cities such as Stockholm, Göteborg, or Malmö to realize that you are in an urban area. Right in the center of Stockholm, you can fish for salmon or go for a swim. In Göteborg's busy harbor you can sit aboard a ship bound for the archipelago and watch fish jump out of the water; in Malmö hares hop around in the downtown parks. It is this pristine quality of life that can make a visit to Sweden a step out of time, a relaxing break from the modern world.

— Updated by Rob Hincks

AT A RECEPTION for visiting dignitaries, the mayor of Stockholm surprised his guests by serving them glasses of a clear liquid that turned out to be water. It came, he explained, from the water surrounding this island city, and the purpose of the tongue-in-cheek gesture was to demonstrate that modern cities can afford clean environments. In fact, Stockholm has won the European Sustainable City Award in competition with 90-odd other cities, and a large swathe of Stockholm, including the vast royal domains, has been declared a national park for the benefit and enjoyment of the populace.

There were sound, practical reasons for building Stockholm on the 14 islands that command access from the Baltic Sea to Lake Mälaren. Back in the 13th century, after the Vikings had retired from plunder and discovery, Estonian pirates had taken to pillaging the shores of the lake, which extends deep into the Swedish heartland. Birger Jarl, the ruler who founded Sweden's first dynasty, put a stop to all that by stockading the islands the pirates had to pass. His effigy lies in gilded splendor at the foot of the city hall tower.

Stockholm without water would be unthinkable. It's the water that gives it beauty, character, life. The north shore and the south are, to be truthful, rather Germanic in character, not too different from, say, Zurich or Berlin. But watch them from across a busy waterway, mirrored in the blue lake, and they become invested with a lively charm.

The pearl in the oyster, however, is the small island known as Gamla Stan, or Old Town, dominated by the tawny-color, massive Royal Palace, designed by Nicodemus Tessin in the 17th century and completed in the 18th. In the Middle Ages so many German merchants settled here that a law was passed to limit their number on the city council to less than half the members. The winding streets are lined with old houses in yellow, ocher, and the occasional oxblood red. Some of the city's most attractive small hotels, gourmet restaurants, and lively jazz clubs are here. To many people, the greatest treasure, dating to 1489, is found inside Storkyrkan, the Stockholm cathedral, next door to the palace: a larger-than-life, polychrome wooden statue of St. George slaying the dragon.

Skeppsholmen, a smaller island east of Gamla Stan and once the nation's principal navy base, is an idyllic place for a stroll and great for art-lovers. The Museum of Modern Art by the Spanish architect Rafael Moneo opened in 1998 and is one of the great contemporary museums. It blends in well with other structures, such as the "old" modern museum, a former armory and a trendsetter since its opening in 1958; it is now becoming the Museum of Architecture. Also on Skeppsholmen is the exquisite East Asiatic Museum, another Tessin creation, which houses one of the world's finest collections of Chinese art.

After you cross the bridge from Skeppsholmen on your way back to the city center, you'll walk past the National Museum. You'll do well to stop there—not just for its Rembrandts and Swedish masters of centuries past, but also for its new atrium restaurant, one of the city's best, in the piazzalike inner courtyard.

The piers of Stockholm's islands are lined with so many vessels of every category, from cruise ships and seagoing roll-on/roll-off vessels to island-hopping steamboats and pocket-size ferries, that it would seem impossible to squeeze in another motorboat, sailboat, or sloop. There were more than 100,000 of them at last count, and still the number keeps growing. The waterborne traffic jam when they return on a Sunday night in summer after a weekend at sea is something to behold.

Most Stockholm sailors travel no farther than one of the 25,000 islands and skerries that make up the Stockholm archipelago, extending 73 km (45 mi) east into the Baltic Sea. A red-timber cottage on one of these islands in the Baltic is most Swedes' idea of ultimate bliss, and there they seek to re-create the simple life as they imagine their forefathers to have lived it.

A fair approximation of archipelago life is just a 25-minute ferry ride from the city center. This is Fjäderholmarna, or Feather Island, an islet that not long ago was a navy munitions dump. The rock is worn smooth by retreating Ice Age glaciers, there's a clump of yellow reeds at the water's edge, and on the rock is the inevitable red cottage, windows and corners trimmed with white, against a backdrop of dark green foliage. There's a restaurant serving excellent Swedish specialties and a small colony of craftsmen making high-quality souvenirs.

Take a boat trip west from the city, and you're in a different world, verdant and tranquil. An hour away and you're at Drottningholm Palace, also designed by Nicodemus Tessin and now the residence of the royal family. The palace and its formal French garden are impressing and the little Chinese Pavilion enchanting, but the real gem is the 200-year-old and perfectly intact Drottningholm Court Theater, where period performances of operas by Mozart, Gluck, and other 18th-century composers are presented every summer. The orchestra wears wigs, the singers appear in original costumes, and the ingenious old stage machinery produces thunder and storms.

As you wander through the reception areas and dressing rooms, you'll be struck by the sparse, cool elegance of the decor and furnishings, a style borrowed from Louis XV but stripped down to the bare essentials. It may strike you, too, that this is not very different from modern Swedish interiors and design. Then you will have discovered a well-hidden truth: the Swedes, who take such pride in being modern, rational, and efficient, are secretly in love with the 18th century.

— Eric Sjogren

Eric Sjogren, a Swedish travel writer based in Brussels, is a frequent contributor to the *New York Times* and other publications.

ASTRID LINDGREN

APPROPRIATELY, the career of Astrid Lindgren, Sweden's best-known children's writer, author of the *Pippi Longstocking* books and many others, has a fairy-tale beginning. Once upon a time, Lindgren's seven-year-old daughter, Karin, ill in bed with pneumonia, begged her, "Tell me a story . . .tell me the story of Pippi Longstocking."

"Neither she nor I know where on earth she got that name from," says Lindgren. "That was the first time I ever heard it. I made up the character right there and then, told her a story, and only wrote it down much later."

Thus was born one of the most memorable characters in children's fiction, her adventures translated from Lindgren's native Swedish into more than 50 languages.

"A few years later I was awarded a prize for the stories and offered to share it with Karin," recalls Lindgren, "but by then she decided that she was too old. She said she was bored with Pippi."

With younger children all over the world, however, Pippi continues to strike a responsive chord: a little girl of indeterminate age with a gap-toothed smile, freckled face, and wild mop of ginger hair from which a braid juts lopsidedly out over each ear.

Phenomenally strong, irrepressibly cheeky, she lives independently of adults, with a horse and monkey in a tumbledown house, supporting herself from a hoard of gold coins. She has no table manners and doesn't go to school. She does just what she likes when she feels like doing it.

"Bertrand Russell once said that children dream of power the way that adults dream of sex," says Lindgren. "I was impressed with that at the time, and I think I must have had it in mind when I created Pippi."

Despite vociferous protests from educationalists and child psychologists, Pippi won immediate favor with kids. Lindgren has since created several other memorable characters, but Pippi remains the basis of her enormous popularity in her home country.

It would be well-nigh impossible to find a Swede who has not heard of Lindgren. She is *Tant Astrid,* Aunty Astrid, a gray-haired, nearsighted little old lady who is a symbol of hearth and home, of faith in traditional values and of love of rural Sweden, with its deep, dark pine forests, wide blue lakes, and meadows dotted with red-painted wooden houses.

The independent spirit that created such an unconventional character as Pippi Longstocking still exists within this grandmother, however, and using her awesome popularity, Lindgren has been partly responsible for the fall of one Swedish government and for forcing a second one in 1989 to draft radical new legislation protecting the rights of pets and farm animals, about which she has a bee in her bonnet.

She remains refreshingly unspoiled by all the adulation and attention she receives.

"When I go out, people come up to me in the street and tell me how much they've enjoyed my books, and children will hug and kiss me," she says. "Of course, that's very nice, but you know, somehow I always feel it's not happening to *me.*

"It's as though someone else had all that celebrity and I am standing alongside her."

The mere suggestion that she wields power brings a steely glint to her blue eyes. "Power? I have only the power of the word," she says. "I wouldn't want power in the real sense. That's the worst thing I know. People always abuse it."

Yet there is more than suspicion that, Pippi-like, she revels in the influence she, an ordinary (or perhaps one should say, extraordinary) citizen, can use to inject rebellious ideas into the heads of her youthful public and bend Sweden's rulers to her will.

One of her characters is *The World's Best Karlson.* Lovable figment of a little boy's imagination, Karlson is a jovial type who laughs at reality and flies around the house aided by a propeller set in the middle of his back. The Karlson books have become particularly popular in Russia, where *Literaturnaja Gaseta,* a literary review, has described the character as "the symbol of innocent, uncorrupted childhood, the childhood we as adults find so difficult to remember and accept."

The Satirical Theater in Moscow staged a play based on the character in the 1960s, and Lindgren says that when she visits Russia, taxi drivers always talk to her about Karlson.

Lindgren was delighted to hear that when former Swedish prime minister Ingvar Carlsson visited Moscow, many Russians were disappointed because he wasn't the *real* Karlson.

* * *

HOWEVER, SAYS LINDGREN, it is the stories of the Bullerby children that most closely approximate her own childhood. These feature the adventures of children from three families in a little village somewhere in Sweden and eulogize rural life set against a fondly painted picture of seasonal contrast. The Bullerby children are Lindgren's *nicest* characters: playful but, unlike Pippi, unwilling to overstep the line.

Bullerby is based on the little village of Sevedstorp, set amid the dense pine-and-spruce forests that cover the southern Swedish province of Småland, birthplace of her father, Samuel August Ericsson, who by the time Astrid was born, in 1907, had moved to the nearby town of Vimmerby.

Home was a simple clapboard house, painted red and with a glassed-in porch, surrounded by well-tended flower beds, daisy-strewn lawns, and apple trees. Her father had started life as a hired hand but wound up running his own farm. The family was reasonably well off, though there was rarely money left over for luxuries. Samuel Ericsson was an excellent storyteller, and many of the anecdotes he told his children surfaced later in Lindgren's books. Her mother, Hanna, wrote poetry in her youth and at one time dreamed of becoming a schoolteacher.

Lindgren was one of four children. She had an elder brother, Gunnar (born in 1906), and two younger sisters, Stina (born in 1911) and Ingegerd (born in 1916). All displayed literary talents of some kind or another: Gunnar became a member of

parliament renowned for his political satires, Stina a translator, and Ingegerd a journalist.

The innocent childhood fun and games described in the Bullerby books are, by and large, those of Astrid herself and her brother and sisters. "We played the whole time from morning to night, just like the children in the Bullerby stories," she says.

She enjoyed a warm relationship with Samuel August, a fact that is reflected time and again in her books, peopled in the main with warm, understanding, though often gruff fathers. She describes their mother, on the other hand, as a rather distant person, recalling that Hanna hugged her only once when she was a child. It was from her that she inherited her willpower, energy, and stubbornness, she says.

The creator of Pippi Longstocking rebelled against Hanna's authority just once as a child: "I was quite young—perhaps three or four—and one day I thought she was stupid so I decided to run away and hide in the outside toilet. I wasn't there for too long, and when I came back in, my brother and sisters had been given sweets. I thought this was so unfair that I kicked out in Mother's direction. I was taken into the front room and beaten."

When she started at the local school at the age of seven, in 1914, she was overcome with shyness (a traditional Swedish handicap) when the teacher called out her name and, instead of answering "yes," burst into tears.

The priest in charge of registering the new arrivals told her she could go and sit down instead of standing with the other children. "I absolutely didn't want to go and sit down." The tears subsided, and she now sees the incident as the day she broke through her "wall of shyness."

She was a conscientious pupil, remembered by classmate Ann-Marie Fries, the model for Madicken, another of her characters, as "unbelievably nimble. I remember her in the gym; she could climb from floor to ceiling like a monkey."

Astrid also began to show evidence of literary talents. Her essays were frequently read to the rest of the class, and when she was 13, one of them was even published in *Wimmerby Tidning,* Vimmerby's local newspaper. This one was titled "Life in Our Backyard" and described two small girls and the games they played. "They joked and called me Vimmerby's answer to Selma Lagerlöf, and I decided that if there was one thing I would never be it was an author."

She recalls her teens as a melancholy episode. "Like most teenagers, I thought I was ugly," she says, "and I just *never* fell in love. Everyone else was in love."

She left school at 16 and was given a job at *Wimmerby Tidning* reading proofs and was even allowed to do some reporting when she was assigned to cover some local events such as weddings and funerals.

In 1926 Astrid's blissful childhood came to a very definite end when, at the age of 18, she had an affair and became pregnant. In recent years Sweden has developed a reputation for liberality in such matters, but in those days, pregnant and unmarried, she created a huge scandal in Vimmerby, a small town steeped in traditional Lutheran values.

Astrid left home and traveled to the capital, Stockholm. "Of course, my parents weren't pleased, but I wasn't thrown out or anything like that," she explains. "Wild horses wouldn't have kept me there."

She knew nobody in Stockholm. "I was terribly alone at first," she says. "I had left behind all my friends. I was very unhappy. Childhood is one thing," she says philosophically. "Youth is something else."

She took solace in reading the works of Norwegian author Knut Hamsun. Hamsun's book *Hunger* made a deep impression on her. She still names it as her principal literary influence. Lonely and poor herself, she identified strongly with Hamsun's graphic descriptions of the life of a starving young writer in Norway.

In an essay for the mass-circulation Stockholm evening newspaper *Expressen* in 1974, she recalled sitting under a bird-cherry tree outside a church, reading *Hunger.* "That was the greatest literary experience I've ever had," she says.

She gave birth to a son, Lars, whom she handed over to foster parents in Copenhagen, returning to Stockholm to study shorthand and typing and to land a job at a local firm working for the father of Viveca Lindfors, the Swedish-born actress.

"I soon started to make friends in Stockholm, and I went to Copenhagen as often as I could to see Lars. There was never any question of his being adopted. He was my son and I loved him deeply," she says.

On one occasion she left her job during working hours to take the train to Copenhagen, only to be spotted by her boss. She was fired.

However, her luck seemed to have turned. Astrid found an editorial job with KAK, the Swedish automobile association. There she met Sture Lindgren, whom she married in the spring of 1931. Her son came to live with them, and in 1934 she gave birth to her daughter, Karin.

* * *

THE FAMILY LIVED IN the part of Stockholm known as Vasastan, at first in a small apartment close to the main railway line to the north of Sweden, later in a spacious, light apartment overlooking a park. Lindgren still lives there today, surrounded by her books and memorabilia of her lifetime as an author.

It was in the winter of 1941 that Karin asked her to tell the story of Pippi Longstocking. "Much later I was out walking in the park when I slipped and sprained my ankle," she recalls. "I was forced to lie in bed, so I began to write down the stories I had told to Karin."

She typed a manuscript and sent it to Bonniers, one of Sweden's leading publishing houses. It was refused. Undaunted, she wrote a girl's story, *Confidences of Britt Mari,* which she entered for a contest organized by another, much smaller publishing house, Rabén and Sjögren. She won second prize, and in 1944 the story was published. Lindgren also began working for the company as an editor.

The following year Rabén and Sjögren published her follow-up, titled *Kerstin and I.* Then in 1945 the company announced a new contest for books aimed at children ages 6–10.

Lindgren revised her Pippi Longstocking manuscript and entered it for the contest, along with a new effort, *All About the Bullerby Children,* in which she lovingly re-created her childhood in Vimmerby. *Pippi Longstocking* won first prize. *All about the Bullerby Children* failed to take an award but was bought for publication. The first Pippi Longstocking book was well received by both critics and public and soon sold out. However, a year later, the follow-up, *Pippi Goes Abroad,* caused a furor, with Lindgren accused of undermining the authority of parents and teachers.

Professor John Landquist, writing in the evening newspaper *Aftonbladet,* accused Lindgren of "crazed fantasy" and said Pippi's adventures were "something disagreeable that scratches at the soul."

Today there is a different perspective. Viví Edström, professor of literature at the University of Stockholm, has described Pippi as "a child's projection of everything that is desirable" and claims her as a major influence on Swedish literature.

"In the still prim and moralizing children's literature of the 1940s, Astrid Lindgren's breakthrough meant that children had a literature on their own terms," says Edström.

The third and last Pippi Longstocking book, *Pippi in the South Seas,* was published in 1948. In this one Pippi sails away to a Pacific island for a reunion with her father, returning to Sweden for Christmas, which she spends alone. It could be an allegory on the fate of nonconformists in Sweden, a country where the good of the collective has always been prized above that of the individual.

Physically, the model for Pippi was a red-haired, freckle-faced friend of daughter Karin, Sonja Melin, who today sells vegetables in Hötorgshallen, one of Stockholm's few surviving indoor markets. "I meet her now and again when I go out shopping," says Lindgren. "She was just so lively as a child. As soon as I saw her, I thought, 'That's my Pippi!' "

Lindgren has created many other well-loved and sometimes controversial characters in the 30 books she has written since.

Mio My Son, written in 1954 (perhaps significantly, two years after the death of husband Sture) is one of Lindgren's most ambitious books: a highly advanced fairy story that explores difficult themes such as fear and death.

In 1985 a journalist asked Lindgren on Swedish Radio, "Isn't *Mio My Son* actually a pretty nasty book?"

She replied, "Of course; that's why children love it."

* * *

ALTHOUGH SHE HAS NEVER ATTEMPTED a "serious" adult novel ("I never really wanted to; I'm not sure I'd be any good at it"), she has not been shy about exploring themes considered improper for children. In 1973 controversy raged once more, this time over *The Brothers Lionheart,* in which a dying child dreams of meeting, in another world, the brother he idealizes who has died heroically in a fire. The two boys ride off to fight the forces of evil.

Shortly after this, in 1976, Lindgren, a lifelong voter for the Social Democrats, caused a still greater fuss when she became embroiled in a row with Sweden's Socialist government.

It all started with a demand from the tax authorities, which would, she calculated, along with her social-insurance contributions, exceed her actual income. She wrote a fairy story for *Expressen,* the Stockholm newspaper. Its main character, Pomperipossa, has always loved her country and respected its rulers. Now she turns against them: "'O you, the pure and fiery social democracy of my youth, what have they done to you?' thought Pomperipossa, 'How long shall your name be abused to protect a dictatorial, bureaucratic, unjust, authoritarian society?' "

The barb went home, and in the Swedish parliament (*Riksdag*) then finance minister Gunnar Sträng (his surname translates into English as "Strict") reprimanded Lindgren. "The article is a combination of inspired fantasy and total ignorance of tax policy," he said. "Astrid Lindgren should stick to what she knows, namely making up stories."

Lindgren hit back: "He may not be good at arithmetic, but he's certainly good at telling fairy-tales. I think we should trade jobs, he and I."

In that year's general election the Social Democrats lost power, after more than 40 years in office. An analysis of the result by the influential Sifo public-opinion research institute named the controversy over Lindgren's story as a major contributory factor.

Ronia, the Robber's Daughter, published in 1981, returned to a "straight" fairy-tale format, the story of a boy and girl from two different, warring bands of robbers who run away together. This was turned into an award-winning Swedish film by comedian/director Tage Danielsson. Eleven of her books have been filmed, and Lindgren herself still takes an active interest in each project.

She has been positively deluged with prizes, including in 1989 the Albert Schweitzer Award, given for her work on behalf of animal rights. At a time in life when most people would be content to wind down, she joined forces with veterinarian Kristina Forslund in a campaign to persuade Sweden to introduce more stringent rules on animal husbandry.

A string of articles and open letters soon brought the government to its knees. Prime Minister Carlsson announced new legislation that he dubbed "Lex Astrid" and called on Lindgren personally to tell her about it.

Despite laws considered the most advanced in the world, Lindgren is not satisfied. She describes them as "toothless." "They are full of loopholes," she says. "Now we have to fight to get them tightened up."

Although hampered by failing eyesight, she began the 1990s with a new children's play written for Stockholm's Royal Dramatic Theater, plans to film *The Brothers Lionheart,* and thoughts of writing a new book.

"It depends [on] whether I feel inspired. I write quite quickly, in shorthand at first, then I type it. I do a chapter, then rewrite until it flows properly. After that I continue with the next one. A word processor? I couldn't use one of those; I'm not a bit technically minded, I'm afraid.

"I really don't know what I would have been if I had not become an author." She smiles, perhaps thinking of her battles with authority, the Pippi Longstocking side of her personality coming to the fore. "Maybe I could have been a lawyer. I might have been rather good at that."

— Chris Mosey

BOOKS & MOVIES

Books

Relatively few Swedish writers have been translated into English, and the ones who have generally fall into the classic category, leaving the contemporary genre sadly underrepresented.

The classics include 1909 Nobel Prize laureate Selma Lagerlöf, whose *The Wonderful Journey of Nils Holgersson*, written on request as a geography textbook for schoolchildren, takes the reader together with a little boy called Nils Holgersson on an adventure through the entire country.

The plays of Swedish writer August Strindberg greatly influenced modern European and American drama. Perhaps the most enduringly fascinating of these, *Miss Julie* (1888), mixes the explosive elements of sex and class to stunning effect.

Vilhelm Moberg's series of novels about a poor Swedish family that immigrated to America, *The Emigrants* (1949), *Unto a Good Land* (1956), and *The Last Letter Home* (1956–59) give insight into what life was like in the second half of the 19th century, when Sweden was one of the most backward agrarian countries in Europe and one-quarter of its population left for North America.

Proletarian writer Moa Martinson rose from illegitimacy and poverty to become an acclaimed novelist. Two of her novels, her debut, *Women and Appletrees* (1933), and the novel often regarded as her best, *My Mother Gets Married* (1936), have been translated into English. Both novels tell of the struggles of working-class women in a time when women had little say in the decisions affecting their lives. In *Women and Appletrees,* three generations of women struggle to overcome poverty, hardship and loneliness.

My Mother Gets Married is the first of Martinsson's autobiographical trilogy. It is a wrenching portrait of poverty, brutal, boozing men and the stigma of illegitimacy. Mia is six years old when her mother gets married for the first time. The book follows her into young adulthood with a language that draws heavily on oral tradition.

Eyvind Johnson's autobiographical four-volume epic about Olof (1934–37), a logger in the Swedish north and, like Johnson himself, alone from an early age blends fairytale and realism. The series was the basis for the author's 1974 Nobel Prize award (*The Year was 1914, Here is Your Life!, Don't Look Back!,* and *Postlude to Youth*).

1951 Nobel Prize laureate Pär Lagerkvist's novels are as refined as they are timeless. *Barabbas* (1950) is about man's desire to believe, told through the story of the man whose place Jesus took on Golgata. Staying close to the biblical story, Lagerkvist still manages to subtly question every truth.

Evil is the theme of Lagerkvist's *The Dwarf.* Written in 1944, it is Lagerkvist's protest of war and warning of what can happen when evil is unleashed. The dwarf, a servant at a medieval court and a heartless, Machiavellian, scheming character, takes no responsibility for the deeds he carries out on the behalf of his master, the Prince. Despite the medieval setting, *The Dwarf's* theme continues to resonate.

Lagerkvist's mythical *The Sibyl* (1956) struggles with good and bad, the divine and the human. A man is cursed and believes in the curse. He seeks the help of an oracle who shows him that God is both love and hate and that the two are not contradictory.

Only one of poet and novelist Karin Boye's novels, the masterly futuristic *Kallocain* (1940), has been translated into English. Often compared to George Orwell's *1984,* Kallocain is a depiction of a world under totalitarian rule seen through the eyes of idealistic scientist Leo Kall. Convinced he is furthering the common good, Kall perfects the truth drug Kallocain. Where Orwell is purely political, Boye's take on totalitarianism is much more existential.

Göran Tunström's *The Christmas Oratorio* (1983) spans three generations of the Nordensson family. Incredible journeys, doomed love, and freak accidents fill the lives in this story, which, like most of Tunström's novels, start out in the province of Värmland. With his amazing prose, fluctuating from poetic to fantastic to realistic, Tunström has secured his place in Swedish literature.

Since his poetry was first published in 1954, the writer and poet Tomas Tranströmer's work has been much admired in Sweden. Unfortunately, only his more obscure titles have been translated into English, including the collection titled *For the Living and the Dead*.

Captain Nemo's Library (1991), by Per Olov Enquist, is a fine family drama set in the 1940s on the northern coast of Sweden.

Hugely popular in Sweden and exported abroad are the TV dramatizations of the police thrillers about police chief Martin Beck written by the husband-and-wife team of Maj Sjöwall–Per Wahlöö from 1965 until Wahlöö's death in 1975. One of Sjövall-Wahlöö's thrillers, *The Terrorists*, was even prophetic with a scene in which a Swedish prime minister is shot, a precursor to the assassination of Olof Palme in 1986. All of Sjövall-Wahlöö's books (*The Laughing Policeman, Roseanna, The Locked Room, The Man on the Balcony, The Man Who Went Up in Smoke,* and *The Terrorists*) have been translated into English.

Other Swedish writers in the thriller genre whose works have been translated into English are Jan Guillou (*Enemy's Enemy,* from 1989, and *Vendetta: Coq Rouge VI,* from 1991), Kerstin Ekman (*Black Water,* 1996, set in the secluded landscape of the Swedish north) and Henning Mankell's 1998 work *The White Lioness: A Mystery*.

Mikael Niemi's *Popular Music from Vittula* (2001) is a raw, amusing, and sometimes surreal account of the author's childhood in Tornedalen, in the north, close to the Finnish border. The area around Vittula is no place for the weak. If they want any respect at all, real men need to learn how to work, fight, and hold down their alcohol.

For a historical background, try *A History of the Vikings* (Oxford University Press, 1984). The book recounts the history of the seafaring traders and plunderers whose journeys stretched as far from Scandinavia as Constantinople and North America. Gwyn Jones's lively account makes learning the history enjoyable.

Myth and Religion of the North, by E. O. G. Turbille-Petre, explains the history and the evolution of the diverse mythological tales and pagan religions of Sweden.

One of the most exhaustive and comprehensive studies of Sweden published in English in recent years is *Sweden: The Nation's History,* by Franklin D. Scott (University of Minnesota Press). Chris Mosey's *Cruel Awakening: Sweden and the Killing of Olof Palme* (C. Hurst, London, 1991) gives an overview of the country's recent history with a focus on the events surrounding the assassination of Palme and the farcical hunt for his killer.

Movies

Mention Swedish film, and most people automatically think of Ingmar Bergman. A mainstay of the Swedish cultural scene for 50 years, Bergman has shaped Swedish filmmaking like no other director. From his first triumph in Cannes in 1956 with *Smiles of a Summer Night,* Bergman has continued to please his critics. Three of his movies have won the Oscar award for best foreign film over the years: *The Virgin Spring,* in 1960, *Through a Glass, Darkly,* in 1961, and *Fanny and Alexander,* in 1983.

Bergman's movies were always daring and different. *The Summer with Monika* caused a big scandal upon its release in 1952 because of an exposed breast. The most memorable of all of Bergman's films, however, might be *The Seventh Seal,* a medieval tale where the main character, a noble knight just back from a crusade, buys more time from Death by challenging him to a chess game. The crusader's resistance of the inevitable and the separation he feels from God are rather enduring themes.

Fanny and Alexander was the first in a trilogy about Bergman's parents. The second part, *Best Intentions,* came in 1992, and the conclusion, *Private Confessions,* in 1996. *Private Confessions* was directed by Bergman's friend and one-time lover, Liv Ullmann, a star of many of his movies and herself an acclaimed director.

If Bergman gave Swedish directors a reputation for seriousness, some might say gloom, the younger generation is altering that image. Beirut-born Swedish director Josef Fares's *Jalla Jalla,* from 2000, is a hilarious low-budget production with a cast of Fares's friends and family about the arranged engagement between a young immigrant park worker, Roro, and the girl his father picked out for him. The sudden engagement causes some friction, to say the least, between Roro and his Swedish girlfriend, and Roro and his best friend have only days to set things straight. Only 25 when he made *Jalla Jalla,* Fares has been dubbed the wonder child of Swedish film.

Equally funny is Måns Herngren's and Hannes Holm's 1997 *Adam and Eve.* Four years into their relationship, Adam and Eve find out that eternity is a very long time, and sometimes a bit boring. They both realize change is needed, but classical gender differences lead them seek change in very different ways.

Sometimes the best perspective is offered at a distance. For a decade British-born director Colin Nutley has amazed Swedish moviegoers with his discerning depictions of Swedish society. His big breakthrough came in 1993 with *House of Angels,* in which a cabaret singer and her gay best friend show up at a funeral in a small Swedish village. The man in the casket, the villagers find out, was the singer's grandfather, and as the sole relative she moves into his house. The pair's perceived decadence causes unease in the community, and they are told straight-out to leave. Avoiding the usual stereotypical pitfalls, Nutley explores bias and fears without becoming preachy or overbearing.

Nutley made headlines overseas again in 2000, when his *Under the Sun* was nominated for an Oscar for best foreign film. There is nothing new about this sweet and subtle love story, set against a 1950s countryside backdrop, and this is on purpose. The movie borrows its title from Ecclesiastes: "What was will be again; what has been done will be done again; and there is nothing new under the sun."

Another Swedish director to win recognition abroad is Lasse Hallström. Although *My Life as a Dog* (1985) failed to win an Oscar, it got the New York Film Critics Circle award for best foreign-language film in 1987. Hallström's big break in the United States came with *What's Eating Gilbert Grape,* starring Johnny Depp and Leonardo DiCaprio. His most

remarkable movies after *Gilbert Grape* are *Cider House Rules* (1999), *Chocolat* (2000), and *The Shipping News* (2001).

Human trafficking is the topic of Lukas Moodysson's latest movie, *Lilya 4-Ever.* Based on a true story, the movie tells the disconcerting story of a teenage girl who, trying to escape hardship in the former Soviet Union, finds herself forced into prostitution and trafficked to Sweden. Shot in-your-face documentary style, the movie leaves no one unaffected. The movie swept most of the awards at the annual Swedish film awards ceremony in 2003 but failed to get a nomination to the Oscars.

Moodysson 1998 debut *Show Me Love* was called "a young master's first masterpiece" by none other than Ingmar Bergman. Shot with a grainy, home-movie-like quality, *Show Me Love* is a love story between two teenage girls in a small Swedish town where nothing ever happens. The conventional plotline of the love that can't be, at least not in a small town, and the deeper themes of suburban alienation, teen angst, and the disconnect between well-meaning parents and their children avoid becoming clichéd through Moodysson's subtle storytelling.

His 2001 follow-up to *Show Me Love,* the charming *Together,* solidified Moodysson's reputation as one of Sweden's brightest new filmmakers. In that film the leader of a mid-'70s commune tries to keep the place together after his sister and her children move in, introducing into the collective such evils as toy guns, television, and Pippi Longstocking.

Perhaps Sweden is better known abroad for its stars than for its directors.

The greatest of them all was Greta Garbo, a silent film star in Sweden before immigrating to Hollywood in the 1920s. With movies such as *Anna Karenina* (silent in 1927 and with sound in 1935), *A Woman of Affairs* (1929), *Queen Christina* (1934), *Camille* (1937), and *Ninotchka* (1939), Garbo became the epitome of a Hollywood star.

The next Swedish-born actress to conquer Hollywood was Ingrid Bergman in an American 1939 remake of her Swedish breakthrough *Intermezzo.* She went on to star with such Hollywood big names as Humphrey Bogart (*Casablanca*), Gary

Cooper (*For Whom the Bell Tolls*), Bing Crosby (*The Bells of St. Mary*), and Gregory Peck (*Spellbound*).

Other Swedish actresses to light up movie screens worldwide over the years have been Anita Ekberg (*La Dolce Vita*), Lena Olin (*The Unbearable Lightness of Being, Chocolat, The Ninth Gate*), and Pernilla August (*Star Wars, Episode II*).

James Bond has always been fond of Swedish costars. Maud Adams (*The Man with the Golden Gun, Octopussy*), Britt Ekland (*The Man with the Golden Gun*), Mary Stavin (*A View to a Kill*), Kristina Wayborn (*Octopussy*), and Isabella Scorupco (*Goldeneye*) have all starred with the British agent.

For the sake of equality, a few male Swedish actors need a mention. Stellan Skarsgård (*Breaking the Waves, Good Will Hunting, Dogville*), Max von Sydow (whose long list of movie credits is as disparate as *The Exorcist* and *Snow Falling on Cedars*), and Peter Stormare (*Fargo, Dancer in the Dark, Armageddon*) have proved the most enduring in the Hollywood competition.

VOCABULARY

	English	Swedish	Pronunciation
Basics			
	Yes/no	Ja/nej	yah/nay
	Please	Var snäll; Var vänlig	vahr snehll vahr vehn-leeg
	Thank you very much.	Tack så **mee**-keh	tahk soh mycket.
	You're welcome.	Var så god.	vahr shoh **goo**
	Excuse me. (to get by someone)	Ursäkta.	oor-**shehk**-tah
	(to apologize)	Förlåt.	fur-**loht**
	Hello	God dag	goo **dahg**
	Goodbye	Adjö	ah-**yoo**
	Today	I dag	ee **dahg**
	Tomorrow	I morgon	ee **mor**-ron
	Yesterday	I går	ee **gohr**
	Morning	Morgon	**mohr**-on
	Afternoon	Eftermiddag	**ehf**-ter-meed-dahg
	Night	Natt	naht
Numbers			
	1	ett	eht
	2	två	tvoh
	3	tre	tree
	4	fyra	fee-rah
	5	fem	fem
	6	sex	sex
	7	sju	shoo
	8	åtta	oht-tah
	9	nio	nee
	10	tio	tee
Days of the Week			
	Monday	måndag	mohn-dahg
	Tuesday	tisdag	tees-dahg
	Wednesday	onsdag	ohns-dahg
	Thursday	torsdag	tohrs-dahg
	Friday	fredag	freh-dahg
	Saturday	lördag	luhr-dahg
	Sunday	söndag	sohn-dahg
Useful Phrases			
	Do you speak English?	Talar ni engelska?	tah-lahr nee ehng-ehl-skah
	I don't speak . . .	Jag talar inte svenska . . .	yah tah-lahr **een**-teh **sven**-skah

I don't understand.	Jag förstår inte.	yah fuhr-**stohr** **een**-teh
I don't know.	Jag vet inte.	yah **veht een**-teh
I am American/ British.	Jag är amerikan/ engelsman.	yah ay ah-mehr-ee-**kahn**/ **ehng**-ehls-mahn
I am sick.	Jag är sjuk.	yah ay **shyook**
Please call a doctor.	Jag vill skicka efter en läkare.	yah veel **shee**-kah **ehf**-tehr ehn **lay**-kah-reh
Do you have a vacant room?	Har Ni något rum ledigt?	hahr nee noh-goht **room leh**-deekt
How much does it cost?	Vad kostar det?/ Hur mycket kostar det?	vah **kohs**-tahr deh/hor **mee**-keh **kohs**-tahr deh
It's too expensive.	Den är för dyr.	dehn ay foor **deer**
Beautiful	Vacker	**vah**-kehr
Help!	Hjälp	yehlp
Stop!	Stopp, stanna	stop, **stahn**-nah
How do I get to . . .	Kan Ni visa mig vägen till . . .	kahn nee **vee**-sah may **vay**-gehn teel
the train station?	stationen	stah-**shoh**-nehn
the post office?	posten	**pohs**-tehn
the tourist office?	en resebyrå	ehn-**reh**-seh-**bee**-roh
the hospital?	sjukhuset	**shyook**-hoo-seht
Does this bus go to . . . ?	Går den här bussen till . . . ?	gohr dehn hehr **boo**-sehn teel
Where is the W.C.?	Var är toilett/ toaletten	vahr ay twah-**leht** twah-**leht**-en
On the left	Till vänster	teel **vehn**-stur
On the right	Till höger	teel **huh**-gur
Straight ahead	Rakt fram	rahkt **frahm**

Dining Out

Please bring me . . .	Var snäll och hämta åt mig	vahr snehl oh hehm-tah oht may
menu	matsedeln	maht-seh-dehln
fork	en gaffel	ehn gahf-fehl
knife	en kniv	ehn kneev
spoon	en sked	ehn shehd
napkin	en servett	ehn sehr-veht
bread	bröd	bruh(d)
butter	smör	smuhr
milk	mjölk	myoolk
pepper	peppar	pehp-pahr
salt	salt	sahlt
sugar	socker	soh-kehr
water	vatten	vaht-n
The check, please.	Får jag be om notan?	fohr yah beh ohm **noh**-tahn

INDEX

NOTES

NOTES

NOTES

NOTES

NOTES

NOTES